New Testament History

A Narrative Account

Ben Witherington III

Baker Academic

A Division of Baker Book House Co
Grand Rapids, Michigan 49516

© 2001 by Ben Witherington III

Published by Baker Academic
a division of Baker Book House Company
P.O. Box 6287, Grand Rapids, MI 49516–6287
www.bakeracademic.com

Paperback edition published in 2003
ISBN 0-8010-2769-1

Printed in the United States of America

All rights reserved. No part of this publication may be reproduced, stored in a retrieval system, or transmitted in any form or by any means—for example, electronic, photocopy, recording—without the prior written permission of the publisher. The only exception is brief quotations in printed reviews.

The Library of Congress has cataloged the hardcover edition as follows:
Witherington, Ben, 1951–
    New Testament history : a narrative account / Ben Witherington III.
        p.   cm.
    Includes bibliographical references and indexes.
    ISBN 0-8010-2293-2 (cloth)
    1. Bible. N.T.—History of Biblical events. 2. Bible. N.T.—History of
contemporary events. I. Title.
    BS2410 .W55 2001
    225.9′5—dc21   2001037486

To those institutions and their faculties that have nurtured me—

the University of North Carolina at Chapel Hill,
Gordon-Conwell Theological Seminary,
Harvard Divinity School,
Princeton Theological Seminary,
Duke Divinity School,
and the University of Durham

Also to A. J., a good friend and colleague,
and to R. D. H., who has been the hands of Jesus in my life.

Contents

Preface

At first blush it might seem perfectly obvious what "New Testament history" is and what the contents of a book about New Testament history would contain. On closer inspection this is not the case. Are we talking about a history of the New Testament documents themselves, or perhaps a history of the times in which the New Testament books were written? Or are we talking about an ordering and chronicling of the events mentioned in the New Testament? And if we are discussing the latter, how much of a running start does one need? Should we begin with the era of the Maccabees, or go even further back to the time of Alexander the Great, or even the exile? One may ask the same sort of question at the other end of the spectrum. Do we stop the discussion around A.D. 100, since all the New Testament documents seem to have been completed by then? Or do we carry on until we have chronicled the events that led to the collecting and closing of the New Testament canon? Further still, should New Testament history begin when, properly speaking, the New Testament era begins, at Pentecost, thereby leaving out the rehearsing of the life and times of Jesus himself? For better or worse, I have concluded that this latter approach, which focuses solely on the nascent stages of what came to be called early Christianity, is inadequate. We must begin at least with the beginning of the life of Jesus, because understanding the historical connection between Jesus and the movement he spawned is crucial to understanding anything that one might choose to call "New Testament history."

Naturally, it is not possible for this book to cover all of these subjects within a reasonable amount of space, so I have contented myself with focusing on the New Testament era itself from about 6 B.C. to A.D. 100 with some necessary cursory treatments of the antecedents and postludes to this period. My approach to the matter will involve a focus not only on historic individuals and events, but also on social movements and crosscurrents that illuminate those persons and events. The New Testament peoples and their activities must be seen within their proper social and religious contexts if they are to be understood properly. The Jesus movement as a messianic movement was not an isolated phenomenon on the landscape of early Jewish history. Nor was the rise of the church an example of *creatio ex nihilo*. Things must be seen in their proper contexts.

We must also be prepared to say some things about our source material, for a historical work is only as good as the sources upon which it relies to reveal the truths about persons and events of antiquity. This means, of course, that this book cannot reveal everything we always wanted to know about Jesus or Paul or the early Christians but were afraid to ask. Many questions will remain unanswered because they are not addressed or because their answers are not hinted at in the sources. We must be content with what light the sources do shed on our subject matter and not let our conclusions outrun the viable and reliable evidence.

This book is possible only because of the hard work of experts in the fields of Jewish history and Roman history whom I have had to rely upon time after time. They will see their fingerprints throughout this work, and I wish to express my sincere gratitude for their invaluable help. Particularly, I would like to thank E. Schürer, G. Vermes, J. Hayes, S. R. Mandell, P. Richardson, and L. Grabbe for their work on Jewish history; P. Green for his work on the history of Philip and Alexander; and M. Goodman, F. Millar, and M. P. Charlesworth for much hard work on Roman history. My attempt in this book to integrate Jewish, Roman, and Christian history while at the same time showing how the books of the New Testament played their role in this history would have been impossible without the help of these scholars and many others.

We turn now to the task at hand, reminding ourselves of the opening words of the only work (a two-volume historical monograph) on a portion of New Testament history that we find within the canon itself:

> Many have undertaken to draw up an account of the things that have been fulfilled among us, just as they were handed down to us by those who from the first were eyewitnesses and servants of the word. Therefore, since I myself have carefully investigated everything from the beginning, it seemed good also to me to write an orderly account for you . . . so that you may know the certainty of the things you have been taught. (Luke 1:1–4)

Ben Witherington III
Easter 2001

Abbreviations

AB   Anchor Bible

ABD   *Anchor Bible Dictionary.* Edited by D. N. Freedman. 6 vols. New York, 1992

ABRL   Anchor Bible Reference Library

ANET   *Ancient Near Eastern Texts Relating to the Old Testament.* Edited by J. B. Pritchard. 3rd ed. Princeton, 1969

BAR   *Biblical Archaeology Review*

CIJ   *Corpus inscriptionum judaicarum*

CIL   *Corpus inscriptionum latinarum*

DJG   *Dictionary of Jesus and the Gospels.* Edited by J. B. Green and S. McKnight. Downers Grove, Ill., 1997

DNTB	*Dictionary of New Testament Background.* Edited by C. Evans and S. Porter. Downers Grove, Ill., 2000
ICC	International Critical Commentary
IG	*Inscriptiones graecae.* Editio minor. Berlin, 1924–
ILS	*Inscriptiones latinae selectae*
JBL	*Journal of Biblical Literature*
JSNTSup	Journal for the Study of the New Testament: Supplement Series
JTS	*Journal of Theological Studies*
NAC	New American Commentary
NewDocs	*New Documents Illustrating Early Christianity.* Edited by G. H. R. Horsley and S. Llewelyn. North Ryde, N.S.W., 1981–
NTS	*New Testament Studies*
SBLSP	*Society of Biblical Literature Seminar Papers*
SEG	Supplementum epigraphicum graecum
SemeiaSt	Semeia Studies
SJLA	Studies in Judaism in Late Antiquity
SNTSMS	Society for New Testament Studies Monograph Series
TNTC	Tyndale New Testament Commentaries
WBC	Word Biblical Commentary
WUNT	Wissenschaftliche Untersuchungen zum Neuen Testament

Prolegomenon

Of History, Historians, and Biographers

The term "history" can refer to a variety of things. "History" can refer simply to the flow of events in the past that are perceived to have had some sort of ongoing significance. It is taken for granted that not everything that happens in a human life is of "historic" significance. Thus, for instance, what Robert E. Lee had for breakfast on the first day of the battle of Gettysburg will not likely be revealed in the accounts of that important morning. Now, had his breakfast made him ill, so that he would have been unable to direct the Southern army on that day, then what he had for breakfast might be said to have some historic significance. Even trivial matters become important if they affect the crucial decisions and actions of those who shape history. The familiar aphorism is a good reminder on this front:

> For want of a nail, the horseshoe was lost. For want of a horseshoe, the horse was lost. For want of a horse, the messenger was lost. For want of

the messenger, the battle was lost. For want of the battle, the war was lost, and all for want of a nail.

In this study, when I use the term "history," I will be referring usually to written history, not to the events themselves. Thus, for example, when I speak about Luke's history of the early Christian movement as chronicled in Acts, I am not referring directly to the things that happened, but rather to a particular person's chronicling of the things that happened. This is not an inconsequential distinction, because written history is always a matter of the reporting of facts plus the interpretation of those facts. And indeed, even the facts a historian chooses to include in a report already involves a process of critical sifting and interpreting of data. There is no such thing as uninterpreted history. History writing is never like an old episode of *Dragnet*, where Joe Friday could insist, "Just the facts, ma'am, just the facts." The question that must be raised about any piece of written history is this: Is the presentation such that the truths about what happened and why are illuminated or even revealed by the account, or are those truths obscured by the presentation? There are good historians and bad historians, but none who present us with interpretation-free and value-free accounts. Sometimes a historian is accused of "bias" because his or her frame of reference or interpretive approach seems to skew the data or interpret it unfairly. Such a charge is not infrequently warranted, but every historical account is written from some particular point of view. This needs to be recognized from the outset. More and less "objective" accounts of ancient historical events are possible, but a strictly "neutral" or uninterpretive account is not.

No one who begins a biography of Jesus with the words "The beginning of the good news of Jesus Christ, the Son of God" or concludes an account with "these things have been written so that you might believe" is attempting to be neutral about the subject matter. The question that should be raised about such accounts is not whether they amount to a form of advocacy—because of course they do—but whether the interpretation of Jesus offered illuminates or obscures the historical subject matter that is being treated.

This leads us to an important conclusion: we have no ancient sources about Jesus and early Christianity from "neutral" observers. Whether we are dealing with Roman writers like Tacitus or Jewish writers like Josephus or the New Testament writers themselves, none of these writers is attempting to give us an "objective" assessment of the data, if by "objective" one means value free or purely neutral. Thus, all the relevant ancient data must be critically sifted and evaluated. This is not to say that the opposite of "objectivity" in regard to such

Illustration P.1 One of the Qumran scrolls found at the Dead Sea.

sources is "radical subjectivity," with people creating stories out of whole cloth. It simply means that one must be aware of and take into account the points of view of the writers who present us with our data on Jesus and early Christianity. We must always "consider the source" of the information as we evaluate its interpretation of the data.

Also, it must be noted that we do not have copious sources of information about early Christianity. The Roman writers seldom comment on the matter, and Jewish writers who do comment on the matter (such as Josephus) appear to have had their accounts tampered with by later Christians who copied the accounts down through the ages. Nonetheless, some valuable material may be garnered from these sources about Jesus and the movement he spawned. Then, of course, we have the New Testament accounts themselves, written by those who were participants in the movement. They offer "insider" information, and from an insider's perspective as well. Sometimes, as we all know, insider information can be the most valuable and most revealing about a particular historical matter. Napoleon met his Waterloo in part because his opponent knew well his tendencies and had good spies.

Fortunately, we are not limited to written sources about New Testament history. We have also a wealth of archaeological, epigraphical, and numismatic evidence, which can help us reconstruct the original social and religious settings of the events. There is always a danger of too much background information becoming the foreground of one's historical analysis;[1] nonetheless, a thick description of the social and religious setting can help provide the necessary context for the proper interpretation of the various words and deeds of Jesus and his followers. For example, the aphorism "Render unto Caesar the things that are Caesar's, and unto God the things that are God's" (Mark 12:17) in its original setting is not likely to have meant an endorsement by Jesus of the notion of two legitimate spheres of authority in the world—human and divine. Jesus believed that all things belong to God and that his dominion was breaking into human history. He was not an early advocate of the separation of church and state!

Something needs to be said at this juncture about the limits of historical inquiry. The most that a historian can establish about events in the past is a good probability one way or another that this or that event did or did not happen. There is no such thing as absolute certainty about such matters, if we are talking about the kind of certainty intellectual inquiry of historical sources can deliver. Thus, the reader needs to be aware that when in this study I say, for instance, "The historical evidence favors the probability that Jesus had an inner circle of twelve disciples," I have put the matter this way, not because I have any serious personal doubts about this matter, but because a historian must not allow his or her piety to outrun the evidence as it can be marshaled on a particular historical matter. To put the matter another way, I as the author of this monograph believe a good deal more than I can prove. A New Testament history book is, or should be, about what one can show with good probability is or is not the case. Much that is true about the historical Jesus is not historically demonstrable because the evidence is meager. Thus, the readers must content themselves with the fact that the historically demonstrable truths about Jesus and early Christianity are at best only a subset of what was historically true about these matters.

When dealing with ancient sources, we cannot be content to know the religious and social settings out of which these sources have come. We should also know something about how the ancients viewed the writing of history and biography, for in the Gospels and Acts apparently we are dealing with three ancient biographies and one two-volume historical monograph (Luke-Acts). What kind of historical information we can extract from these sources will depend to some extent on what kind of data they were trying to deliver and what historical and biographical

1. A danger rightly stressed by P. Barnett, *Jesus and the Rise of Early Christianity: A History of New Testament Times* (Downers Grove, Ill.: InterVarsity, 1999), passim.

conventions they were seeking to follow. Thus, a short exposition on these matters is in order here.

The problem of anachronism is a serious one when it comes to evaluating materials in the Bible because there is a widespread assumption in the conservative Christian community, ever since the Reformation, that God's Word requires only a good, clear mind, an open heart, and the guidance of the Holy Spirit to be understood. No particular additional resources (beyond the reader and the text) need be consulted or should intervene.[2]

This assumption lends itself to various forms of anti-intellectualism when it comes to the serious study of the Bible as an ancient historical document. Lacking sensitivity to the ancient conventions about history writing, many contemporary readers assume modern ones to be in play when reading the text. Perhaps the most notorious example of this sort of error is the case of the Christian writer who in a famous book, *The Battle for the Bible*, concluded that Peter must have denied Jesus six times (something no individual Gospel suggests), because otherwise this writer was unable to account for the varying descriptions of denials and cockcrows in the Gospels. Bringing modern historiographical expectations to the text makes it difficult to appreciate or even recognize the ancient conventions and genre traits that are in play. The modern desire for precision must not be imposed on ancient authors, who often, though not always, preferred to write in a generalizing fashion.

To take another example, the ancients were usually perfectly content to use adverbs and other terms for time in a metaphorical or less-than-precise way. Luke, for instance, is satisfied with saying that Jesus was "about" thirty when he began his ministry (Luke 3:23). This general lack of concern for precision is what makes the more precise time references in the passion narratives stand out all the more distinctly. Up to the passion narratives, Mark's favorite term to indicate the flow of time was "immediately" (*euthys*), a term the evangelist uses relentlessly, even when often what he means is simply "next." When a modern person tries to press ancient general time notices beyond the general sense the original author was trying to convey, it can only result in distortion.

Furthermore, one could say that the way ancient Jews viewed the day and time was very different from ours. For the New Testament authors, all of whom were Jews (with the possible exception of Luke) the day began at sundown, not at midnight! The whole rhythm of life was

---

2. This assumption, of course, plays right into the cultural flow of a postmodern milieu, where radical subjectivity has now been baptized and called good, and the standing mantra is "There are only texts."

different for them. They began the day with a time for worship, or evening fellowship around a table and then rest. It is from the Romans that we have come to reckon the day as beginning at midnight, and we also owe the Romans for the notion that one should get up and go to work at sunrise (this is even when Roman courts began their daily work—cf. the trial of Jesus). Likewise, in regard to the beginning of the year, Jews began their calendar year in the fall, not, as the Romans did, in January. Thus, for Jews the year began with harvest and finished with the summer, a very different way of looking at the cycles of life than we have. This is why Westerners are often confused by biblical phrases like "reaping and sowing" to describe the activities of the year, where they would expect the reverse order of those events.

But it is not just the conceptions of time that differed in antiquity. There were also conceptions about history different from what we find in modern history books, not the least of which is the belief that God was in control of history, orchestrating when certain things happened, especially crucial salvific events. Thus, when we hear the phrase "but when the time had fully come, God sent his Son" (Gal. 4:4), we realize that the apostle would not have subscribed to modern secular notions of either no deity involved in human history or at most a watchmaker God who wound up the universe and then left it to its own devices. To the contrary, it was passionately believed that God intervened repeatedly in human history and indeed was in control of the entire tapestry of events—past, present, and future. This being so, it behooves us to consider closely how ancients dealt with matters biographical and historical.

Let us start with a description of ancient biographies and what their genre traits were, since, I would argue, Matthew, Mark, and John all appear to be such documents, while Luke-Acts appears to be an ancient historical monograph. "The first qualification for judging any piece of workmanship from a corkscrew to a cathedral is to know what it is— what it was intended to do and how it is meant to be used."[3] C. S. Lewis was quite right in this remark, and it is especially apt when it comes to dealing with either an oral presentation or a written document.[4] These sorts of considerations apply especially when the possibility of anachronism is a serious danger, that is, when one is dealing with ancient

3. C. S. Lewis, *A Preface to Paradise Lost* (Oxford: Oxford University Press, 1942), 1. I thank Christopher Bryan, *A Preface to Mark: Notes on the Gospel in Its Literary and Cultural Settings* (Oxford: Oxford University Press, 1993), 9, for reminding me of this fine quotation.

4. The next few paragraphs appear in another form in the introduction to B. Witherington III, *The Gospel of Mark: A Socio-Rhetorical Commentary* (Grand Rapids: Eerdmans, 2001).

documents. Works of ancient history or biography should each be judged by their own conventions.[5]

The word "genre" means a literary kind or type. It refers to a sort of compact between author and reader whereby the author, using various literary signals, indicates to the reader what sort of document is being read and how it should be used. The genre signals in the text provide the reader with a guide to the interpretation of the text.[6] To make a genre mistake is to make a category mistake, which skews the reading of the document.

"The genre of a particular work is established by the presence of enough generic motifs in sufficient force to dominate,"[7] so that when the reader picks up the document, he or she will know soon thereafter whether to expect to derive from it phone numbers, or definitions of words, or entertainment, or historical or biographical information, or even some combination of such things. It follows from this that it is important to discover what kind of document Mark, or Matthew, or John is.

We must remind ourselves that the possibility of the Gospels being ancient biographies must be assessed on the basis not of modern biographical conventions but of ancient ones.[8]

The one thing to keep in mind is that ancient *bioi*, like modern biographies, center on a particular person and seek to present an adequate and accurate characterization of that person. An ancient biography would include information about other persons and groups of people, but the major focus throughout the work would be on the central character. What was considered revealing of that person's character and

5. Some major flaws in certain forms of reader-response criticism are that it tends to ignore the compact between author and audience, often ignores that the author had some purposes and some information to convey when writing the document, and assumes that it is the reader who can and must decide what sort of things, including what sort of meaning, one can derive from a text. This is one reason why various reader-response approaches to the Gospels have failed so miserably to come to grips with the genre question. Historical information that would help sort this issue out is ignored or neglected. Instead, the Gospels are treated as if they are works of modern fiction.

6. See H. Dubrow, *Genre*, The Critical Idiom 42 (London: Methuen, 1982), 118; cf. R. A. Burridge, *What Are the Gospels?* SNTSMS 70 (Cambridge: Cambridge University Press, 1992), 53.

7. Bryan, *Preface to Mark*, 13.

8. This was precisely the problem with the assessments of R. Bultmann and other form critics like W. Marxsen, *Introduction to the New Testament: An Approach to Its Problems*, trans. G. Buswell (Oxford: Blackwell, 1968), 125, who, on the basis of modern biographical considerations, complained that the Gospels reflect the "absence of everything required for a biography (sequence of events, development, Jesus' appearance, etc.)." The first two items Marxsen listed were characteristics of ancient historical works, not ancient biographies, while the third is a concern of modern biographers but not necessarily of ancient ones.

personality would be included; what was not so, likely would be left out. Thus, while a biographer might well include a short story or anecdote about a person that was not of any larger "historic" significance, an ancient historian was unlikely to do so.[9]

The aims of the ancient biographer, such as Plutarch, were often hortatory. They sought to inculcate mimesis, positive or negative. The message was "Go and do likewise" (if the biographical subject was virtuous), or in some cases "Go and do otherwise." To be sure, some overlap of features and aims occurred between biography and history, or between biography and moral philosophy, or between biography and encomiums (speeches), but still, the reader could distinguish a life from a tract of moral philosophy. The point is, as Burridge stresses, "Ancient βίος was a flexible genre having strong relationships with history, encomium and rhetoric, moral philosophy and the concern for character."[10]

The historian's concern was with movements, historical developments, cause and effect, synchronisms—that which was historic and epoch making. The ancient biographer also drew on historical data about the central figure, but did so with different aims and purposes. For instance, we should not be surprised that Mark, Matthew, or John seems almost unconcerned about explicating how event A was related to event B, which seems to have followed it. Rather, each of these evangelists sought to ask and answer this question: Who was Jesus, what was he like, and why is he worth writing a biography about?

In evaluating Mark, Matthew, and John as biography, we must have a firm handle on these Gospels' chronological and social settings, broadly speaking. Whatever their precise dates, Mark, Matthew, and John were written after the beginning of the Roman Empire and during the period of the rise of the Roman biographical tradition, following in the footsteps of the Greek biographical tradition. What the Roman tradition added to the discussion was a greater concern for family traditions, the need for the demonstration of public honor, and, sometimes in the latter two-thirds of the first century, a focus on the hero's patient suffering and death under a tyrant (see, e.g., Thrasea Paetus's *Life of Cato*). "The genre of *exitus illustrium virorum* became fashionable under oppression by Tiberius, Nero,

9. Notice Plutarch's famous remarks at the beginning of his *Life of Alexander* 2–3: "For it is not Histories I am writing, but Lives; and in the most illustrious deeds there is not always a manifestation of virtue or vice, no, a slight thing like a phrase or a joke often makes a greater revelation of character than battles where thousands fall. . . . Accordingly, just as painters get the likenesses in their portraits from the face and the expression of the eyes, wherein the character shows itself, but make very little account of the other parts of the body, so I must be permitted to devote myself rather to the signs of the soul of a person, and by means of these to portray the life of each."

10. Burridge, *What Are the Gospels?* 69.

and Domitian. Such a focus on the subject's death [often an untimely death] is an important parallel for the Passion narratives in the gospels."[11]

Each of these three Gospels has been called a passion narrative with a long introduction. These Gospels have this form partly because they were written in an environment where there would be a certain sympathy in the empire for the chronicling of a life that could be shown to be a good or virtuous life that unfortunately suffered an untimely and unjust end at the hands of some authority figures. In fact, Mark devotes some 19 percent of his narrative to the passion narrative compared to 15 percent by Matthew or Luke—proportionally more emphasis in Mark on the last week of Jesus' life than in the other Synoptics.[12] John's Gospel, however, places even heavier emphasis on the last week of Jesus' life, beginning in chap. 12 and continuing until chap. 20 (the whole second half of the Gospel).

A variety of external and internal features of these Gospels points us in the direction of biography of some sort. First, they are the right length (Mark has 11,242 words, Matthew 18,305, John 16,150).[13] Matthew actually is at the upper limits for a biography (Luke at 19,428 being at the upper limits for what a single scroll could contain), but Mark is closely similar to the average length of one of Plutarch's *Lives*. Second, these works, even at a glance, clearly are continuous prose narratives, which places them in the category of history, biography, or romance. These Gospels clearly are not moral tracts, speeches (encomiums), or even plays, though John is more like a drama than the other two Gospels in question. Mark and Matthew have a basic chronological and even geographical progression—from a largely northern ministry to a final visit to Jerusalem, from Galilee to Jerusalem. Third, notice how rarely Jesus is not the center of attention of any given narrative. Take, for instance, Mark's Gospel (an exception would be the story about Herod in chap. 6, but even there Jesus is discussed at 6:14–16). Jesus or his teaching is the subject of over 44 percent of all the verbs in Mark's Gospel,[14] and in almost any given narrative, Jesus is either the center of attention or discussion, or not far from the spotlight. These books are the

11. Ibid., 77. J. Marcus, *Mark 1–8*, AB 27A (New York: Doubleday, 2000), 67, thinks that Mark 16:1–8 may not be a suitable ending for a biography, and he is largely correct. This does not affect our discussion, however, if Mark 16:1–8 is not the Gospel's original ending.

12. It is useful to compare Plutarch's life of Julius Caesar at this point, where there are signs in the heavens before his tragic murder, including an eclipse of the sun, showing the gods' disapproval of this action (*Caesar* 69.3–5).

13. See R. Morgenthaler, *Statistik des neutestamentlichen Wortschatzes* (Zürich: Gotthelf, 1958), 164, table 3.

14. See the chart offered by Burridge, *What Are the Gospels?* 271, whom I largely follow throughout this section of the introduction.

good news about Jesus, and they seldom stray any distance or length of time from their main subject.

Fourth, each of these Gospels follows the ancient biographical convention of using indirect portraiture to reveal the central figure. By this I mean that the evangelist largely lets Jesus' words and deeds speak for themselves. He does not intrude upon the story with a great deal of authorial commentary, nor do we find much first-person commentary by Jesus about himself.[15] Fifth, Mark and Matthew are characterized by the use of short anecdotal stories that focus on a word or deed of Jesus, and whether we call these pronouncement stories or, more appropriately, *chreiai*, the stringing together of these condensed narratives was indeed characteristic of ancient biographies. Here John differs, but it can be seen as more of a philosophical biography, dealing with dialogues and monologues involving the one who is the Word on earth.

Sixth, the usual subjects for ancient biography were public figures such as emperors and generals, or literary figures such as rhetoricians and poets, or sages and philosophers. Bryan suggests that an outsider reading Mark, even more so Matthew, likely would assume that the work was a biography about some sage.[16] This is equally true of John. It was not unexpected that sages would be misunderstood and suffer at the hands of society, being treated as the nonconformist outcasts that they often managed to be (see Lucian, *Demonax* 11.65). Finally, in regard to Mark's somewhat rough Greek or John's somewhat simplistic style, it must be borne in mind that *bioi* in the first century A.D. were by nature popular literature. They did not need to be seen as being in the same league as Virgil's *Aeneid* or Homer's *Odyssey*, or being as precise as a careful work of history like Thucydides' *History*. The goal was to create a lasting impression through the impact of the whole *bios*.

One would not expect of an ancient biography a "womb to tomb" chronicling of a person's life. Nor would one expect much time or focus on the early childhood development of the person in question, since it was believed that character was basically static and did not develop over time, but rather, was merely revealed. The author would not necessarily be concerned to recount even all the historic events that transpired in the main character's life, since the goal was to reveal who this person truly was, through a portrait of words and deeds,

---

15. John's Gospel of course has a good deal more first-person commentary than the Synoptics. See, e.g., the demonstration by Burridge, ibid., 143–45, that direct character analysis or physical description of a figure or first-person commentary was not a sine qua non of ancient biographies. Rather, it was common to present samples of the person's words and deeds.

16. Bryan, *Preface to Mark*, 37.

Illustration P.2 Portrait of a first-century cynic philosopher or sage.

not to give an exhaustive life account. A representative sampling of a person's life activities that revealed character would be more than sufficient. Finally, if the person's death took place in some glorious or inglorious fashion, ample space had to be devoted to explaining the significance of the event because it was widely believed in antiquity that how one died revealed one's true character and, more importantly, what God or the gods (in a pagan biography) thought about that person. Needless to say, since Jesus was crucified and no one in antiquity saw this as a noble way to die, much explaining was required of Matthew, Mark, and John if their hero figure was to be viewed sympathetically by a first-century recipient of one of their Gospels. Judged by ancient standards then, Matthew, Mark, and John all look rather clearly like ancient biographies of the more religious or philosophical sort.

What, then, of Luke-Acts? Ancient historiography, by comparison to ancient biography, focused more on events than on persons and personalities. It was concerned to record significant happenings, but also to probe and, if possible, explain the cause of these happenings. Luke's concern about causation is manifest in both volumes of his work, as the theme of God's determined plan or counsel arises again and again, as does a stress on the fulfillment of Scripture—or, to put it another way, a stress on the historical manifestation of God's earlier promises, prophecies, and plans.

Had Luke been about the business of writing a biography of Jesus and of his successors, we would have expected Luke 1 to have looked quite different, and Acts 28 as well. As for the latter, a biographer never would have left the reader hanging in regard to what happened to Paul after two years of house arrest in Rome. As to the former, Jesus is not at all the focus or subject of the first major section of Luke 1. In an ancient biography it was expected that the main character would be mentioned at or very near the beginning of the work to alert the reader to the nature or subject of the work. But what we are told in Luke 1:1–4 is that this work will be about the "things which have happened among us," which is to say that the focus will be on events. Notice that only Luke among the Gospel writers shows any real interest in historical synchronisms (Luke 3:1; Acts 18:2), or in the historical development of Jesus' life (Luke 2:41–52, particularly the last verse).

There were various sorts of ancient approaches to history writing, including two main traditions: the Greek tradition of Thucydides, Polybius, and Ephorus, and the Roman tradition of writers like Livy, Tacitus, and Suetonius. Broadly speaking, the Greek tradition bore the most resemblance to the modern tradition in that it involved research, the consulting of eyewitnesses, the comparing of sources, and the like. The Roman tradition was more often undertaken by a retiring public figure interested in writing his memoirs and perhaps checking a few local records and individuals, but not traveling and consulting eyewitnesses in far-flung locations. Then, too, Roman historians tended to focus on the history of one city—Rome. They would chronicle its life on a year-by-year basis.

For the Greek historian the hallmark of real history writing was personal observation and participation in events, involving travel, and thus it was a task of one's best years, not something reserved for the twilight years undertaken from the comfort of one's villa. Wealth and social contacts were essential to being a Roman historian, but not so with the Greek tradition. In the Greek tradition interest and involvement with one's subject matters were the essential criteria, and it is noteworthy that the author of Acts claims only a limited involvement in the events he chronicles (through the presence of the "we" passages in the second half of Acts). Otherwise, he seems to rely on sources such as Paul and Peter. Greek historiography also tended to focus on more universal history, rather than on one city or geographical or ethnic group. Thus, it would appear that Luke is deliberately following in the Greek tradition of historiography, even though, unlike Thucydides or

Polybius, he is not mainly interested in military or political history, but rather in the social and the religious history of one particular movement of his day.

One thing that definitely distinguishes modern historiography from almost all forms of ancient historiography is that the ancients did not hesitate to include the divine or the supernatural in their narratives of historical events. Yet notice that Luke, unlike some ancient writers, does not discourse about the fabulous in a way that makes it immune to historical scrutiny. He insists that the miraculous deeds and divine interventions recorded in his account were not "done in a corner" and that various eyewitnesses could be consulted about these matters. This contrasts with the ancient writers who wrote about "supernatural" events on remote islands or faraway countries, locations that none of their readers could possibly check to find out if the account was veracious.[17]

In contrast to modern historiography, the ancients were much less concerned with (1) chronological precision; (2) exhaustive or comprehensive accounts; (3) value-free commentary; (4) ascribing all events to purely natural causes; (5) the avoidance of rhetorical devices and effects. Indeed, almost all good ancient historians would expect these five features to regularly characterize their works. Ancient historiography was a rhetorical exercise to some extent, and it was undertaken to persuade someone about something. History was not discoursed on for its own sake. It is not a surprise that Luke's rhetorical skills are most in evidence in the speech material and in his famous prologue (Luke 1:1–4). Otherwise, he is rather constrained by the narratives he found in his source material.

Perhaps something in particular needs to be said about the presence of speech material in ancient biographical and historical sources. In an age before electronic recording devices, when a notable speech was made (unless it was an address of an emperor or the carefully prepared encomium of a rhetorician), one could not expect to find a written record of the matter after the fact. Even a cursory glance at the speeches in Acts shows that at most they are summaries of speeches, not transcripts of whole speeches, for with rare exception they take only a minute or two to recite.

With the Gospel materials we are on somewhat different ground, since Jesus seems mainly to have taught in parables and aphorisms— shorter, more memorable forms of speech. Nevertheless, we need to be aware that it was according to ancient historical and biographical con-

17. See B. Witherington III, *Acts of the Apostles: A Socio-Rhetorical Commentary* (Grand Rapids: Eerdmans, 1998), 1–32.

ventions to summarize the essence of a speech, perhaps quoting one or two memorable highlights. We must not, then, overpress the evidence in the Gospels and Acts in regard to verbal precision; but on the other hand, it is not true that there was an ancient historical convention that expected writers to compose fictitious speeches for the main characters in their narratives. If Luke was a careful ancient historian—and I believe he was—we may expect from him adequate and accurate summaries of what was said on one occasion or another based on the reports of witnesses whom the author consulted, or occasionally based on his own presence on the occasion. We may also expect, since all the earliest Christians were Jews, that they tended to pass down their sacred traditions, including especially the words of Jesus and the apostles, in a fashion that could be called conservative and careful. The differences between parallel accounts of Jesus' teachings remind us, however, that ancient authors felt more free than do moderns to edit their material in ways conducive to their larger literary or, in this case, theological purposes.

The Greek tradition of historiography had a practice of arranging material by geographical region and/or ethnic group. We see this practice especially in the work of Ephorus, and we find it also in Acts, and it reminds us that Luke is not following a strict chronological ordering of events in either of his works. The order he presents is, broadly speaking, chronological, but within that broad framework another ordering principle is at work, namely, dealing with things on a region-by-region basis. Thus, notice how in Luke's Gospel we basically find Jesus first in Galilee, then in Samaria, and then in Judea and Jerusalem, so that the Gospel has a "going up to Jerusalem" trajectory. Acts, by contrast, has a "from Jerusalem to the world" trajectory, moving from one region to another, branching out from those closest to Jerusalem to those more remote. Thus, Luke has neatly divided up his work into what would fit on two papyrus scrolls—the first dealing with the geographical theater in which Jesus operated, and the second dealing with the geographical regions where the early Christian movement and its ministry spread through the auspices of missionaries such as Philip, Peter, and, especially, Paul.

It is also a mistake to underplay the indebtedness of Luke to the Septuagint, the Greek translation of the Old Testament, which was the Bible of most early Christians. Luke has rightly been called a writer of salvation history, and to a significant extent he sees the Gospel story as the continuation and fulfillment of the story of God's dealings with his people as recorded in the Old Testament. The Septuagint not only affects the style in which Luke writes and serves as the only version of the

Bible he regularly quotes from, but also gives him an approach to history writing that did not characterize Greek or Roman writers.

Luke is a monotheist profoundly convinced that the God of the Hebrews is the God of Jesus and his followers, and that the promises made in Old Testament times to God's people are now coming to fruition in the ministry of Jesus and his followers. Thus, he believes that he is writing in the eschatological age when the hopes and fears of all the years are coming to fulfillment in and through the people he is writing about. The sense of the divine plan being worked out and manifested permeates the narrative from Luke 1 through Acts 28. It is also true that Luke's preoccupation with the subject of the salvation of the world, both Jew and Gentile, unites him with the biblical heritage and distinguishes him from the major concerns of secular historians of his time and place. Luke, then, stands profoundly indebted to both the Greek and Jewish historiographical tradition, and no account of his handling of his source material can afford to overlook these factors.

Aware of the sort of primary sources we will be dealing with and what their limitations and orientations are, we are now prepared to undertake the task of chronicling New Testament history, a task that immediately takes us first to source material we have not even mentioned yet, sources both Jewish and pagan about the events that transpired between the time of Alexander the Great and the birth of Jesus.

Chapter 1

From Alexander to Alexandra and Beyond

356–67 B.C.

To the casual reader of the Bible who proceeds directly from Malachi to Matthew, it can come as something of a shock to discover the gap of several hundred years between the end of the narrative in the Hebrew Scriptures and the beginning of the narrative in Matthew. It is not just the time lag that surprises, however, but also the difference in the character of the people of God. During the time of Ezra and Nehemiah, the Hebrews had returned from Babylonian exile and tried to reestablish themselves in Israel. While they may well have picked up various Persian customs and indeed many gained some facility in Aramaic, none of that could account for the following two facts: (1) the entire New

29

Testament is written (by Jews!) in Greek; (2) the most widely used version of the Old Testament by the turn of the era was also in Greek—the Septuagint. How had it happened that Jews had become so Hellenized between the end of the Old Testament era and the beginning of the New Testament era? To answer this question we must consider the remarkable figure of Alexander the Great and the legacy he and his successors left to early Judaism.

Illustration 1.1 Jewish History before Roman Occupation

Date	Event
1000–960 B.C.	Reign of David
722–721 B.C.	Assyrian conquest of Israel; Assyrian exile begins
575–450 B.C.	Babylonian exile
332 B.C.	Alexander the Great conquers Palestine
311 B.C.	Ptolemaic Empire in Egypt dominates Palestine
198 B.C.	Antiochus III of Syria takes Palestine
168 B.C.	Antiochus IV tries to abolish Jewish faith
166 B.C.	Judas Maccabeus starts rebellion
164 B.C.	Jerusalem reopened—Feast of Hanukkah
143 B.C.	Simon, Judas's brother, routs forces of Antiochus VI
134–104 B.C.	Rule of John Hyrcanus
103–76 B.C.	Rule of Alexander Janneus
76–67 B.C.	Rule of Alexandra
63 B.C.	Roman general Pompey conquers Jerusalem

Alexander

Born in 356 B.C. in Pella, Alexander was the son of King Philip II of Macedon. His father, while not quite the world ruler Alexander became, provided the pattern of aggressive military behavior that his son later would follow. One of the main motivating factors for this warlike behavior of both Philip and Alexander seems to have been that Mace-

Illustration 1.2 The chief symbol of classical Greek culture—the Parthenon.

donians were viewed by the Greeks who lived in the city-states south of Macedon as uncouth of speech, unsophisticated in culture, ethically unreliable, politically inept, and militarily weak. In other words, Philip and Alexander suffered from a cultural inferiority complex, and they were determined to prove the Greeks wrong at every point of their characterization of Macedonians. It needs to be borne steadily in view that the ancients viewed human personality as determined by geography, generation, and gender. By and large, they did not judge people as individuals, but according to their ethnic or geographical group. What we would call a stereotype, they would call an ethnic character type (cf., e.g., the evaluation by a Cretan poet of the character of his own people in Titus 1:12).

At the birth of Alexander, Philip had just come off of four years' worth of military triumphs that had transformed Macedonia from a backwater into one of the most powerful states in all of the Greek mainland. It would be helpful if we knew more about the childhood of Alexander, but most of the evidence we have from Plutarch and others is the stuff of legend. There is some reason to think that he was indeed precocious as a young man, and we know that he identified himself with Achilles, who was said to be an ancestor of his mother. On his father's side, the lineage was traced back to Heracles (whom we call Hercules), thus providing Alexander with two powerful figures from his past to emulate. But the one he admired and emulated the most was his own father.

Of his tutors, two stand out as worthy of comment. There was Leonidas, a strong disciplinarian who placed great emphasis on physical training and endurance. The most famous anecdote of this period was that Alexander complained that Leonidas's idea of breakfast was a long night march, and of supper a light breakfast.[1] Yet this physical regimen was to serve him well when he went out on campaign. I will say more of his other and more famous tutor, Aristotle, shortly.

Another important trait of Alexander was that he had a remarkable memory, seldom forgot a slight, and certainly never forgave one. When Leonidas chastised the boy for throwing too much incense into the sacrificial fire and sarcastically suggested that he could be so extravagant only after he conquered the spice-bearing regions of the world, Alexander answered years later by conquering Gaza and sending his former teacher eighteen tons of incense and spices. Alexander was not a man to be taunted or crossed. Nor was he a man who ever lacked courage. The story of the young man Alexander taming the wild horse Bucephalas when others much older than he had failed is typical.

In March of 346, after various notable Macedonian military triumphs had come to the attention of the Athenians, the famous rhetorician Isocrates published his *Address to Philip*, calling for a crusade by all true Hellenes against Persia. Isocrates had made such an appeal before (in 380) to the democratic states of Greece to no avail, but now his speech notes the advantages of one-man rule as a way of uniting all of Hellas. Indeed, in a notable piece of rhetorical flourish he encourages Philip to consider all Hellas "your fatherland," a piece of advice Philip was to take quite literally as he took over Greece. Philip liked the sound of these suggestions, but he knew there was preparatory work to be done first. Accordingly, in the winter of 343-342 Philip sent out an invitation to a boyhood friend to return to the Macedonian court and become the main tutor of his son. This man had studied with the famous Plato and had been serving for some time as an emissary between Philip and other rulers. His name was Aristotle. Philip decided that Alexander needed to be removed from the distractions of the court and the capital, and so Aristotle and Alexander were sent to a small village north of Beroea to complete his education. Alexander was already concerned even as a young teenager that he get the proper training so that he might be a great king.

Undoubtedly, Alexander learned many things from Aristotle. Recall that in his *Politics*, Aristotle argues that the only justification for a mon-

---

1. See P. Green, *Alexander the Great* (New York: Praeger, 1970), 35.

archy rather than a republic is that a particular leader have such outstanding *areté* (moral excellence) that a royal ruler becomes preferable to a more democratic arrangement. Aristotle was, furthermore, extremely ethnocentric. The Persians were barbarians ruled by their passions, and when Alexander conquered them, he was to rule them like a despot, while it would only be necessary to lead the Greeks. *Barbaroi* (a word that originally meant non-Greek-speaking peoples), reasoned Aristotle, were slaves by nature and needed to be treated as such. The opposite of a barbarian was a well-educated Greek-speaking person who valued most highly the virtues of self-denial and self-control. This basic teaching Alexander put rigorously into practice, treating Greeks as near equals and all others as peoples who required an iron authoritarian hand to rule them. Alexander studied a variety of subjects with Aristotle: medicine, biology, geometry, astronomy, and rhetoric (particularly the art of arguing both sides of a question equally well). For three years Alexander studied with Aristotle, and what he learned then would shape him for the rest of his life, especially the lesson about the inherent superiority of the Greek language and culture to all other forms of human expression.

When one considers the later period in Alexander's life, with all of his military victories across Asia Minor into Babylonia and indeed on to India, it is good to bear in mind that it was not his idea but Philip's to engage in a panhellenic crusade against Persia. Alexander, to be sure, though only a lad of eighteen, had been instrumental in the victory against the Greek forces at Chaeronea in 339, which in effect united Greece under Philip's rule; but it was Philip's dream originally to be the great Persian conqueror and he who originally had set up the Hellenic League. But Philip and Alexander were all too well aware that Greece would remain a divided land, not least because Darius already had some fifteen thousand Greek mercenaries on his payroll in 338, which is more than twice as many Greek men as the Hellenic League would initially muster to fight against Darius!

Yet Philip was undaunted, and in the early spring of 336 his troops crossed over into Asia Minor and met with success; indeed, they were welcomed with open arms by some of the Greek cities, including Ephesus, which placed a statue of Philip next to that of Artemis in the great temple of Artemis in the city. Coupled with a coup in Persia that led to the assassination of Darius II, things looked good for Philip's crusade against Persia. But in June of 336 all this was to change suddenly when one of Philip's own bodyguards stabbed him when the games were about to be celebrated. Historians have long debated whether Alexander, or Alexander's mother, or others might have long been plotting

The Hellenization of the Holy Land

The Hellenizing of the Holy Land was not merely intensive in some places but also extensive. From Tel Dan in the far northern part of the land comes a bilingual inscription from the late third or early second century B.C. The text is in Greek (at the top) and Aramaic, and reads, "To the god in Dan, Zoilos discharges his vow." Notice that the god in question is not given a name, which in theory could mean that the Hebrew God is being referred to, but most scholars have thought it more likely that some pagan or non-Jewish Semitic (Nabatean?) god is meant. The name Zoilos may be a barbarism for Silas. Whatever we conclude about the god addressed in this inscription, the fact that the inscription is in both Greek and Aramaic suggests that we are dealing with a Jewish, or at least a Semitic, person who also knows some Greek. We see evidence already well before the time of Christ of the influence of Hellenism on the region, even when it came to matters of religion. (*NewDocs* 1:105)

against Philip, since he seemed determined to raise up another heir to rule instead of allowing Alexander to do so, but the verdict on this must be "unproved."[2] In any event, the outcome was that Alexander assumed the mantle of kingship and the task of completing the job his father had begun in conquering Persia. It took him a while to consolidate his control of his kingdom, but in the early spring of 334 he was finally ready to cross the Dardanelles into Asia Minor and begin the campaign.

In regard to Alexander's activities in the region of prime concern for this study, we know that after the long siege and capture of Tyre in 332, he proceeded down the coastal plain with only Gaza offering resistance. According to a surely legendary account, Josephus (*Ant.* 11.326–339) reports that Alexander visited Jerusalem and was greeted by an elaborately robed high priest named Jaddua, who presented to Alexander the acknowledgement of the capitulation of the city. The tale further relates that Alexander offered sacrifice in the temple and read the Book of Daniel, in which his conquest had been recorded! What is noteworthy about this account, which is surely mostly fiction, is that it contains no evidence of conflict between the representative of Hellenism and the representative of Judaism.[3] It is probably true that Alexander largely left intact the Persian structures of governance in Jerusalem, and perhaps also true that he allowed some Jews to join his military

2. See ibid., 66.
3. See J. Hayes and S. Mandell, *The Jewish People in Classical Antiquity: From Alexander to Bar Kochba* (Louisville: Westminster John Knox, 1998), 24.

forces, permitting them to continue to observe their own religious customs (see Josephus, *Ant*. 11.338–339).

Alexander then proceeded on to Egypt, where he was crowned pharaoh in November of that same year (332). His first royal act, prompted by a dream, was to plan the building of a great port city (Alexandria). Especially from Egypt was the Hellenizing influence to radiate into the promised land over the succeeding centuries. It is no accident that the translation of the Hebrew Scriptures into Greek took place in the Jewish community in Egypt and from thence came to influence the believing community in Jerusalem, Judea, and even Galilee.

When finally Alexander engaged and defeated Darius III in 331, it became evident that he would be a world ruler quite unlike the Persian kings. His desire was for a unified world culture of a Hellenized type, to which end he forced ten thousand of his Greek soldiers to marry ten thousand Persian women. The experiment does not seem to have accomplished a great deal in itself, but it revealed the pattern that Alexander saw as desirable. His successors were to implement the policy of Hellenization to one degree or another over the coming century and a half.

It is not necessary to chronicle the long string of battles and victories Alexander was involved in during the last decade of his life (333–323), but several crucial points need to be made: First, Alexander conquered the entire region surrounding Israel, including Syria and Egypt. Second, the Hellenizing influence on the region was not limited to the time of Alexander's conquests, but continued during the era of his successors, the Ptolemies and the Seleucids, who consolidated the cultural impact of the Greek invasions. Third, while Alexander was a conqueror, and his true genius was as a field commander, his successors were rulers and administrators, and it is to them that we may credit the lion's share of Hellenizing influence on Jewish peoples both in the Holy Land and in the Diaspora. Fourth, and perhaps the most crucial point to bear in mind, many Jews during the period of 332–67 B.C. came to believe the claim that Greek culture and language were superior forms of human culture and expression and sought to emulate that culture by (1) adopting Greek educational practices (including learning rhetoric); (2) embracing Greek views about physical education and training, to the extent of being willing to build gymnasia even in Israel and to participate in Olympic style games (even if it required surgery to remove the marks of circumcision!); (3) accepting Greek ideals about independence and democracy. Let us consider how this transpired during the time of Alexander's successors, 323–167 B.C.

Alexander's Successors

Ptolemy, a high-ranking Macedonian general and longtime confidant of Alexander, was perhaps the wisest of his successors. Rather than becoming embroiled in disputes over who would rule the entire Alexandrian empire, Ptolemy chose to try to gain control over the region he saw as most strategic and promising within that empire— Egypt. It was Ptolemy who stole the body of Alexander and took it to Egypt, where he constructed a great tomb in Alexandria for his former friend. Ptolemy was initially content with the title of satrap (a Persian term) over the region, until in 321 he was challenged for the territory by another former comrade of Alexander, Perdiccas. This attack on his realm was unsuccessful, and in due course it precipitated Ptolemy assuming the title of king in 305. To further legitimate his control over the region, each of the succeeding kings in the Ptolemaic dynasty was to assume the name Ptolemy, and the queens were all to call themselves Cleopatra. If one were to take Egypt as a test case as to whether Hellenization could happen successfully in a land with radically different language and customs and a long and proud history and heritage, the answer must be an emphatic yes.

In fact, Ptolemy II and III managed to take dominion over Cyrenaica, Cyprus, many of the Aegean isles, and parts of Asia Minor and Israel. The domestic policy of the Ptolemies was to leave in place as much of the native culture as possible, and also to leave control over the running of the economic and business affairs of the country in the hands of the natives. Yes, there was a centralized bureaucracy for the collection of taxes and for public works projects such as expanding the canal system to increase the amount of arable land, but this affected the day-to-day living of most Egyptians very little. More intrusive was the control of banking and of imports and exports, as well as of the production of various kinds of oil. But the Ptolemies knew that if they were to successfully Hellenize Egypt, they also had to Egyptianize themselves, and so they adopted and adapted many of the old pharaonic customs and habits.

From the outset, Ptolemy I's plan was to make Egypt into a showplace of learning and culture for the Mediterranean world, and so he and his successors offered major inducements of patronage so that the artists and educators and rhetoricians of the Greek world would move to Alexandria. One of the great drawing cards was the development of an unparalleled library with its huge collections of scrolls. Soon enough, even great figures from Athens, such as Demetrius of Phalerum, relocated to Alexandria so that they could practice their philosophy and statecraft in this new Hellenistic environment. Like the Romans after them, the Ptolemies were wise enough to encourage the continuation of the traditional Egyptian cults without change, but they added to this their own patron deity, Sarapis, which involved a syncretism of Egyptian and Greek religion.

Through commerce more than military exploits, Egypt under the Ptolemies had considerable influence over what transpired in Israel. "The Temple state, comprised of Judah and Jerusalem, was incorporated into the highly organized economic administration of the Ptolemies. The community was subject to the system of heavy taxation, royal monopolies, and land lease policy that the Ptolemies maintained."[4]

Jews also found life in Egypt acceptable as they were allowed to practice their own religion, as was also true in Israel. Naturally, the Ptolemaic influence waxed and waned as stronger and weaker rulers came and went. Near the very end of the Ptolemaic period there still stood the imposing figure of Cleopatra VII, who had revived the sagging economy and was well supported by her native peasants. Her downfall came, however, due to her ambition to become queen of the entire Mediterranean world, which led to the courting of first Julius Caesar and then Marc Antony. When both of these had died, and Octavian (i.e., Augustus) could not be enticed, Cleopatra sealed the fate of the Ptolemaic dynasty by taking her own life, thus in effect handing Egypt over to the rising power in the west—Rome.[5]

The other major dynasty deriving from the partitioning of the Alexandrian Empire was the Seleucid dynasty. This kingdom basically extended from Asia Minor east to the limits of Persian territory. In fact, this kingdom had two capitals (one at Antioch in Syria, the other at Seleucia on the Tigris in Mesopotamia). Like the Ptolemies, the Seleucids remained Greek in language and culture but in their style of autocratic rule they followed the example of their Persian predecessors, and perhaps most importantly, they began to be worshiped as gods as early as Antiochus II (who ruled from 261 to 247 B.C.). The major rulers of this dynasty were Seleucus I (312–280 B.C.), Antiochus I (280–261 B.C.), Antiochus II, Antiochus III (223–187 B.C.), and, most notoriously from a Jewish point of view, Antiochus IV (175–163 B.C.), who dubbed himself Epiphanes ("god manifest"). It is important to note that already in his day, Seleucus I began the policy of founding cities in Asia Minor designed to foster the spread of Hellenism in the region. As part of the same operation he settled Jews in these cities to whom he gave citizen-

4. Ibid., 32. See particularly the papyrus from 260 B.C. (p. 33) that documents the policy of tight economic control of the region.
5. See D. B. Sandy, "Ptolemies," *DNTB*, 273–75.

ship rights (Appian, *Syriaca* 57). Hellenized Jews at the turn of the third century B.C. were already being used as agents of Hellenization in Asia Minor. It is perhaps also of significance that Syrian Antioch proved to be the first city where Jewish and Gentile Christians seem to have shared fellowship meals together (cf. Galatians 1–2), and that same city is where the name *Christianoi* first seems to have been applied to Christians (Acts 11:26). In a city that had long sought to foster *oikoumenē* (community) between various ethnic groups through the syncretizing influences of Hellenism, it is not surprising to find such things happening.

Furthermore, Greek cities were established in and around the Holy Land to further the influence of Hellenism on the region. In some cases this meant the reconstituting of existing cities such as Gaza or Acco (renamed Ptolemais) or Beth Shean (Scythopolis) or Gadara in a more Greek mold, and in other cases the founding of new cities in the Trans-Jordan such as Philadelphia, Pella, and Philotera. Each of these cities not only had a Greek constitution or political organization, but also was organized around the gymnasium with a focus on socializing the youth into Greek culture (the body of youth being called the *ephēbeion*).

After 250 B.C. the Seleucids gradually lost control of the land east of the Euphrates, which made them concentrate all the more on the lands in the region of Syria and Asia Minor. The Seleucids had won a decisive victory at Paneion (Caesarea Philippi) over the Ptolemies in 198 B.C., and Israel was governed by these rulers from Antioch for the next fifty years. By the end of 198 the Seleucids, through Antiochus II, were in rather firm control of Israel militarily, and they went about dictating policy to the local town councils (*synedrion*), siding with one and then the other of the Jewish priestly lines in these councils as they sought to have power. The one exception to this rule seems to be Jerusalem and a few square miles outside of it, which was called Judea. Under the Persians this city-state had had considerable internal autonomy (cf. Ezra 7:14), a policy that was largely continued by the Seleucids. It had been organized as a temple-state with the Pentateuch serving as its constitution. The high priest was in charge of this minuscule kingdom except, of course, for military matters, which rested in the hands of the imperial governor. Yet the reminder of Hayes and Mandell is salutary: "Clearly there was far more Hellenization in the Jewish Temple state than 1 or 2 Maccabees or even Josephus openly acknowledged."[6] This was true both before and during the Maccabean era.

Less than nine years after the Seleucids gained a firm grip on the Holy Land, in 190 B.C. they suffered a crushing defeat at the battle of

6. Hayes and Mandell, *Jewish People*, 13.

Magnesia, causing them to lose control of Asia Minor to the rising power in the West—Rome. But the peace proved to be more costly to the Seleucids than the war, for the terms imposed in 188 at Apamea not only formalized the loss of Asia Minor but also forced on the Seleucids a huge tax to be paid twelve times a year. This enormous financial burden was to a large extent responsible for the way Antiochus IV related to the various candidates vying for the high priest's post in Jerusalem. First there was the bribe that Jason (note the Greek name), the brother of the then existing Zadokite priest Onias III, offered to Antiochus to make him high priest. Antiochus accepted; he could hardly afford to do otherwise. But Jason had also promised, with the bribe, to accelerate the pace of the Hellenization of Judea. Only a few years later, in 171 B.C., a man named Menelaus, who could not even claim Zadokite heritage and who was an even more ardent Hellenizer, offered an even bigger bribe to have himself made high priest. This bribe was also accepted. It should also be kept in mind that tax farming was already a practice of both the Ptolemies and the Seleucids well before the Romans were involved in the region. The Romans in this matter, as well as in others, simply continued the practices of their predecessor rulers.

But Antiochus IV was not satisfied with controlling just Israel. He took his troops and attempted to annex Egypt, an effort that likely would have succeeded had not the Romans intervened on the side of the Ptolemies in 168 B.C. When news of this defeat reached Jerusalem, there was an attempt to reinstate Jason in the office of high priest, ousting Menelaus. Antiochus was in no mood for such "treason," and on his way back from Egypt he demolished Jerusalem's city walls, looted the temple treasury, and sought to give the city a new constitution, including a new cultic orientation. The temple was again placed under the control of Menelaus, only now the god to be worshiped there was Olympian Zeus, also identified as the Syrian god Ba'al Shammen ("the lord of heaven"). From December 167 to December 164 Judean Jews endured some of the darkest days in their history. The activities going on in the temple during this time came to be called the "abomination of desolation," or put another way, the "appalling sacrilege" (cf. 1 Macc. 1:54; Dan. 11:31; Mark 13:14). The extent of the progress of Hellenization in Judea at this juncture is shown by the fact that the Judean "aristocratic and educated classes in particular willingly consented to the Hellenising programme of Antiochus Epiphanes, and indeed promoted it."[7]

7. E. Schürer, *The History of the Jewish People in the Age of Jesus Christ (175 B.C.–A.D. 135)*, vol. 1, rev. and ed. G. Vermes and F. Millar (Edinburgh: Clark, 1973), 145.

Needless to say, many Jews did not accept this desecration of their holy place and paid for the rejection of the royal decrees with their lives. The Hasmoneans[8] were a priestly family who rejected the radical Hellenizing policies of Menelaus. The elderly Mattathias not only refused to offer the sacrifice prescribed by Antiochus IV, but also killed a Jew and an officer on the spot who were undertaking such a sacrifice in the town of Modein. Mattathias immediately fled to the hills and died soon thereafter. His five sons, and in particular his son Judas, would lead the rebellion against Antiochus.

Judas's guerrilla tactics proved successful against the much larger armies of Antiochus—so much so that Antiochus sought to come to terms with Judas (who had earned the nickname Maccabeus, "hammer"), having suffered several defeats in 166–165 B.C. In December of 165 Judas led his small army into Jerusalem and purified the temple. The ban on the worship of Yahweh was rescinded, and the traditional worship was resumed in the temple in Jerusalem in 164 even though Antiochus did not formally recognize Jewish religious liberty until 163. The purification and restoration of the cultus in Jerusalem is celebrated today as the Feast of Hanukkah (or Dedication). It is important to note that the Maccabees were not concerned just with the Jews of Judea. There must have been a considerable number of devout Jews in Galilee who had close fellowship with Judean Jews, because "one of the first acts of the Maccabees after the restoration of the cult was to bring help to fellow-Jews in Galilee and Gilead who were oppressed by heathens, Simon going to Galilee and Judas to Gilead (1 Macc. 5:9–54)."[9] Yet the tenuous nature of Judaism in Galilee at this time seems to be demonstrated by the fact that Simon, after defeating the Gentiles in Galilee, led all the Jews and their families out of Galilee, settling them in Judea (1 Macc. 5:23). At that juncture the Maccabees were not prepared to Judaize Galilee or Gilead.

Yet having gained a taste for freedom, the Maccabees decided to struggle for political as well as religious independence, a struggle that was to continue for over twenty years. Judas won a major victory over the Seleucids at Beth Haran, northwest of Jerusalem in 161 B.C., but he lost his life soon thereafter in a subsequent battle at nearby Elsa. The youngest of the Maccabee brothers, Jonathan, succeeded Judas as the leader of the rebel army, a role he played for the next three years. In 157 the Seleucids made peace with Jonathan, and in 152 he was named high priest in Jerusalem as well as administrator of Judea. Jonathan engaged in a policy of diplo-

8. The name seems to have come from a family ancestor named Hashmon or Hasmon.
9. Schürer, *History of the Jewish People*, 142.

Illustration 1.3 The western retaining wall of the Herodian temple—known as the Wailing Wall.

matic appeasement, supporting various Seleucid rulers or pretenders to the throne, all the while increasing the amount of territory under Jewish control. In 143 one of those pretenders, Tryphon, saw Jonathan as a threat to his own power and sought to crush him. Through deception Jonathan was taken prisoner near Beth Shean and later executed.

Many of the Jewish insurgents had been uneasy with Jonathan because not only had he had dealings with the Seleucids, but he also owed his priesthood and administratorship to his negotiations with them. The case was different with Jonathan's successor, Simon, the second son of Mattathias. He successfully negotiated a full peace treaty with the Seleucids in 142 B.C., making Judea politically independent, but only Simon among the original five brothers was still alive to celebrate that day. This peace treaty precipitated the expulsion of all Seleucid representatives from Jerusalem that same year. In 141 the Jewish people and their priests chose Simon to be their high priest and governor, and it was stated that this priesthood would stay in Simon's family. All seemed well for almost six years, until Simon's son-in-law assassinated him.

But the Maccabees were not to be shifted from power through an act of treachery. Simon's youngest son, John Hyrcanus, was quickly established as the next ruler before his rivals could get their act together. He was to rule from 134 to 104 B.C. If Judas had been like a David to his people, it could be said that John Hyrcanus was like a Solomon, for he freed Judea from all remnants of Seleucid influence and expanded his realm to include Samaria, Idumea, parts of Galilee, and even some territory east of the Jordan. Furthermore, John deliberately set out to Judaize these territories and so reclaim their peoples as well as the land for Judaism. Though John never proclaimed himself king, he had coins struck with his name on them, and he ruled over a court, having designated himself high priest and leader of the Jewish nation.

We should note that John himself had a definite affinity for some Greek ideas, as is shown by his changing of his sons names from Hebrew names to Greek ones. His imitation of other world rulers, and of some of the Greek ideals, antagonized more traditional Jews who held to the earlier Hasmonean notions about purity. It was during this period that the group known as the Pharisees began to form and to protest the Hellenizing practices, which they saw as endangering Judaism.

Little can be said about Aristobulus I, the son and successor of John Hyrcanus, except that he married Salome Alexandra. His brother Alexander Janneus (again note the Greek name) became high priest and ruler through marrying his brother's widow, Salome. He ruled from 103 to 76 B.C. and followed the expansionist and Judaizing practices of John Hyrcanus, extending the borders of Israel beyond even their Solomonic extent. His reign, however, was marred by his dictatorial manner and by the internal strife and intrigues that plagued the court. He lost his life while besieging a Greek city. His wife, Salome, succeeded him and ruled from 76 to 67, and she supported the Pharisees, who had become her closest advisors on religious matters.

Unfortunately, Salome's life ended just before the outbreak of civil war between her two sons, Aristobulus II and Hyrcanus II, who were rivals for the throne. Actually, trouble had begun before Salome's death, for she had appointed Hyrcanus II high priest before she died, and then sought to make him ruler as well. Aristobulus II, however, had powerful supporters and was having none of this. He in effect seized the government and forced his brother into an arrangement whereby he would be the political ruler and Hyrcanus would remain the high priest in power. But an Idumean named Antipater, seeking to feather his own nest, offered to help Hyrcanus II regain the political power he had ceded to Aristobulus II. A general civil war ensued from 67 to 63 B.C. Yet the forces of Antipater proved insufficient, and so another source of military might, the army of the Roman general Pompey, was enlisted to settle the matter. In 63 Pompey entered the fray, captured Jerusalem, exiled Aristobulus II and his immediate family as well as many other Jews, and reconfirmed Hyrcanus II as the high priest. But

Illustration 1.4 Maccabean coin.

Pompey did not restore Hyrcanus II to political power; indeed, he reduced the size of Hyrcanus's kingdom.

This uneasy arrangement lasted until the death of Pompey in 48 B.C.
At that point Hyrcanus II and Antipater sought the support of another
famous Roman general, Julius Caesar, who in turn made Antipater
procurator of Judea and reconfirmed Hyrcanus II as high priest, also
granting him a limited amount of political power. The Jewish territories formerly seized by Pompey were returned, and all Roman soldiers
were withdrawn from Judea. Unfortunately, Caesar himself was assassinated in 44, which led to a further coup in Judea, with Antipater
being killed and Hyrcanus II being captured by the surviving son of
Aristobolus II, Antigonus, the last remnant of the Hasmonean line.
Though Antigonus proclaimed himself king of Judea in 40 B.C., the
Roman senate was not at all pleased with his actions against those
whom Rome had earlier confirmed in power, and so it was that in 39
the Idumean Herod the Great was proclaimed by the senate as king of
Judea. But Herod had to unseat Antigonus, and so more war ensued for
two years until Antigonus was captured and put to death in 37. Herod
then brought back the now aged Hyrcanus II to be the high priest, but
he fell afoul of Herod's suspicions and was executed in 30 for conspiracy. Thus it came to pass through this labyrinthine process that (1) Israel became a partially Hellenized realm; (2) Israel came to be ruled
first by Alexander's successors, then briefly by Jews, then finally by the
Idumean Herod; and (3) Judea came to be a province ultimately ruled
first by client kings, then by procurators or prefects.

Conclusions: Early Jews and the Legacy of Hellenism

At this juncture I summarize some of the important points about the Hellenizing of Jews during the period under scrutiny in this chapter. The major conclusion of M. Hengel's landmark study *Judaism and Hellenism*[10] has stood the test of time. We cannot set Judaism over against Hellenism as if they were binary opposites, nor is it satisfactory to contrast a Hellenized Judaism found in the Diaspora with Palestinian Judaism. All Judaism in the wake of Alexander and his successors was Hellenized to one degree or another. The effect of Hellenization was extensive, even when it was not always intensive. The following clues make clear that Hellenization was a fact of life during the time of the Maccabees, even in Judea: (1) the *Letter of Aristeas* takes for granted that the Judean scholars summoned to Egypt to translate the Hebrew Scriptures into Greek had full command of the Greek language; (2) the grandson of Jesus ben Sira who translated the Book of Sirach into Greek was Judean by birth; (3) the Greek translator of the Book of Esther was also Judean by birth, according to the subtitle of the book in the Septuagint; (4) it is likely that the Eupolemus whom Judas Maccabeus sent to Rome as head of a Jewish delegation (1 Macc. 8:17; 2 Macc. 4:11) is the same Eupolemus of whose written works we have Greek fragments.

The helpful summary of L. Grabbe is on the mark in these matters: (1) Hellenism was a cultural orientation, Judaism a religion, and frankly, some aspects of Hellenistic culture were irrelevant to Jewish life and practice and would have been seen as neither good nor bad, even by the most pious and orthodox. The distinction in 1 Maccabees between Hellenizers and Judaizers reminds us that some were less resistant and some more resistant to Greek culture, but even the Maccabees themselves adopted and adapted some Greek ways. Judaizers were those who opposed specific Hellenistic ideas or practices affecting their religion. (2) The reactions of Judaizers to Hellenization varied, depending on whether one has in mind the Hasidim, the Maccabees, the partisans of Onias, or those who refused to defend themselves. Not even Menelaus (see above) rejected the label "Jew," though most observant Jews would have considered him a bad Jew. (3) To be Hellenized in the sense of knowing the Greek language and adopting some aspects of Greek culture did not mean that one had ceased to be a Jew, as is clear from the example of Philo of Alexandria, and the message of the *Letter of Aristeas* suggests that Jews could take part in a Hellenistic world without compromising their Judaism.

10. 2 vols., trans. J. Bowden (Philadelphia: Fortress, 1974).

(4) We must not, however, exaggerate the intensity of Greek influence in Jewish culture in Israel, for Greek did not displace the ancestral languages of Hebrew and Aramaic, even though it was used some for commerce and various other forms of communication with non-Jews. (5) As they somewhat accommodated to Hellenistic culture, "the Jews always maintained one area that could not be compromised without affecting their Judaism, that of religion. In the Greco-Roman world only the Jews refused honor to gods, shrines, and cults other than their own. . . . For the vast majority, this was the final barrier that could not be crossed; we know from antiquity of only a handful of examples of Jews who abandoned their Judaism."[11]

A Closer Look: *The Pharisees*

The term "Pharisees" seems to derive from the Hebrew root *prs*, which means either "separate" or "interpret"—probably the former. Thus, the Pharisees were the "Separate Ones," probably because of their attempt to distinguish themselves in the careful observance of the law from Gentiles and from less observant Jews. The term does not seem to have been a self-designation, but rather, a label applied to them by others. It is outsiders like the writers of the New Testament or Josephus who call these Jews Pharisees.

The Pharisees first appear on the landscape of early Judaism during the time of the Hasmonean rulers. Josephus reports that they were initially very influential with John Hyrcanus (134–104 B.C.) in giving him guidance about how Jewish law and life should be interpreted (*Ant.* 13.288–298). Apparently, the Pharisees were under the patronage of Hyrcanus and served as his advisors in various matters. One Pharisee, Eliezer, criticized John's policies, and this led to a dispute with some Sadducees, in particular with Jonathan, a Sadducean friend of John Hyrcanus. Jonathan won the argument with Eliezer, and this led to the diminution of the influence of the Pharisees on the ruler at this point.

Conflict between the Pharisees and the ruler continued during the reign of Alexander Janneus (103–76 B.C.), the son of Hyrcanus. It is telling, however, that on his deathbed Janneus advised his wife, Alexandra, who was to be his successor, to make peace with the Pharisees so that

---

11. L. Grabbe, *Judaism from Cyrus to Hadrian*, vol. 1 (Minneapolis.: Fortress, 1992), 169–70.

they might help her by controlling the people (*Ant*. 13.399–417). This same passage reveals that what the Pharisees were really seeking was control over the laws that governed everyday Jewish life. Under Alexandra, the Pharisees would have substantial powers, including the ability to free prisoners and recall exiles, though they could not punish anyone on their own authority.[12] But this political power was to be short-lived, for Alexandra's successors did not turn to the Pharisees for support.

Under Herod the Great (37–4 B.C.), two Pharisaic leaders, Pollion and his disciple Samaias, supported Herod strongly, but this was a sort of backhanded slap in the face directed against the Sanhedrin due to its weak leadership (*Ant*. 14.163–184; 15.1–4). These two Pharisees became prominent clients of Herod, and his good relationships with them led to the exemption of all Pharisees from a loyalty oath to Herod. Josephus relates that toward the end of Herod's reign there were about six thousand Pharisees (*Ant*. 17.41–42), which suggests they had become a significant social movement. The descriptions Josephus provides of the Pharisees suggest that they were not part of any revolutionary movement and that their beliefs and practices were highly traditional in nature. Indeed, the Pharisees were noted not only for their knowledge of the law and of ancestral customs, but also for their meticulous attention to their practice of the law. It seems clear that even well before the New Testament era, the Pharisees were a group highly respected by the Jewish people and at least on occasion served as the voice of the people to their leaders.

The careful work of J. Neusner sifting through the rabbinic corpus has shown that the pre–A.D. 70 Pharisees were a group especially focused on issues of dietary laws, ritual purity for meals, and observance of the Sabbath, an impression confirmed by the New Testament itself.[13] Note that it is precisely on these sorts of matters that Jesus took issue with the Pharisees. If we were to describe the Pharisees in a broad way, we may say that they sought to live as if they were priests and as if the laws that applied to the priests in the temple applied to ordinary Jews in their homes. They sought to spread a Levitical view of holiness throughout the land, and in a sense they thereby called for a sort of priesthood of all Jewish believers. The Pharisees also claimed to be those who passed on faithfully the oral traditions given to Moses on Mount

12. See the discussion by A. Saldarini, "Pharisees," *ABD* 5:289–303.
13. J. Neusner, *The Rabbinic Traditions about the Pharisees before 70*, vol. 3 (Leiden: Brill, 1971), 304.

Sinai. By claiming to have both the correct interpretation of the Mosaic law and the ability to explain and even expand the law by means of oral tradition to meet new dilemmas and situations, they asserted explicit and extensive authority over their fellow Jews. In particular, it was the scribes (or *haberim*) among the Pharisees who were the Torah scholars to whom the Pharisees turned for precise rulings on various matters. They had little tolerance for anyone who threatened the assumptions upon which their authority was based. Josephus reports that the Pharisees also believed in bodily resurrection, in rewards and punishments after death, and that some of them apparently believed in a certain degree of divine determinism or divine providence (cf. *J.W.* 2.119–166; *Ant.* 18.11–25; 13.171–173, 297–298).

Josephus consistently implies that the Pharisees were generally of a lower station in terms of social position than the Sadducees. They could be clients of a ruler, but they usually lacked direct political power. So far as we can tell, they had members in the Sanhedrin, but they did not control it, for that was the provenance of the high priest, and we know that his closest allies were the Sadducees. One must not assume that Pharisaism during or before the New Testament era was a monolithic entity. But the Pharisees' influence even in the temple is clear because the priests performed the Day of Atonement sacrifice according to the Pharisaic outline of how it ought to be done. The later remark in the Mishnah correctly reveals how seriously the Pharisees took oral tradition as well: "It is more culpable to teach against the ordinances of the scribes than against the Torah itself" (*Sanh.* 11:3).

In fact, a variety of Pharisees existed, differing in social status, education, and views on various subjects. There were more strict and less strict Pharisees in and before Jesus' day, as the debates between the house of Shammai and of Hillel show. The Hillelites appear to have been the more lenient Pharisees, and there is some reason to think they steered Judaism in a more quietistic, Hellenistic, and philosophical direction.[14] The Shammaites appear to have been more the hard-liners, with perhaps even a revolutionary or violent contingent among them, to which Saul of Tarsus may have belonged. It would be a mistake, however, to think that politics in the narrow sense of the term was the primary focus of the Pharisees in Jesus' day. Politics mainly concerned them insofar as it affected their practice of Torah. Their real agenda was the hallowing of everyday life in all its aspects within the existing structure of society, not apart from it (unlike

14. See B. Witherington III, *The Christology of Jesus* (Minneapolis: Fortress, 1990), 58–59.

the Qumranites). Jesus, as we will see, had a good deal in common with the Pharisees, and we need not think that he was at odds with all Pharisees, nor that he had no adherents or admirers among the Pharisaic movement, nor that he thought they all were hypocrites. Nevertheless, as we also will see, major philosophical differences definitely stood between Jesus and the Pharisees as they each sought to reform God's people in light of their profoundly held convictions about future judgment and the eschatological events.

Chapter 2

The Rise of the Herodians, the Birth of Jesus, and the Dawn of an Empire

63–4 B.C.

When Pompey the Great took Jerusalem in 63 B.C., probably few thought that this foreshadowed the coming of a continual Roman presence in the region for the next several hundred years.[1] Yet before the Roman Empire ever came to be, a dark cloud of Roman presence

1. I am indebted to J. Hayes and S. Mandell whose fine work on the subject matter of this chapter made my work here much easier.

already was hovering over the ancient Near East. Western Mediterranean culture was on a collision course with eastern Mediterranean culture.

Illustration 2.1 Jewish History during Roman Occupation

Roman Rulers/Emperors	Date	Jewish Rulers
Pompey/Caesar (63–31 B.C.)	63 B.C.	Herod the Great (37–4 or 2 B.C.)
Augustus (31 B.C.–A.D. 14)	4 B.C.	Kingdom divided—Archelaus (4 or 2 B.C.– A.D. 6): Judea, Samaria, Idumea; Antipas (4/2 B.C.– A.D. 39): Galilee, erea; Philip (4/2 B.C.– A.D. 34) Iturea, Trachonitis
	A.D. 6	Judea turned over to prefects/procurators
Tiberius (14–37)	14	
	26	Pontius Pilate (26–37), fifth prefect
Gaius Caligula (37–41)	37	
	39	Herod Agrippa I (39?–44)—Herod the Great's kingdom reunited
Claudius (41–54)	44	Fadus procurator over Judea (44–46)
	46	Tiberius Alexander, procurator (46–48)
	48	Cumanus (48–52)
	50	Herod Agrippa II takes over parts of Galilee, Perea
	52	Felix, Roman procurator in Judea (52–58)
Nero (54–68)	54	
	60	Festus (60–62)
	62	Albinus (62–64)
	64	Florus (64–66)
	66	Jewish War (66–70); Vespasian sent in 66
Galba/Otho/Vitellius (68–69)	68	

Vespasian (69–79)	69	Vespasian to Rome; Titus conquers Jerusalem
	74	Flavius Silva conquers last Jewish fortress, Masada
Titus (79–81)	79	
Domitian (81–96)	90	Herod Agrippa II dies

It is also fair to say that no one living in the early first century A.D. would have guessed that the birth of a carpenter from Nazareth just before the turn of the era was ultimately going to prove of more importance historically than the birth of Octavian or any of the emperors who followed him. To say that the period we are chronicling in this chapter is one of the most important periods in all of human history is to say too little. At the very least, for those who are the offspring of so-called Western culture, this is the inception of the most important and formative period in all of human history in terms of politics, religion, and culture.

The Rise of the Herodian Clan

After his conquest of Judea and Jerusalem, Pompey set about to reorganize the way the region was administered politically. Some of his actions may be seen as punitive. He was aggravated at having to besiege the temple precincts of Jerusalem for three months before it was finally taken. Yet it is significant that unlike other areas in the vicinity, Judea was not attached to Syria, but rather was allowed to maintain a separate identity. Hyrcanus II was allowed to keep the office of high priest and a portion of his civil authority, but the country itself was reduced to the old boundaries of Judah, and the Hellenistic cities conquered by the Maccabees reverted to their prior status as Greek cities. The Greek cities in the interior on both sides of the Jordan were grouped together into a league called the Decapolis.[2] Most importantly, Judea was placed under Roman tribute, and in short order a sum of more than ten thousand talents was extracted from them. The actions of Pompey make clear that he wished to maintain the area as a client state, not turn it into a Roman province.

The Romans themselves did not at this juncture seek to rule directly in the region, and so the rise of Antipater, the father of Herod the Great, becomes an important part of the story. We are told by Josephus that

---

2. Jesus was to visit at least one, if not more, of these cities.

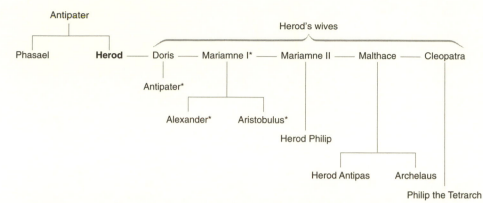

Illustration 2.2   Herod the Great's family tree. (Asterisks indicate execution by Herod.)

Antipater was an Idumean (*J.W.* 1.123; *Ant.* 14.8). This, however, does not mean that he may not have been at least nominally a Jew, because John Hyrcanus had taken Idumea and there had been many conversions to Judaism (*Ant.* 13.254). Antipater had served earlier as governor over Idumea under King Alexander Janneus and Queen Alexandra. Unlike Aristobulus II and Hyrcanus II, Antipater realized that the arrival of Roman forces in Syria and the Holy Land meant that a truly independent Judea was a vain hope. So it was that after some years of machinations and plottings by the remaining Hasmoneans, Julius Caesar in essence reconfirmed Hyrcanus II as the high priest, and Antipater became the de facto procurator of Judea.[3] Antipater was granted permission to restore the fortifications of the city, and the tax burden was reduced so that he could afford to do so. In addition, Julius Caesar made Judea exempt from the levying of Roman auxiliaries, and several cities were returned to Judean control, including Joppa (*Ant.* 14.195–210).

Perhaps the most significant act of Antipater was his appointment of his two sons as governors, Herod in Galilee and Phasael in Jerusalem and its vicinity (*J.W.* 1.203; *Ant.* 14.158). From the outset, Herod showed his true colors—energetic, impulsive, and given to take action quickly, frequently in ruthless fashion. In Galilee there was a leader of bandits (apparently peasants and landless persons) named Hezekiah, who had been creating mayhem on the Syrian border. Herod not only captured him but also had him and his followers executed (*J.W.* 1.204; *Ant.* 14.159). This greatly pleased the Roman governor in Syria, Sextus Caesar. The action, however, alarmed the aristocracy in Jerusalem be-

---

3. See J. Hayes and S. Mandell, *The Jewish People in Classical Antiquity: From Alexander to Bar Kochba* (Louisville: Westminster John Knox, 1998), 117–18.

cause "they saw how powerful and reckless Herod was and how much he desired to be a dictator" (*Ant.* 14.158–165; *J.W.* 1.204–207).[4] For this action the Sanhedrin summoned Herod to trial in Jerusalem, because an action by the Sanhedrin was required before the death penalty could be imposed on a Jew (*J.W.* 1.208–209; *Ant.* 14.165–167).[5]

It is not clear what happened when Herod appeared in Jerusalem for trial. He may have been tried and acquitted, the trial may have been postponed, or Herod may even have fled to escape a guilty verdict. What we do know is that Sextus Caesar wrote Hyrcanus asking him to acquit Herod (*Ant.* 14.169–179; *J.W.* 1.210–211). Herod went and stayed with Sextus, who then appointed him governor over the Decapolis and the city of Samaria. Having gathered some troops, Herod then marched on Jerusalem, probably to take revenge on the aristocrats who had insisted on his trial, and perhaps to depose Hyrcanus as well. But through the intervention of his father, Antipater, and his brother Phasael, he was persuaded to back off, and the impetuous young man retreated to Galilee (*Ant.* 14.177–184; *J.W.* 1.212–215).

The next few years leading up to 40 B.C. were times of utter chaos in the Holy Land. The Roman struggles between Brutus and Cassius on one side and Marc Antony and Julius Caesar on the other spilled over into Syria, and led to the strange, brief alliance between Herod and Hyrcanus II to prevent one of the remaining offspring of Aristobulus II from ruling in Judea. Antony, who was supposed to be in charge of the Roman forces in Syria, was too busy wooing Cleopatra to do so, and into the power vacuum came other forces—particularly the Parthians. During this period Antipater was poisoned, and Herod, Phasael, and Hyrcanus found themselves besieged within the city of Jerusalem by Parthians led by Antigonus. We should note that many Jews volunteered to fight with the Parthians against the Herod family (*J.W.* 1.250).

4. Here and elsewhere it is clear that I think that Josephus is basically reliable in his portrayal of Herod as a ruthless, egocentric ruler. Although some good points are made by P. Richardson, who shows that a few admirable things can be said about Herod, I am unconvinced by his attempt to portray Herod in a favorable light. Especially unconvincing is his attempt to portray Herod as a good Jew. A good Jew of Jesus' day was not like Herod, who Richardson admits "shared the religious outlook of most Roman citizens. He had little hesitation in acknowledging Octavian in the cult of Roma and Augustus, and he supported other temple cults such as Pythnian Apollo" (P. Richardson, *Herod: King of the Jews and Friend of the Romans* [Columbia: University of South Carolina Press, 1996], xiii). In other words, Herod was not a monotheistic Jew, and pointing out that in some ways he was Torah-observant while he was in Judea does not prove otherwise.

5. This shows what a different situation the Sanhedrin was in during Jesus' day, for by the time of Jesus' trial they had long since been stripped of the power of capital punishment, a divestment that likely took place when Judea was made a Roman province rather than a client state.

Illustration 2.3 Masada (with Roman seige ramp in the foreground) was one of Herod's fortresses.

While Phasael and Hyrcanus were eventually persuaded by the Parthian commander to leave the city, Herod and his family fled under cover of darkness and finally reached Masada, where he left his family with eight hundred troops and supplies while he himself set out for Petra (*Ant.* 14.348–362; *J.W.* 1.261–267). Hyrcanus was carried away to Parthia as a prisoner, having had his ears cut off (thus disqualifying him to be high priest [cf. Lev. 21:17–23]), and Antigonus either poisoned Phasael or he committed suicide. When Herod arrived in Petra, he was rejected by the Nabatean ruler Malchus I, and so he headed for Egypt. There he was well received by Cleopatra, who apparently hoped to have Herod retake Judea for her, but Herod demurred from such a task and instead set sail for Rome, even though it was late October and past the normal sailing season, in order to stake his claim to be ruler of Judea (*Ant.* 14.374–376; *J.W.* 1.277–279). Once Herod was in Rome, Antony and Octavian championed his cause before the senate, and the senate unanimously approved him as "king of Judea" (*Ant.* 14.377–389; *J.W.* 1.280–285). Herod left Rome with what he wanted, after only a one-week stay.

If we ask why the Romans had been willing to so strongly support Herod, when in fact Antony, while in Syria, had received many visits from Jewish groups asking Antony to oppose Herod and his family, the reasons seem to be as follows: (1) the Hasmonean family was in shambles, and no one remained as a viable candidate for the throne; (2) Antony and his family had always had good relationships with this Idumean family; (3) the Romans preferred at this stage of their existence to have others do the dirty work of containing Jewish hotheads and keeping the Parthians at bay, not least because ever since the time of Gaius Marius, the Roman army had been based not on conscription but on paid employment—a very expensive proposition; (4) Herod was unqualified to be the high priest, and thus he could not hold both the office of high priest and ruler (the Romans preferred that all power not be left in the hands of one client king); (5) the Romans saw in Herod a potential source of ongoing revenue, as he was ruthless enough to extract it from the populace and aristocrats if need be.[6]

Though declared king of Judea, Herod returned to the region with the task of winning back the country, which was under the control of Antigonus. He landed at Ptolemais and instantly began raising an army. The Roman commander in the area, Silo, was ordered to help Herod, but he did so without enthusiasm. Herod first set out to secure the coastal plain, taking Joppa, then he proceeded south and west, entering Idumea. He rescued his relatives, who were under siege at Masada, and then turned north to besiege Jerusalem. This effort failed initially, partly due to the lack of real help from Silo, and so Herod stopped the siege and retreated to Galilee (*Ant.* 14.394–412; *J.W.* 1.290–302).[7]

Galilee, however, was no safe haven for Herod. He faced much opposition, and at one point we are told that many of Herod's partisans and the nobility of Galilee were dragged from their homes and

6. Here I am basically following the conclusions of Hayes and Mandell, *Jewish People*, 125.

7. It is, of course, very important to read Josephus critically (see A Closer Look—Time and Calendars in Antiquity, below). Much scholarly debate has centered on whether *Jewish Wars* or *Antiquities of the Jews* is nearer the historical mark concerning the portrayal of Herod. I would urge that Josephus wrote *Wars* in the 70s under the patronage of Vespasian, and the work should be seen as an apologia for the Jewish people. In this work, Josephus deliberately masked some of his real views in an attempt to protect Jews and Judaism, which had just suffered the disaster of A.D. 70. In *Antiquities*, we find Josephus writing in the 90s (the work was finished under Domitian sometime in 93–94). It was through external urging that he took up the task, and he had had more time to assess the actual historical situations of the events of the earlier part of the first century. By and large, *Antiquities* does not serve the purpose of Roman political propaganda (i.e., unlike *J.W.* 3.108, where we are told explicitly that that work was written to deter other Jews from revolting against Rome). *Antiquities* concludes its account at the outset of the Jewish war in A.D. 66. (See B. Witherington III, *The Christology of Jesus* [Minneapolis: Fortress, 1990], 81–83.) In general, we may trust the portrait of Herod found in the *Antiquities* more than that found elsewhere in Josephus's writings.

drowned in the sea of Galilee. General insurrection was going on in
both Galilee and Judea at the time (*Ant.* 14.413–450; *J.W.* 1.303–307).
The turning point in the struggle really came when Marc Antony put a
new commander in Syria, Sosius, who was actually prepared to assist
Herod in establishing his claim. Sosius sent two legions ahead and followed with most of the rest of his army (*Ant.* 14.447). In due course,
Galilee was subdued, Antigonus's army was defeated, and Jerusalem
was besieged. The resistance was fierce, and not until the summer of
37 B.C. was the city taken.[8] The Romans, as well as Herod, were furious
that there had been such resistance, thus "the Jews on Herod's side
were anxious not to leave a single adversary alive. And so they were
slaughtered in heaps, whether crowded together in alleys and houses
or seeking refuge in the temple; no pity was shown either to infants or
the aged, nor were weak women spared, but even though the king sent
word around, urging them to forbear, not one of them held his hand,
but like madmen they fell upon persons of every age" (*Ant.* 14.480). Antigonus surrendered and was delivered to Antony, who had him executed. Interestingly, Dio Cassius reports that before Antigonus was beheaded, he was scourged while being tied to a cross, a punishment "no
other king had suffered at the hands of the Romans" (*Roman History*
49.22.6).[9]

Herod's rise to the throne had required much brutality and bloodshed, and things did not immediately become much easier for him
after having taken Jerusalem. Hayes and Mandell have divided Herod's
reign into three periods: (1) 37–30 B.C., a period of trying to settle internal problems and of dealing with difficulties in cementing his authority
because of the roles of Antony and Cleopatra in the region; (2) 30–10
B.C., a period of some prosperity and success, though with domestic
troubles; (3) 10–4 B.C., a time of both domestic and international troubles and turmoil.[10]

After the taking of Jerusalem, Herod encountered much animus
among his new subjects. There were to be difficulties with the remaining Hasmoneans as well, not to mention Cleopatra, who had designs on
his new realm. In fact, opposition was so extensive that Antony had to
leave a Roman legion encircling the city of Jerusalem "to protect the
king's position" (*Ant.* 15.72). It is interesting that two of Herod's closest
allies proved to be the Pharisees Pollion and Samaias. Pollion rebuked
the Sanhedrin for calling Herod before them, and the two recom-

8. On this date, see L. Grabbe, *Judaism from Cyrus to Hadrian*, vol. 2 (Minneapolis:
Fortress, 1992), 326–28.

9. Perhaps this served as a precedent for the later treatment of Jesus.

10. Hayes and Mandell, *Jewish People*, 129.

mended that Jerusalem be surrendered to Herod when he laid siege to it (*Ant*. 15.3–4).

It is clear that Herod, once in power, would stop at almost nothing to secure his position. For example, he brought in a priest from Babylonia named Hananel and installed him as high priest, despite Caesar's earlier promise that the priesthood would stay in the Hasmonean family (*Ant*. 14.194–195). This move infuriated Herod's wife and her mother, whose son Aristobulus III was passed over in this maneuver. Through pressure by way of Cleopatra and Antony, Herod was persuaded to remove Hananel and install Aristobulus, which produced an enormous popular response from the people (*Ant*. 15.50–52). This in turn raised all of Herod's fears and insecurities, and so he had Aristobulus drowned at a swimming party at Jericho, where his winter residence was (*Ant*. 15.53–56; *J.W*. 1.437). This act led to Herod having to explain himself to Antony, and apparently he bribed his way out of trouble on this occasion (*Ant*. 15.57–67, 74–79).

In the winter of 37–36 B.C. Marc Antony married Cleopatra, and she began to lobby more strongly for the restoration of her realm to its former Ptolemaic extent, which is to say that she began to lobby to be made ruler over Jerusalem and Judea. Antony agreed to giving her some control of part of Judea (including, apparently, the coastal region including Joppa, and the balsam and palm plantations near Jericho), and Herod felt it wise not to resist at that point. Herod was sent by Antony to do battle with Malchus and the Nabateans, an endeavor that led to some defeats, though total disaster was averted (*J.W*. 1.364–365), and in fact Herod showed some of his military skill in this conflict.

The period of 30–10 B.C. can be rightly called Herod's best years, in terms of successfully establishing himself and achieving some of his goals. With the death of both Antony and Cleopatra, and the turning of Egypt into a Roman province, a new era dawned in the reign of Herod. Herod, showing his political astuteness, appeared before Octavian at Rhodes, submitting to his authority, and confessed that he had been Antony's friend, but suggested that he would be an even more loyal friend of Octavian (*J.W*. 1.387–390). Octavian was obviously impressed with Herod, who could in fact point out that he had helped Octavian in the struggle against Antony by halting the advance of Antony's gladiators to Egypt (*Ant*. 15.195; *J.W*. 1.392). The end result of his audience with Octavian was that Herod was reconfirmed in his position as king of Judea, a result that disappointed many of his Jewish subjects (*Ant*. 15.198). Later that same year it was Herod who helped supply Octavian as he proceeded to invade Egypt (*Ant*. 15.199–201; *J.W*. 1.394–396). When Octavian proved successful in Egypt and elsewhere, and became

Illustration 2.4 Herod the Great coin found near Ramla.

Augustus (27 B.C.), this served to secure Herod in his position for the rest of his reign.

Octavian on three occasions granted Herod more land, to the point that by 20 B.C. he was in control of territory as extensive as the Hasmonean kingdom at its apex. Herod became the linchpin in Octavian's strategy for controlling the crucial landbridge region between Syria and Egypt at the east coast of the Mediterranean. Herod was designated Augustus's "ally and friend," which was in fact a legal status giving Herod virtually unlimited power and control as a client king over his own domain (*Ant.* 17.246). "Only foreign alliances and the waging of war required the full approval of Rome."[11]

The impression must not be left that after his meeting with Octavian all was smooth sailing for Herod. He returned from Rhodes to find his wife, Mariamne, and other of the Hasmoneans still harboring desires to reestablish a Hasmonean in power, either priestly or political. Herod's relationship with his wife finally reached the breaking point, and he had her tried and executed (*Ant.* 15.202–236). Soon thereafter, Herod executed his Hasmonean mother-in-law, Alexandra (*Ant.* 15.240–251).

Under these sorts of circumstances, it is not surprising that Herod was rather paranoid, and so the refortification of his kingdom and the building of some citadels seemed a logical move, not least because most of the fortifications, even in Jerusalem, were run down or crumbling after years of strife and neglect. Thus it was that Herod built the Antonia Tower (named after Marc Antony) in Jerusalem, refortified the

11. Ibid., 136.

city walls, and built three large towers into these walls, naming one after his brother (Phasael), one after his wife (Mariamne), and one after a close friend (Hippicus). These actions were followed by building programs on a massive scale. The fortress Herodium was built outside Bethlehem, the fortress Masada was further strengthened, the fortress Machaerus was built in the Trans-Jordan region, and several other such fortresses were constructed. The city of Samaria had had good relationships with Herod since his coronation, and Herod rewarded the loyalty by turning the city into one of his major citadels, complete with a new temple to Augustus, constructed for the im-

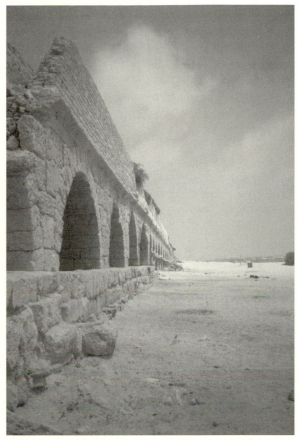

Illustration 2.5 The Roman aqueduct at Caesarea Maritima, one of the cities Herod built.

perial cult to be practiced there (*Ant*. 15.292–298; *J.W.* 1.403). It was for actions such as these that Josephus and others rightly had doubts about whether Herod could be considered a true Jew.

Herod also undertook the total rebuilding of a harbor or seaport at Strato's Tower, renaming it Caesarea, after the emperor. This huge undertaking, which required dredging and reshaping the very landscape of the shore, took more than ten years and was completed and dedicated somewhere between 12 and 9 B.C. It provided Jews with a first-class seaport, opening up avenues for much more foreign trade. It is not surprising that this strategic spot later became the political capital of Judea. But Herod was not to know of this development; indeed, it is likely he would have been dismayed by it, considering all the time, effort, and money that he poured into the reconstruction of the city of

Jerusalem, including the building of his own palace, a theater, an amphitheater, and even a hippodrome (*Ant.* 15.267–319). The crowning achievement of Herod's building program, however, was his rebuilding of the temple (*Ant.* 15.380–425), a project that seems largely to have been finished during his lifetime but continued on a lesser scale for decades after his death.

The older Herod got and the nearer to death, the more paranoid he became about relatives and others seeking to take his throne from him. Somewhere around 7 B.C., Herod had his two sons whom Mariamne had provided to him executed on the charge of treason (*Ant.* 16.361–394; *J.W.* 1.538–551). Even later Herod was to execute Antipater, his son by another wife, Doris, only a few days before Herod himself passed away. His indecision about the succession is clear from the fact that he drew up three different wills in the last two years of his life.

But it was not just family troubles that plagued Herod during the last years of his reign. He fought a war against Trachonite bandits, but also against their Nabatean supporters, and when he crossed the Nabatean border to do so, he violated the Pax Romana, and Augustus strongly disapproved of this action. Indeed, the emperor refused to receive Herod's ambassadors who came to plead his case in Rome. Two years passed before their case was finally heard.

Furthermore, there were religious troubles. When Herod had previously sworn allegiance to Rome and the emperor, he had exempted some Pharisees and Essenes who objected to such a loyalty oath, but after the Nabatean debacle, when they again refused to swear such an oath, Herod fined them, and some Pharisees were executed, apparently for treasonous behavior (*Ant.* 17.41–45). As Herod began to decline in health, several Jewish teachers, possibly Pharisees, incited a group of young people to pull down the golden eagle erected by Herod over one of the temple gates. These youth, along with those who incited them, were burned alive, and even the high priest was dismissed from office (*Ant.* 17.149–167).

The final disposition of Herod's estate was a recipe for disaster, as he left the realm not to one or two but three of his sons. Herod died in Jericho, probably just before Passover in 4 B.C. (*J.W.* 2.10; *Ant.* 17.213). He was buried at one of his favorite fortresses, the Herodium.

In their assessment of Herod's reign, Hayes and Mandell say that his actions toward his family "appear to have been fueled by a sense of insecurity and inferiority. As the product of Hasmonean ineptitude, Idumean opportunism, and Roman contrivance, Herod had no firm base within his kingdom that could count him as its own, and vice versa."[12] It is, however, no justification for Herod's lethal treatment of his family to say that Aristobulus I and Alexander Janneus behaved even worse in this regard. It may be the case that Herod never escaped the stigma of having become king by means of a hostile takeover of Jerusalem and Judea with the aid of Rome.

If we are to evaluate Herod's apparent respect for some Jewish beliefs, institutions, and customs, even to the point of rebuilding the temple, alongside his apparent lack of respect for the same once he was outside the realm of Judea, we can only say that Herod's desire to be seen as a Hellenistic monarch who fully participated in the Greco-Roman world clearly outweighed whatever loyalty he may have had toward Judaism. The fact that Herod provided a good deal of employment through his building projects and twice during his reign reduced taxes (*Ant.* 15.365; 16.64), and that he refused to let his sister marry a Nabatean commander because he refused to convert to Judaism, shows that even Herod had enough sense to know that he could go too far in straining his relationship with the devout Jews in his realm. If he wished to remain in power, there had to be a certain amount of placating Jewish religious sensibilities.

Finally, as for the famous aphorism of Augustus about Herod that it was better to be Herod's pig (*hys*) than his son (*huios*) (Macrobius, *Saturnalia* 2.4.11), this should likely be seen as a remark reflecting Augustus's knowledge of how Herod had executed some of his sons, and how Jews in general did not kill and eat pork. It may tell us nothing about whether or not Herod kept a kosher table.[13] Thus, when even Richardson admits that "Herod's piety . . . did not extend to matters of theology, Torah, the future, or God's role for Israel—let alone issues such as sin, redemption, and atonement"[14]—nor apparently, did it extend to scrupulousness about matters of orthopraxy—we have good reason to doubt whether Herod could in any sense be deemed a good or consistently observant Jew.

The Birth of Jesus and the Slaughtering of the Innocents

According to Matt. 2:1–8, Jesus of Nazareth was born during the reign of Herod the Great, and since we know that Herod died sometime before 2 B.C. (though the precise date may be debated, 4 B.C. seems most likely), this produces the anomaly that Jesus was, so to speak,

12. Ibid., 145.
13. In my view, it is unlikely that Herod observed kosher food regulations, not least because he was always entertaining Gentiles.
14. Richardson, *Herod*, 295.

born B.C. How has the calendar become so skewed? A closer look at the reckoning of time and these dates is in order here.

A Closer Look: *Time and Calendars in Antiquity*

The reckoning of time in antiquity went through a variety of permutations and combinations until Julius Caesar, on the basis of the Egyptian solar calendar, standardized a 365-day year with an extra day inserted on leap years. Both the church and Western culture in general followed this solar calendar until the reforms of Pope Gregory XIII, which were set forth on February 24, 1582. Since that time we have followed the Gregorian calendar.

The trouble in regard to the date of the birth of Jesus really began in A.D. 525, when Pope John I asked a monk named Dionysius to prepare a standardized calendar for the Western church, reckoned from the date of Jesus' birth. Relying on the Julian calendar and the traditional date of the founding of the city of Rome, Dionysius set A.D. 1 as corresponding to 754 A.U.C. (*anno urbis conditae*, i.e., from the founding of the city of Rome), with Jesus' birth date being set as December 25, 753 A.U.C. Unfortunately, Dionysius was certainly wrong about the year (he was off by at least several years) and may well have been wrong about the day also.

The key factors in determining the date of Jesus' birth are: (1) the date of Herod's death; (2) the date Luke assigns to the beginning of John the Baptist's ministry coupled with the age he assigns to Jesus (cf. Luke 3:1–3, 23); (3) the astral phenomenon that the magi are said to have seen, if it was a result of a natural occurrence such as a conjunction of planets. Josephus tells us that Herod the Great was proclaimed king of Judea in 40 B.C. and that he reigned approximately thirty-seven years (*Ant.* 14.381–385; 17.191). Josephus also tells us that Herod died shortly after an eclipse of the moon (*Ant.* 17.167). No such event transpired in 3 B.C., but there was one on March 12/13, 4 B.C. Josephus goes on to add that Passover was celebrated shortly after Herod's death (*Ant.* 17.213; *J.W.* 2.10). The first day of Passover in 4 B.C. would have been April 11. Thus, it is likely that Herod died between March 12 and April 11 in 4 B.C. This in turn means that Jesus was born sometime prior to March of 4 B.C.[15] In my view, the infor-

15. On the complexities of these matters, see B. Witherington III, "The Birth of Jesus," *DJG*, 60–74.

mation in Luke 2:1–2 does not help us very much to further clarify this matter, for Luke seems to be saying that he is referring to some census prior to the famous census of Quirinius in A.D. 6 or 7 (a census he dates well after the turn of the era in Acts 5:37), in which case the date of that earlier census is not specified.

Luke tells us that John the Baptist began his ministry during the fifteenth year of Tiberius's reign. Augustus died in the summer of A.D. 14, and Tiberius assumed the throne later that year. This places the inception of John's ministry in A.D. 29, or if inclusive reckoning of regnal years is involved (partial years counted as whole years), possibly as early as A.D. 27. Since both Mark 1:14 and Luke 3 suggest that Jesus' ministry began after John's (though how long after is not known), Jesus' ministry could not have begun before A.D. 27, if not later. Luke then tells us that Jesus was about thirty when he began his ministry. The Greek word *hōsei*, translated "about," indicates an approximation that would allow a few years on either side of thirty. The Talmud (*b. Sanh.* 106) says that Jesus began his ministry at the age of thirty-three to thirty-four. If this is close to correct, then Jesus by this reckoning would have been born about 4 B.C. Luke tells us that John the Baptist was born during the reign of Herod the Great as well (cf. Luke 1).

As for the astral phenomenon, various theories have been advanced. The theory that the magi saw a conjunction of Jupiter and Saturn that was visible in the region in 7 B.C. is possible, but modern astronomers have made clear that this conjunction would not have been close enough to appear as a single star. It is not impossible that J. Kepler's original speculation has some merit. He suggested that the magi witnessed the birth of a new star or supernova, an event that we know did transpire in 5–4 B.C. But according to Matthew, this star led the magi to the precise locale of Jesus' birth, which hardly sounds like a natural astrological occurrence. In any case, the Matthean story suggests that the magi visited Jesus at some point after his birth, perhaps even a year or more later. If this is so, the astral phenomena would not necessarily help us determine the time of Jesus' birth very precisely. In light of all the above data, it appears most likely that Jesus was born somewhere around 4 B.C. In regard to the day of Jesus' birth, it is natural to be suspicious about December 25, since this was the pagan day for celebrating the Saturnalia, and we know that Christians in the early middle ages tried to replace pagan feasts with Christian ones. Luke 2:8 might suggest a date other than in winter, since normally flocks would be outside during the months between March and November, but *m. Šeqal.* 7:4 suggests that sheep around Bethlehem might well be outside during the winter also. The first real witness to the tradition that Jesus was born on December 25 is Hippolytus (A.D. 165–235), a date that John Chrysostom (A.D. 345–407) supports as well. All we can say is that such a date is possible, but we have no compelling early evidence in the Gospels or elsewhere that points definitely in this direction.

As I have outlined in the excursus, converging lines of evidence suggest that Jesus was born probably in 4 B.C., though an earlier date is not impossible. The location of Jesus' birth has been argued about by various scholars of late (e.g., J. D. Crossan and other members of the Jesus Seminar). As we consider this matter, we should note that Matthew and Luke, probably independently of each other, attest to the tradition that Jesus was born in Bethlehem. While this location might have been conjured up on the basis of Mic. 5:2, only Matthew makes anything of this prophetic connection and only he really stresses that Jesus was Son of David.

The question becomes, What should we make of the tradition that Joseph and Mary had to travel to the ancestral home to register for the tax census? There is nothing a priori improbable about Herod seeking to levy taxes, and doing so in a Jewish manner that may have required a trip to the ancestral home. We know that late in Herod's reign, he faced various problems and was in constant need of funds to support his building and military ventures, not to mention the tribute he paid to the emperor and the various special projects he funded in Greece and elsewhere to establish and improve his honor rating as a world ruler.

Clearly, one of the most difficult historical problems in the Gospels is dating the census mentioned in Luke 2:1–2. The problems with Luke's statements are these: (1) There is no evidence of an empirewide census taken during the reign of Augustus. (2) Quirinius was sent by Augustus to be governor of Syria (and so of Judea) in A.D. 6, not somewhere between 6–4 B.C. After A.D. 6 he did indeed take a notable census in the region. Josephus himself tells us that Quirinius did a survey tour of Israel to assess the property of the Jews (*Ant.* 18.1–2). (3) There is no evidence that Quirinius was governor of the region twice, or that he undertook a census of the region twice. Luke may have confused Quirinius with P. Quintilius Varus, who was legate in Syria from 6–3 B.C., but elsewhere Luke shows that he knows the difference between a cognomen like Quirinius and a mere nomen like Quintilius (cf. Acts 13:7,

Census Records of the New Testament Era

Census registers are another useful source of evidence to understand the culture in which Jesus and his earliest followers lived. From Alexandria, we have some second-century A.D. records of a man and his family registering for the census by making a declaration of property owned. This makes quite clear that the census was for taxation purposes. We cannot determine from this evidence whether the other family members were present or needed to be present for this registration. (*NewDocs* 1:79)

24:1). In any case, a Roman census would not likely have required Jews to return to an ancestral homeplace, nor is it likely that the Romans would have undertaken a census on their own in Herod's realm while he was still ruling.

Before we too rapidly dismiss Luke's record as historically inaccurate, several important considerations need to be borne in mind. First, Acts 5:37 shows that Luke knows that Quirinius's census took place considerably later, prompting the revolt of Judas the Galilean in A.D. 6–7. Second, if Luke is not simply indulging in rhetorical hyperbole, it is not absolutely necessary to take Luke 2:1 to mean that the whole empire was enrolled at once. What the Greek suggests is that Caesar decreed that "all of the Roman world be enrolled." The present tense of the verb *apographō* and the use of *pas* suggest that what Caesar was decreeing was the extension of the enrollment already going on in some parts of the empire to the rest of the empire. Historian A. N. Sherwin-White reminds us, "A census or taxation-assessment of the whole provincial empire . . . was certainly accomplished for the first time in history under Augustus."[16] Luke then would be referring in a general way to this unprecedented ongoing event. Third, there is some evidence of a census of Judea during the governorship of Saturnius between 9 and 6 B.C. We know that Herod had lost some of his autonomy after 10 B.C. when he fell into disfavor with Augustus due to the war with the Nabateans. It is possible that Rome might have imposed a taxation on Herod as a reprisal for his violation of the Pax Romana in the region.

Another important consideration is that Luke's precise wording in the Greek of Luke 2:2 is curious. He could be referring to the first or the former census that was taken under Quirinius, or it is even possible

16. A. N. Sherwin-White, *Roman Society and Roman Law in the New Testament* (Grand Rapids: Baker, 1978), 168–69.

grammatically to take the word *prōtē* to mean "prior to" or "before" the more famous census of Quirinius that led to Jewish revolt. We know that Qurinius had been made consul in 12 B.C., and a consul in the eastern provinces could have wide-ranging authority. It is not impossible that as consul he ordered a census even during the waning years of Herod's reign, forcing Herod to undertake the act, which he did in Jewish fashion. The conclusion one must come to is that Luke 2:1–2 cannot be dismissed as historically impossible, especially if Luke is simply identifying Quirinius by his later, more notorious census and his later, more familiar role in the region once Judea was part of a province. Thus, the birth of Jesus in Bethlehem, an event confirmed by two likely independent accounts in Matthew and Luke, is certainly possible.

If we ask where in Bethlehem Jesus may have been born, several points need to be stressed. According to Matt. 2:11 Jesus was found in a house by the magi, but this likely transpired at some time later and perhaps elsewhere than where Jesus was born. Luke 2:7 needs to be seen in the larger context of Luke 2:4–7, which does not suggest that Mary went into labor immediately or even shortly after she and Joseph arrived. To the contrary, the text says, "while they were there," Mary went into labor. Thus, the familiar image of Joseph and Mary arriving in Bethlehem and being unable to find a place to stay on the night of the arrival probably is not well grounded in the text. Furthermore, the word *katalyma* in Luke 2:7 can mean "guest room, house, inn." It may be doubted that there were any inns in Bethlehem in Jesus' day, since it was not on any major roads, and inns were found on major roads, especially the Roman ones (e.g., there was an inn near Jericho, a major crossroads for both north-south and east-west traffic [cf. Luke 10:30, 34]). Moreover, when Luke wants to speak of a commercial inn, he uses a different word, *pandocheion* (Luke 10:34). When Luke does use *katalyma* in his Gospel, it clearly means a guest room (cf. Luke 22:11 to 1 Sam. 1:18 LXX). Note also that the early Arabic and Syriac translations of the New Testament have never translated *katalyma* as "inn." The translation "guest room" rather than "house" makes good sense, especially because we know that most ancient Near Eastern homes had the manger within and at the back of the house, not in a separate barn. The animals slept in one large enclosed space, which was divided so that the animals would be either behind or below the main living space.

In this case, then, we should envision Mary and Joseph staying in the home of relatives or friends, and since the guest room was taken due to the census going on (note the definite article here: there was no room in *the* guest room), they were placed in or near the space where the animals were kept, with the baby being laid in a stone manger. This

Illustration 2.6 A stone manger with hitching posts, found in Judea.

means that a good deal of the mythology surrounding this story has no basis in the text, especially the notion of Mary and Joseph being cast out from civilized accommodations and taking up temporary residence in a barn.

Several other aspects of the birth and infancy stories need to be dealt with from a historical point of view. We need to dismiss the view that the stories in Matthew 1–2 and Luke 1–2 are of some ilk different from other Gospel stories. In fact, they reveal the same mixture of the mundane and the supernatural we find elsewhere in the Gospels, and the stories are narrated with the same sort of theological perspectives as well.[17] Like the passion narratives, the birth narratives, particularly Matthew's, are interlaced with scriptural citations precisely because these were portions of the Jesus story that would most need justification and explanation. Early Jews were not looking for a messiah miraculously born of a virgin.

It needs to be remembered that the Matthean and Lukan birth accounts share certain fundamental notions, including the betrothed couple Mary and Joseph, the virginal conception, the Davidic descent of Joseph, the birth in Bethlehem during Herod's reign, the angelic revelation of the name Jesus, and Jesus' upbringing in Nazareth. This is

17. See Witherington, "Birth of Jesus," 60–61.

true even though the majority of material in these two birth narratives is not common to both.

Let us consider the stories of the virginal conception from a historical point of view. We note the citation of Isa. 7:14 in Matt. 1:23. The pre-Christian interpretation of this text by Jews seems to have seen its fulfillment in Hezekiah, the son and successor of Ahaz. There is no evidence that early Jews saw this as a prophecy about a virginal conception. There is good reason for this. The Hebrew word *almah* in Isa. 7:14 refers to a young woman of marriageable age. The idea of her virginity is probably implicit, but *almah* is not a technical term for virgin, nor does it exclusively focus on that aspect of the woman's character. The Hebrew word *bethulah* comes nearer to being such a term. Furthermore, the term *almah* never refers to a married woman in the Old Testament, but does always refer to a woman who is sexually mature. There are no Old Testament texts where *almah* clearly means a woman who is sexually active, although it is possible that Song of Sol. 6:8 implies this. We may safely conclude that *almah* normally, if not always, implies a virgin, and this will explain why the LXX translates the word with *parthenos*. Yet, note that in Gen. 34:3 LXX, Dinah is called a *parthenos* even though she has been seduced by Shechem, though after the rape she is simply called *paidiskē*. What one can say on the basis of the linguistic evidence is that it is improbable that Matthew deduced the notion of a virginal conception on the basis of his meditation on the Isaianic prophecy either in the Hebrew or in the Greek. To say "a virgin will conceive and give birth" need imply no more to an early Jew than that a woman who had not previously had intercourse did so and thereby got pregnant. The notion of the virginal conception seems already to have existed prior to Matthew's connection of the idea with this Isaianic text, as its independent attestation in Luke without such a scriptural connection confirms.

A commonly heard argument says that the story of Jesus' birth is simply a variant of the myths of origins told about figures in the Greco-Roman world, such as the stories about Augustus. The truth, however, is that none of the pagan stories are about a virginal conception, a notion that lends itself to the accusation of the child being illegitimate. The pagan stories are usually about some kind of act of *hieros gamos*— a divine being descends to earth in the guise of a man, mating with a human woman. But this is not at all what Matthew or Luke suggests happened in the case of Mary, which is about miraculous conception without any form of intercourse and without the aid of any male figure, divine or otherwise. The Lukan account speaks of the Holy Spirit overshadowing Mary, which may suggest divine protection (cf. Luke 9:34), and certainly suggests a divine bestowal of something miraculous. What is not suggested in either of the two Gospel accounts is some sort of mating, not least because the Holy Spirit is never portrayed as a human figure or as a being that ever assumes a human form. Furthermore, there is no evidence from Jewish infancy stories about Moses or others of the notion of virginal conception, and, as already noted, Jewish messianic expectations do not seem to have anticipated such an event.

There are also serious problems for those who maintain that the virginal conception is a theological idea without grounding in historical reality. One must ask, Why would early Christians, members of an evangelistic religious group, create so many problems for themselves and open wide the door to the charge of illegitimacy by inventing the idea of Jesus being born of a virgin? The charge of illegitimacy was certainly a reality in the time of Origen, as his debate with Celsus shows, but I would suggest that it was already a live issue in New Testament times (cf. John 8:41; and possibly Mark 6:3). Notice how both Matthew and Luke feel under some pressure to refer to the virginal conception, even to the point of awkwardly including the idea in their genealogies (on which, see below). Explanation is also required, if Jesus was not born of a virgin, as to why early in the second century Christians so widely and readily accepted the notion (cf. Ign. *Smyrn.* 1:1). Other New Testament texts perhaps reflect a knowledge of the virginal conception as well (cf. Rom. 1:3; Gal. 4:4; Phil. 2:7; John 1:13; 6:41–42). More directly, in a patriarchal society it was not usual to call a man the son of his mother, even if the father had died, and so Mark 6:3 seems to reflect a knowledge that Jesus was not physically the son of Joseph. Matthew 1:18, of course, attempts to make very clear that Joseph was not responsible for the siring of Jesus. Furthermore, on any normal reading of Matt. 1:25, with the verb "to know" being in the imperfect tense, this text suggests that after the birth of Jesus, Joseph ceased from abstaining from sexual relations with his wife ("he was not knowing her until . . ."). The mention of Jesus' brothers and sisters (e.g., Mark 6:3), who are never called by the Greek word for cousins, is most naturally taken as meaning that Mary did not remain a virgin after the birth of Jesus. There is also nothing in the Lukan account to suggest that Mary had anything other than a normal pregnancy and delivery. Indeed, the story in Luke 2:22–40 about the trip to the temple for Mary to perform the ceremony of purification in fulfillment of the law (Lev. 12:2–8) suggests that Luke thought she had a normal delivery requiring ritual cleansing. It is important to use the term "virginal conception," not "virgin birth," as that is the juncture at which the miracle transpired, for the birth seems to have been perfectly normal.

When all is said and done, it is easier to explain the Gospel evidence on the assumption that the virginal conception was a historical event that the Gospel writers tried to explain, albeit somewhat awkwardly, than to assume that this is a theological idea dreamed up by some early pious Christian. If Jesus had been known to be illegitimate, it would hardly be possible—if the writers had any personal integrity—for Luke or Matthew to present Jesus' conception as they have done, especially Luke, who presents Jesus' conception as more miraculous than John the Baptist's. Matthew's narrative likewise would collapse without the notion of the virginal conception, for Jesus' conception is presented as such a holy thing that a righteous man like Joseph could be persuaded to accept it and accept Jesus as his legal son, and thus a son of David. The sort of apologetics and adjustments in genealogies we find in Matthew and Luke suggest writers struggling to come to grips with an idea whose historical reality they could not doubt, but had to explain.

It has been traditional since at least the time of Annius of Viterbo in A.D. 1490 to assume that Matthew's genealogy traces Jesus' lineage through Joseph (his legal genealogy), while Luke's genealogy traces his lineage through Mary (his natural genealogy). In Luke's case, however, this requires that one take the Lukan phrase "as was supposed of Joseph" as a parenthetical remark in Luke 3:23, but it also requires that the author use the word *huios* (son) in v. 23b to mean both son and grandson in the same breath, leaving out any mention of Mary's name. In other words, it does not appear that Luke was trying to present a genealogy through Mary's side of the family. It is possible that we have two genealogies from Joseph's side of the family, and one popular conjecture is that Luke traces the line through Joseph's father, while Matthew traces the line through Joseph's maternal grandfather. Another conjecture is that Matthew presents Jesus' legal or royal genealogy, while Luke presents his actual physical predecessors.

But it may be counterproductive to treat these genealogies as we would modern ones, for clearly they serve different purposes in their respective Gospels, and their differences are far more notable than their similarities. To try to reconcile the two may be wrongly to ignore that they are different in nature and in function. Here are some of the most notable differences: The Matthean genealogy (1) introduces the whole Gospel, including the birth narratives, and traces the line from Abraham through Joseph to Jesus using the term "begot" (this is a genealogy meant to show Jewish pedigree in a linear fashion); (2) has an artificial division of the names into three groups of fourteen; (3) has a notable insertion of several women, and possibly some brothers, while at the same time lacking some names from the relevant Old Testament genealogies; (4) has an awkward circumlocution at the end of the genealogy reflecting Matthew's belief in the virginal conception. By contrast, the Lukan genealogy (1) follows the baptism and introduces the ministry of Jesus, and thus is not really part of the birth narrative; (2) repeatedly uses "son of" without any verbs tracing the line backwards from Jesus up to Adam and God; (3) begins with a circumlocution indicating that Luke knows that Jesus was not really Joseph's son (not surprisingly, since the order is the opposite of Matthew's); (4) inserts a Rhesa and an extra Cainan into the genealogical list (cf. Gen. 10:12–31; 11:12; 1 Chron. 1:24).

It appears that Matthew seeks to portray Jesus as a true Israelite in the line of David, while Luke wishes to stress that Jesus is a true human being. The crucial point of both genealogies, however, is not so much to say or explain something about Jesus' ancestors as about his character. The Matthean genealogy should be seen in light of the passage that follows (Matt. 1:18–25), which makes clear that the point is to highlight that Jesus is both the Son of David and the Son of God. It may be that the virginal conception has led Matthew to include various women in the genealogy in preparation for mentioning Mary in an otherwise male-dominated patriarchal genealogy. The women listed were either famous figures or related to famous figures, and this prepares the reader for thinking of Mary as a special instrument of God. More to the point, these women were involved in irregular unions and yet were vehicles of God's messianic plan. In other words, the mention of these earlier women is part of Matthew's apologetics on behalf of Mary and the irregular event that happened when she became the mother of the Messiah.

Luke, by contrast, attempts to place Jesus in the broader context of humanity rather than in Judaism per se. This is perhaps because Luke is writing for a Gentile audience,[18] and wishes to stress Jesus is their Savior as well. In fact, it is Luke, as a historian, who seeks to present Jesus as the ideal human being, who is not only one with all humanity but also grows in wisdom and stature, and is to be seen as a model of how people ought to relate to God, to others, to temptation, and so on. Perhaps Luke sees Jesus as the new Adam, the founder of a new race of humankind. Luke seems to have added "son of God" to his genealogy to stress that not only is Jesus' full humanity clear (he is a son of Adam), but also his origins are ultimately from God (hence, son of God). The genealogies in

18. See B. Witherington III, *The Acts of the Apostles: A Socio-rhetorical Commentary* (Grand Rapids: Eerdmans, 1998), 63–65.

both Gospels serve primarily theological and christological purposes and only secondarily historical ones. The evangelists were not concerned to present exhaustive lists of Jesus' actual ancestors, but to highlight certain aspects of his heritage that would best make clear for their respective audiences Jesus' significance and nature.

Before leaving the subject of Jesus' birth, one further incident needs to be considered from a historical point of view: the story about the slaughtering of the innocents in Matt. 2:16–18. As we have already seen, there is plenty of evidence to suggest that Herod was paranoid about potential rivals to his throne, and especially so toward the end of his life. At the very least, then, this story is historically plausible. We should also stress that Bethlehem was a very small town, meaning that we should not envision the slaughtering of dozens of children; indeed, one dozen may be the most that would have been involved. Furthermore, it must be remembered that this event, if historical, transpired after the time of Jesus' birth and after the visit of the magi, and so presumably after the time when the town was crowded with registrants for the census. It is not an argument against the historicity of this story that Josephus does not mention it. His silence may reflect his ignorance of the matter, which would have been a small-scale action at most. Richardson argues that the account in Matt. 2:3–4 suggests an improbable relationship between Herod, the temple authorities and their scribes, and the Sanhedrin, but in fact, Richardson himself has pointed out that Herod had a firm hand on the temple authorities and the Sanhedrin, and would have had occasion to consult them on religious matters (e.g., he must have done so about the training of the priests for the building of the temple).[19] A Herod who would not scruple at executing some of his own sons would have had few qualms about executing a few Jewish children if one of them was viewed as a potential threat to his throne. Thus, we can only say that while the historical substance of this story cannot be confirmed by outside sources, the essence of the story comports with what we know about Herod and his paranoia. Even the story about the flight into Egypt gains plausibility when we compare Herod's own story, for at one juncture, as previously noted, he did the same.

The Rise of the Roman Empire

It has been said that when Caesar crossed the Rubicon in 49 B.C., he set Rome on a course toward monarchy.[20] It was soon thereafter,

19. Richardson, *Herod*, 296–97.
20. M. Goodman, *The Roman World 44 B.C.–A.D. 180* (London: Routledge, 1997), 28.

in 48 B.C., that Caesar was elected *dictator* by the people, following in the footsteps of the tyrant Sulla. But very unlike Sulla, who went into retirement once his legislative agenda had been passed, Caesar stayed in office, having himself voted dictator for life in 44 B.C., a move that any with republican sentiments could only view as ominous, especially in the wake of his acceptance of the establishment of a priesthood for his worship. Thus it was that on the Ides of March (March 15) 44 B.C., Brutus and Cassius, two of Pompey the Great's allies, stabbed Caesar to death in the senate's meeting place in Pompey's theater. Although the hope had been that things would return to normal in a republican way, a considerable power vacuum was left after Caesar's sudden death, and various individuals could have been expected to vie for the top position. What was not expected was the meteoric rise of Marcus Octavius, who between 44 and 31 B.C. rose from obscurity to the position of emperor, with more power than even Julius Caesar had possessed.

Julius Caesar was in fact the great uncle of Octavius, and since Caesar was childless, Octavius became like a child to him, even at age sixteen joining him in Caesar's Roman triumph in 46 B.C. Thus, while it may have been a shock to many, it is not entirely surprising that Octavius was named chief heir to Caesar's enormous fortune. Cicero at once saw the danger and said of Octavius that he was a talented young man who should be praised, honored, and removed (*Letters to Friends* 11.20.1)! Octavius began by privately raising two legions of his own, partly made up of some of Caesar's veterans brought out of retirement. They were soon put into use against the forces of Marc Antony, which were seen as a threat by the consuls then in power in Rome, for Antony was taking action against the conspirators who killed Caesar. While Antony was beaten badly enough to force his retreat into Gaul, both of the consuls who had gone with Octavius to Mutina to do battle were killed in the conflict. Octavius, wasting not a moment, went straight back to Rome and demanded the consulship, even though he was barely twenty years of age. There was little or no resistance. A law was quickly passed making him the legitimate heir of Julius Caesar; he was granted the name Gaius Julius Caesar Octavianus, and he was made consul.

But while all this had transpired in part because of the admiration that some had for Octavius's attack on Antony, and apparent sympathy with the "liberators" Antony was after, within a few short weeks, Octavius was singing a very different tune—agreeing to cooperate with Antony and Lepidus. Through a private agreement these three became a triumvirate. A law was passed granting the three men a five-year task to set up the state properly. This in effect meant that the normal system of lawmaking and elections was put on hold. When the five-year period was over, there was simply a renewal of the original arrangement.

The task that the triumvirate needed to undertake first was dealing with Brutus and Cassius, who had a great army in the east and had extorted massive funds from the provincials. Leaving Lepidus in charge in Rome, Octavius and Antony brought matters to a head at Philippi in Macedonia in 42 B.C., where they won a decisive victory against Caesar's killers. In October of 40 B.C., an agreement was reached between Antony and Octavius that seemed to further cement their alliance, for Antony agreed to marry Octavia, the sister of Octavius. But in fact, Octavius had designs on Antony's provinces, even though the three men had divided up the realm among them. For example, when Antony's legate in Gaul died unexpectedly, Octavius simply took over the province and the troops there. Then, in a campaign against Sextus Pompey, who had a considerable fleet in Sicily and may have been attempting to control the corn trade, Octavius and Lepidus defeated Pompey in Sicily. Lepidus rightly claimed that Sicily should be under his control, but Octavius, apparently through bribery, won over Lepidus's troops, forcing Lepidus to retire under close supervision to an obscure spot.

Octavius then turned his attention to Antony, who was licking his wounds after losing a third of his army in his crusade against the Parthians. Their point of engagement was Actium in Greece in September 31 B.C., and Antony and Cleopatra only managed to escape from the battle with a few ships. Octavius's pursuit was relentless, and when Antony and Cleopatra were finally trapped in Alexandria, they committed suicide rather than surrender. The triumvirate was at an end, and Octavius, returning to Rome, disbanded half the legions in his command and was given the title Augustus by the senate. He continued to be consul year after year, and in effect to be in complete control. He was voted repeatedly the commander of the forces in all the major provinces, and occasionally, as in 27 B.C., when he beat some recalcitrant tribes in Spain, he went out with some legions to do battle. He rejected the title that his stepfather Caesar had taken, dictator, when it was offered by the plebes in 22 B.C. In truth, he did not need such a title, so absolute was his power. The only thing that seemed to threaten his reign was serious illness, and there was a period of such illness in 23 B.C. when it was feared he would not live.

No one stays in power for as long as Augustus did without strong assistance, and perhaps the most notable of Augustus's "strong men" was Marcus Vipsanius Agrippa, a general who was mainly responsible for

Illustration 2.7   Augustus coin.

most of Augustus's major victories in the 40s and 30s B.C. in Illyrium and elsewhere. The illness in 23 B.C. led to the promotion of Agrippa to increasing prominence and visibility, and so much trust was there in this relationship that three times between 27 and 12 B.C. when Augustus was out of Italy, Agrippa was left in charge. In 21 B.C., Agrippa married Augustus's daughter Julia. But unfortunately, Agrippa died unexpectedly in 12 B.C. It was a personal and a political tragedy because this occurred less than a year after Agrippa had been made, by constitutional law, Augustus's equal in his authority to intervene in the provinces not formally assigned to him when the good of Rome required such action (the so-called *imperium proconsulare maius*). This law is of note for our study not least because it meant that in a troubled or volatile area like the Syrian province, it was always possible that even a local proconsul like Pontius Pilate might suffer the loss of honor resulting from Caesar sending forces into his own region, indicating his own incompetence.

It was in the end Augustus who gradually seems to have persuaded Rome of something that that state had never been convinced about before: genetic continuity at the top of the power structure was a key to the stability of the realm. Augustus seems to have believed this to be true, perhaps because of his situation in relationship to his great-uncle Julius Caesar.[21] Despite the desire on Augustus's part, he was never able to produce a male heir of his own. His second wife, Livia, whom he married in 39 B.C., brought with her into the marriage two sons by previous marriage, Tiberius (born in 42 B.C.) and Drusus. Tacitus later chronicled what happened in the tangled web of these relationships: "After Agrippa

21. See Goodman, *Roman World*, 42.

departed his life, and premature death (or their stepmother Livia's treachery) cut off Lucius and Gaius Caesar—the former while on his way to our armies in Spain, the latter while returning, weakened by a wound, from Armenia—since Drusus had long since perished, Nero [that is, Tiberius] alone remained of the stepsons and everything centered on him" (*Annals* 1.3). While it has always been true that politics makes strange bedfellows, this was supremely true in the case of Augustus's family, for Julia, Augustus's only biological child, was made to marry Tiberius after Agrippa died, to further cement the family connections.

It has often been suggested that the real power behind the throne from the 30s B.C. was Livia, who seemed to be an expert at finding ways to eliminate rivals so that one of her offspring could rule. The marriage of Julia to Tiberius was a very unhappy one. Tiberius was so unhappy that he refused to continue to fight in Augustus's army or to live in Rome with Julia, and he retired in 6 B.C. to Rhodes. His sexual preference was for men, in any case, and Julia took out her frustrations by having a series of adulterous relationships, both of them making a mockery of Augustus's attempt to have his family model traditional Roman family virtues. But Augustus was more successful in the way that he extended the circle of power and patronage by engineering a series of judicious marriages in the wider circle of his family with many of the old patrician families of Rome.[22]

Part of the way that Augustus maintained his prestige was by continuing his efforts at expanding the boundaries of the empire by winning "glorious" victories. There were in fact various regions that were beset with turmoil and rebellion after A.D. 6, including Judea, Asia Minor, Africa, Sardinia, and the Balkans. Like Alexander, Augustus dreamed of a world empire, but of course the world was not going to simply lie down at the feet of Rome. Wars, heavy-handed extraction of tribute and taxes, and the like would be the means of forcing provinces into line. It needs to be said, however, that the Roman emperors did not have the same ideological vision as Alexander. Though there would be the rise and spread of the emperor cult during the first century A.D., by and large Goodman's conclusion deserves to be endorsed:

> Emperors had little interest in imposing ideology—social, political, or religious—and had no means to impose surveillance on the whereabouts of all the inhabitants of the empire. But in their concern to ensure their own safety, comfort, power and prestige, emperors employed a huge military force whose main but unstated purpose was the suppression of dissent.[23]

22. See ibid., 46.
23. Ibid., 81.

There were, of course, mentally imbalanced rulers such as Gaius Caligula, who sought to impose on Jews the worship of himself and his statue in the temple in Jerusalem, but the Roman policy in general had always been to allow indigenous peoples to worship their own gods, so long as they did not fail to pay their taxes or seek to overthrow the Roman client rulers or governors. This policy of a sort of religious freedom was not uniquely applied to Jews, although since they were the only significant group of monotheists in the empire, it took a unique form with them as the rise of the emperor cult became a significant trend in the first century A.D. The Jews would not offer sacrifices *to* the emperor, but rather offer them *for* the emperor. This was simply a wider application of the general Roman policy of letting ethnic groups pursue their own indigenous form of religion.

How was Augustus to maintain control of so vast a domain? By maintaining a huge standing army, of course. It is estimated that up to 100,000 legionnaires were kept in readiness to fight at all times, some twenty-eight legions, and this was after Augustus had dismissed over half his troops in 29 B.C. when he declared that Rome was entirely at peace.[24] At his death in A.D. 14, twenty-five legions remained stationed in the following manner: one in Africa, three in Spain, four in lower Germany, four in upper Germany, three in Pannonia, two in Dalmatia, two in Moesia, four in Syria, and two in Egypt. Note that the Holy Land was surrounded by six legions, for clearly, it was seen as a strategic and hot spot in the empire.

But how was the emperor to fund this huge standing army? By raising taxes, of course, since the army was paid, not conscripted. The first of many provincial censuses took place in 27 B.C. in Gaul, and it was the relentless and systematic way that the census and tax collection was pursued throughout the empire that led to revolts in Gaul, Judea (in A.D. 6–7), and Pannonia. The taxes were largely levied on agricultural produce in the regions outside Italy. "One should not underestimate the difficulty involved in imposing a quick new system of fiscality and monetization on the whole of north-west and central Europe, and in introducing to the eastern parts of the empire regular censuses and a poll tax, both of which were previously unknown in some areas, although long established in others, such as Egypt. . . . Easier to impose were the indirect taxes (portoria) payable on goods in transit at ports, imperial frontiers and various boundaries between provinces or groups of provinces."[25]

24. See ibid., 82.
25. Ibid., 101.

The Roman preference was always to have the local elite do the dirty work in terms of collecting taxes and the like. In return, the elite were allowed a measure of self-government, some control over food supplies and over communal property (or property transactions), and participation in local entertainment. In highly stratified societies it was the elite who had the most to gain by cooperating with Rome.

Besides assuring the flow of money to Rome, the main task of the provincial governor was to administer justice, usually by traveling from town to town and holding court. The justice system, like the economic system, was highly biased in favor of the well-to-do, and of course, the language of law was Latin, which made it difficult for provincials to always know what was going on. The Romans, unlike the Macedonians, did not seek to impose their language or culture on all the conquered territories in day-to-day life or in business. It is perhaps precisely because they did not have an agenda like the earlier Hellenizers that it became necessary to have Roman colony cities, settled by retired soldiers, dotted throughout the landscape of the empire, to ensure that the Roman way of life could exist in the provinces, at least for Romans who found it necessary to live outside Rome.[26]

It is interesting that Augustus left written advice to Tiberius (see Tacitus, *Annals* 1.11) not to expand the empire beyond its existing frontiers, advice he largely followed, as did Caligula. All campaigns for new territory went into abeyance, until Claudius decided to invade Britain. Sometimes it is possible to tell something about the stability of a region by the title of the provincial governor. The term "procurator" indicated someone in a civilian role, while the term "prefect" indicated a formally appointed military person in charge of a region. Note that the first provincial governor appointed by Augustus to Judea in A.D. 6 was a prefect.

There were, of course, also client kings who helped in the administration of the empire, and Goodman is right that they must be seen as part and parcel of Roman provincial administration. Once the empire began, they were not really independent rulers who only had alliances with Rome. Rome could remove them from power whenever that became necessary.[27] Such kings were especially prevalent in the eastern part of the empire, both in Asia Minor and in and around Judea. Part of the Roman strategy was to install in governance those who would be continually beholden to Rome for their ultimate source of power or authority. This meant, in the case of Judea, for example, installing a whole new family in power—the Herodian clan. "In such a case, loyalty to Rome was ensured. Hence descendants of Herod were appointed to

26. The analogy with U.S. army bases in Europe and the Middle East is somewhat apt.
27. Goodman, *Roman World*, 110.

kingdoms in Armenia, Asia Minor, and a variety of other places with which they had no previous contact at all."[28] Difficulties could arise when a client king and a provincial governor appointed by the senate both stood in the same region, for the client kings were always led to believe that they had a certain degree of local autonomy and independence, and so it is no surprise that a clash occurred between the governor of Syria, Vibius Marsus, and Herod Agrippa I in A.D. 44 over territorial control and jurisdiction. The advantage of allowing a client king to rule was that he had to raise and pay for his own army, but on the other hand, his jurisdiction seems to have had to pay less to the imperial treasury than did a directly governed province. This was no solace to the locals, though, because the client kings collected their own revenues for their own purposes as well. In other words, it is unlikely that the tax burden in Galilee was much less than in Judea overall.

By the time Jesus actually began his ministry, Judea had been a Roman province for some time, and Galilee had been ruled by the client king Herod Antipas. In the next chapter, we will consider how the three sons of Herod the Great fared in ruling his domain, and we will examine the period that led up to the ministries of John the Baptist and Jesus.

28. Ibid., 111.

Chapter 3

The Herodians and Their Prophetic Adversaries: John and Jesus

4 B.C.–A.D. 27

The Herodians and the First Procurators

The final form of Herod the Great's will had Archelaus succeeding Herod as king in Judea, Antipas becoming tetrarch over Galilee and Perea, and Philip being tetrarch over the least desirable part of the realm—Gaulanitis, Trachonitis, Batanea, and Panias (*Ant*. 17.188–189; *J.W.* 1.664). These arrangements, however, were tentative until ratified by Rome, and everyone knew it, and so a period of turmoil and uprising

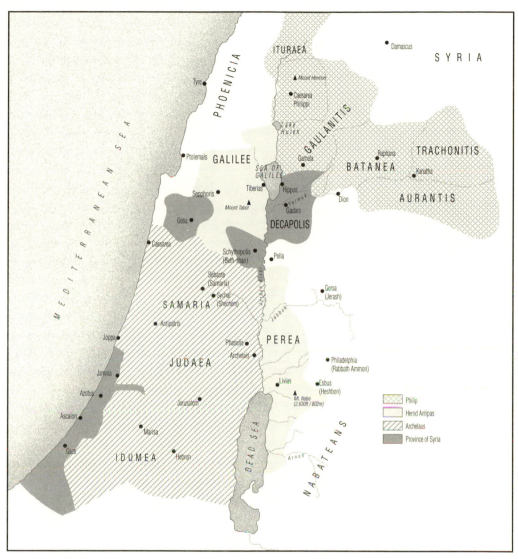

Illustration 3.1 Palestine in the Time of Christ.

ensued. Various demands were made on Archelaus to reverse some of the injustices and questionable actions of Herod the Great. For example, there was a demand for reduction of taxes, release of prisoners, and the removal of the last high priest appointed by Herod, a man named Joazar (*Ant.* 17.200–208; *J.W.* 2.4). The Roman military commander Sabinus made a serious error of judgment when at the time of Pentecost he came to Jerusalem, looted Herod's treasury, occupied the citadels in the city, and burned the porticoes of the temple. The Jewish populace, with the help of Herodian troops, besieged Sabinus in Herod's palace (*Ant*. 17.221–223, 250–268; *J.W.* 2.16–19, 39–54).

The turmoil in Jerusalem was seen as a signal for general revolt and anarchy throughout the region, and various persons sought to make themselves rulers of some portion of Herod the Great's realm. For example, Judas, the son of the rebel leader Hezekiah, whom Herod had executed in 47 B.C., took by force the royal arsenal at Sepphoris in Galilee and sought to seize the region (*Ant*. 17.271–272; *J.W.* 2.56). Simon, a handsome Herodian slave, was proclaimed king by a group of followers. An army was raised, and Simon set ablaze several royal palaces, including Herod's winter palace at Jericho. Simon was tracked down by a Roman military force and was beheaded after he had created havoc in Perea (*Ant*. 17.273–276; *J.W.* 2.57–59). A shepherd named Athronges claimed the title of king, supported by four siblings and a considerable force of other supporters, and began executing Romans and royalists in Judea (*Ant*. 17.278–284; *J.W.* 2.60–64).

Peace was restored only when Varus, the Roman legate in Syria, brought two legions and various auxiliaries into the Holy Land and suppressed the uprisings. He came to Jerusalem, broke the siege against Sabinus, and crucified some two thousand Jewish insurgents. These events remind us that, especially during interregnums, the Holy Land could become a cauldron of dissent, with various illegal actions transpiring[1] and various royal or messianic pretenders seeking to make their claims. The Romans had to take such claims seriously, whether they were made by a person such as Judas, or whether they were made on behalf of someone such as Jesus as Nazareth. "Messianic aspirations and apocalyptic visions undoubtedly triggered disturbances and gave rise to self-appointed and follower-proclaimed leaders."[2]

All of this had transpired while Archelaus was away in Rome gaining confirmation from the senate and Augustus. However, he had to help deal with Athronges himself when he returned (*Ant*. 17.284; *J.W.* 2.64). Yet when he came back, it was clear that Augustus had made some alterations in what Herod had proposed in his will. For one thing, Archelaus was made ethnarch—not king—of Judea, Idumea, and portions of Samaria (including Sebaste). Archelaus was not given a status superior to his brothers, but simply treated on par with them. This was perhaps in part because Antipas had also gone to Rome and pleaded to be made king over the whole realm since that was in accord with

---

1. As we shall see, James was to become a victim of such a period between rulers.
2. J. Hayes and S. Mandell, *The Jewish People in Classical Antiquity: From Alexander to Bar Kochba* (Louisville: Westminster John Knox, 1998), 148.

Herod's earlier will and since Archelaus was incompetent to rule (*Ant.* 17.224–239; *J.W.* 2.20–32). Antipas was granted an independent realm including Galilee and Perea. It is interesting that on this same occasion the Samaritans, as reward for not participating in the recent uprising, were granted a 25 percent reduction in their taxes. Philip, as we have noted, was given the least desirable part of the realm.

There is little doubt that Archelaus inherited the most difficult task of the three Herods: governing Judea and Jerusalem. Antipas's assessment of his brother's abilities proved, unfortunately, all too true, for Archelaus ruled only until A.D. 6, and during his decade as ruler the only notable things he seems to have accomplished were the rebuilding of Herod's winter palace in Jericho and the repair of the temple porticoes. Archelaus offended many by his various choices of high priest (there were three in rather quick succession after Joazar, including a return of Joazar in the end), and also by his marrying his brother's wife, which seems to have particularly infuriated the Pharisees, for whom Lev. 18:16 and 20:21 and Deut. 25:5–6 had the binding force of civil law.[3] Leaders in both Judea and Samaria sent delegations to Augustus to protest Archelaus's reign; he was summarily banished to Vienne in Gaul, and his realm was placed under the direct supervision of the province of Syria.

The New Testament seldom refers to Philip's territory, never mind Philip himself, but it is interesting that of the Herods, only Philip succeeded in reigning until he died, in A.D. 33 or 34. His realm was composed predominantly of Gentiles, and apparently they, unlike some of Archelaus's subjects, had no occasion to complain about Philip's actions, or lack thereof. Like his father, he undertook two major building projects early in his reign. He fortified Bethsaida and renamed it Julias (after Augustus's daughter), and more importantly, he rebuilt the city of Paneas and renamed it after the emperor and himself—Caesarea Philippi. Perhaps it was because his territory was predominantly Gentile,[4] but Philip was the only one of the Herods allowed to mint his own coins, on which he put images of the emperors Augustus and Tiberius and a facsimile of a temple.

It is not certain, but apparently Philip married only once, to a relative, Herodias,[5] who later abandoned him for Herod Antipas—the

---

3. See ibid., 151.

4. Ibid.

5. Here, Josephus (*Ant.* 18.137) and Mark (6:17–29) seem to disagree, with Josephus saying that Philip was married to Salome, and Mark that he was married to Salome's mother. Confusingly, Josephus also says at *Ant.* 18.136 that Antipas was married to Herodias, which is what Mark 6:17–29 also claims. It appears this dilemma is to be resolved by the suggestion that Salome married yet another Philip—Philip the Tetrach (*Ant.* 18.136–137).

cause célèbre that provoked the Baptist's criticism, leading eventually to his beheading. Philip died childless, and his realm was placed under the legate in Syria, until Caligula decided to turn it over to his friend Herod Agrippa I.

The longest-ruling of the sons of Herod the Great was Antipas, who lasted until A.D. 39, and was deposed at that point only due to his desire to be more than tetrarch. During the reign of Tiberius he was considered a close "friend" of the emperor (*Ant.* 18.36). Josephus reports no acute tensions during his reign (cf. *Ant.* 18.27–38, 101–126, 240–256; *J.W.* 2.167–168, 181–183). Antipas, like his father, was famous, or infamous, for his building projects. Not only did he rebuild Sepphoris, but also he built a new capital on the Sea of Galilee, which he named Tiberias. Unfortunately, he built this city on a Jewish cemetery, offending all the pious Jews in the region. Antipas did manage to get in hot water for marrying a Nabatean woman, a daughter of King Aretas IV, intending, no doubt, to cement peace in the region. Later, when he ditched this woman for Herodias, the angry Aretas took military actions against his realm, and Jews became angry as well, since Antipas had violated the prohibitions against marrying a brother's wife while he was still living. Aretas's actions were successful against Herod's forces, and they led to a complaint to Tiberius, who declared that Aretas had violated the Pax Romana by his attack on Herod's realm and should be captured, dead or alive. Aretas seems to have successfully avoided such capture, for it is this same Aretas (who ruled from 9 B.C. to A.D. 40) whom Paul was to run afoul of.

We are told by Josephus that Antipas, goaded by Herodias because Caligula had granted his relative Herod Agrippa I the title of king, was prompted to ask to be designated king by Caligula as well. Agrippa interceded, however, and told Caligula that Antipas was engaging in treasonous actions involving amassing arms and troops, and so Caligula had him exiled to Lyons in Gaul, and Agrippa was handed his territory (*Ant.* 18.240–252).[6]

A **Closer** Look: *Josephus the Jewish Historian*

Much of what has been chronicled in this study thus far depends heavily on the accounts of Josephus, and here is an appropriate place to take stock of his work and his reliability as a historian. Elsewhere I have dealt with the issue of Luke's reliability in comparison to that of Josephus on the historical

6. In *J.W.* 2.183, Josephus says that Antipas was exiled to Spain.

matters that they both discuss,[7] and I am unconvinced that Luke knew Josephus's work, not least because Luke was likely not writing at as late a date as Josephus wrote his definitive work, the *Jewish Antiquities* (in the 90s). Nor do I think that we need as a rule to give Josephus the preferential nod over Luke in historical matters. Both writers are apologetical historians, and both writers' works must be read critically. It is clear that when Josephus wrote the *Antiquities*, he was operating in a place (Rome) and in a cultural milieu that gave strong preference to historical works that were rhetorically skillful in composition. Josephus was well aware of this and recognizes the necessity of his exposition's ability to charm (*Ant.* 14.2–3). I think it likely that Josephus was following the model of Dionysius of Halicarnassus, who likewise wrote a twenty-volume historical work in the 90s and was seen as a model for historians writing in a Hellenistic mold, which clearly Josephus was trying to do. As a rhetorical historian, he took certain liberties with his sources, not the least of which is the rhetorical inflation of the numbers of people involved in one event or another. Here it is useful to cite S. Cohen's final summary, which follows a careful evaluation and comparison of all of Josephus's works:

> Josephus normally revises the language of his source. . . . The result is Josephan Greek, not a mechanical crib of the source. . . . With revision of language some revision of content is inevitable. Details are added, omitted, or changed, not always with reason. Although his fondness for the dramatic, pathetic, erotic, and the exaggerated is evident throughout, as a rule Josephus remains fairly close to his original. Even when he modifies the source to suit a certain aim he still reproduces the essence of the story. Most importantly he does not engage in the free invention of episodes. . . . When analyzing Josephan chronology we must always keep in mind the possibility that Josephus deliberately departed from the historical sequence for literary reason. . . . We have emphasized another aspect of Josephus' work; his inveterate sloppiness. Texts suitable for tendentious revision as well as passages which contradict his motives are sometimes left untouched. The narrative is frequently confused, obscure, and contradictory.[8]

Cohen's careful analysis, amply illustrated by examples from Josephus's works, makes clear that we cannot take Josephus's accounts at

---

7. See B. Witherington III, *The Acts of the Apostles: A Socio-rhetorical Commentary* (Grand Rapids: Eerdmans, 1998), 235–39.

8. S. Cohen, *Josephus in Galilee and Rome: His Vita and Development as a Historian* (Leiden: Brill, 1979), 232–33.

face value. The reader of Josephus is confronted at various points by the same sort of synoptic problem as in the Gospels because he offers two, often differing, accounts of many of the same events in *Jewish Wars* and *Jewish Antiquities* (and sometimes a third in his autobiography). Which of these two accounts is usually likely to be more accurate? In my view, though *Wars* was written nearer the time of the events in question, clearly it was a propaganda piece aimed at damage control and shielding Judaism from further reprisals after the disaster of A.D. 70 in Jerusalem. For instance, in *Wars,* Josephus deliberately downplays the role of the Pharisees to protect them, for they were the sect of Judaism he seems to have most resonated with, and at one point even sought to join (*Life* 12, 21). He seeks to pin blame for the Jewish wars on the more militant Jews, and even states that he was writing *Wars* to deter other Jews from revolting (*J.W.* 3.108). Notice that Josephus avoids connecting Judas and zealotry with Pharisaism in *J.W.* 2.118–119, but admits in *Ant.* 18.23 that the group that Judas founded agreed with the Pharisees in all matters except that they had a militant passion for liberty (cf. *Ant.* 18.3–4). It seems to me that in case after case, it is wiser to trust Josephus's later, less propagandistic account in *Antiquities,* a work that he wrote under external urging, when he was at the zenith of his career and had had many years to reflect on the historical events of the first century, some of which he had been directly involved in, in Judea and Galilee, during and before the Jewish wars of A.D. 66–70.[9] I will have occasion to say more about the synoptic problem in Josephus when I discuss the matter of Jewish zealotry.

When Judea became part of a province in A.D. 6, many Jews were happy, for a decade earlier they had requested to be delivered from Herod and simply be considered part of the Syrian province (*Ant.* 17.314). As an imperial province, as opposed to a senatorial one, Judea and Samaria both came under the emperor's direct oversight. Note that the highest-level official in charge of Judea at this time was in Syria, not in Judea where lower-level officials, prefects from the equestrian order, actually administered on the scene.[10] Judea had traded a king for midlevel management. Perhaps the worst news about the change was the increase in taxes payable to Rome, including a head tax. The various sorts of taxes that the people were subject to included land taxes,

9. See B. Witherington III, *The Christology of Jesus* (Minneapolis: Fortress, 1990), 81–84.
10. See Hayes and Mandell, *Jewish People*, 153.

customs, border duties, and the personal head tax. It was in A.D. 6 or 7 that Quirinius, appointed by Augustus, carried out the infamous census in preparation for new tax levies. At the same juncture, Coponius was made prefect of Judea.

A large and violent response to this census was led by a man named Judas from Gamala (who is nonetheless called Judas the Galilean) and a Pharisee named Saddok (*Ant.* 18.4–25; *J.W.* 2.118). Acts 5:37 suggests that Judas was killed in armed conflict with the Romans and his followers were scattered. Both after the death of Herod and after the dismissal of Archelaus these zealots arose, seeking to reestablish an independent people of God. The memory of the Maccabees and their ability to overcome significant opposition to bring freedom to Israel was still fresh in many people's minds. But was there really an ongoing, religiously motivated Zealot movement from the time of the latter years of Herod's reign until the end of the Jewish war, or was it rather a matter of isolated eruptions of banditry on various occasions during the New Testament era? To address this question we must consider more closely what both Josephus and the New Testament suggest about the matter.

A **Closer** Look: *Zealots or Bandits?*

It has become fashionable of late among scholars to deny the existence of a Zealot movement in the Holy Land during the first half of the first century A.D.[11] Recall my earlier statement that on the whole, Josephus's *Antiquities* likely presents a more accurate portrait of the sects of early Judaism than his earlier *Wars*, which clearly is more of a propaganda piece meant to deter further revolt and do damage control on behalf of Jews in the empire in general. Josephus says quite explicitly in *Ant.* 18.23–25 that Judas the Galilean was no mere bandit or brigand, but rather, that he and his followers were in agreement with the views of Pharisaism, except that they believed in taking up arms to gain freedom. Josephus is careful in *J.W.* 2.118–119 to avoid making this connection with Pharisaism, but he does portray Judas as founder of a fourth philosophical sect (alongside the Pharisees, Sadducees, and Essenes) that included the following in its credo: (1) avoiding the census, because submitting to the census is submitting to slavery; (2) advocating that the theocracy, where God alone is the supreme leader of Israel,

11. See, e.g., R. Horsley, *Jesus and the Spiral of Violence: Popular Jewish Resistance in Palestine* (San Francisco: Harper and Row, 1987).

be reestablished (serving God and serving Rome were incompatible); (3) violence for the sake of freedom and independence, especially when it involves a just act of vengeance; (4) the necessity of suffering and martyrdom to reestablish a free nation.

Were there only the connection between Judas and Pharisaism, it might be possible to dismiss it as insignificant, but Josephus also says that during the Jewish war in the 60s, the revolutionary government then in charge in Jerusalem sent two Pharisees to Galilee to take action against Josephus, who then was a provincial commander (*Life* 195–197). To this we may add the further connection between zealous and violent action and at least one form of Pharisaism when we consider the example of Saul of Tarsus, who was prepared to take violent action against fellow Jews in order to preserve early Judaism from pollution. Furthermore, Josephus in *Ant.* 17.271–272 candidly admits that Judas's plundering of the armory in Sepphoris was part of his "zealous pursuit of royal rank." In other words, messianic motivation prompted his zealotic actions.

Even a cursory reading of *Antiquities* reveals that Josephus does not intend for his audience to think that the actions of Judas in A.D. 6 were isolated incidents with no relationship to or bearing on later revolutionary actions. Acts 5:36–37 confirms this impression. In Josephus's words, Judas and Saddok at the very least planted the seeds of the later troubles, which presumably means the activities in the 60s (*Ant.* 18.9–10). Josephus also connects the *sicarii* (the so-called daggermen) with both Judas and the later events at Masada. Indeed, the whole impression left by *Ant.* 18.4–25 is that Judas and his followers were religiously observant Jews who wished to recognize only God as their true leader and master. It is impossible to characterize the movement that Judas began as purely social or political in character.

At this juncture we note the probable family link between Judas and the later revolutionaries. For example, Menahem, apparently the son of Judas the Galilean, is the one who assumes leadership of the *sicarii* (*J.W.* 2.425–434) leading them to Masada. According to *J.W.* 2.444, Menahem was followed by "the zealots," which here may have its generic sense rather than referring to a particular sect or party of the Jews. What we can say about this last text from *Wars* is that it suggests an integral connection between Judas, Menahem, the *sicarii* at Masada, and some of those who in the 60s were called Zealots.[12]

12. See the detailed discussion in Witherington, *Christology of Jesus*, 85–87.

Thus, it appears that despite the protests and reservations of some scholars, M. Hengel's conclusions are fully warranted: "The Jewish Freedom movement between 6 and 70 A.D. had a certain uniform ideological basis. They stood near to Pharisaic piety and bore the impression of a strongly eschatological outlook."[13] It is quite believable that these "zealots" (though the movement was not labeled this way before the 60s) based their actions on the zealous deeds of Phineas and the Maccabees. What had long been festering in Judea and Galilee finally erupted in the 60s into full-scale war. John the Baptist and Jesus operated in a volatile environment where the ideology of the Maccabees—the ideology of freedom and theocracy—was alive and well.

The evidence about the exact nature of the social situation between the time when Coponius was made prefect in Judea in A.D. 6 and when Pontius Pilate assumed that office in A.D. 26 is not abundant. We know that there were not any large concentrations of Roman soldiers right in Judea or Galilee during this period of time, and we know that the Romans settled on Caesarea Maritima as their administrative capital. The Romans reserved to themselves the appointment of the high priest, and there must have been some unrest during the time, for four high priests were appointed in rapid succession, the last of whom, Caiaphas, served for years (*Ant.* 18.34–35). But in fact, before Quirinius left Israel for Syria after his famous census, he appointed one Ananus as high priest (*Ant.* 18.26). His son Eleazar was one of the four high priests who served in rapid succession, and Caiaphas was Ananus's son-in-law. Thus, the Romans made some effort to keep the office in something of a hereditary line. Tacitus tells us that during the period of A.D. 6–26 both Judea and Syria applied for relief from their tribute burden (*Annals* 2.42.5). It is also noteworthy that about A.D. 1 Herod's sister Salome died. The Romans had granted her a group of cities to provide for her income and living (Jamnia, Phasael, Azotus, and Archelais), but she willed them to the emperor Augustus's wife (*Ant.* 18.31). "What this did was create large and very profitable estates owned directly by absentee Roman landlords. To see such wealth and acreage, in Yahweh's land, controlled and administered by foreign Romans must have greatly rankled landless Jewish masses."[14]

Jesus—the Early Years

Very little can be said about happenings in general in Judea and Galilee during the period between the death of Herod and the arrival of Pontius

13. M. Hengel, *Die Zeloten*, 2nd ed. (Leiden: Brill, 1976), 412.
14. Hayes and Mandell, *Jewish People*, 155.

Illustration 3.2 Herodian stone (with Hebrew inscription) on the Temple Mount.

Pilate, nor can much be said about the lives of Jesus and John the Baptist during this period. We must examine what little evidence we have, however, and consider the larger social context out of which the Baptist and his movement arose.

Are there clues about Jesus' early years? Let us consider for a moment two items in no real dispute: Jesus' personal name, and the fact that his parents were observant Jews. The Greek name Iesous is a shortened version of the Hebrew name Yeshua, or as we would put it, Joshua—the name of the man who led the invasion of the promised land and was the first real leader of the theocratic state. The name means "Yahweh is salvation." This was, to judge from the twenty-one different Jesuses men-

tioned in Josephus's works, a very popular name in the first century, attesting to the desire of God's people to live without foreign control or overlords.[15]

Luke 2:39 shows that Jesus' parents were observant Jews, which normally would mean that Jesus was circumcised on the eighth day after his birth and then dedicated in the temple (Luke 2:21–22). We know that he was taught to read the Scriptures, for several texts mention him doing so (cf. Luke 4:16–20; Mark 6), and we may be sure that he was taught to recite the Shema (Deut. 6:4–5), the credo of early Jews. Jose-

15. Interestingly, the name Yeshua disappears from Jewish writings after the first century A.D., and the longer form of the name, Yehoshua, is substituted. This is probably because of the significance that the name came to have in early Christianity.

phus says that Jewish children in Jesus' era were thoroughly grounded in the laws of the nation, even to the point of memorizing and repeating them (*Ag. Ap.* 2.178). But at the same time, it is likely correct to conclude from a text like John 7:15 that Jesus had not studied with some famous Jewish teacher, and had not gone to Jerusalem to do so. Nonetheless, as the child of observant Jews, Jesus would have had opportunity to go to various festivals and learn much just by observing. For example, his reaction to the traders' activities in the temple surely must stand against a background of his having visited the temple when such activities were not going on. Then, too, we may conclude from his being asked to read and comment on the Scriptures in his hometown synagogue (Luke 4:16–20) that it was known that he was a literate child of observant Jews, could read the Scriptures, and could be expected to say something appropriate.[16]

Though later apocryphal documents, such as the *Infancy Gospel of Thomas*, have a good deal to say about the "hidden" years of Jesus' childhood and youth, these documents amount to little more than pious fiction and are recognized by almost all scholars as of little or no historical worth. The canonical Gospels themselves have only one story from Jesus' youth, which likely has some historical substance—Luke 2:41–52.

The likelihood of some historical substance being behind this story is enhanced by the fact that it reflects badly on Jesus' parents: they seem to have neglected to make sure he was in the group of pilgrims going home to Galilee, and they do not understand him. In particular, Mary, whom Luke wishes to portray ultimately as a disciple of Jesus (Acts 1:14; note also Luke's omission of Mark 3:21 from his Markan source), in these birth narratives is shown to lack full understanding of Jesus and his actions (cf. Luke 1:29, 34; 2:33), though like a good disciple she reflects on what she does not understand (Luke 2:50–51).

Notice that the story in Luke 2:41–52 has no gratuitous miraculous elements, unlike the apocryphal tales about Jesus making real birds out of clay, and the like, a point that must count in favor of the historical substance of the story. A trip by a pious Jewish family with their son come of age to the temple was customary as part of Jewish parents' obligation to acquaint the son with his religious duties. Furthermore, it was customary for Galileans to go up to the city of Jerusalem in large parties, not least because of concerns for safety on the road (cf. Luke 10:30). The story has yet another earmark of authenticity: Jesus to some extent dis-

---

16. The Mishnah (*m. ʾAbot.* 5:21) says that children were taught to read the Scriptures from age five, and at age thirteen one is fit for the commandments.

engages from his parents' authority, a motif confirmed elsewhere in other Gospel traditions (cf. Mark 3:31–35; John 2:4). It is also possible that Luke in 2:19 and 51 is trying to indicate Mary as the source for these stories. Finally, the motif of Jesus following the will of God alone is familiar from other Gospel stories (again, see Mark 3:31–35).

Luke 2:41–52 is in some ways like John 2:1–12 because the story ends with Jesus doing what his parent wants without verbally indicating that he would do so. The tensions between the claims of the physical family and the family of faith are evident, with Mary speaking of Jesus' father (Joseph) and Jesus replying in terms of his actual Father (God). Notice that while Jesus is portrayed as something of a prodigy in his spiritual knowledge, he is also said to grow intellectually (in wisdom), physically (in stature), and spiritually (in the favor of God as well as of people).

From this singular story we may draw a few limited conclusions. Jesus' childhood is likely to have been in many respects like that of other children of devout Jewish parents—a period of training, growth, development, and learning, especially about the faith. The truly remarkable element in the story is not a revelation that Jesus works miracles, but that Jesus has an extraordinary knowledge of and relationship with God, something that astounded his parents and his teachers. This is an important point, for it is this special and intimate relationship with the Father that comes to light at crisis moments in Jesus' adult life (baptism, transfiguration, the garden of Gethsemane, on the cross). This feature characterized Jesus' life throughout its all-too-brief span.

John the Baptist and the Desert Rabbis

To visit the salt flats of the Dead Sea is to encounter one of the starkest landscapes anywhere on earth. The visitor who leaves the flats and heads into the hills still finds the landscape to be mostly unrelentingly arid and rocky, this region making up what came to be called the Judean wilderness. The temperatures here can be in excess of 100°F in the summer. It hardly seems like a spot to start a renewal movement, but this is precisely what the Qumran community sought to do. They established a base camp in the salt flats where they would wait for God to act against the irremediably corrupt temple hierarchy and cleanse the land, with the help of the "sons of light"—the Qumranites.

Long before the discovery of the Qumran scrolls in 1947, scholars were well aware, through the writings of Josephus, of a group called the Essenes, even though they are not directly mentioned in the New Testament. But what is the relationship between the Essenes whom Josephus describes and the Qumran community? A closer examination is in order.

A **Closer** Look: *The Essenes and the Qumranites*

The earliest reference to the Essenes outside of their own documents is found in the pre–A.D. 40 writings of Philo (*Good Person* 75–91; *Hypothetica* 11.1–18). Perhaps more important for our purposes is the reference to the Essenes dating from the A.D. 70s from Pliny the Elder in *Natural History* (5.15). Pliny says that the Essenes could be found on the west bank of the Dead Sea, north of Masada and of Ein Gedi, which is precisely where modern archaeologists have found the Qumran remains. Thirteen different times Josephus has occasion to refer to the Essenes; indeed, he refers to them more than to the Pharisees. Two lengthy passages on them are found in *J.W.* 2.119–161 and in *Ant.* 18.18–22. The Essenes are also mentioned in later Christian literature (e.g., Hippolytus, around A.D. 200, in *Refutation of All Heresies* [9.18–28]), and referred to as a heretical Jewish sect.

Both Josephus and Philo indicate that there were more than four thousand Essenes (Josephus, *Ant.* 18.20; Philo, *Good Person* 75), which, if even close to being a correct estimate, means that they could not all have been located at the Dead Sea site. We are also informed that there was a three-year probationary period, and during the first year one had to live according to the rules but outside the Essene community. In the second and third years of probation one could go through the *mikvaot*, or ritual baths, that members used, but could not share in the common fellowship meals. Final admission involved taking very serious oaths (*J.W.* 2.137–142), and expulsion from the group was always possible if one did not strictly obey the elders and the community rules.

All of the sources already mentioned refer to the fact that entrants to the sect turned their property over to the group, and even food and clothing were to be shared. Property overseers were elected in the group (Josephus, *J.W.* 2.122–127; Philo, *Hypothetica* 11.4, 10–12; *Good Person* 85–87; Pliny, *Natural History* 5.15). The same sources all suggest that the Essenes were essentially an all-male group and that they did not marry, although Josephus does mention another group of Essenes who did marry (*J.W.* 2.160–161). The daily regimen of the

Illustration 3.3 The Scriptorium at Qumran.

group included rising before dawn, prayer, work until midday, purificatory bath, a common meal, work until evening, and an evening meal (*J.W.* 2.128–133). Basically, the Essenes were involved in agricultural work, though they had artisans, shepherds, beekeepers, and scribes (Josephus, *Ant.* 18.18–22; Philo, *Hypothetica* 11.8–9). It appears that the Essenes also offered their own sacrifices quite apart from those offered at the temple in Jerusalem (*Ant.* 18.19).

In regard to the beliefs of the Essenes, Josephus mentions that they regarded the names of the angels as important (*J.W.* 2.142), believed that things were divinely determined in advance (*Ant.* 13.172), and had prophets in their midst who made very accurate predictions (*J.W.* 2.159).[17] The question then must be pressed, Are these the same sectarians as the people who produced the Qumran scrolls?

First, the archaeological evidence indicates that the Qumran community in the salt flats of the Dead Sea existed there between the second century B.C. and A.D. 68. Josephus tells us that the group was first extant during the reign of Jonathan of the Maccabees, or around 145 B.C. (*Ant.* 13.71), and he mentions that he also participated in the group as

17. On all the preceding on the Essenes, see T. Beall, "Essenes," *DNTB*, 43–48, which I have largely followed here.

a youth (circa A.D. 53). This data comports with the archaeological data for Qumran.

Second, the Qumran evidence about admissions procedures, participation in the common meal, and obedience to the elders all closely resemble the description Josephus gives (cf. 1QS 6:13–23; 5:2–7:17). We also know that the Qumranites practiced the sharing of property (1QS 1:11–12; 5:1–2; 6:17–22), though there is some evidence that members were allowed to retain some private property (CD 9:10–16). That hundreds of coins were found in the administration building but none in the living quarters at Qumran supports the communal property conclusion. On the issue of marriage there is some dispute about the Qumran evidence. On the one hand, only male skeletons have been found on the site, but on the other hand, the Damascus Document and the Rule of the Community speak of marriage (cf. CD 4:19–5:7; 1 QSa 1:9–12). There is, however, no dispute about the clear evidence at Qumran for the practice of ritual washings (cf. 1QS 5:13–14; CD 11:21–22), and of common meals (1QS 6:2–5). I have not mentioned the founder of the Qumran community, known only as the Teacher of Righteousness, but so far as the evidence from Josephus and the Qumran scrolls goes, this person seems to have been a priest who had a falling out with the Maccabees, split off from the Maccabean community, and went out to the Dead Sea area, taking a significant number of loyal adherents with him.

Third, as Josephus indicated about the Essenes, this sectarian group was very bookish (*J.W.* 2.136, 159), especially focusing, of course, on the Hebrew Scriptures, but also studying other sources. This comports nicely with the evidence found at Qumran in many scrolls. Clearly, too, interest was great at Qumran in angels (cf. *1 Enoch*, *Thanksgiving Hymns*, *War Scroll*, and *Songs of the Sabbath Sacrifice*, among other scrolls). Equally clearly, the Qumranites believed in divine determinism (cf. 1QH 1:7–8; 7:31–32; 15:12–15, 17; 1QM 17:5; 1QS 3:15–16). One can hardly doubt the prophetic orientation of the Qumran community, not only because of their collection of prophetic books, but also because of the pesher commentaries on such books (e.g., 1QpHab).

On the basis of this evidence we should conclude with a high degree of likelihood that the Qumran community at the Dead Sea was part of the Essene sect. But it is also true that there is now evidence of an Essene presence in Jerusalem, and even an Essene gate into the temple precincts.[18] They appear to have been located to the south of the Mount Zion section of the city, which is near the site of the upper room and where the early Christians seem to have met as well. We will have occasion later to consider the suggestion that the earliest Christian community was influenced by Essene practices. Here it is sufficient to say that the Essenes/Qumranites seem to have been a prominent, eschatologically oriented sect, eagerly preparing and looking forward to the time when God would purify his people and bring them back into a right state of holiness.

Was John the Baptist at some point a part of the Qumran community? The evidence that he was is not compelling, but it is suggestive. First, we know that the Baptist was plying his trade in the Judean wilderness, the same region where the Qumran community was, although John 1:28 and 3:23, with the references to Bethany and Aenon, suggest that he was operating somewhat north of their locale. Second, there is the text used in the earliest Gospel, Mark, to introduce John the Baptist. Mark 1:2–3 quotes Mal. 3:1 and Isa. 40:3. The latter text in particular seems to have been a theme verse for the Qumranites. They were preparing the way of God's coming in the Judean wilderness.[19] John may be said to have been doing the same. He shared in a common eschatological outlook that now was the time when the fulfillment of the prophecies and promises of God would begin to transpire. Third, there is the matter of food. Both John and the Qumranites manifested ascetical dietary tendencies. Fourth, there is the eschatological orientation of John and the Qumranites. Both believed that God's judgment on Israel was imminent and that repentance was necessary. Fifth, there is the matter of John's water ritual. Although Qumran's water ablutions were basically daily purification rites, there does seem to have been an initiatory water rite practiced on the probationers there, on which, possibly, John could have modeled his water ritual. Finally, according to Luke 1, John came from a priestly family. This may be significant because the Qumran community not only was founded by someone in a priestly line, but also strove to have all its members live in a priestly manner and prepare for the coming of both a priestly and a kingly mes-

18. See the discussion in B. Pixner, "Jerusalem's Essene Gateway," *BAR* 23 (1997): 23–26. See also B. Capper, "The Palestinian Cultural Context of Earliest Christian Community of Goods," in *The Book of Acts in Its Palestinian Setting*, ed. R. Bauckham (Grand Rapids: Eerdmans, 1995), 341–50.

19. We should note that the Hebrew of Isa. 40:3 suggests that the text should be read, "The voice of one crying: 'In the desert prepare the way of the Lord.'" In this reading of the text, the preparation, rather than the crying, is what is transpiring in the wilderness.

sianic figure. In other words, it was natural for a pious young man of priestly stock to be attracted to such a group of people.

Furthermore, when we encounter John, even if he was at one time a Qumranite, he is one no longer, as shown by the fact that he is alone, and is making an effort to call the nation directly to repentance rather than just withdrawing from the polluted majority of Israel. Also, he allows both the clean and unclean, the righteous and the sinners, to come into contact with him. And, John apparently had no Levitical program in mind for his baptisands to follow, nor had he a revolutionary program to cure the nations ills. He was not a reformer in the same manner that the Pharisees or Zealots were. Nor was he a miracle worker, as John 10:41 reminds us.

Here we first examine what Josephus has to say about John the Baptist before considering the New Testament evidence. Josephus devotes only one paragraph to John (*Ant.* 18.116–119), which is, of course, significantly less attention than John gets in the New Testament. First and foremost, Josephus makes no connection between Jesus of Nazareth and John. He mentions that John was noted for his baptizing, but does not mention that the river Jordan was where John was doing so. It is possible that John chose the eastern, or Perean, side of the Jordan to baptize people because it was outside the Roman province (though within the territory of Herod Antipas) (cf. John 1:28; 10:40). Josephus also says that John was imprisoned beyond the Jordan at the fortress known as Machaerus, which suggests that it was near where John had been operating and where he was taken prisoner.

One of the major tendencies of Josephus, when he is dealing with matters of Jewish belief, is his attempt to present things in a way that makes sense to a Greco-Roman audience. For example, instead of speaking about things like resurrection, a specifically Jewish notion, he is more likely to speak about a belief in immortality.[20] In the case of John, Josephus de-eschatologizes his teaching. John goes from being an apocalyptic prophet of doom to being a teacher of morality, exhorting people to live righteous and pious lives. Furthermore, rather than the baptism for repentant sinners that John offers in the Gospels, Josephus suggests that John's baptism was a sort of confirmation ritual for a conscience that had already been cleansed. It is also interesting that Josephus, who certainly knew about the furor that Antipas's marriage to Herodias caused, nonetheless attributes

20. P. Barnett writes "This is typical of Josephus who regularly translates apocalyptic elements in Judaism into political and philosophical terms" (*Jesus and the Rise of Early Christianity: A History of New Testament Times* [Downers Grove, Ill.: InterVarsity, 1999], 122).

Illustration 3.4 Jordan River near the Sea of Galilee.

Antipas's arrest of John to a fear that he might instigate a popular rebellion, whereas the New Testament attributes John's arrest to his reproach of Antipas for that marriage.

According to Luke 3:1–2, John began to prophesy and baptize in the
fifteenth year of Tiberius's reign as emperor, which, depending on
whether partial regnal years are being counted, would mean that John
began to act and speak in A.D. 27 or 28. In my judgment, John's ministry transpired probably in A.D. 27 and 28, [21] possibly continuing into
early A.D. 29, and Jesus' ministry began probably in A.D. 28 (the overlap
period with John) and concluded with his crucifixion in A.D. 30.[22]

Something now needs to be said about John's water ritual and its
radical nature. If, as both Josephus and the New Testament indicate,
this rite was connected with repentance and God's forgiveness of sins,
then in effect John was offering people a way to obtain right standing
with God quite apart from the agency of the temple apparatus in Jerusalem. We should remember that John's rite bore most resemblance to

21. B. Meyer is correct that it could have begun as early as the fall of A.D. 27 (*The Aims
of Jesus* [London: SCM, 1979], 11).
22. For the view that Jesus died in A.D. 33, which allows us to push forward John's
ministry to A.D. 28–29, see Barnett, *Jesus and the Rise*, 123–24. I am unconvinced by his
arguments that Jesus had a ministry of three to four years' duration.

proselyte baptism, a ritual practiced only on Gentiles! John's calling of all kinds of Jews to baptism suggests that he was in agreement with the Qumranites that the nation of Israel was seriously corrupt, not holy at all. The nation needed more than remedial attention to minor problems; it needed to start over from scratch with God (see, e.g., Matt. 3:7–10). Yet unlike the Qumranites, John allows all sorts of persons to come into contact with him.

It is a serious mistake to underestimate the importance of John the Baptist when considering the rise of the Jesus movement. In the earliest Gospel, John and his ministry are quite properly seen as "the beginning of the gospel" (see Mark 1:1–14), an idea that the later Gospels also promote in one fashion or another. John is the one who sets things in motion and prepares Israel for the coming of their God and his reign, for judgment was to begin with the household of God, and only thereby, and perhaps thereafter, would there be redemption. It is probably true that the largely positive presentation of John in the Gospels is due to Jesus' own positive appreciation of John and his ministry.[23]

According to Mark 1:5, people were coming to the Jordan from Jerusalem and Judea to be baptized by John. This suggests that his ministry must have been near Judea, probably on the other side of the Jordan and somewhat north of Jerusalem, placing John in Antipas's territory. The reference to Judeans and Jerusalemites coming to John may be significant. At this time, that part of the Holy Land was part of a Roman province, and yet it contained the Holy City. Its priesthood and even the vestments of the priest were under Roman control. Pious Jews in that realm would have known that something was seriously wrong morally or spiritually for them to be living under occupation. By contrast, in Galilee at least there was the facade or illusion that Jews were being ruled by someone at least partly Jewish.

In regard to Jesus, what I have just said suggests that Jesus was baptized by John in or near Judea. I would propose that John 3:22–4:3 is probably correct in hinting at a period in Jesus' life in which he was either a disciple of John or a co-laborer with him beyond the Jordan before embarking on his own, largely Galilean, ministry once John was imprisoned.[24]

If Mark 1:6 is anywhere near the mark historically, it appears that by his clothing and food, John was self-consciously presenting himself like one of the prophets of old, in particular one of the northern prophets, specifically Elijah (cf. the leather belt in 2 Kings 1:8). Even less in

---

23. See W. Wink, *John the Baptist in the Gospel Tradition*, SNTSMS 7 (London: Cambridge University Press, 1968), 111.

24. For a more detailed discussion, see Witherington, *Christology of Jesus*, 34–38.

doubt is that John's baptism was for the remission of sins, quite apart from the sacrifices in the temple. This may explain why even tax collectors and Romans, according to Luke 3:12–14, came to John for baptism (cf. Matt. 21:31–32), and would further explain why not only the temple hierarchy but also the Pharisees would be at odds with John and his methods of dealing with sin and uncleanness.

Another facet of the Markan account that appears in the other Gospel accounts as well is that John did not see himself as the definitive revealer of God, but rather, expected some sort of sequel to his own ministry. Someone or something would come after him. From Mark and the Q material it is not clear whether John envisioned God directly intervening with a baptism of fire, or through another human agent of God. The saying about the sandals, if it actually goes back to John, would support the conclusion that John expected a human agent to follow, whom John was unworthy even to serve as a slave.

Ten percent of the earliest collection of Jesus' sayings, the material known as Q, mentions or is devoted to John and his words and deeds. Before we deal with some of this important material found in Matthew 3 and Luke 3, some explanation must be given about the sayings source known as Q.

A **Closer** Look: *Q and A on Q*

It is clear enough from reading early Jewish literature that a regular practice of the disciples of great teachers and sages was to make collections of their famous sayings. Some of these early Jewish sages, such as Hanina ben Dosa or Honi the Circle Drawer, bear a certain resemblance to Jesus. Furthermore, anyone who has studied the Mishnah knows that various famous teachers had their most famous aphorisms or sayings not only memorized by their students but eventually set into writing. The famous saying about the disciple being a plastered cistern, never losing a drop of the distilled wisdom of his master, is of course an exaggeration, but nevertheless reminds us that rote memorization was common among the disciples of early Jewish teachers. Thus, there is a social context and pedagogical process in which it is quite believable that at some point before any of the Gospels were written, a collection, largely of sayings material, was made of Jesus' most memorable teachings.

The term "Q," short for *Quelle*, which is German for "source," is the cipher that scholars use to refer to the material that Matthew and Luke have in common but did not find in their Markan source. This material, which includes, for example, the Sermon on the Mount, often appears quite similar, even word for word in the First and Third Gospels, which suggests to most scholars that Matthew and Luke shared a common sayings source.[25] Indeed Luke states that he did use sources (Luke 1:1–4), and there is no reason to doubt that Matthew did likewise.

The collection of Jesus' sayings tells us that early on people recognized that while what Jesus did, as a miracle worker or even during the last week of his life, was important about Jesus, so also, what he taught was crucial for the ongoing Jesus movement. Indeed, Jesus' actions required an interpretive context. The healings of Jesus without the connection to the coming dominion of God would not have had the same significance. Below is an outline of the material common to Matthew and Luke but not found in Mark (or John, for that matter).

SECTION I
Luke 3:2–9/Matt. 3:1–10
Luke 3:15–17/Matt. 3:11–12
Luke 3:21–22/Matt. 3:13–16
Luke 4:1–13/Matt. 4:1–11
Luke 6:20–49/Matthew 5–7
Luke 7:1–10/Matt. 8:5–10
Luke 7:18–23/Matt. 11:2–6
Luke 7:24–28/Matt. 11:7–11
Luke 7:31–35/Matt. 11:16–19

SECTION II
Luke 9:57–62/Matt. 8:19–22
Luke 10:1–24/Matt. 9:37–38; 10:5–16; 11:20–24; 11:25–27; 13:16–17
Luke 10:1–12/Matt. 9:37–38; 10:5–16
Luke 10:13–15/Matt. 11:20–24
Luke 10:16–20/Matt. 10:40
Luke 10:21–24/Matt. 11:25–27; 13:16–17
Luke 11:2–4; 11:5–13/Matt. 6:7–13; 7:7–11

25. Some scholars think it is possible that Matthew used Luke or, more probably, Luke used Matthew, but this is a distinctly minority opinion. Against this opinion is that some of the non-Q material found in Matthew but not in Luke would have served some of Luke's purposes, as would some of Matthew's purposes been served by some of the non-Q material found in Luke but not Matthew.

SECTION III
Luke 11:14–26/Matt. 12:22–30, 43–45
Luke 11:29–32/Matt. 12:38–42
Luke 11:33–36/Matt. 5:15; 6:22–23
Luke 11:42–52/Matt. 23:4, 6, 7, 13, 22–23, 25–31, 34–36

SECTION IV
Luke 12:2–3/Matt. 10:26–27
Luke 12:4–7/Matt. 10:28–31
Luke 12:8–12/Matt. 10:19, 32–33
Luke 12:22–31/Matt. 6:25–33
Luke 12:32–34/Matt. 6:19–21
Luke 12:35–40/Matt. 24:43–44
Luke 12:42–48/Matt. 24:45–51
Luke 12:49–50
Luke 12:51–53/Matt. 10:34–36
Luke 12:54–56/Matt. 16:2–3
Luke 12:57–59/Matt. 5:25–26
Luke 13:34–35/Matt. 23:37–39

SECTION V
Luke 13:18–21/Matt. 13:31–33
Luke 13:23–27/Matt. 7:13–14; 22–23
Luke 13:28–30/Matt. 8:11–12; 20:16
Luke 14:15–24/Matt. 22:1–10
Luke 14:5–27/Matt. 10:37–38
Luke 14:34–35/Matt. 5:13
Luke 15:3–7/Matt. 18:12–14
Luke 15:8–10

SECTION VI
Luke 16:13/Matt. 6:24
Luke 16:16–17/Matt. 11:12–13; 5:18
Luke 16:18/Matt. 5:32
Luke 17:1–4/Matt. 18:7, 21–22
Luke 17:5–6/Matt. 17:20

SECTION VII
Luke 17:22–23/Matt. 24:26

Luke 17:24/Matt. 24:27
Luke 17:37/Matt. 24:28
Luke 17:26–30/Matt. 24:37–39
Luke 17:31–32/Matt. 24:17–18
Luke 17:33/Matt. 10:29
Luke 17:34–35/Matt. 24:40–41
Luke 19:11–27/Matt. 25:14–30
Luke 22:28–30/Matt. 19:28[26]

A careful examination of this material shows that it includes some narrative but is mostly aphorisms, parables, and sayings of various sorts. Also, Jesus is presented as a prophetic sage in this collection of material, and indeed, as the incarnation of God's wisdom upon the earth.

The short sermon of John found in Matthew 3 and Luke 3 is full of invective and dire warnings about coming judgment. John calls his audience snake spawn—not the usual way to win friends and influence people. John warns his listeners that they must repent and live a life that shows they have repented of their sin, and not presume to say, "We have Abraham as our Father." John is making clear that heredity cannot settle the issue, since God could raise up true Israelites even from stones. Certainly, here John is addressing Israelites, not Gentiles or proselytes. Matthew's account suggests that this sermon was addressed to some particular group of Jews; perhaps, if Luke 7:29–30 is any clue, it might be addressed in particular to the Pharisees among the crowd, for the term "brood of vipers" suggests a particular group of persons.

Indeed, the sermon suggests that John is surprised that this particular group has come for baptism and so to avoid the wrath of God soon to fall on God's people. Apparently, John thinks that someone else has told this group of Jews about his message of imminent judgment. Although wrath is emphasized in this speech, John does allow that a winnower will gather some wheat. Once again, John does not say whether the one coming after him will be a human or divine agent of judgment or winnowing. Notice that Matt. 13:41 depicts angels gathering the wicked.

26. On these divisions, see B. Witherington III, *Jesus the Sage: The Pilgrimage of Wisdom* (Minneapolis: Fortress, 1994), 219–21. Generally, scholars believe that Luke best preserves the order of Q, hence the Lukan texts are listed first, while I would argue that Matthew usually best preserves the wording of Q.

One of the most interesting aspects of this sermon is its similarity to the parable of the tares (Matt. 13:24–30). Both stress the coming and final rule and judgment of God. Both call for immediate response so that one might be counted as wheat rather than chaff. Repentance and conversion are required of individual Jews if they are to avert spiritual disaster. It is fair to say that John, like the Qumranites, believed that the leadership of Israel was highly corrupt and required conversion. In regard to the saying about baptism, it seems clear that John contrasts his own with the future, more dramatic or effective baptism with the Holy Spirit and with fire.

Luke 7:18–23/Matt. 11:2–6 provides us with a window on the interrelationship between John the Baptist and Jesus. The story has all the earmarks of authenticity because it is unlikely that Christians would make up a story about John having doubts in regard to who Jesus is. Also, it shows that John continued to have disciples even after Jesus began his separate ministry, so that Jesus' movement could not be said to be just the continuation of John's movement. John inquires of Jesus if he is "the one who is to come," probably an allusion to Mal. 3:1. If so, Jesus' response suggests that John is thinking of the wrong Scripture, for Jesus quotes Isaiah. Yet it is also possible that John is using Qumranite language about the coming messianic figure (1QS 9:11; 4QPBless 3). Perhaps the reason for John's question is that John expected a coming judging figure, but Jesus has come healing and proclaiming good news.

The citation Jesus offers is a composite, with bits from Isa. 29:18–19; 35:5–6; 61:1; 26:19. The important point about these citations is not simply that Jesus has precedent for being a healer, but that he sees himself as not merely living in the age of scriptural fulfillment, but indeed, bringing it about. This story is, of course, told for the sake of what it reveals about Jesus, not about John, for we are not told how John reacted to Jesus' response.

Luke 7:24–28/Matt. 11:7–11 is a separate tradition from the one just discussed, and it too tells us a great deal about John, in this case through the eyes of Jesus, who in essence calls John the greatest man ever born, and more than an ordinary prophet. We have confirmation in this passage that John was in the Judean wilderness and that he wore the clothes of prophets, not of kings. Indeed, there seems to be a contrast between Herod Antipas, with his fine raiment, and John. There may even be a reference to a coin minted by Herod that had a reed on it. If so, Jesus sees Herod as a shaky ruler, blowing whichever way the wind blows.

The most important part of this passage for our purposes is that John is called a prophet, but also more than a prophet. Jesus perhaps saw John as the special eschatological prophet who would come before the end, preparing God's people for the final and climactic act of divine redemptive judgment. But notice also what this saying implies about Jesus' self-understanding. It implies that Jesus saw himself as the Coming One, or at least some sort of messianic figure who would follow the last great eschatological prophet. The age of the law and the prophets was passing away and the dominion of God was coming, and John had one foot in each age, according to Jesus. The contrast in Matt. 11:11 is not between two groups of people but between two ways of evaluating them—those merely born of women, and those who are also in the dominion of God. The point is that even the greatest human being judged in human terms does not have as great a status as the least of those transformed and included in the dominion of God. Jesus seems to be picking up and expanding John's contrast between human descent and repentance and faith as a prerequisite for participating in the coming dominion of God.

Another Q passage that tells us something about John and Jesus is the strange material found in Luke 16:16/Matt. 11:12–13. This saying makes clear that Jesus taught in a context of controversy. The gist of the earliest form of the saying seems to be this: the law and prophets were until John; since then, the divine dominion has suffered violence, and the violent take it by force. One possible meaning of this saying is that local revolutionaries were attempting to force God's dominion to arrive, in part by taking over sections of the Holy Land or perpetrating acts of violence against the Romans. Another possible meaning is that John and Jesus had suffered from those who use violence to achieve their aims, people like Herod Antipas. If the latter is the correct meaning, it places John and Jesus together in a context of being at risk. Additionally, this saying might mean that Jesus sees John as the last of the old order of things, the age of the law and prophets. The inbreaking of the dominion of God meant a new, eschatological state of affairs.[27] That dominion was already in some sense present.

Luke 7:31–35/Matt. 11:16–19 makes evident how much Jesus viewed John as a person of God with divine authority, and shows how Jesus was ready to compare his own ministry to that of John, in this case by contrasting the styles of ministry. We learn that "this generation," a term meaning "this wicked generation" (cf. Luke 11:29–32, 50–51; 17:25; Mark 8:12, 38), does not appropriately respond to either John's

27. The material in this section can be found in fuller form in Witherington, *Christology of Jesus*, 46–49.

or Jesus' style of ministry. This saying apparently comes from late in Jesus' ministry, when he had been rejected by the majority of his audience. Probably, we should correlate the dancing to Jesus' celebratory form of ministry (including having fellowship even with sinners and tax collectors), while the mourning would correspond with John's more ascetical approach and focus on grieving over sin. Neither extreme pleased the audience. John was labeled a fanatic, and Jesus a libertine or immoral. Clearly, John and Jesus had different visions of how to go about their ministries, but both received a negative response.

As we draw the discussion about John to a close, something must be said about the interesting material in John 3:22–4:3. According to E. Linnemann, this passage tells us the following: (1) Jesus worked as a baptizer, or at least allowed and encouraged his disciples to do so; (2) Jesus drew a greater crowd as a baptizer than did John; (3) Jesus stayed in Perea for a considerable period of time, allowing himself not only to be baptized by John, but also apparently to be a follower of John for a while; (4) the later parallel baptismal practices became a problem, and Jesus, not wanting to compromise John's baptismal ministry, stopped his when the Pharisees noted that Jesus was having more success; (6) Jesus learned from John about this new way of right standing with God through repentance and baptism; (7) this learning led Jesus to the conclusion that the repentance of tax collectors and sinners was the sign of the inbreaking of God's dominion, and he must take up preaching about it in Galilee.[28] What are we to make of these suggestions? It does not appear that Jesus actually became John's disciple, though accepting baptism at his hands shows that he endorsed the Baptist's actions and ministry program. What is suggested is a parallel practice in Perea during the same period of time. Mark 11:27–33 confirms that Jesus saw John's baptism as having divine approval. Then, too, it is believable that Jesus withdrew from the parallel practice so as not to compromise John's work, seeing his own preliminary efforts as a supplement to what John was trying to accomplish. Clearly, the baptism by John of Jesus was a "watershed" event in Jesus' life. And in the next chapter we must examine the beginnings of Jesus' Galilean ministry.

---

28. E. Linnemann, "Jesus und der Täufer," in *Festschrift für Ernst Fuchs*, ed. G. Ebeling et al. (Tübingen: Mohr, 1973), 219–36.

Chapter 4

The Coming of the Prefect and of the Perfect: Pilate of Rome and Jesus of Nazareth

A.D. 26–29

Under Pilate, All Was Not Quiet[1]

A prefect, as noted before, was a military man in charge, and the one assigned to the Judean province in A.D. 26 was Pontius Pilate. Recent attempts have been made to rehabilitate the image of Pilate, but they

1. This is a recasting of Tacitus's language to say the opposite of what he says about the state of the empire under the reign of Tiberius (*Histories* 5.9).

107

Illustration 4.1 An inscription, found in Caesarea Maritima, mentioning the prefect Pilate.

have been unsuccessful.[2] Pilate was a man of equestrian rank, sent as the fifth prefect to what most Romans considered a minor and less desirable provincial assignment. He governed from A.D. 26–37, or during the entire tenure of the ministries of John the Baptist and Jesus of Nazareth. During the first six years of that period—the period most crucial for this study—the Syrian legate of Rome, Lamia, was not even in Syria, but rather, back home in Rome. Needless to say, he would have been difficult to contact if Pilate suddenly needed legion support from Syria. Thus, H. K. Bond argues that this explains why Pilate needed to be so ruthless in nipping any potential uprising in the bud.[3] However, though this may provide a partial explanation for Pilate's behavior, there is plenty of evidence that Pilate, like so many Romans, was anti-Semitic, and it is no accident that Josephus stresses, in his less propagandistic work, the *Antiquities*, that Pilate was finally recalled because he set himself against the Jewish law and committed crimes to that end (*Ant*. 18.85–89). The setting up of the iconic standards in Jerusalem in Herod's palace and the taking of funds from the temple treasury are but a part of a larger pattern of behavior reflecting Pilate's insensitivity to Jewish feelings and his willingness to use brutality rather than diplomacy to accomplish his own aims. Luke 13:1

2. See H. K. Bond, *Pontius Pilate in History and Interpretation*, SNTSMS 100 (Cambridge: Cambridge University Press, 1998).

3. Ibid., 15.

cites an incident all too typical of anti-Semitic prefects in eastern provinces.[4]

It is true that tensions had been rising between the prefect and the Jewish people during the rule of Gratus, Pilate's predecessor, and so Pilate inherited a volatile situation already made worse by bad governance. It needs to be kept steadily in view that A.D. 26 is also the year that Tiberius retired from active governing to the island of Capri, leaving the prefect of his praetorian guard, Aelius Sejanus, wielding great authority. What we know for sure about Sejanus is that he was strongly anti-Semitic, and likely to give Pilate encouragement to act out his own anti-Semitism in that troublesome Jewish province.

Philo's description of Pilate includes the following character sketch: he was "naturally inflexible, a blend of self-will and relentlessness," given to "briberies, insults, robberies, outrages and wanton injuries, executions without trial constantly repeated, ceaseless and supremely grievous cruelty" (*Embassy* 301–302). Even allowing for a certain measure of exaggeration and bias, we must conclude that Pilate was no able and fair-minded governor of Judea.

Consider, for example, the act of Pilate in his very first year in office. He sent troops by night carrying images of the emperor into Jerusalem (*Ant.* 18.55–59; *J.W.* 2.169–174). A large protesting crowd of Jews soon besieged his residence in Caesarea, demanding the removal of the images. Only after a confrontation in the stadium there that followed strenuous diplomatic effort did Pilate finally agree to remove the images. This story tells us a great deal about Pilate. That he undertook this action under cloak of darkness shows his awareness that he was doing something that would infuriate the Jews. That it took enormous pressure before he was prepared to remedy the situation likewise reveals reams about his character and lack of sensitivity to Jews.

The report of the reaction to Pilate's confiscation of temple funds for the sake of building a new aqueduct is even less flattering to Pilate's image. When the Jewish crowds protested this action, Pilate responded with soldiers armed with clubs but dressed as civilians, injuring many, killing some (*Ant.* 18.60–62; *J.W.* 2.175–177). This action shows that Pilate was perfectly willing to resort to subterfuge to bully Jews into submitting to his actions. Had he used troops directly to quell the protest, it would have been much easier for a Jewish embassy to protest to the

4. Note the assessment of J. Hayes and S. Mandell: "The evidence we possess suggests Pilate's high degree of insensitivity to Jewish religious and social customs as well as of impetuosity of behavior" (*The Jewish People in Classical Antiquity: From Alexander to Bar Kochba* [Louisville: Westminster John Knox, 1998], 156).

© Editrice Pontificio Istituto Biblico, Roma

Illustration 4.2 Modern Samaritans celebrating Passover on Mt. Gerizim.

legate in Syria, but disguising soldiers as civilians gave Pilate the opportunity for plausible denial of the protest against the brutality. He
could simply say that pro-Roman Jews beset anti-Roman Jews.

Notice, too, the action that got Pilate recalled A.D. 37 (*Ant*. 18.85–
89). Pilate blocked a procession of Samaritans who wished to as-
cend Mount Gerizim, resulting in a battle, casualties, and the execution of the Samaritan leaders and even of influential Samaritans not
involved in this particular event. The appeal of the Samaritans to Vi-
tellus, then legate in Syria, was successful, and Pilate, a Roman citizen, was sent to Rome for trial.[5] From first to last Pilate was by no
means a competent or fair-minded governor of Judea. On the contrary, he was devious, anti-Semitic, and brutal. It is against this
background that one must judge his behavior recorded in the passion narrative in the Gospels. Hayes and Mandell may well be right
that Pilate's reign was what led to the formation of the "Herodian"
party (Mark 3:6; 12:13), which seems to have been those lobbying
for the restoration of Herodian rule in Judea.[6] Grabbe is definitely
right that Tiberius's change of policy in regard to the length of a provincial governor's stay (Augustus allowed them only a three-year
term) was not a helpful one. Pilate had been left in power long after

5. Like Paul of Tarsus.
6. Hayes and Mandell, *Jewish People*, 157.

Illustration 4.3 Tiberius coin.

he should have been displaced, and that led to more abuses of power.[7]

Jesus of Nazareth in Galilee

Nazareth was the village of Jesus' youth in lower Galilee (Matt. 2:23; Luke 1:26; 2:4, 39), not far north of the Jezreel valley. It is about equidistant from the Sea of Galilee and the Mediterranean (only fifteen miles from the former). It is identified in the Gospels as the village of Mary and Joseph (Luke 2:39, 51), an identification few have disputed, since Nazareth is not a name one would pick out of the air to be the hometown of a messianic figure. Only four miles away was the capital city, rebuilt by Antipas in 4 B.C., Sepphoris, "the ornament of all Galilee" (*Ant.* 18.27), but a city predominantly Gentile in character, in a region ringed by Greek city-states (Tyre, Sidon, Scythopolis) and principalities (Gaulanitis and Samaria).

Nazareth seems to have been uninhabited after the Assyrian invasion in 733 B.C. until the second century B.C. It was during the rule of John Hyrcanus (134–104 B.C.) that the city was finally resettled by Jews, for the region of Galilee had been reconquered by this Hasmonean ruler. It has been suggested by P. Barnett that the name Nazareth derives from the Hebrew word *netzer* (branch), indicating that it was resettled by those of Davidic ancestry (see Isa. 11:1 about the branch and the root of Jesse). The connection between the word *netzer* and

7. Notice L. Grabbe's comments that Pilate was the exception to the rule that generally Tiberius had appointed good governors, and that Pilate was in power too long (*Judaism from Cyrus to Hadrian*, vol. 2 [Minneapolis: Fortress, 1992], 421–22).

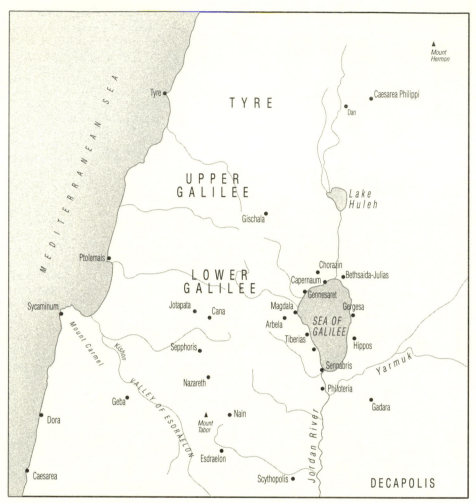

Illustration 4.4 Galilee in the Time of Christ.

Nazareth seems apparent in texts like Mark 10:47 and Luke 18:37–38.[8]
Mary and Joseph, if of Davidic descent, may have found this a natural
place to settle at some point.

The archeological evidence suggests a maximum population of Nazareth at the beginning of the first century A.D. of about 480 persons.[9]
The general picture drawn from the archaeological data is of a village
devoted almost exclusively to agriculture, though some artisans would

8. P. Barnett, *Jesus and the Rise of Early Christianity: A History of New Testament
Times* (Downers Grove, Ill.: InterVarsity, 1999), 93.
9. See J. F. Strange, "Nazareth," *ABD* 4:1050–51.

Illustration 4.5 This handmill found in Capernaum is made of Basalt and was used for grinding grain.

have populated the village as well. This was a village where everyone would have known one another's business and lives. In terms of the village's honor rating, that would appear to have been very low indeed. The comment of Nathanael in John 1:46 is perhaps typical: "Can anything good come out of Nazareth?" It was not a notable or noteworthy town among the cities in Israel. But what of the nature of Galilee itself? What was the historical Galilee like in Jesus' day socially, economically, politically, religiously? The following sketch will help to place Jesus in his proper setting.

S. Freyne, in his recent definitive essay on Herodian economics in Galilee,[10] points out that under Herod the Great the economy of the nation developed rapidly, and his son Antipas seems to have concentrated most of his efforts in lower Galilee in terms of building and developments, and we may talk of the Romanization of parts of the region. In the main, what Galilee had to offer was, of course, agricultural products, and what was developing in Jesus' time was something of a small market economy, with the principles of supply and demand in operation. Food shortages were always present in the empire, and although

10. S. Freyne, "Herodian Economics in Galilee," in *Modelling Early Christianity*, ed. P. F. Esler (London: Routledge, 1995), 23–46.

Egypt was the breadbasket for Rome, Galilee supplied many of the regional markets with grain. We know for sure that there were Herodian estates—large farms belonging to Herod—and that the surplus grain, corn in particular, was used to pay the tribute to Rome and also to pad the personal income of Antipas's family. These large estates had estate managers, such as Chuza (Luke 8:3), and it appears certain that small family farms, if not taken as debt payments or bought up, were marginalized by the big estate farms. In the case of Nazareth, it and other nearby villages with farms would have had to supply the city of Sepphoris with provisions.

But it was not only grain that Galilee could supply to a market; there is plentiful evidence in lower Galilee of olive growing, as seen in the remains of numerous olive presses. It appears that Galilee supplied both itself and parts of Phoenicia with olives and olive oil. Furthermore, Galilee was famous for a certain kind of fish (*coracin*) that when salted could be exported in all directions and for great distances. There was also a famous fish sauce, very popular in Rome, called *garum*, shipped in jars or amphorae (*J.W.* 3.516–520). In other words, fishing was big business in Galilee, and it spawned or supported subsidiary businesses, such as the pottery business. "The fact that Jesus recruited his first followers from those who were engaged in such an enterprise shows that his message was not addressed solely to the peasant farmers, something that needs to be borne in mind in evaluating its alternative value system. . . . It is surely significant that in leaving their nets, families and hired servants the first followers of Jesus were actually rejecting the values of the market economy as these operated in Galilee then, and that they were highly commended within Christian circles for doing so."[11]

Currency is, of course, another economic issue. Although no legions were stationed in Galilee, Herod had his troops (note the chiliarchs in Mark 6:21), and invariably troops were paid in coin, and in turn they bought goods with coin. In addition, the large number of people traveling through Galilee would have used coin to supply their needs. But perhaps for some Jews in the region bartering with goods still would have been one, perhaps the main, way to make exchanges for what they needed. Yet Jesus never mentions bartering in any of his sayings and does mention coins. We know that at least three times Herod Antipas minted coins: A.D. 19/20, 26/27, and 38/39. All these coins were minted in Tiberias, near the fishing villages, and none bear any likenesses of humans or of animals. The two earlier strikings have palms, or reeds, or wreaths on

11. Ibid., 35.

them.[12] But the largest number of coin finds in the lower Galilee region are of Tyrian coins, especially the half-shekel, pointing to the importance to Galilee of trade with Tyre. Although currency seems to have been prevalent as a means of exchange in Jesus' setting (cf. Mark 6:36–37; Luke 10:35), Jesus himself seems to have regarded money with suspicion. Hoarding money is described by Jesus as being futile; his disciples are to rely on standing hospitality, not money, when they travel; Jesus overturns the tables of the money changers. These atti-

Illustration 4.6 Tyrian half-shekel used to pay the temple tax.

tudes are all the more interesting in light of the increasingly monetary nature of Galilee's economy.[13] Perhaps Jesus' hostility was partly due to money leading to an increasingly stratified society, with the rich getting richer and the poor getting poorer. Perhaps, as Freyne suggests, Jesus avoided cities like Sepphoris and Tiberias altogether not so much because of their Gentile or Greco-Roman character, but because of the value systems they represented. Herod's development of a market economy was marginalizing traditional family farms, and in the process, extended family structures, a fact that may explain why in his teachings, Jesus emphasizes the rebuilding of family as family of faith. Freyne's summary bears close scrutiny:

> Jesus and his renewal movement is best understood as offering another set of values in addition to the two competing ones which we have seen within the social world of Antipas' Galilee. Insofar as it might be expected to have had a widespread appeal in that particular setting it was potentially threatening to both. The very radical nature of its social programme challenged the values that the Herodian market economy espoused, and the revision of the traditional religious categories of Temple, Torah, and land which it demanded would have undermined the centrality of Jerusalem and the unqualified loyalty that it was able to foster among its rural adherents. The fact that Jesus' message proved as unacceptable to the lat-

12. The earliest coin has the reed on it, which may be helpful to know, because if Jesus alluded to this coin in his saying about the Baptist (Luke 7:24; Matt. 11:7), then obviously, he made the remark after the coin had been widely circulated in Galilee, that is, after A.D. 20. On this correlation, see G. Theissen, *The Gospels in Context: Social and Political History in the Synoptic Tradition*, trans. L. Maloney (Edinburgh: Clark, 1991), 29–31.

13. Here I follow Freyne, "Herodian Economics," 41.

ter as to the former is perhaps indicative of the reserve with which Galilean peasantry viewed its radical social agenda, despite the sense of alienation from the dominant system that must have been experienced, and the seeming inability or unwillingness of the cult-based system to stop the drift toward penury. The wandering charismatic/healer/holy man, Jesus may well have fulfilled a definite social need in the villages of Galilee, but in a climate in which people clung precariously to some things though all was in danger of being lost, his call to freely abandon all would appear to have been too demanding and too utopian.[14]

In regard to the political situation in Galilee, I have already said a considerable amount, but here a few further remarks are in order. Even if the Galilee of Jesus' day was not in a state of constant hostilities, things there were far from bucolic. The image of a gentle Jesus, meek and mild, wandering around Galilee offering nice, entertaining stories called parables, or engaging in academic debates, fails to convey the sensitive and hostile atmosphere in which Jesus regularly operated, nor does it convey the effect that Jesus' teaching and actions would have had in that atmosphere. In particular, politics and religion were deeply intertwined in Galilee, as in Judea, and any sort of messianic claims or ideas were regularly and readily viewed as threats to the political status quo. It is no surprise, in view of his teachings and actions, that Jesus was crucified. What is surprising is that it did not happen sooner, but perhaps that is a function of the amount of time Jesus spent in Galilee as opposed to Jerusalem, the epicenter of political anxiety in the Holy Land.

One of the major reasons that rulers in this region, whether prefects or client kings, were likely to be anxious is that Judea was a new kind of province, a province of the second rank, which meant being ruled through the use of auxiliary troops, not legions, except in emergency situations, in which case there would be an appeal to the legate in Syria. Because it was a second-rank province, Judea never got the most highly qualified governors, as the senatorial provinces did, but only prefects of the equestrian class, who were often incompetent and frequently insensitive.[15] In the case of Galilee, Herod, so long as he kept the tribute and taxes flowing to Rome and did not violate the Pax Romana, was very much left to his own devices. The problem for both Herod Antipas and Pilate was that a landed aristocracy that had the respect of the general populace was necessary to gain support for the policies of Rome, but unfortunately, the aristocrats were simply creatures

14. Ibid., 45.
15. See F. Millar, *The Roman Near East, 31 B.C–A.D. 337* (Cambridge: Harvard University Press, 1993), 44–50.

of Herodian making, known to be cronies of the ruling Idumean family.[16] It is safe to say that these aristocrats by and large did not command the respect of the general populace, not least because they were aiding and abetting Herod in taking over smaller family farms and turning them into Herodian estates. These "leaders of Galilee," as they are called in Mark 6:21, shared the Greco-Roman value system of Herod Antipas and were the courtiers or retainers of Antipas whom he had set up in power on estates or in the capital cities of Sepphoris or Tiberias. The point is that a significant gulf stood between the governing and the governed in Galilee and Judea, which was not bridged by mutual respect or trust. Nor were the intermediaries between the two groups of much help, because mostly they were tax collectors! Jesus viewed with suspicion not only Antipas (whom he called "that fox"), but also the ruling class. In short, he shared the views and the value system of the common person in Galilee. This needs to be kept in mind as we proceed in this chapter.

Not a lot can be said about the religious leaders in Galilee, although the evidence suggests the presence of scribes and some Pharisees in the region, and certainly there were synagogue rulers in various places. The latter rabbinic structure of leadership that arose after A.D. 70 must not be read into Jesus' time. In Jesus' day there were teachers, scholars, sages, holy men, prophets, synagogue rulers, and messianic claimants, but no ordained rabbis. What we can say with great confidence is that the Jews of Galilee, like the Jews of Judea, were in general a highly religious group of people, and many of them were very observant Jews. Many Galileans regularly made the long journey on foot to the festivals in Jerusalem; many made their major life decisions on the basis of their religious beliefs; many had learned considerable portions of the Torah and prized its teaching above all else. Most Jews were more likely to respect and follow the advice of the religious leaders of their day than they were to respect the governing authorities, whether Herodian or Roman. Torah, temple, and territory were at the heart of Jewish religion in Jesus' day. But the Holy Land was not free at the time; the temple was in corrupt hands and correct observance of Torah was a matter of much debate. I will say a good deal more about Jesus' interaction with the religious leaders shortly.

The beginning of Jesus' unique ministry, apart from any associations he had with John the Baptist, seems to be grounded in a visionary experience he had while being baptized by John. On one occasion when Jesus was questioned by people about his authority, he responded with

---

16. See M. Goodman, *The Ruling Class of Judaea: The Origins of the Jewish Revolt against Rome, A.D. 66–70* (Cambridge: Cambridge University Press, 1987), 40.

a counterquestion about the authority of John's baptism (Mark 11:27–33 and par.). This counterquestion seems to imply that Jesus' authority rested on what happened when John baptized him, that in essence he was commissioned for ministry on that occasion. At the very least, this passage suggests that Jesus saw John's baptism as a turning point in his own adult life, a point at which he got empowerment and authorization for the ministry he undertook.[17]

The student of apocalyptic literature immediately recognizes that the earliest form of the story of Jesus' baptism, found in Mark 1:9–11, has various features typical of that literature—the opening of the heavens, the voice from heaven, the reference to the Spirit coming down suggesting communication and communion with God. Similar ideas appear in Rev. 1:10, 4:1–2; 10:1; 21:2–3. Both sources have the rending of the heavens before the voice from above is heard, and in fact, the coming of the Spirit precedes the voice in both sources as well. It is when the seer is in the Spirit that he hears the voice. It is, then, no accident that in Mark 1 the Spirit came down upon Jesus and then he heard a voice from heaven. Also, the heavens must be opened before beings or messages can emerge from there.

The Markan account depicts the baptism involving a private communication between Jesus and God, unlike the Matthean portrayal, in which God addresses the public. The address from heaven in Mark says "You are my beloved Son" (Mark 1:11), whereas in Matthew it says, "This is my beloved Son" (Matt. 3:17). Certainly, the Markan account is more primitive, and equally certainly, it summarizes a visionary experience of Jesus.

Some explanation must be given as to why Jesus in particular felt compelled to begin his own ministry after being baptized by John when others did not feel so compelled, and what stands out about Jesus' baptism is the accompanying visionary experience. We may add that there would have been a need for Jesus to retell this story and interpret it for his followers so they would understand what prompted his unique ministry. Also, it may be stressed that it is hardly likely that later Christian writers would make up the idea that Jesus underwent a baptism for remission of sins (cf. Mark 1:4–5 with 1:9–11).

The voice from heaven offers a partial quotation from Ps. 2:7, confirming to Jesus that he was God's special chosen one. The original setting of the quotation refers to an individual elevated to the position of king over Israel. At the level of experience, Jesus is being portrayed as an apocalyptic prophet, but the content of his vision has to do with a

17. For a fuller form of what is found here, see B. Witherington III, *The Christology of Jesus* (Minneapolis: Fortress, 1990), 148–55.

messianic vocation of some kind, apparently in a Davidic mold. Indeed, if Jesus had such a vision, it would be hard for him not to conclude that he was God's Anointed One, the *mashiah*. It is this experience that provides a clear explanation for the course of action Jesus takes after the baptism, for the baptism itself does not provide such an explanation or impetus. This vision explains the source of Jesus' power for ministry as well—the Holy Spirit. Jesus thought of himself as God's Son, guided by God from above and empowered by the Spirit, who came down upon him on that memorable day.[18]

But what did Jesus use that power for? The short answer is to help and heal Jews and others. As a prophetic figure, he acted in ways like those other northern prophets Elijah and Elisha, which is to say that he was known for his deeds of power. Some scholars have been tempted to ignore the exorcism material in the Jesus tradition, which is a big mistake. Our earliest historical sources about Jesus' activities, Mark and Q, both strongly attest that Jesus was an exorcist. Furthermore, the extracanonical data, including non-Christian data, are in agreement with this portrayal (see *b. Sanh.* 43a, which claims that Jesus was killed for practicing sorcery). Let us consider the exorcism material briefly.

G. Twelftree demonstrates that unlike other early Jewish (and non-Jewish) exorcism material, exorcism stories in the Synoptics do not include the use of mechanical devices to produce an exorcism, or the invocation of an external authority to perform the act (cf. *Ant.* 8.46–49 on Eliezar the exorcist). Within the Jewish tradition, exorcism was particularly linked with Solomon and his wisdom (i.e., in this case, esoteric knowledge about secret formulas that removed demons). Perhaps the most important of Twelftree's observations is that Jesus explicitly connects exorcism with eschatology.[19] For example, the important Q saying found in Matt. 12:28 (cf. Luke 11:20) comes to mind: "If I by the Spirit of God cast out demons, then the dominion of God has broken into your midst." In other words, Jesus sees it as part of his ministry to take on the powers of darkness, for only so would God be reigning in a particular person's life who formerly was possessed.

The coming of God's dominion involves the rescuing of people from darkness of various sorts. This comports well with the brief parable in Mark 3:27, where Jesus speaks of first binding the strong man so that he might release his captives. Apparently, Jesus believed that this binding took place during his days of temptation in the desert, and this

18. See ibid., 153–55.
19. See G. Twelftree, *Jesus the Exorcist: A Contribution to the Study of the Historical Jesus*, WUNT 2.54 (Tübingen: Mohr [Siebeck], 1993).

event might be coordinated with the saying of Jesus about seeing Satan fall like lightning from heaven. Jesus, like other early Jews, saw three stages to defeating Satan: binding Satan, releasing Satan's captives, and then destroying Satan. As I have already noted, this implies that Jesus, through these exorcisms and other acts of power, was inaugurating the eschatological age, the coming of God's final divine saving and ruling activity (the dominion) on earth. In the volatile atmosphere of Galilee, language about God's dominion or saving reign coming in power and about exorcisms could only alarm many of the power brokers in the region, for Jesus was demonstrating that he was plugged in to an alternate power source.

A Closer Look: *Of Miracles and History*

The miracle narratives in the Gospels are found in all layers of the tradition, although it is interesting that there are no exorcism tales in the Fourth Gospel. In evaluating such stories from a historical point of view it must be remembered that what we are evaluating is not the miracles themselves (which happened long ago and are no longer accessible to us as unique events, assuming they are based in reality), but the reports of these miracles. Are the reports more or less credible? Most scholars are willing to say that Jesus performed deeds that were viewed as miracles in his day. Indeed, most would say that he had a notable reputation as a miracle worker, although some would qualify that saying that we are talking about psychosomatic cures and therapy of various sorts (e.g., the therapy of touching when dealing with untouchables like lepers). Sometimes historians have criticized the critical acumen of the ancients, suggesting that they were incapable of distinguishing between natural and supernatural occurrences. In some instances this complaint has some merit, but we should note that a person who talks about a particular event being a miracle, in the midst of a variety of events that he or she does not view as miraculous, is a person who is indeed exercising critical acumen about such matters.[20]

For the most part, the types of miracles Jesus is said to have performed are not unprecedented. Various prophets and healers before him did such things, and apostles and prophets and healers did so after him. This means that the miracles themselves raise the question but do

20. See the discussion in Witherington, *Christology of Jesus*, 156–57.

not fully provide the answer of who Jesus was. They show a man of God imbued with power, but they do not show what sort of man of God he was. Even Jesus' adversaries did not dispute that he worked miracles, including exorcisms, but they attributed these to his connection with the powers of darkness (see Mark 3). Jesus' mighty deeds were seen as either of God or of Satan. "Such extreme verdicts are not reached in respect of any old nondescript 'average person'; they presuppose some sort of 'marvellous phenomenon' perceived and acknowledged as such by all parties."[21]

There are a variety of good reasons why Jesus' miracles should not be seen as a form of magic. In the first place, the texts make clear that Jesus performed his miracles by using an external source of power, the Spirit of God, not by mere force of his personality. Nor is there any evidence of Jesus using spells, conjuring tricks, magical formulas, herbs, rings, curse tablets, and the like. Notice that Jesus does not follow the later Christian example of praying or invoking the sacred name in order to do a miracle. Furthermore, Jesus' miracles are usually associated with faith, a basic trust in Jesus that he can help. Also, Jesus did not do miracles to draw crowds; indeed, the earliest Gospel, Mark, suggests that Jesus sought to escape such crowds so that he could concentrate on the main focus of his ministry, preaching and teaching (see Mark 1:35–38). Yet a Q saying such as Luke 10:13–15/Matt. 11:21–23a shows that Jesus saw his miracles as more than just deeds of compassion. They were bringing a foretaste of the promised eschatological blessings, and they were also a means of calling people to repentance.

From a historical point of view, what is most important is not the miracles themselves, which were not unprecedented, but Jesus' unique interpretation of the miracles as signs of the dominion's inbreaking, and also as signs of who he was: the fulfiller of Old Testament promises about the blind seeing, the lame walking, and the like. The miracle tales provide one further piece of evidence that Jesus did not see himself in ordinary human categories. He saw himself, as he saw John, as more than a prophet. Indeed, his commissioning vision led him to see himself as God's beloved Son.

It is by no means just the miracles that suggest that Jesus saw himself as some sort of eschatological figure destined to have a crucial role

---

21. E. Schillebeeckx, *Jesus: An Experiment in Christology*, trans. H. Hoskins (New York: Vintage, 1981), 182.

in human history. This same implication comes in Jesus' repeated and preferred use of the phrase "Son of Man" as a form of self-identification. I need to discuss this matter briefly before turning to Jesus' teaching and teaching style as clues to his historical significance.

Very few scholars would dispute that Jesus' main spoken language was not Greek but Aramaic. It follows from this that the phrase in question when dealing with Jesus' preferred self-designation is not the odd Greek phrase *ho huios tou anthrōpou* ("the son of the human being"), but rather, the Aramaic phrase that led to it, *bar ʾenashaʾ*. It is my view that the source of this self-identification phrase for Jesus is the apocalyptic literature that shaped his worldview. In particular, I believe that Jesus was drawing on Daniel 7, though he may also have been familiar with the kind of material about the Son of Man that one finds in the Similitudes of *1 Enoch*. In fact, I would draw the historical conclusion that Daniel 7 was critical to the shaping of Jesus' self-understanding and his understanding of his mission, for only here in the Old Testament do we find the two phrases most commonly found on the lips of the historical Jesus: Son of Man, and dominion of God.

The Son of Man figure mentioned in Daniel 7 is, in my view, a representative of and for Israel in the presence of God.[22] The beasts in that text symbolize the pagan empires of the world, but the human being symbolizes God's people, and in particular the representative of God's people. The implication is of a more human and humane figure than one finds among the pagan rulers and leaders. By calling himself a human figure, Jesus was not merely indicating his full humanness and susceptibility to suffering, but rather, was placing himself in a particular eschatological role as the representative standing between Israel and God. This representative is to be given a dominion, or kingdom, by God—indeed, an everlasting dominion. He is to rule over nations and be given divine glory. The promise of such a figure to God's exiled people gives hope for their vindication and final triumph over their foes, leading to their reigning with the representative on earth. The promise as brought to fruition in a land ruled either by a Roman prefect or client king would be seen as ominous for and by such rulers, if they understood its meaning. In this context we can see why Jesus' choice of Son of Man terminology had definite political overtones for those who were not tone-deaf to the resonances of apocalyptic literature and its key phrases. If Jesus is the Son of Man proclaiming the inbreaking of God's dominion in the present, the implication is that in due course he would supplant the beastly rulers in the land. In fact, Mark 14:62 suggests that the Jewish authorities understood all too well the political

22. See Witherington, *Christology of Jesus*, 238–39.

overtones of Jesus' claim to be the Son of Man mentioned in Dan. 7:13–14. Such claims helped to get Jesus executed.

A brief look at a couple of Son of Man sayings is in order to fill out what we can say about the historical Jesus' self-presentation. For example, the Q saying in Luke 9:58/Matt. 8:20 reminds us not only of Jesus' itinerant lifestyle, but also that Jesus was poor and often rejected normal Jewish hospitality. Jesus has accepted a vocation that requires him to face hardship over and over. Yet to judge from Luke 9:44b, Jesus anticipated not just hardship, but rough handling and being turned over to the authorities. But notice that the passive form of the verb, "be delivered into human hands," indicates that it is God who ultimately is the one delivering up the Son of Man.

Mark 10:45, if it is an authentic saying of Jesus, reveals much about how he viewed his vocation. The idea of a human sacrificial death atoning for the sin of other people was very much alive in early Judaism (cf. 4 Macc. 6:27–29; 17:21–22; 2 Macc. 7:37–38; *y. Yoma* 38b; 1QS 5:6; 8:31; 9:4). Elsewhere, I have argued at length for the authenticity of this saying, and so will concentrate on its meaning here.[23] First, Dan. 7:13–14 can be in the background here because the Son of Man in that saying represents the suffering people of God, even though he is promised dominion and glory. The idea of a ransom is a familiar Jewish concept, in terms of ransoming life back (cf. Exod. 21:30; 30:12; Num. 18:15; Lev. 25:51–52). While this saying is usually associated with Isaiah 53, it actually seems closer to Isa. 43:3–4. The phrase *anti pollōn*, "on behalf of many," conveys a sense of substitution. The overall concept is not one life given for some rather than for all, but one dying instead of the many (i.e., everyone else). This in turn would imply that Jesus did not feel he needed to die to ransom himself. In other words, he is not arguing for his death atoning for his own sins. A similar sort of phraseology and concept can be found in *Ant.* 14.107. To sum up, we learn from this saying and from Luke 9:44b that it is God's plan that Jesus die and that out of that death a great good would come—the redemption of many.

In some ways, Mark 14:62 is the most important Son of Man saying, being the one most clearly grounded in Dan. 7:13–14. Jesus here responds probably positively to the high priest's question, but changes the terms of reference to his preferred self-designation: not messiah, but rather Son of Man. This may reflect Jesus' attempt to avoid stereotyping or being placed in a pigeonhole in regard to the kind of messianic figure he was claiming to be. He would forge his own image of the role of the eschatological messianic figure. This saying envisions the

23. Ibid., 251–56.

Son of Man having a future role in the judgment of Israel, in particular of the Jewish officials who were now judging Jesus![24] Jesus' mission would not be completely fulfilled either in his life or in his death, but would carry on beyond death. This is a remarkable claim, but not an impossible one for an early Jew who believed in resurrection, as Jesus surely did. I will say more about the historical nature of the trial narrative in the next chapter.

Lest there be skepticism about Jesus seeing himself in some sort of messianic light, we should remember that various messianic pretenders and contenders arose during Jesus' lifetime. I have already referred to the figures that arose during Jesus' youth, and now should mention Theudas, the Egyptian, and the Samaritan. These three figures postdate Jesus (the first two during the rule of the procurator Fadus, the third much closer to Jesus' time during the reign of Pilate). All three performed symbolic actions suggesting God's eschatological presence, and all three drew great crowds, as did Jesus. I will say more about these figures in chapter 11, but here we should note that Jesus operated in a social context in which it was perfectly possible for him to view himself in some sort of messianic light.[25] In fact, a fair-minded reading of the historical evidence strongly suggests that he did, and this immediately provides us with some historical continuity between Jesus' historical self-representation and the beliefs of his first followers about him after his death.

Now I must say a few things about Jesus' public teaching, which has certain characteristic features. For example, he often prefaced a particular saying of his with the word "amen." We find no one else using this practice in the New Testament. It is found in all layers of the Gospel tradition—13 times in Mark, 9 in Q, 9 in L, 9 in M, 25 in John (always as "amen, amen").[26] In dramatic contrast to this is the Old Testament use of "amen," which is only "used" to confirm the truth of someone else's remarks, as is also the case elsewhere in the New Testament (cf. 1 Cor. 14:16; 2 Cor. 1:20; Rev. 5:14; 7:12). Perhaps the closest biblical parallel to Jesus' usage is the prophetic phrase "Thus says the Lord," but in all those sayings it is followed by the remarks of someone other than the prophet himself, whereas Jesus prefaces his own remarks with "amen," which basically means "in truth" or "truly." What sort of person confirms the truthfulness of his own remarks in advance of making those remarks? The answer would seem to be a person who believed he had independent authority and did not require the endorsement of other teachers or prophets or the audience to

24. On the authenticity of this saying, see ibid., 257–59.
25. See ibid., 90–92.
26. "L" stands for material unique to Luke, and "M" for material unique to Matthew.

confirm the truthfulness of his remarks.

A second feature of Jesus' teaching comports with this conclusion. Notice that Jesus does not use formulas like "On the authority of Rabbi Gamaliel, who spoke on the authority of Rabbi Hillel, the meaning of this phrase is . . ." Rather, he simply says, "I say to you." What these two speech traits suggest is that Jesus spoke as a person who had more than a prophetic consciousness, though certainly Jesus was a prophetic figure in various regards.

A third feature of Jesus' speech that is characteristic, if not unique, is his use of the Aramaic term *abba* to address God. We know of a growing tendency in Jewish literature, especially approaching the first century A.D., to address God as Father, perhaps particularly in Wisdom literature (cf. Wis. 14:3; Sir. 23:1, 4; 51:10; 3 Macc. 6:3, 8; 4Q371, 372). But the use of *abba* is not the same as the use of the more formal *ab* or *abi* (father). *Abba* means something like "father dearest," connoting both intimacy and endearment. Jesus' use of this term is seen at a moment of great anxiety in Mark 14:36. But it appears that Jesus also must have taught his disciples to use this term in address to God, as the Lukan form of the Lord's prayer address suggests (Luke 11:2), as does the occurrence of the term in the very earliest Christian documents (Gal. 4:6; Rom. 8:15). The implication of this usage is not just that Jesus manifested an unusually close relationship with God, but that in some

Illustration 4.7 Remains of the Jewish synagogue in Capernaum (third century A.D.).

fashion he made it possible for his disciples to relate to God in those intimate terms as well.[27]

Obviously, Jesus was widely known for his public teaching being in sapiential form, particularly in the form of parables and aphorisms. This is a metaphorical way of teaching, and what stands out is the frequency with which Jesus resorted to this manner of teaching. There is a sliding scale between a simple metaphorical analogy on one end of the scale and a detailed allegory on the other. On the whole, Jesus' more complex parables (the so-called narrative parables, such as we find in Luke 10 and 15) seem to have several points to make, and on occasion we find parables that are rather allegorical in character (Mark 4, the parable of the sower), but none of Jesus' parabolic teaching is like a full-blown allegory, where every detail of a tale has some symbolic significance.

Teaching in parables and aphorisms or pithy short sayings ("It is easier for a camel to go through the eye of a needle than . . .") is, of course, an indirect form of speaking. There may have been several reasons, historically speaking, why Jesus would use this as his mode of public address. Jesus spoke in a volatile environment, and every indication we have suggests that he wished to define his ministry and reveal his message on his own terms. He did not wish to be labeled with stereotypical terms. Therefore, he set out to use metaphorical speech coupled with a unique form of self-reference—the phrase "Son of Man." Then, too, the terms of discourse were familiar enough to spark discussion with a Jewish audience, but unfamiliar enough to spark an intent listener into active thought about the meaning of the words. This is likely also why Jesus characteristically closed his remarks with "Let those who have two good ears, hear." Jesus, in most of his public discourse, presented himself as a sage, and as such was somewhat enigmatic, and deliberately so. This also comports with the fact that his religious experience involved apocalyptic visions, yet another form of metaphorical and symbolic expression. Jesus would not have pleased those who wanted simple, plain, direct speech. Jesus' parables were about the inbreaking of God's eschatological reign on earth, and occasionally his own role in that event plays a part in a parable (Mark 12:1–9). In a volatile environment outsiders would have a hard time penetrating the parables and deciphering his speech. This may have made it possible for Jesus' ministry to go on longer than it would have if he had been as direct in his critique of the powers that be as John the Baptist was.

27. See Witherington, *Christology of Jesus*, 216–21.

As this chapter draws to a close, we must consider two prominent relationships that Jesus had: with his disciples, and with the Pharisees. Though few scholars doubt that Jesus had an inner circle of twelve disciples, clear confirmation for this comes from outside the Gospels, in 1 Cor. 15:5. In fact, so set in stone was the tradition that there were twelve, that Paul calls them "the twelve," when actually by Easter morning they were but eleven. Since Paul had had conversations with Peter, James, and John (see Galatians 1–2), it is impossible to believe that Paul is just passing on a tradition here that he did not know the validity of. Furthermore, Judas is regularly mentioned as "one of the twelve" in various layers of the tradition (cf. Mark 3:14–19; Luke 6:13–16; Matt. 10:2–4; John 6:67–71). This historical evidence supports the view that there must have been an inner circle of disciples of a set number. On a close reading of the Gospels, what seems chiefly to distinguish the Twelve from other disciples is that the Twelve are given the opportunity to actually participate in Jesus' ministry.

Let us consider for a moment the calling of the Twelve in light of Mark 1:17 (and par.): "And Jesus said to them, 'Follow me and I will make you fish for people.'" This saying indicates that Jesus recruited followers, something that other early Jewish teachers and sages apparently did not do. There is Old Testament background to Jesus' words (Jer. 16:16; Ezek. 29:4; 38:4; Amos 4:2; Hab. 1:14–17) that lends an ominous tone to his saying. Especially the Jeremiah and Ezekiel texts refer to catching people for judgment. We must remember that in the Jewish way of thinking, water, particularly chaos water, is seen as the enemy of God (e.g., Ps. 74:13). Therefore, to fish for followers is to rescue people from the chaos water, that is, from the realm that contains monsters and leads to the underworld, the place of death. In short, people are being rescued from the realm of darkness. It would appear that the call and the commissioning of the Twelve came at the very same juncture. They were called to follow; they were commissioned to catch people.

We may question at this point, Why would Jesus pick twelve as the inner circle? Surely, it must have something to do with the twelve tribes of Israel. But notice that Jesus does not include himself among the Twelve; rather, he is above them, gathering and commissioning them. Notice too that the function of the Twelve is not just to follow or be with Jesus, but to catch people. But what people? Apparently, they were commissioned to rescue fellow Israelites, for it is within Israel that Jesus sent out the Twelve, two by two. This comports with the remark "I was sent only to the lost sheep of the house of Israel" (Matt. 15:24). This suggests that the Twelve were being sent to the tribes of Israel. They had as their task not to be Israel, but rather, to free Israel. "If Jesus saw his basic program as winning back the lost sheep of Israel, not converting the world, in light of the fire from heaven that was hovering on the horizon, then the use of the metaphor is quite understandable."[28]

The Twelve were Jesus' agents, and here the Jewish conception of *shaliah* comes into play (cf. *m. Roš. Haš.* 1:3; 4:9; *m. Yoma* 1:5). The concept is of a legal agent who represents the sender, and who has authority to speak and act for the sender within certain parameters. A saying like Matt. 19:28 and par. makes evident that not only would the Twelve fish for followers, but also they would play another role in relationship to Israel at the eschaton: judging the twelve tribes. In the *shaliah* concept, the idea is this: one's reaction to the agent is as if one had reacted the same way to the sender. So those who rejected or mistreated, or accepted and helped, the Twelve were in effect doing the same thing to Jesus.

Let us consider for a moment the composition of the Twelve as listed in our earliest source in Mark 3. Simon is given first mention, along with his nickname, Cephas (see John 1:42; Matt. 16:18), in Greek, Petros, which is unattested in the era before Jesus as a Greek personal name. It is not clear whether this nickname is intended as a double entendre or not (the rock, or rocky), and in fact the word *cepha* primarily means "stone" rather than "rock." Notice that the nickname Peter is used from this point on in Mark (3:16; 5:37; 8:29, 32, 33; 9:2, 5; 10:28; 11:21; 13:3; 14:29, 33, 37, 54, 66, 67, 70, 72; 16:7), except that Jesus addresses him as Simon in the Gethsemane scene, with the return to Peter's formal name possibly reflecting the seriousness of the occasion and Jesus' disappointment (14:37).[29] It has been suggested that Simon's renaming as Peter is to be viewed like the renaming of the patriarchs (e.g., Abram to Abraham, noting that Abraham is referred to as "the rock" in Isa. 51:1–2),[30] in which case Jesus may be bringing about the eschatological rebirth of Israel with new patriarchs.

Nor do we know why James and John are called the Sons of Thunder (Mark 3:17), though various conjectures have it that the nickname referred to their fiery temperament (cf. Mark 9:38 to Luke 9:54). This naming seems different from Peter's because it is applied to both brothers, and in fact does not amount to a change of name, for they retain their names throughout the Gospels.[31] Half of the Twelve may well have been made up of pairs of brothers, that is if James and Levi/Matthew of Alphaeus were brothers and Levi was one of the Twelve. The

28. Ibid., 131.
29. See J. Painter, *Mark's Gospel: Worlds in Conflict* (London: Routledge, 1997), 67.
30. J. Marcus, *Mark 1–8*, AB 27A (New York: Doubleday, 2000), 268.
31. See R. Guelich, *Mark 1–8:26*, WBC 34A (Dallas: Word, 1989), 162.

traditional nature of the list seems clear from the fact that Levi is not mentioned here, at least by that name. Bartholomew is not a name but a patronymic, meaning "son of Thalmai," so we do not know this man's personal name. There is difficulty also with the name Thaddaeus, which does not occur in Luke, but rather, in its place, Judas the son of James (Luke 6:16; Acts 1:13). Simon the Cananean (which likely does not mean Canaanite) presumably refers to Simon the zealous one or patriot. He may have been, at least formerly, involved in revolutionary circles. Judas is identified by the fact that he handed Jesus over. The term "Iscariot" might mean a person from Kerioth, a town possibly in Idumea or possibly in Judea (cf. Josh. 15:25, near Hebron; Jer. 48:24, in Moab; but in either case he is not a Galilean), but it also might mean that Judas was one of the *sicarii*, or dagger men, the extreme faction and hit men among the revolutionary party.[32] This latter view seems to be supported by the variant reading *Skariōth* at Mark 3:19 and Luke 6:16 (Matt. 10:4 has a similar variant, *Skariōtēs*).[33] If Kerioth in Idumea is correct, then Judas, like Herod the Great, may not have been a full-blooded Jew, or at least not a native of Israel.

The overall impression is that the Twelve were a socially diverse group that included both fishermen and their nemesis the tax collector, and both a tax collector and those who opposed paying any taxes to Rome or the overlords, indeed, those who had supported opposing such oppressors even by violent means. In any event, though the list begins in good fashion, it ends in depressing fashion. One of the hand-picked Twelve is remembered for one thing only—he betrayed Jesus. "There is a warning to the reader not to expect too much of these disciples."[34] Yet at the outset these men are enlisted in the war against the powers and principalities, although there is enough dark undercurrent to already prompt a worry that they may become casualties in that apocalyptic war.[35]

Clearly, however the Twelve were by no means the only disciples of Jesus, nor even the only traveling disciples. This is evidenced by a text like Luke 8:1–3, where women such as Mary of Magdala and Joanna the wife of Herod's estate manager are seen traveling with and supporting the disciples. This is one of the shocking facts about Jesus' ministry—he had all sorts of followers, including

32. See Witherington, *Christology of Jesus*, 96–98.

33. See Guelich, *Mark 1–8:26*, 163.

34. Painter, *Mark's Gospel*, 69.

35. The last several paragraphs are found in another form in B. Witherington III, *The Gospel of Mark: A Socio-rhetorical Commentary* (Grand Rapids: Eerdmans, 2001), 151–53.

women.[36] And Jesus did not make radical demands only of the Twelve; he made radical demands of many disciples, as Luke 9:59–60/Matt. 8:21–22 shows. It seems on the surface that in this saying Jesus was counseling a treatment of parents that no other early Jewish teacher would have sanctioned. Indeed, most such teachers would have taken this saying as a violation of the "honor your father and mother" commandment. One of the chief filial duties in response to that commandment was thought to be providing an honorable burial for one's parents. For example, *m. Ber.* 3:1 insists that attendance to the duty of burying the dead supersedes even the most binding of religious obligations. The point in Jesus' saying, however, is a matter of priorities. It was far more crucial to come and follow Jesus than to bury one's parents.

Thus, Jesus' call to follow him has even more urgency involved than the call of Elisha by Elijah. Elisha at least was allowed to make a farewell gesture to his family (1 Kings 19:20). What Jesus' teaching likely shows is something of his radical approach to the Mosaic law. Jesus seems to have believed that the eschatological situation was such that the law could be superseded in various respects. The teaching of Luke 9:59–60/Matt. 8:21–22 comports well with likely authentic material such as we find in Mark 3:31–35, which suggests that for Jesus, loyalty and duty to the family of faith supersede loyalty and duty to physical family. Jesus says that whoever does the will of God is a member of his family. It is important to recognize the radicality of some of Jesus' teaching, for it helps to explain from a historical point of view why Jewish authorities might wish to take action against him. We can begin to see why Jesus' teaching might upset a group so thoroughly grounded in the Mosaic law as the Pharisees. Let us turn to a brief examination of Jesus' relationship with them.

Though it appears that Pharisees were located mainly in Jerusalem and Judea, a controversial teacher in Galilee who might be contravening some of the Pharisaic teachings might well prompt them to go north to check on this matter. Matthew 23:15 and *Ant.* 20.34–49 would indicate that the Pharisees had a penchant for proselytizing as well. Pharisees would be especially likely to be interested if Jesus performed actions on the Sabbath that they would object to, or if he fellowshiped with those whom they deemed unclean (both of which Jesus is reported to have done). In various ways, Mark 7 is the crucial text for understanding this matter more clearly. The impression one gets from looking at all the references to Jesus' encounters with Pharisees is that he was regularly in controversy with them.

36. See the full-length treatment of this subject in B. Witherington III, *Women in the Ministry of Jesus*, SNTSMS 51 (Cambridge: Cambridge University Press, 1984).

Mark 7 is in fact a collection of Jesus' teachings on several related subjects. The criticism of Jesus' disciples for failing to wash their hands before eating seems to come from the hyper-Levitical segment of the Pharisees, who believed that the "tradition of the elders" prohibited this action.[37] The issue in Mark 7:15–23, however, is clean and unclean food. At stake here is the teaching of the Torah itself, not merely oral tradition. Jesus seems to assume an authority over Torah that allows him to declare that all foods are clean, and indeed, he insists that the focus now must be on matters of moral purity. The intriguing thing about Jesus' teaching on the law is the sovereign freedom with which he handles it—sometimes reaffirming it, sometimes intensifying it, sometimes abrogating parts of it.

This sovereign freedom is probably also the explanation for why Jesus felt free to heal on the Sabbath (see Mark 3:1–6), even though technically that constituted work. In Jesus' view, the Sabbath was a day for giving people rest and restoration from what ailed them. Thus, he also believed that the disciples' plucking grain on the Sabbath was not a problem (Mark 2:23–28).

One may ask what sort of person takes this sort of stance toward the law, and the answer surely must be someone who saw himself as more than just a teacher or ordinary prophet. It must be someone who saw himself as an agent of God bringing in the eschatological situation where new occasions would teach new duties, and a new covenant would prevail. From a historical point of view, the less radical a teacher Jesus was, the more inexplicable it becomes that Jewish authorities would take action against him. But if the converse is true—if Jesus did indeed travel with women disciples, critique even the law, fellowship with sinners and tax collectors—then it is understandable why he became a marked man. In the next chapter, we must consider the passion and resurrection narratives, and why Jesus' life ended as it did. Here, however, we have seen that a radical teacher and healer operating in a volatile environment, and in controversy with Jewish authorities, was likely to attract a good deal of attention, and heated attention at that.

---

37. See R. Booth, *Jesus and the Laws of Purity: Tradition History and Legal History in Mark 7*, JSNTSup 13 (Sheffield: JSOT Press, 1986), 214–16.

Chapter 5

The Trials and Tribulations of Jesus

A.D. 29–30

The Chronology of Crucifixion

Before we can examine the historical substance of the passion narratives, we must sort out the crucial chronological issue of exactly when Jesus was crucified. Broadly, of course, we can easily answer that it took place sometime during the rule of Pontius Pilate, which means between A.D. 26 and 37, a fact that Tacitus the Roman historian confirms (*Annals* 15.44). But we need to be far more specific. All four Gospels narrate that Jesus was executed on a Friday, the day before the Sabbath (Matt. 27: 62; Mark 15:42; Luke 23:54; John 19:31, 42). Furthermore, all four Gospels indicate that Jesus' death took place during or just before the major Jewish feast of Passover, that is, in spring. Thus, we need to ask on what occasions between A.D. 26 and 37 did

132

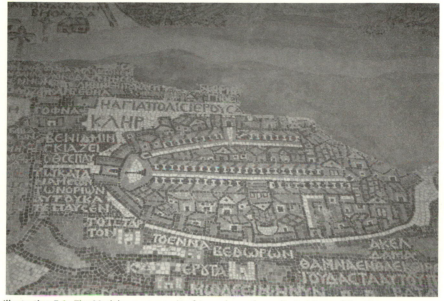

Illustration 5.1 The Medaba map mosaic of Jerusalem—the earliest picture of the city.

Passover occur on a Friday. Before we answer that question, other considerations are in order.

We may be able to date the death of Jesus more specifically because of the relationship between the ministries of Jesus and John the Baptist, and our knowledge of the date of the death of Herod Philip. On the latter, it appears reasonably clear that Herod Philip was dead no later than A.D. 34. If the synchronism in Luke 3:1–2 contains historically reliable information on the relationship between the time of Jesus' ministry and the reign of Herod Philip, as most scholars would accept, then Jesus' ministry was likely over before the death of Herod Philip.[1] This means that Jesus died no later than about A.D. 33.

In regard to the dating of Passover on a Friday in this general time period, we have two primary choices, A.D. 30 and 33. If we choose the later date, a problem is created in regard to the length of Jesus' ministry and its relationship to that of John the Baptist. We have no evidence suggesting that Jesus' ministry was any longer than three years. Furthermore, we know that John the Baptist was executed by Herod Antipas and that he was active while Pontius Pilate ruled in Judea. This means that the Baptist's ministry was taking place during and after A.D.

1. On these issues, see the discussion in J. P. Meier, *A Marginal Jew: Rethinking the Historical Jesus,* vol. 1, ABRL (New York: Doubleday, 1991), 372–84.

26, when Pilate came to Judea, and at most would put his execution somewhere around A.D. 27 or 28.[2] This in turn places the beginning of Jesus' ministry about A.D. 28. On this showing, A.D. 33 is probably too late to be the date of Jesus' death. The later date also makes for a significant problem in the chronology of events surrounding the beginning of the church and the time when Saul of Tarsus was converted. Thus, I conclude that Jesus died on Nisan 14 (April 7) in A.D. 30.[3] This means that I, with most scholars, believe that the Johannine chronology of these events is more precise than the Synoptic one. Jesus was executed before sundown on April 7, A.D. 30, the Day of Preparation, when the lambs were slaughtered for the Passover feast. By sundown, when the Sabbath and the Passover began, Jesus was already buried. The events that led up to the execution of Jesus must have transpired in A.D. 29–30.

Of Passion Narratives and Preliminary Events

In the last chapter, I chronicled in a selective fashion some of the words, deeds, and relationships that Jesus had during his active ministry in and around Galilee. I stressed that the situation was volatile, and that Jesus was a rather radical teacher in various respects, not to mention that he was an exorcist and healer, which made him a powerbroker of some consequence. With this reputation, and in this situation, Jesus goes up to Jerusalem. In all likelihood, Jesus was well familiar with the reputation of Pilate and his anti-Semitic bent. It did not take much foresight on the part of Jesus to realize that he was putting himself in harm's way by joining the Passover pilgrims in A.D. 30, unless, of course, Jesus planned to go to the feast incognito and say and do nothing in public while there.

Scholars generally agree that probably the earliest continuous narrative written about Jesus by the first Christians was the passion narrative. In fact, each of the Gospels has often been dubbed "a passion narrative with a long introduction." Well before Mark ever put together

2. See ibid., 374–76.

3. In part these conclusions hinge on whether we follow the Johannine chronology of passion events or the Synoptic one. I agree with both J. P. Meier and R. E. Brown that the Johannine chronology makes better sense of all the data, and this in turn may mean that Jesus was executed on Passover Eve, or the day when the lambs were slaughtered for Passover. It must be kept in mind that the Jewish day ran from sunset to sunset, not from midnight to midnight. If Jesus died at or about 3 p.m., he died before the onset of Passover, assuming it began on Friday evening. This in turn means that the meal Jesus shared with his disciples, if it was a Passover meal, was nonetheless not eaten on Passover itself. It is probably not necessary to resort to the conjecture that Galileans calculated Passover slightly differently from Judeans.

the earliest Gospel, somewhere around A.D. 68, a continuous passion narrative was circulating in the early churches. For the historian it is necessary to seek the pre-Markan form of the passion narrative, that is, the form of the narrative before Mark added his special traditions and did his editing on the material.

Probably the three most likely Markan additions to the basic narrative are the notice about the young man who ran away, which may be the signature of the author of Mark's Gospel (14:51–52), the reference to Alexander and Rufus (known to Mark's audience?) (15:21), and the rending of the curtain and the comment of the centurion (15:38–39). We may debate whether the passion narrative proper originally began with the triumphal entry into Jerusalem or whether it began closer to the time of death itself, with, say, the arrest of Jesus. For our purposes, we need to begin with the triumphal entry and consider Jesus' action in the temple, which seems to have been the chief cause of his eventual arrest. Then we will consider the passion narrative proper. Above all, for the historian, it is crucial to consider how it could have happened that Jesus came to be crucified as "King of the Jews." What series of events and judgments could have led to this outcome? I suggest that if Jesus did not make a grand entrance into Jerusalem and/or take some symbolic action in the temple, it is hard to explain the conclusion to his life.

First, we know that it was a common custom among the Jews for disciples of a great teacher to commandeer an animal so that the teacher might ride while the disciples walked.[4] Jesus' disciples might well have done this for him. Second, the earliest account of this event in Mark does not have Jesus hailed as the Lord; at most, he is hailed by the crowd as one who comes in the name of the Lord, which may suggest that they saw him in some prophetic light. But it also could be argued that Jesus was simply being accompanied by pilgrims singing the pilgrim songs, one of which was based on Ps. 118:26–29 and is known to have been used during the Feasts of Tabernacles and Passover. Psalm 118:26 and the quotation of it may be no more than a greeting used by pilgrims as they approached the city.

If Jesus intentionally rode into town on a donkey as a symbolic gesture, what would it have symbolized? There is evidence from several places in the passion narrative, both here and in the discourse in the garden of Gethsemane, that Jesus may have conceived of his role in the light of certain Scriptures from Zechariah, in this case, Zech. 9:9. Notice that at no point earlier in the Gospel narratives has Jesus ever ridden, and that this particular riding goes against the tradition of the pil-

4. See B. Witherington III, *The Christology of Jesus* (Minneapolis: Fortress, 1990), 105.

grims walking into the city. Jesus is deliberately elevating himself above the crowd. This act, like that in the temple, appears to be some kind of prophetic sign. It is not clear, however, that the crowds took the hint. As for what this action might mean, one could see it as an antirevolutionary action, in light of Zech. 9:9. Jesus comes into town as the peaceful shepherd king, rather than as the warrior riding in on his charger. This would comport with Jesus' more pacifistic teaching as it is enshrined at various points in Matthew 5–7 (see esp. Matt. 5:9, 38–48). Thus, Jesus, bringing his career to a close, does in the end reveal himself, but not in terms of the most popular form of early Jewish messianic expectation. In fact, Jesus may be the first to ever use Zech. 9:9 as a form of messianic expression. In view of the novelty of this action, and the likelihood that its significance was not immediately apparent, it would appear from a historical point of view that it is not this action that led to Jesus' demise. We turn now to the prophetic action in the temple.

It was the view of S. G. F. Brandon that Jesus and his disciples went into the temple accompanied by a crowd, and that when Jesus' action was witnessed by the crowd, the crowd pillaged the temple.[5] Although no source says anything about a crowd pillaging the temple in response to Jesus' action there, this narrative comes the closest to portraying Jesus as some kind of revolutionary. The temple was the delicate epicenter of early Judaism, and actions taken against it were always likely to have grave consequences. Also, the temple would be watched even more closely during feast times, especially because various Jews believed that this temple and its hierarchy were hopelessly corrupt and would be judged by God, an opinion that Jesus appears to have shared (cf. *1 En.* 89:73–90:29; 4QFlor 1:1–12). Even those who clearly supported temple worship might object to this particular temple and what was transpiring in it. Then, too, there is evidence from Josephus (*Ant.* 18.85–87; *J.W.* 6.283–287) of some eschatological expectation for a messianic figure to do something about the temple so as to legitimize a messianic claim.

Evidence from *m. Sanh.* 9:6 suggests that a violent act was acceptable in the temple precincts to prevent someone from stealing one of the sacred vessels. There is also the famous inscription at the juncture of the court of the Gentiles and the inner courts warning Gentiles against entering further into the temple upon pain of being instantly dispatched. Finally, Acts 21:27–30 shows mob violence in the temple against a person perceived as violating its sanctity. In other words, dra-

---

5. S. G. F. Brandon, *Jesus and the Zealots: A Study of the Political Factor in Early Christianity* (Manchester: Manchester University Press, 1967), 333.

matic actions in the temple as a reaction to pollution were both known and seen as justified. In this social situation, Jesus' own actions are quite believable and understandable.

Since we know that early Christians after Easter continued to involve themselves in the life of the temple (see Acts 2:46), it is entirely unlikely that they would have invented a story about Jesus taking some sort of forceful action against the temple. Temples were protected by the Romans all over the empire, including this Jewish temple. The Roman view was that the gods were not to be mocked; on the contrary, they were to be properly honored. If even symbolically Jesus had temporarily interrupted the procedures that led to sacrifices, the Romans would have viewed this as a revolutionary action.[6]

The outer court of the Herodian temple was exceedingly large, some 300 meters wide by 450 meters in length. There is evidence that this area had only recently begun to be used as a sort of agora for the sale of sacrificial animals. In fact, the practice may have originated as late as A.D. 30 under the instigation of Caiaphas, who wanted more resources for the temple coffers.[7] We know that there were already markets on the Mount of Olives to buy sacrificial animals.

It is possible that Jesus took a limited action in one corner of this part of the temple that would have not attracted the response of the Roman troops in the adjacent Antonia fortress, but perhaps only the attention of a few temple police. Brandon's scenario requires a much larger-scale action than the Gospels depict. What is depicted in the Synoptics and in John is Jesus overturning the money-changers' tables and driving out the vendors of birds and animals. This action in itself suggests some sort of cleansing of the temple is required, and the saying that accompanies the action suggests this as well. While I think that cleansing is part of the significance of Jesus' action, I also think that in the main it must be seen as a prophetic sign-act symbolizing the coming judgment on the temple. Jesus is foreshadowing the day when business as usual in the temple will be fully interrupted, for the temple will be judged. We know from Mark 13:1–2 and par. (cf. John 2:19) that Jesus apparently did predict (correctly) the demise of the temple within a generation. Clearly, Jesus' action should not be seen as an attempt to destroy the temple on that occasion, but it certainly could have symbolized the temple's coming destruction.

As for how Jesus' action would have been perceived by the authorities, it is very possible that they construed it as Jesus whipping up the

---

6. See E. M. Smallwood, *The Jews under Roman Rule: From Pompey to Diocletian*, SJLA 20 (Leiden: Brill, 1976), 148–54.

7. See the discussion in Witherington, *Christology of Jesus*, 109–10.

Jerusalem

Pliny once called Jerusalem "the most illustrious city of the east" (*Natural History* 5.70), though he could only have been referring to the city prior to its destruction in A.D. 70. This was not, however, a huge city, except during the times of a major festival. Archaeological surveys suggest that in the time of Herod the Great the city had about thirty-six thousand residents, about sixty thousand at the time Jesus was executed, and about seventy-six thousand at the time of Herod Agrippa II. In other words, it was a gradually growing city during the New Testament era. Its population would inflate for short periods, perhaps as much as tenfold during Passover and other major feasts. This is why the presence of troops during the feast days was seen as essential during the time when Judea was a Roman province. It is interesting that when Jerusalem became a city of refuge late in the Jewish war, Tacitus says that there were some 600,000 people in the city in A.D. 70 (*History* 5.13). Clearly, this may have been much more than would have been present at a feast. One estimate suggests that some eighteen thousand lambs could be sacrificed in the temple on the day before Passover, and one lamb would serve for about ten people. Thus, some 180,000 participants may have been at the feast in the city at one time.[1]

The city of Jerusalem was, of course, not a port city, being some forty miles from the Mediterranean coast. Nor was it on the main north-south coastal road traveled by the traders. Jerusalem was, however, well-situated to be a capital city, for it had a good elevation and was surrounded by the natural defenses of valleys on three sides, being vulnerable only from the north. It was also a natural place to have as a religious center, being a "high place." Certainly, in Jesus' day and after, the temple was a major drawing card and source of income for the residents working on it, and of course for the priests serving in the temple. Jerusalem can be said to be the most important religious center in the east during the early empire.

Josephus describes Jerusalem in his day as mainly consisting of two parts: the lower city and the upper city. The lower city included the City of David, the Ophel, and the Tyropoeon Valley. The upper city was basically on the hill now called Mount Zion. Basically, the upper class (high priest's family, temple nobility, Sadducean aristocrats) lived in the upper city, nearer to the temple, the palace, the fortress, the theater, and the hippodrome, while the lower class lived in the lower and older part of the city. Only in the first century B.C. did people begin to move in significant numbers from the City of David up to the area that was to become the upper city. Most of the wealthy in Jerusalem belonged to the influential

---

1. Josephus's highly inflated figures of 256,500 lambs slaughtered shortly before the time of the Jewish war to serve for some 2,700,000 people (*J.W.* 6.424–425) should be taken as a good example of typical Josephan rhetorical hyperbole.

priestly families. The lower class also included some of the poorer priests and Levites, as well as merchants, artisans, and unskilled laborers. If we ask what sort of person might have had a house in the upper city to host Jesus and the Twelve for a Passover meal, the likely answer is a member of a priestly family.

Jerusalem was, of course, a predominantly Jewish city, the largest such city in the empire. But the city was bicultural. Most residents spoke and understood only Aramaic, some were bilingual, with Greek being their second language, and some spoke only Greek. The ossuary scripts and other such evidence support these conclusions. Both the educated and the merchants learned Greek for business purposes if for nothing else. Coins were minted in Palestine with Greek inscriptions, many Palestinian Jews had Greek names, and the pottery and architecture of the city show Greek influences. The pursuit of things Greek was not uncommon in Jerusalem, especially among the well-to-do, who might even go to the gymnasium or the hippodrome or the theater. A significant number of Jews had migrated to Jerusalem from all over the empire, some doing so in their old age so that they could be buried there. Some Jews who came for a feast stayed and made a life in Jerusalem, and not surprisingly, if they spoke only Greek, they participated in a synagogue in which the liturgy and homily were in Greek.

Although the Romans maintained a presence in Jerusalem in the Antonia fortress, they kept pretty much to themselves and did not amalgamate or normally fraternize with the general populace. Theirs was something like the experience of American soldiers living on an American army base on foreign soil. The city was thoroughly Jewish, but that Judaism was to a greater or lesser extent Hellenized, depending on the particular Jew in question. Without a doubt, Jews of Jesus' day could not have imagined the horror of what would happen in the second century after the Bar Kochba revolt, when Jerusalem was made a pagan city called Aelia Capitolina and Jews were summarily banned from the city.

visiting pilgrims against the establishment, and also against the city dwellers who earned their livelihood through the temple—money-changers, animal vendors, and the like. In a city whose teeth were already set on edge by the presence of the close watch of the Romans, any sort of words or actions against the temple would have been seen as a threat against the priesthood, the aristocracy (Sadducees) that supported it, the city workers who counted on income from the temple, and the Roman authorities. It is interesting that in the early history of Judea it was always prophets from somewhere out of town, not from Jerusalem, who criticized the temple (e.g., Micah, Jeremiah, and Uriah [see Jer. 26:20]). If we couple Jesus' action in the temple with his radical theocratic teaching on the inbreaking of the eschatological reign of God in Jerusalem, we have a plausibility structure that quite readily could spell the demise of Jesus.

The Long, Dark Road to Golgotha

The stories in the passion narrative are painted in dark and somber tones, perhaps especially the story of Jesus' prayer in Gethsemane, a story that seems to be independently attested in Heb. 5:7–8: "During the days of Jesus' life on earth he offered up prayers and petitions with loud cries and tears to the one who could save him from death, and he was heard because of his reverent submission. Although he was a son, he learned obedience from what he suffered."

Perhaps the first important thing to say about the passion narratives is that they freely admit that Jesus' inner circle of the Twelve denied, deserted, or betrayed him in his hour of need.[8] This is hardly the sort of story early Christians would make up about their progenitors in the faith. By contrast, the women who followed Jesus in and from Galilee (Mary of Magdala and others) were last at the cross, first at the tomb, and first to see the risen Lord. This clear contrast in the narrative between the response of the male and female disciples likewise is not what one would expect if this story were basically pious fiction. Notice also that the passion narratives are dotted with quotations from the Old Testament stating that this or that part of the story fulfilled Scripture. This strongly suggests that early Christians had lots of explaining to do about why the story turned out as it did, since it appears that early Jews certainly were not looking for a crucified messiah. Indeed, the idea of a "crucified anointed one of God" would have been seen as an oxymoron, since it was believed that crucifixion was a sign that a person was cursed, not anointed, by God. Thus, the passion narrative is full of surprising twists and turns.

The real beginning of the end comes with the story of the Last Supper. It is the last time Jesus is together with the Twelve as twelve. It serves as Jesus' last meal before his execution. This story is independently attested outside the Gospels in 1 Cor. 11:23–26, where clearly Paul is citing a tradition that goes back before the time of his writing 1 Corinthians in the early-to-mid–50s. In other words, it is a tradition that arose within twenty years of Jesus' death. From the Pauline form of the tradition we learn that Jesus was betrayed (by one of the disci-

---

8. I do not see the Beloved Disciple in John's Gospel as an exception, as he is, in my judgment, not one of the Galilean disciples or of the Twelve, but a Judean disciple. It may have been in his house in Jerusalem where the Last Supper was held.

ples present), and that he gave a new symbolic interpretation to the bread and wine that were part of a Passover meal (cf. 1 Cor. 5:7). Much debate has addressed whether the meal shared between Jesus and the Twelve could have been a Passover meal, and in my view, it was. It was simply a Passover meal celebrated in advance of the normal day, which probably means that the disciples would have had to perform the ritual sacrifice themselves, something far from impossible. Historically, the most crucial point about the Last Supper story is that the way Jesus interpreted the elements suggested that his death would have some sort of special or salvific significance for his disciples. If one accepts Mark 10:45 as a saying of Jesus, this interpretation is a believable action on his part. It indicates not only that Jesus knew he was going to die, but also that he believed that the outcome of his death would be positive.

To get at the historical nub of this portion of the passion narrative, we are going to follow closely the Markan account for a while to see what comes to light.[9] Several factors about the Last Supper narrative seem anomalous. First, there is the apparently clandestine nature of the preparations. The disciples are to follow a man who is occupied with an unusual task (carrying a jar of water)[10] to a destination that he, but not the disciples, will know.[11] Note also that the text says that the man will meet them, not the reverse, which suggests that he will be looking for them. Second, there is the matter that the master seems to be sending them to prepare for a Passover prior to the appropriate time. Last, there is Jesus' remark about "my room," as if Jesus already had a predetermined and familiar place in mind. Yet the disciples obey Jesus without question here, as if Jesus' orders are not cryptic.[12] It is interesting that while in the rest of Mark 14 we find references to "the twelve," in vv. 12–16 we find references only to "the disciples," presumably including Judean disciples.[13]

Perhaps we have here an indication that Jesus had been to Jerusalem before and had a familiar place where he took meals within

9. The following material appears in another form in B. Witherington III, *The Gospel of Mark: A Socio-rhetorical Commentary* (Grand Rapids: Eerdmans, 2001), 370–76.

10. Men might carry water in a skin, but not in a jar meant to gather water for household purposes, which was a woman's task. See R. Gundry, *Mark: A Commentary on His Apology for the Cross* (Grand Rapids: Eerdmans, 1993), 821.

11. See C. Myers, *Binding the Strong Man: A Political Reading of Mark's Story of Jesus* (Maryknoll, N.Y.: Orbis), 360–61.

12. Which in itself favors the clandestine explanation, with the disciples in on the secret plan, rather than prophetic foresight, which only Jesus has.

13. See M. Hooker, *A Commentary on the Gospel according to St. Mark* (London: Black, 1991), 332.

the city (for the Passover had to be eaten, if at all possible, within the Holy City), and in fact arrangements complete with secret signal had been made in advance for him and his disciples to show up in a particular house on that night.[14] The likelihood that this is a correct conclusion is increased by a careful reading of the Fourth Gospel, which suggests not only that Jesus made repeated trips up to Jerusalem during his ministry, but also that he had a Judean disciple whom he was especially close to, the Beloved Disciple (not one of the Galilean disciples), in whose house he reclined as a guest at the head of the table during Passover week.[15] Since the Passover meal seldom finished before midnight and needed to be taken within the city walls of Jerusalem, Jesus would have remained within the jurisdiction of the priestly authorities late into the night.[16] Indeed, if there is any validity to the tradition about the upper room being on Mount Zion, he would have been taking Passover within a stone's throw of Caiaphas's house.

A careful reading of Mark 14:12, which has two temporal clauses, suggests that Mark is speaking to his audience in a non-Jewish way of thinking about days. The Jewish way was to reckon a day from sundown to sundown, the Roman way from midnight to midnight. By the Roman way, the first day of unleavened bread (Nisan 15) and the day of the slaughter of the lambs (Nisan 14) were one and the same, for the former began on the evening of the latter.[17] There is much to commend in some of A. Jaubert's suggestions that the meal that Jesus had with his disciples was a Passover meal, not celebrated on the normal day, but rather, earlier, perhaps following the calendar found in Jubilees and perhaps at Qumran. Although I disagree with Jaubert that this Passover day was Tuesday rather than Thursday, I think she is correct that Jesus was crucified, as John says, on the day of the slaughter of the lambs—Nisan 14. I further think that part of the confusion comes from the fact that the Johannine account depicts a meal taken earlier in the week, which was not a Passover but a Greco-Roman style banquet, complete with extensive symposium, that is, with teaching.[18]

14. L. Hurtado writes, "Such secrecy was required, probably, because Jesus knew the authorities were looking for an opportunity to arrest him away from large public gatherings" (*Mark* [New York: Harper and Row, 1983], 220–21).

15. See the discussion in B. Witherington III, *John's Wisdom: A Commentary on the Fourth Gospel* (Louisville: Westminster John Knox, 1995), 1–15, 235–38.

16. Hurtado, *Mark*, 221.

17. See Hooker, *Mark*, 334.

18. See Witherington, *John's Wisdom*, on John 13; cf. A. Jaubert, *The Date of the Last Supper*, trans. I. Rafferty (Staten Island, N.Y.: Alba House, 1965).

A **Closer** Look: *What Kind of Passover?*

It is all too easy to get embroiled in controversy as to whether the Last Supper was in fact a Passover meal. In my view, it was, though celebrated early.[19] The earliness may be one good reason why it was celebrated in secret, for this would have meant that the disciples or their friends would have had to slaughter the lamb themselves, not have it done in the temple precincts. Yet, they were in Jerusalem. A circumvention of the sacrificial protocol would itself have been an affront to the priestly authorities. Sacrificing animals for the feast outside of Jerusalem was not an unknown practice, for we find it at Qumran, at Mount Gerizim, in the Diaspora, and presumably in Galilee as well by those who were devout but unable to travel the ninety or so miles to the festival in Jerusalem.

It is, however, somewhat strange that neither the lamb nor the rite of purification is mentioned in these verses in Mark that describe the meal. Is this because Jesus celebrated the meal with the other Passover elements but without the lamb? He was, of course, reinterpreting the Passover elements in a new way, and so it is not impossible that other innovations (e.g., no lamb) might have been involved. Still, it seems unlikely that the meal would have been held without the lamb, which was, so to speak, the main course. Thus, we must reckon with the possibility of an "illegal" Passover meal, celebrated early and without the due process of the temple sacrificial rites, for the lamb had been slaughtered and dressed elsewhere.[20] This is yet another piece of evidence supporting the view that Jesus was a radical Jew, unafraid to alter tradition and even set aside portions of the Torah as no longer binding in the wake of the coming of God's eschatological saving activity.

Mark tells the story of the meal in telegraphic fashion. Mark 14:17 says that Jesus came with the Twelve in the early evening to take the meal. That it says the Twelve came with Jesus may mean that the two disciples sent ahead to prepare the way were not from among the Twelve—perhaps Judean disciples.[21] The first remark from Jesus' lips

19. For a fresh discussion arguing that the Last Supper was a Passover meal, see M. Casey, *Aramaic Sources of Mark's Gospel*, SNTSMS 102 (Cambridge: Cambridge University Press, 1998), 219–52, which includes a strong argument for an Aramaic substratum to this story.

20. If Jesus had relatives down the road in Bethlehem (where lambs were raised for sacrifice in Jerusalem), could he have relied on them to perform the sacrificial act?

21. See J. Painter, *Mark's Gospel: Worlds in Conflict* (London: Routledge, 1997), 184.

at the supper in this Gospel (14:18) is that one of the Twelve is going to betray him. This may suggest the meal was taken exclusively with the Twelve.[22] At a meal in this highly stratified world of male culture, the persons closest to the guest of honor or host were considered the most important guests. It is, then, a measure of the depth of the perfidy that it would be the one who dipped the bread in the bowl with Jesus who would betray him (14:20).

Mark 14:22–26 provides us with the earliest Gospel description of the Last Supper meal itself. Scholars have often debated how much Mark himself has redacted his source in light of later Christian practice, especially in regard to the words over the bread and the cup. It is instructive to compare this primitive Gospel account to that found in our earliest source for this material, 1 Cor. 11:23–26. Often noted is that the Lukan form of these sayings (Luke 22:19–20) is closer to the Pauline material than the Markan form is,[23] which may suggest that Mark has indeed done some editing for the sake of his largely Gentile audience. This would be consistent with the pattern of Markan editorial work found elsewhere in the Gospel,[24] and reminds us that the earliest Gospel does not always provide the earliest form of a saying or narrative. The matter is more complex than that.

The first thing that needs to be said about Jesus' reinterpretation of the elements of the Passover is that he does not reinterpret the lamb or the bitter herbs; rather he focuses on the bread and the wine. Second, it is hard to make too many fine points about the words of institution on the basis of the various Greek texts because Jesus probably spoke in Aramaic. Thus, for instance, Jesus would have said something like, "This—my body," for the verb "is" found in the Greek would not be in the Aramaic. Furthermore, the phrase "my body for you" probably cannot be said in Aramaic any more than the phrase "my blood of the covenant" can.[25] What can be gathered from the reconstruction of the original is that Jesus was giving to

22. It is my view that the meal portrayed in John 13 involving the Beloved Disciple happened earlier in the week, while this clandestine Passover took place on Thursday night and likely involved only the Twelve plus Jesus. Probably, servers also would have been involved—perhaps the Beloved Disciple's family members if this meal occurred at the same site.

23. In my view, this is not merely because Luke had another source for some of his passion narrative material, but also because he was a sometime companion of Paul. See the introduction to B. Witherington III, *The Acts of the Apostles: A Socio-rhetorical Commentary* (Grand Rapids: Eerdmans, 1998). But there is also evidence that the Lukan form has been influenced by the Markan version at Luke 22:20, where Luke combines the Pauline and Markan statements. See E. Schweizer, *The Good News according to Mark*, trans. D. Madvig (Richmond: John Knox, 1970), 300.

24. Cf., e.g., Mark 10:2–12 and par.

25. See Schweizer, *Mark*, 301–3.

> ## Ransoming Souls
>
> One of the great values of studying ancient papyri and inscriptions is
> that one comes across words found in the New Testament, but in differ-
> ent contexts, which helps us understand the range of meaning of a word,
> especially when it has particular religious associations. One such key
> term is the Greek word *lytron*, "ransom," which is familiar to the reader
> of the New Testament, especially from a text like Mark 10:45. For exam-
> ple, we may consider the inscription "Galliko, female slave of the Askle-
> pian village of Keryzeis (dedicates this as) a ransom of Diogenes." Here,
> clearly, the term "ransom" has a religious significance. A slave is making
> a propiatory dedication in order to ransom a relative or friend named Di-
> ogenes. It is possible, since the god Asklepios is mentioned, that Diogenes
> is not well, and Galliko is trying to buy back his life by this dedication to
> the god of healing. (*NewDocs* 2:90)

his disciples in advance, in symbolic form, the benefits of his death, and
asking them to take these into themselves. J. Jeremias puts it this way:

> When at the daily meal the *paterfamilias* recites the blessing over the
> bread . . . and breaks it and hands a piece to each member to eat, the
> meaning of the action is that each of the members *is made a recipient of
> the blessing by this eating;* the common "Amen" and the common eating
> of the bread of benediction unite the members into a table fellowship.
> The same is true of the "cup of blessing" which is the cup of wine over
> which grace has been spoken, when it is in circulation among the mem-
> bers: *drinking from it mediates a share in the blessing.*[26]

It also seems clear that Jesus saw his death as the act that instituted
or ratified the new covenant. Thus, this meal, while perhaps foreshadowing the eschatological banquet (on which cf. Isa. 25:6; 65:13; *1 En.*
62:14; *2 Bar.* 29:8; *Pirke Avot* 3:20), is actually about instituting a new
covenantal relationship between God and God's people. This assumes
that the old one was no longer in force or enforceable, or at the very
least that it needed replacing. "For suddenly we realize that Jesus is *not*
after all participating in the temple-centered feast of Passover (note
that Mark never mentions the eating of lamb). Instead he is expropri-
ating its symbolic discourse (the ritual meal) in order to narrate his
new myth, that of the Human One who gives his life for the people."[27]

26. J. Jeremias, *The Eucharistic Words of Jesus*, trans. N. Perrin, 3rd ed. (London: SCM, 1966), 232.
27. Myers, *Binding the Strong Man*, 363.

The story is once again laden with irony because the implication of the theological assertion about the expiating blood of Jesus poured out for many (Mark 14:24) is that death (the ultimate pollutant in the Jewish purity system) is the means of ultimate cleansing.[28]

If indeed this story accurately represents Jesus' understanding (whatever the particulars about the authenticity of the words of institution), what astounding faith and trust he must have had to have believed that his death would accomplish such a thing, and then to be so supremely confident that he could symbolically distribute the benefits of that death in advance of it happening! This high moment must be compared to his moment of struggle in the Garden of Gethsemane.

Mark 14:26 serves as a transition to the next three scenes in the passion narrative, for the setting of those scenes is on the Mount of Olives. The scenes include Jesus' prediction of denial, the threefold implicit betrayal by three disciples' failure to watch with Jesus when he comes three times seeking support, and the betrayal and arrest of Jesus. In short, these scenes become increasingly dark, with the relationship of Jesus and the disciples going from bad to worse to worst. Since these scenes are not crucial to our historical reconstruction, we will pass on to the betrayal itself in Mark 14:43–52.

From the very beginning of this pericope in Mark 14:43 we see the emphasis on Judas being one of the Twelve, thus making his act all the more inexplicable and treacherous. In fact, each time he is mentioned in the Gospel, he is mentioned as the one who handed Jesus over. A crowd is with him, armed with swords and clubs, but it need not have been a large crowd. Mark says nothing about Roman soldiers. Yet, something more than a rabble is implied, because this crowd came with the temple officials. With Judas are chief priests, scribes, and elders.[29] This is the same list of persons mentioned in Jesus' first passion prediction (Mark 8:31), but it is surprising that the elders are not mentioned in the reference to the plot in Mark 14:1–2. That a prearranged signal is needed to indicate who Jesus is may mean that these officials, or at least the temple police (who were Levites), did not know what Jesus looked like, or at least that in the dark a positive confirmation of identity was needed to make a quick arrest.[30] "The secret signal, the surprise attack at night, and of course the heavily armed contingent all imply that the authorities expected

28. See J. Neyrey, "The Idea of Purity in Mark's Gospel," *Semeia* 35 (1986): 91–127, esp. 115.
29. Painter notes that this is the very group that made up the Sanhedrin (*Mark's Gospel*, 191).
30. Ibid., 190.

armed resistance."[31] A kiss was a normal form of greeting between disciple and teacher, a token of real friendship. Judas says, "The one I kiss should be grabbed and led away securely." The intensive verb used in v. 45, *kataphileō*, means "to kiss with every show of affection," thus making the betrayal even worse. It is striking that after the betrayal by the kiss, Judas completely disappears into the night, never to appear again in Mark's narrative.

Mark 14:47 mentions the cutting off of the high priest's slave's ear, but does not name the perpetrator of the deed,[32] and notably, there is no condemnation of the action in Mark, unlike in Matthew and Luke (Matt. 26:52; Luke 22:51).[33] What

Illustration 5.2   A gate looking into the garden of Gethsemane.

this reference further confirms is the involvement of the high priest in this arrest. We should note that even the early Jewish traditions freely admit Jewish involvement in Jesus' death (cf. Josephus, *Ant.* 18.3.3; *b. Sanh.* 43a; 107b; *y. Sanh.* 7:16; *b. Sanh.* 67a).

One of the major historical points of debate in regard to the passion narrative is whether or not Jesus was actually tried before the Sanhedrin. This question is raised not least because John does not record such proceedings (the private interview with the high priest and former

---

31. Myers, *Binding the Strong Man*, 367.

32. This might seem odd, since according to John 18:10–11 the swordsman was Peter, and Mark is presumably relying on a Petrine source; but perhaps Mark wishes to spare the memory of Peter at this juncture.

33. See Myers, *Binding the Strong Man*, 367.

high priest does not qualify—cf. John 18:12–14, 19–27). Luke 22:66–71 suggests a morning hearing before some sort of council, but mentions no verdict being passed against Jesus; the charges leveled against him before Pilate (Luke 23:1–5) are not mentioned in the hearing. Both the Matthean and the Markan accounts perhaps suggest a night hearing or trial before the Sanhedrin. In short, there are at least three very different versions of what happened to Jesus after his arrest and before his being handed over to Pilate. Here, we need to consider the nature and power of the Sanhedrin.

A Closer Look: *The Significance of the Sanhedrin*

The Greek word *synedrion* gives us the word "Sanhedrin," meaning "council." The Jewish sources of information differ on the organization and character of this institution. The Mishnah speaks of two Sanhedrins, both consisting of religious scholars: the Great Sanhedrin, which met in the Hall of Hewn Stones in the temple precincts and consisted of seventy-one members; and the small Sanhedrins of twenty-three members each, which met in various cities. Both the New Testament and Josephus paint a rather different portrait. Josephus sees the Sanhedrin as a supreme political and judicial council at first presided over by the king and then by the high priest during the time when Judea was a Roman province. Herod the Great had been able to hold the high priestly aristocracy under his own control. This led to a very different priestly aristocracy in control during the Roman period. All but two high priests from A.D. 6–66 came from two select families. The Gospels attest to Annas and Caiaphas, and neither the New Testament nor Josephus paints a positive portrait of these men. In order to maintain their posts they had to collaborate with the prefect.

During the Roman period, the high priests and their orders were responsible for collecting not only the tithes for the temple but also the tribute for Caesar. R. Horsley paints a sinister picture of these high priests and their entourage, for they increasingly resorted to violence to maintain their dominant position. Note that when the revolt of the people finally exploded in A.D. 66, the target was not just the Romans but also the priestly aristocracy. The Qumran literature and other sources suggest that the fundamental division in Jewish society was between the ordinary people and those who represented or collaborated with Rome—the priestly hierarchy, their scribes, the tax collectors, and so forth. Jesus' action in the temple clearly gives the sense that he saw things to have gone very wrong there, and his oracle of doom about the temple would have been taken as a critique of its administrators.[34]

One of the major difficulties in assessing the nature and powers of the Great Sanhedrin is uncertainty as to what degree the material in the Mishnah represents practices prior to A.D. 70. Before that date, it seems likely that the Sanhedrin was mainly in the control of the high priest and Sadducees and their scribes, though certainly there was a Pharisaic presence on the council. It is notable that in the Gospel trial narratives the Pharisees are never depicted as Jesus' adversaries; rather, it is the chief priests, scribes, and elders. If a few Jews were partially responsible for Jesus' death, they do not appear to have been Jesus' old adversaries in Galilee.

After A.D. 70 the Saducean party was defunct, as was the Jerusalem Sanhedrin, and Judaism was reshaped by those of Pharisaic orientation. The Mishnah, which was not codified until around A.D. 200, has a tractate on the powers of the Sanhedrin, but it may well reflect later Pharisaic practice or ideal legislation meant to indicate how things ought to be run. In a dated but crucial treatment of the matter, H. Danby showed persuasively that only a few of the mishnaic rules are likely to have been extant in the pre–A.D. 70 period.[35] Thus, that the trial narrative recorded in Mark has twenty-seven apparent violations of later Sanhedrin practice is no proof that there was no such trial. It should be noted that despite the oft-repeated claims that there is a growing tendency in the Gospel tradition to increasingly blame the Jews for Jesus' death, the Gospels' Jewish trial narratives show no such trend. The latest Gospel, John, does not even mention such a trial, and Luke's account is very sketchy. It is in fact the earlier Gospel material in Mark, further developed by Matthew, that strongly points to a Jewish trial and Jewish involvement in Jesus' death.

The existence of both a political and a religious Sanhedrin in Jesus' day seems unlikely. Rather, the Bet Din ("House of Judgment") is probably the development of or the successor to the Great Sanhedrin of Jesus' day. Jews before A.D. 70 did not make the sort of distinctions we do between political and religious matters in the way that was done af-

---

34. See R. Horsley, *The Liberation of Christmas: The Infancy Narratives in Social Context* (New York: Crossroad, 1989), 51–52.

35. H. Danby, "The Bearing of the Rabbinical Criminal Code on the Jewish Trial Narratives in the Gospels," *JTS* 21 (1919): 51–75.

ter the holocaust of A.D. 70. That Josephus records only political trials
before the Sanhedrin may be significant for the analysis of the Gospel
material, or, on the other hand, may simply reflect that Jewish historian's focus. What we may conclude from this discussion is that a night
trial of Jesus before the Sanhedrin resulting in a verdict even on the eve
of Passover is not impossible in the pre–A.D. 70 period, for many of the
later rules likely were not in force (though some clearly were—on the
rending of the high priest's robes, cf. Mark 14:63 and *b. Sanh.* 75b).
Annas and Caiaphas and their fellow collaborators with Rome may even
have been willing to have an illegal trial in order to dispose of Jesus.

We must keep clearly in view that Passover was a celebration of Israel's liberation by God from an oppressive pharaoh. This feast would
quite naturally be a time of heightened tensions and increased desires
for liberation from Rome (see *Ant.* 20.106–107). If Jesus did indeed,
during the celebration of Passover, perform an action in the temple and
prophesy its downfall, Caiaphas, in order to protect his and others'
privileged positions, might well have argued, "It is expedient that one
man should die for the people, and that the whole nation not perish"
(John 11:50).

The questions then become, Was the Jewish trial legal or illegal?
Was Jesus condemned legitimately, or was there an injustice done, perhaps even a rigging of the outcome? The answers to these questions are
bound up with three more questions: (1) Did the Jews at this time have
the power to execute for capital crimes? (2) If they did, why would they
turn Jesus over to Pilate? (3) What constituted blasphemy in Jesus' day,
the later notion of using the ineffable name wrongly (or in vain), or a
broader definition of the act?

This last issue must be tackled first. J. Blinzler has shown that the
term "blasphemy" was applied to a wider range of offenses in Jesus' day
than was the case later (see Mark 2:5–7; John 10:33–36; Acts 12:22–23;
14:14).[36] The later, narrower definition, "The blasphemer is not culpable unless he pronounces the name itself" (*m. Sanh.* 7:5), probably did
not apply in Jesus' day, and certainly the Old Testament material does
not suggest a narrow definition of blasphemy (see Exod. 22:28; Lev.
24:11; Num. 15:30–31); in fact, it does not *define* blasphemy at all. What
we do know from the Old Testament is that the penalty for blasphemy
was stoning, not crucifixion.

It is therefore not unlikely that Jesus could have said something at
the Jewish trial that was considered blasphemy, and certainly, that is

36. J. Blinzler, *The Trial of Jesus,* 3d ed. (Cork: Mercier, 1961).

how Mark portrays the climax of the trial. Notice that the accusations about what Jesus said or did in regard to the temple do not finally settle the matter, but rather, the question of his messianic identity. The text is quite clear that the witnesses did not agree about what Jesus said about the temple, and no legal judgment could have been passed on such equivocal evidence.

Most likely what Jesus said that constituted blasphemy was not his claim to be messiah per se, for that had been claimed by others and was not a capital offense. Rather, the blasphemy most likely was perceived in his claim in Mark 14:62 to sit at the right hand of God, and to come in power to judge the high priest (who was also the high court), suggesting his possession of divine honors, powers, and prerogatives. Only God was expected to come on the day of judgment to judge the world.

Why, then, was Jesus not stoned? This is an especially crucial question in light of the case of Stephen (Acts 6–7), who was accused of blasphemy and was stoned. The answer might be that the feast was about to happen, and perhaps too that the high priest wanted a public and Roman execution to nip the Jesus movement in the bud. And we must now come to some conclusion about the first two questions of three numbered above.

John 18:31 is quite clear: the Jewish authorities claim not to have the power to execute Jesus. The historical veracity of this statement has often been doubted on the basis of four things: (1) the warning inscription in the temple indicating that Jews would immediately execute Gentile trespassers (cf. Josephus, *J.W.* 5.194; Philo, *Embassy* 307); (2) *m. Sanh.* 7:2 records the execution of a priest's daughter for adultery, and this is a pre–A.D. 70 ruling; (3) the execution of James mentioned in Acts 12:2; (4) the stoning of Stephen (Acts 7:54–60).

First of all, no one denies that the Romans allowed an exception or two to their exclusive right to use lethal force—for example, the Jewish rule about violations of the sanctity of the temple. However, the execution of James is not a true exception, nor is the execution of the priest's daughter, because both happened during a time between prefects being in the land, when Jewish authorities took advantage of the interregnum situation. Both these executions occurred while Herod Agrippa I was ruling (A.D. 41–44), but there was no prefect in Judea at the time. In the case of Stephen, a trial seems to have started in good form, but to have degenerated into a mob taking matters and stones into its own hands. In other words, vigilante justice took over.

We must reckon primarily with two facts. First, as pointed out previously, while the Romans allowed a certain amount of local autonomy in provinces on matters inconsequential to them, they did reserve to themselves the power of capital punishment. There is no reason to think that the Judean province was an exception to this rule; indeed, because of its turbulent nature, the Romans were highly unlikely to let go of the power of the sword in that locale. Second, Jewish sources tell us that between A.D. 6 and 70 there was a limitation on Jewish judicial powers (cf. *y. Sanh.* 1:1; 7:2 and *b. Sanh.* 41a; cf. *Meg. Ta'an* 6). Notice that Annas II was dismissed from the priesthood for executing James (*Ant.* 20.197–207).

Thus, we should conclude that although the Sanhedrin could legally pass sentence on Jesus, it could not legally execute him. The Sanhedrin was hardly likely to try to take the law into its own hands during a feast time with Herod and Pilate both in town, especially given the character of Pilate. The Markan account of the Jewish trial, which finished at dawn, rings true from a historical perspective.

We turn now to the Roman trial. Pilate, as the prefect of the province of Judea, had what is called full imperium, including criminal and jurisdictional authority, military power, and the power to levy taxes. His jurisdiction came directly from the emperor and could not be delegated in capital cases. The only real limitation on his power was the Roman law against extortion. Pilate's power in a criminal case was called *coertio* if it dealt with certain public crimes such as adultery, forgery, murder, bribery, and treason. Anything that fell outside this list came under what was called personal *cognitio*, and the punishments exacted under this category were *extra ordinem*. Which form of trial Jesus received is debated, but in my view, it must have been *coertio*, for in the end, Jesus was executed for some form of treason.

Roman trials had no juries, but did have counselors. There had to be a formulation of charges by accusers and then by the judge, who also formulated the penalties. The judgment could be handed down publicly at a tribunal, as in the case of Jesus, or privately in chambers. Matt. 27:19 indicates that Pilate sat on the judgment seat to pronounce the verdict in Jesus' case. In a Roman trial the accusers would allege the facts, and the judge would assess them, in part by inquiring of the accused. There were no defense lawyers or witnesses for the defense in such a trial. When the accused was found guilty, some degree of beating/scourging usually accompanied the main punishment, but was not ordinarily considered part of the punishment (unless the scourging had no punitive sequel). Rather, it was a way to shame the guilty party in public, as was crucifixion.

The portrayal of Pilate in the Gospels is of a cynical and vacillating official who seems to strongly suspect an ulterior or false motive in those people trying to get Jesus crucified. Perhaps it is due to his anti-

Illustration 5.3　Pilate coin with shepherd's crook and reference to Tiberius. Obverse of Pilate coin with olive branch.

Semitism that he seeks to tweak the noses of the Jewish officials by either exonerating Jesus or letting him off with a light scourging. Evidently, and not surprisingly, Pilate did not like being used to settle Jewish squabbles and vendettas.

The Fourth Gospel presents a lengthy dialogue between Jesus and Pilate. It could be argued that the restraint shown in the Gospel portraits of Pilate, as compared to those of Josephus and Philo, is partly due to the evangelists wishing not to inflame Romans or Roman officials against Christianity, which was certainly seen as a *superstitio* by many Romans.

The first question Pilate asks in all four Gospels is, "Are you the king of the Jews?" (Mark 15:2 and par.). It seems clear that Pilate had been informed by the chief priests and elders of the accusation against Jesus. They had couched it in these terms so that it might be seen to be a political charge with a capital crime at stake. If such a charge could be made to stick, it would indeed amount to high treason, and normally would lead swiftly to execution. Notice that only Luke, the historian among the Gospel writers and perhaps a Gentile himself, offers the details of the Jewish charges presented to Pilate (Luke 23:2). The first two charges mentioned (stirring up the people, and forbidding the paying of taxes to Caesar) are not taken up in what follows. The crucial charge, then, is about Jesus being the king of the Jews.

Apparently, Pilate was somewhat baffled by Jesus' failure to defend himself, as self-defense was the only defense for the accused in a Roman trial. All this appears to have transpired at or in front of Herod's Jerusalem palace near Jaffa Gate, not at the Antonia fortress near the temple.[37] The accounts show a series of moves that Pilate makes to avoid or delay giving the Jewish authorities the outcome they desire. Note that Pilate finally caves in only when the crowd cries for Jesus' execution.[38]

Several aspects of the trial have been thought to be historically suspect. One of these is offering to release a prisoner at festival time, and a second one is agreeing to the crowd's request in a capital matter. In response to the first point, we may note Papyrus Florilegium 61.59ff, in which the Roman governor of Egypt says to a certain prisoner that instead of scourging him, he will give him to the people; and *m. Pesah.* 8.6a, which also may suggest that there was a custom of releasing a prisoner at feast time, just before Passover would be eaten.

In response to the second point, note that Roman law offered two different forms of amnesty: (1) *abolitio*, which involved releasing a prisoner not yet condemned; and (2) *indulgentia*, which meant giving pardon to a condemned criminal. It appears that the former would apply in the narrative about Jesus' trial. All four Gospels mention the amnesty during the feast, and so its historical feasibility should not be quickly dismissed. Once Pilate had consulted the crowd about the amnesty, it was a natural, if irregular, sequel to ask the same audience what to do with Jesus, especially if he expected them to clamor for Jesus' release. Even then, Pilate tries to forestall the crowd's cry, but finally to no avail. The cry "You will be no friend to Caesar" is quite believable, as it touched Pilate at his vulnerable point. He was an appointment of Caesar, and to fall from grace with Caesar spelled trouble. With Sejanus's power on the wane, it may be that Pilate thought it unwise to act in an unpopular fashion that might lead to a Jewish delegation to Rome.

It seems reasonably certain that Pilate did not put much stock in the belief that Jesus was guilty of high treason. This is perhaps what the handwashing suggests. If so, then Jesus' death is a judicial murder, not a just execution of a criminal. Jesus himself seems to have given no encouragement to Pilate to execute him. But to whom did Pilate deliver Jesus for execution? John 19:23 suggests he handed Jesus over to a Roman centurion with four underlings. Roman prefects did not have regular legions under their command, only auxiliaries recruited from

37. Thus, the Via Dolorosa begins at the wrong place, though it likely ends at the right one.
38. Though Luke 23:6–12 tells of Pilate turning Jesus over to Herod, he was not required to do so, because under Roman law the accused was to be tried where the crime was committed. It is historically plausible that Pilate might turn Jesus over to Herod to avoid dealing with the matter, and to improve his relationship with Herod.

the non-Jewish inhabitants of the region (mainly Samaritans and Syrians, people definitely at odds with the Jews). This raises the possibility that the centurion at the cross might have been a Samaritan, someone familiar with Jewish messianic traditions and thus in a position to utter something like, "Surely, this was the Son of God"—a cry more likely to be on Semitic than on Gentile lips.

Crucifixion and the Crucified One

"Christus . . . suffered the extreme penalty during the reign of Tiberius at the hands of one of our procurators, Pontius Pilate," says Tacitus (*Annals* 15.44.2–8). We need to recognize from the outset that the Romans did not invent the punishment called crucifixion. The evidence points at least as far back as the Hasmonean period and to figures such as Alexander Janneus (cf. *Ant.* 13:379–380; 4QpNah 3–4, i, 7–8; and possibly 11QT 64:1.6–13). Deuteronomy 21:22–23 is a text that likely originally referred to the displaying of a corpse on a tree after execution rather than to crucifixion per se, or to death by hanging, but by New Testament times the text was used to speak about crucifixion, as in Gal. 3:13. In short, crucifixion was a known means of Jewish punishment before New Testament times, but the Romans had adopted and adapted the practice, and we have no evidence in Josephus or from New Testament times that the Sanhedrin or other Jews practiced this form of execution during this era.

The question then becomes, How did Jesus get himself executed by the Romans, and by a form of punishment that the Romans normally reserved for rebellious slaves, bandits, and runaways? Note, for example, that the two *lēstai* crucified with Jesus were probably, like Barabbas, not mere thieves but revolutionary bandits. M. Hengel has shown that there is no evidence for a positive evaluation of crucifixion in the ancient world.[39] It was certainly not seen as a good way to die, even if one wanted to be a martyr. The evidence from Qumran and the New Testament makes clear that Jews could not possibly have seen crucifixion in a positive light in view of their connecting it with Deuteronomy 21, unless they were Jewish Christians, who would have seen the cross in light of the resurrection. In short, in early Judaism there was no expectation of a crucified messiah; in fact, one who was crucified was assumed not to be the Anointed One of God, because crucifixion meant to be cursed by God. Indeed, if someone wanted to scotch the rumor that Jesus was the Messiah, there was no better way to do so than to

---

39. M. Hengel, *Crucifixion in the Ancient World and the Folly of the Message of the Cross*, trans. J. Bowden (London: SCM, 1977).

When Is a "T" a "T"?

Archaeological inscriptional evidence is often ambiguous and difficult to interpret. A good example is the inscription and sigil found on a first- or second-century ossuary from Jerusalem. The inscription on the bone box reads "Jesus of Aloth" followed by a "T." One archaeologist, E. L. Sukenik, interpreted this to be the sign of the cross, and therefore claimed this inscription as the earliest Christian burial label. However, the "T" in question could certainly be the Hebrew letter taw, which was used as a sign of protection and deliverance by Jews. It is thus perfectly possible that this is a Jewish rather than a Christian inscription. (*New-Docs* 1:112)

have him crucified. Notice that in Luke 24:20–21, the disciples going to Emmaus assume that Jesus' crucifixion made it clear that he was not the one to redeem Israel. Notice too that the disciples would not necessarily have anticipated such a conclusion to Jesus' life on the basis of the passion predictions (Mark 8:31; 9:31; 10:34), if they are historically grounded. Those predictions do not mention crucifixion, but only the killing of the Son of Man. There is no evidence, even in Mark 10:45 or Luke 9:44, that Jesus predicted his death by crucifixion.

A Closer Look: *The Practice of Crucifixion*

As a result of the excavations at Giv'at ha-Mivtar near Jerusalem in 1968–70, we now have some rather clear information about execution by crucifixion during the first century A.D. Nails were used in some cases, driven through the wrists (not the hands) and through the ankles. In the case of the Giv'at ha-Mivtar remains, both ankles were nailed to the cross with one nail. This may also have been the case with Jesus.

The normal Roman procedure, once death by crucifixion had been chosen, was to flog the victim, usually with a flagellum or cat-o'-nine-tails, prior to making the victim carry the crossbar of the cross to the site of execution. In Jesus' case, this flagellation took place earlier on in the proceedings as Pilate attempted to have him flogged and released. Thus, Jesus must have experienced considerable blood loss before execution. This may in turn explain why he expired so rapidly on the cross. The flagellum could, and often did, kill its victim, ripping out flesh right down to the bone with the hooks, bits of rock, and the like that were

Illustration 5.4 Ossified nailed foot of a crucifixion victim.

© Erich Lessing / Art Resource, NY

tied to the ends of the thongs (see Philo, *Flaccus* 75; cf. Josephus, *J.W.* 2.612, which refers to being scourged until the entrails were visible, or until the bones showed). In Roman law, unlike Jewish law, there was no maximum number of lashes; the amount of flogging depended on the malice of the one wielding the flagellum. It appears likely that Jesus was severely scourged, because he was unable to carry the crossbar all the way to Golgotha, and he died soon after being nailed to the cross. This comports with the prediction in Mark 8:31 that he would suffer many things before being killed.

It is not clear whether Jesus died on a T-shaped cross with a slot in the top, or the small "t" shape we are most familiar with. What is clear is that it was not the practice to carry the whole cross to the site of execution, but only the crossbar. Normally, there was also a *seducula*, a small block of wood on which to rest the buttocks, to prevent collapse, but also, from the executioners' viewpoint, to prolong the agony. If the executioners were in a hurry, they might break the legs of the victim, thus hastening death (as was the case in the victim found at Giv'at ha-Mivtar). Jesus, however, died before any such expedient was needed.

There is no absolute medical agreement as to the actual cause of death when one is crucified. It could perhaps be suffocation due to inability to hold oneself up on the cross and breathe. This might explain Jesus' great cry at the end as he's gasping for breath (Mark 15:37). It is also possible that Jesus died of traumatic shock, or heart failure. The gush of blood and water (John 19:34) could have come from the lance piercing his pleural cavity, where the fluid had collected after heart stoppage.

Some of the details about the execution of Jesus deserve closer scrutiny. The *titulus* was a placard attached to the cross that declared the crime of the one crucified. The Gospels vary a bit as to what Jesus' *titulus* read (cf. Matt. 27:37; Mark 15:26; Luke 23:38; John 19:19; John 19:20 says that the inscription was in Aramaic, Latin, and Greek). The oldest extrabiblical sources speak of a *tabula* carried by a criminal to the site of execution, possibly hung around the neck. Public crucifixion was practiced as a deterrent by the Romans, and though law did not require it, they did, in notable cases, display the reason for execution. Normally, a person would be executed in the nude as a further element of humiliation (this may have been true in Jesus' case), though perhaps due to Jewish sensibilities about nudity, a loin cloth may have been left on the victim. It is true that Roman law allowed executioners to keep the clothes of the victim (Ulpian, *Digest* 48.20).

What was written on the *titulus* did not necessarily indicate the judicial verdict (i.e., what Jesus was actually found guilty of), but rather, the public reason for execution. For example, the verdict against Jesus must have been some form of treason, but the *titulus* presented the reason: he claims to be "King of the Jews." There may also have been some mockery involved in the text of the *titulus* in Jesus' case. Mark's version reads "The King of the Jews" (Mark 15:26); Matthew has "This is Jesus, the King of the Jews" (Matt. 27:37); Luke has "This is the King of the Jews" (Luke 23:38); and John has "Jesus of Nazareth, the King of the Jews" (John 19:19).

The charge, then, would have read in the three languages that Jesus was *malka, rex, basileus* of the Jews, not that he was *mashiah, christus, christos*. This means that Jesus, so far as the Romans were concerned, was executed as a political criminal, not as a messianic pretender or prophet. As such, he was guilty of *lese maiestas*, or high treason—claiming to be a king in a realm where there could be no political king but Caesar. This also likely means that Jesus had to have done something beyond his normal teaching or healing to have been executed for such an offense. Claiming to be a messianic figure would have some political implications, and claiming to be a king would have some religious implications. The two were intertwined.

A strikingly parallel case from A.D. 62 during the Feast of Tabernacles has Jesus bar Hanan, a prophet of woe who predicted the fall of the

Illustration 5.5 Myrrh and frankincense—spices sometimes used in connection with burials.

temple, being scourged until his bones showed, and then released by the procurator Albinus (*J.W.* 6.300–305). Other details about the death of Jesus also have parallels. For instance, the offer of myrrhed wine (Mark 15:23) as a narcotic to lessen pain is known from Jewish sources where we are told that Jewish women from Jerusalem administered it to the victim prior to death (*b. Sanh.* 43a; cf. Tertullian, *On Fasting* 12). Also, the offering of *oxos*, or wine vinegar (Mark 15:36), while Jesus was on the cross was likely not an act of malice, as it was the usual thirst-quenching drug of the day, which day laborers often drank (cf. Ruth 2:14). In addition, there is some evidence that a dying person could make a sort of last will and testament or disposition from the cross, as we see happening in John 19:26–27 with Mary and the Beloved Disciple.[40] All this material contains the telltale signs that a historian looks for to discern whether a story has historical plausibility. The story of Jesus' demise has many such features.

40. See E. Stauffer, *Jesus and His Story*, trans. R. Winston and C. Winston (New York: Knopf, 1960), 225–30.

Chapter 6

The Rising of the Son and the Birth of the Church

A.D. 30–33

Resurrection Revisited

What happened after Jesus died and was buried? This is in some ways the most important historical question of all in regard to New Testament history. Any answer needs to explain the rise of the church after the demise, in a disgraceful manner, of Jesus. Then, too, sufficient explanation is needed for the psychological turnaround of Jesus' disciples, who went from being deniers, deserters, betrayers, and those who hid behind closed door to being bold witnesses about Jesus, prepared to die for their convictions about their master. Furthermore, there is a christological conundrum. If the beliefs of the earliest Christians about Jesus were not well grounded in what the historical Jesus suggested about himself in his words and deeds and relationships, why not? Were not the earliest Christians members of the inner coterie of the disciples (the Twelve), or women who were disciples even in Galilee, or members of Jesus' family? Were not these people in a position to know what sort of claims would or would not comport with Jesus' historical self-presentation? It is necessary, then, to have a thorough discussion of the matter of resurrection if we are to find a plausibility structure that properly links Jesus to the earliest Christians, and Jesus' self-presentation to their proclamation about him.

Dealing with the issue of Jesus' resurrection involves both the facts and the interpretation of the facts. For example, it is possible that something extraordinary really did happen to Jesus on Easter morning, but the disciples who claimed to have seen something misunderstood the import of the event. Or, it is possible that nothing actually happened to Jesus and his body, but the disciples thought it did. Or again, it is possible that something happened to Jesus and his body, and the disciples correctly deduced the significance of this event. We note at the outset that no one claimed to have seen the rising of Jesus; rather, they claimed to see the results of that event—the empty tomb, or the appearance of the risen Lord, or both.

We must remember that what a person is, what a person believes himself or herself to be, what a person claims to be, what is believed about a person by others, and what is claimed about a person by others can all be different things. For instance, it is perfectly possible that Jesus believed himself to be the Messiah but was mistaken. It is also possible that Jesus really was the Messiah but never made any claims, or at least any public ones, to that effect. Furthermore, it is possible that the disciples claimed some things about Jesus that were correct assessments but were not grounded in anything Jesus said or did in public. In other words, if the question is who was Jesus and was he raised from the dead, it is never adequate simply to deal with either just the facts or just the interpretation of facts. It is never adequate just to assess what was claimed about, or even by, Jesus historically. The question is, Are the claims true or not? Moreover, how do we get at the question of the veracity of the claims? How do we assess the trustworthiness of the witnesses? Pilate was right to ask, "What is truth?" We seldom even deal with these deeper philosophical issues, much less the ontological issues about Jesus. Let us consider for a moment the crucial question "What is resurrection?"

Illustration 6.1 Remains of the dead at Pompeii covered in ash.

As historically understood, early Jews meant by "resurrection" something that happens to a human body after death, not something that happened to witnesses who encountered the raised person later. We may be uncomfortable with this definition, and some may even attempt, in Bultmannian fashion, a "demythologizing" of such notions, but we need to be clear that that is a hermeneutical move out of tune with how the term was historically understood in early Judaism.

This fact becomes especially clear when we examine such phrases as *ek nekrōn egēgertai* in 1 Cor. 15:12. Paul says that the preaching of the early church was that Christ was raised out of the realm of the dead ones. The word *nekrōn* here does not merely mean death or the grave, but refers to dead persons or corpses. This is made perfectly clear in the latter half of the same verse, where Paul puts the matter a little differently, speaking of resurrection of the dead (*anastasis nekrōn*). In other words, resurrection involves the relationship with the persons Jesus left behind when he was raised, not the relationship he had subsequently with his followers. Jesus was raised from the dead; the other dead persons did not experience this new state of being on this occasion.

Let us consider this from another angle. Paul, writing in the early 50s, but relying on traditions that went back to the earliest Christians from whom he got his information, says that what was of prime importance was that Jesus died for the sins of humanity, was buried, on the third day was raised, and—subsequent to all this—was seen by an enormous number of people at different times and in different places (1 Cor. 15:3–8). Certainly, Paul knew that he had seen the risen Lord at a different time and in a different place than did those whom he listed earlier in the appearance list. Now, it is very difficult to doubt that for a Pharisaic Jewish Christian like Paul, the sequence "died . . . buried . . . was raised" implied not only a truly dead and buried Jesus, but also an empty tomb and a risen Lord. The Pharisaic understanding of resurrection was nothing if not materialistic, and more to the point, those who denied such a view of the afterlife were simply said to deny the resurrection, not to have an alternative interpretation of it (e.g., the Sadducees in Mark 12:18). Yet Paul did not make up this notion; he names it as one of the most crucial things he learned from his Christian forebears and passed on to his own Corinthian converts.

Notice carefully what Paul says about the matter of timing. "Resurrection" took place on a very specific occasion, on the third day after burial, but "appearances" took place on a variety of occasions to various people in various places. In short, resurrection is not even the same as appearances of the risen Lord, never mind subjective visions of the risen Lord. Strictly speaking, no one saw or claimed to see Jesus rise from the dead, the later apocryphal Gospels notwithstanding. What the disciples saw was the results of this event: an empty tomb, and then a risen Lord. The sequence "buried . . . raised" implied both of these for the earliest Christians.

Another factor comes into play in 1 Corinthians 15. Paul was a scholar of the Hebrew Scriptures. He knew well the stories of Elijah and Elisha, stories of people being brought back to life by the power of God through a prophet. Yet Paul persists in saying that Jesus is the first example, "the first fruits," of the general resurrection. Why? Surely, it is because Paul distinguished between the event of being raised from death and the state of resurrection life in a body immune to disease, decay, and death. Only Jesus had experienced the latter, and so only he, properly speaking, could be said to have experienced the resurrection, with its new mode of existence. The others simply had been brought back to their old forms of existence, not gone on to the resurrection state.

Scholars have always debated whether Paul places more emphasis on continuity or discontinuity between the earthly body and the resurrection body, but they have not disputed that in both cases the life spoken of is an embodied form of existence. Close inspection of 1 Corinthians 15 shows that Paul wished to affirm both continuity and discontinuity between the two states. On the one hand, it was the same person in an embodied state in both situations; on the other hand, the resurrection body was imperishable, glorious, powerful, and totally animated and empowered by the Holy Spirit.

Paul was perfectly aware that the bodies of persons who had been long dead were no longer extant. Jews in Paul's time often visited family tombs, and sometimes they placed remains in ossuaries when the flesh had totally decayed, a practice that early Christians also followed. I suggest that this knowledge of decomposition is why Paul does not really speak of or use the phrase "resurrection of the body," but rather, deals with the concept "resurrection in the body" or "the resurrection body." If the metaphor of seed and plant (1 Cor. 15:35–44) conveys any meaning, it is more discontinuity than continuity, though the latter is not denied. In other words, the earliest Christians were not so naive as to believe that it was *necessarily* this same body refurbished that appeared later. But in the case of Jesus, where there was a body to be raised, it provided the material starting point for a transformation that resulted in a live person in a resurrection body. In other words, it was much the same with Jesus as it would be for those who Paul says will be living and thus transformed when Christ returns (1 Cor. 15:50–55).

Thus, our earliest evidence about resurrection and about Jesus does not encourage us to think of early Christians merely having visions or spiritual experiences of Jesus after he died. Our earliest records make far stronger and, to the Greco-Roman world, more startling claims than that (cf. Acts 17:31–32).

Perhaps one example of an early critique of the vision theory is in order. It is telling that the male disciples, in assessing the women's testimony about the empty tomb, concluded that it was an idle tale (Luke 24:11), and that at most, one could speak of a vision of angels (Luke 24:23). Bearing in mind that the report that begins at 24:19 and continues through 24:24 is given by disciples leaving Jerusalem who also are speaking in the past tense about having had hope that Jesus was the one to redeem Israel, we can only conclude that no mere visions, or reports of visions of supernatural beings, or reports of empty tombs were going to change these discouraged disciples' mental state. Only an encounter with the risen Lord would do that. This narrative has a self-effacing quality that critiques the male leadership of the early church and at the same time shows that mere visions or claims of visions were not what changed the lives of the disciples.

This brings us to the Gospels themselves. Here, as in 1 Corinthians 15, the materiality of the risen Jesus is brought out in various ways. The important point is that we have several independent testimonies to this effect, and thus, by the criterion of multiple attestation, there is a high likelihood that this motif goes back to the earliest oral accounts about the encounters with Jesus after his death. For instance, in the Markan account, even if one insists that Mark 16:8 is the end of the record of this Gospel (a point I would dispute, for I think that the original ending is missing in Mark), we still find the words "He has been raised; he is not here. Look, there is the place they laid him" (Mark 16:6). This account associates resurrection with something that happened to Jesus' material body, such that it was no longer present in the tomb. Or again, at Matt. 28:9, we read that the women clasped Jesus' feet and worshiped him. Again, resurrection involves a material being who can be touched. Luke puts the matter even more strongly. Jesus says, "Look at my hands and my feet; see that it is I myself. Touch me and see; for a ghost does not have flesh and bones as you see that I have" (Luke 24:39). The same point arises in regard to the accounts in John 20. In short, all four Gospels stress the materiality of what resurrection entailed for Jesus. The question is, Why?

It is sometimes claimed that the stress on the physicality of the resurrection of Jesus is pure apologetics. I have always been mystified by this claim. If the Gospels were written in the last third of the first century, when the church not only already had a viable Gentile mission but also was already well on the way to being a largely Gentile community, why would a community trying to attract Gentiles make up a resurrection story, much less emphasize the material resurrection of Jesus? This notion was not a regular part of the pagan lexicon of the afterlife at all, as even a cursory study of the relevant passages in the Greek and Latin classics shows. Indeed, as Acts 17 suggests, pagans were more likely than not to ridicule such an idea. I can understand the apologetic theory if, and only if, the Gospels were directed largely to Pharisaic Jews or their sympathizers. I know of no scholar, however, who has argued such a case.

We are thus left with the fact that the earliest Christians, proponents of a missionary religion, nevertheless stressed a material notion of resurrection, including a material notion of what happened to their founder at Easter. I submit that the best explanation for this phenomenon is that something indeed must have happened to Jesus' body, and he must have been in personal and visible contact with his followers after Easter.

If it were merely the case that something happened to Jesus' body at Easter, it could easily have been assumed that he was taken up into heaven like an Elijah or an Enoch. As Gospel traditions such as John 20 make evident, an empty tomb by itself was subject to a variety of interpretations, including grave robbing. The empty tomb story by itself would not likely have generated the belief in a risen Jesus. There also must have been appearances of the risen Lord to various persons.

Perhaps here is the place to say something about the mass vision or hallucination theory. The suggestion that the disciples were victims of a hallucination, or their experience was the ultimate example of wish projections, or they merely saw visions has several problems. First, on all accounts the disciples doubted, deserted, and denied Jesus at the end, with the possible exception of some of his female followers and perhaps the Beloved Disciple (a Judean disciple). They were hardly in a psychological condition to produce a fantasy about a risen Jesus. Their hopes had been utterly shattered by his crucifixion less than three days before. Second, it will not do to suggest a mass hallucination, because all the traditions we have suggest that Jesus appeared at different times and places to different persons, last of all to Paul. I know of no basis for the notion of a contagious hallucination. Third, it is hardly believable that the earliest Christians would have made up the notion that Jesus appeared first to some women. We find no extended discussion in the Gospels of a personal appearance first to Peter or to James the brother of the Lord, but we do have stories about the appearance or appearances to the leading female disciples. Given the patriarchal world of the earliest Christians, it is not believable that a missionary-minded group would make up such a story. Nor is there any basis for the suggestion that these appearance stories were largely generated out of the Old Testament, which hardly mentions the notion of resurrection from the dead. In other words, the evidence as we have it strongly resists attempts to redefine "resurrection," if, that is, we wish to preserve any continuity with the historical Christian witness on this matter.

Whether we are comfortable with it or not, Christianity does indeed stand or fall on certain historical facts—not merely historical claims, but historical facts. Among these facts that are most crucial to Christian faith is that of Jesus' resurrection from the dead. The Christian faith is not mere faith in faith—ours or someone else's—but rather, a belief about the significance of certain historical events. Paul was quite right to say that if Christ was not raised, Christians are the most pitiable of all human beings. They are believers in a lie if Christ is not raised. If Christ is not raised, it also changes the way we may look at God.

Notice how very little the New Testament says about dying and going to heaven, and that when the matter is discussed, for instance in 2 Cor. 5:1–10, Paul makes clear that life without a body in heaven is by no means his own ultimate hope or expectation in regard to how he will spend eternity. Indeed, Paul refers to life in heaven without a body as nakedness, which to an early Jew was hardly the most desirable state of affairs. While it is true that under the influence of Greek thought medieval Christianity often substituted the discussion of immortality of the soul for the New Testament doctrine of resurrection of the body, this is not what the majority of New Testament passages are speaking of when they refer to the afterlife. Indeed, it could be said that in the New Testament life in heaven is seen only as an interim condition.[1] Resurrection is something that happens in the earthly realm to real persons who have died. It is not an event in some other realm (for instance, heaven) and is not immune to historical scrutiny and evaluation. It is interesting that J. Murphy-O'Connor has suggested in a recent book, *Paul: A Critical Life*,[2] that the whole reason that Christians believed in the everlasting existence of the human personality beyond death at all was precisely because they believed that there had to be a person there for God in Christ to raise up on the last day. How very different this is from what one usually hears today about dying and going to heaven.

Any position in which claims about Jesus or the resurrection are removed from the realm of historical reality and placed in a subjective realm of personal belief or some realm that is immune to human scrutiny does Jesus and the resurrection no service and no justice. It is a ploy of desperation to suggest that Christian faith would be little affected if Jesus was not actually raised from the dead in space and time. This is the approach of people who want to maintain their faith even at the expense of historical reality or the facts. A person who gives up on the historical foundations of the Christian faith has in fact given up on the possibility of any real continuity between his or her own faith and that of a Peter, Paul, James, John, Mary Magdalene, or Priscilla. Whatever may be said about such an approach today, its nonhistorical faith is not the faith that the early Christians lived and died for. They had an interest in historical reality, especially the historical reality of Jesus and his resurrection, because they believed their faith, for better or worse, was grounded in it.

Nor was this faith of theirs something conjured up generations or even years later than the time of Jesus' life. Paul was in direct contact with various eyewitnesses of the life, death, and resurrection appearances of Jesus. It is striking that in Paul's letters, nowhere does he have to argue with other major Christian leaders about his views on the res-

1. See B. Witherington III, *Jesus, Paul, and the End of the World: A Comparative Study in New Testament Eschatology* (Downers Grove, Ill.: InterVarsity, 1992).
2. Oxford: Clarendon, 1996.

Magic and Other "Superstitions"

To a large extent, the Romans took what could be called a common-sense approach to foreign religions. Each such religion was viewed as a *superstitio*, which, while viewed with suspicion, should be tolerated unless it became a public nuisance disrupting the life of a city or town. This sort of approach applied to Christianity, but also to the "popular" religion of the day that existed throughout the empire—magic. There were, of course, some places, like Ephesus, where this was more of a problem than elsewhere, but it would be wrong to ignore the very wide impact of magic in the Roman Empire, even in the Holy Land (e.g., consider the case of Simon Magus in Acts 8). The second-century A.D. text of a document written by the prefect of Egypt addresses this problem from an official standpoint. The prefect has heard many complain because they

> consider themselves to be beguiled by the means of divination. So that no risk should follow from their foolishness [I] state explicitly here to all to abstain from this misleading curiosity. Therefore neither through oracles,[1] nor by means of the procession of images or similar trickery, let anyone lay claim to have knowledge of the supernatural, or give himself out as an expert about the obscurity of future events. . . . But if anyone is discovered sticking to this undertaking, let him be sure that he will be handed over for capital punishment. The copy of this letter let each of you make provision to set up in public both in the nome capitals and in each village on a white board with lettering that is clear and easy to read. (*NewDocs* 1:48)

One of the things that made Roman emperors and officials most uneasy was prophecies and predictions, whether accomplished through the magical arts or in some more well-known fashion (e.g., consultation of the oracle at Delphi). It was all well and good for Josephus to predict that Vespasian would be emperor, but other predictions could go against the emperor or disrupt the status quo. Hence, the Egyptian prefect in this case tries to stifle such oracles and make sure they are not believed or heeded. The inscription bears witness to how very religious the ancients were, and how prone they were to give credence to oracles and claims about esoteric and supernaturally given knowledge about the present or future. In such an environment, a prophetic movement like the Jesus movement would have been viewed by Romans with considerable suspicion, not least because it involved predictions about a royal or messianic figure named Jesus.

1. That is, written documents ostensibly emanating in the presence of the deity.

urrection and the risen Lord. Indeed, he suggests in Romans 10, Philippians 2, and elsewhere that the common and earliest confession of all these first Christians was "Jesus is the risen Lord." Furthermore, he suggests in 1 Cor. 15:1–5 that the earliest Christians also held very particular beliefs about the end of Jesus' earthly life and the transition to his present heavenly state as risen and exalted Lord. Paul writes 1 Corinthians 15 within twenty-five years of Jesus' death, while various original eyewitnesses were still around to correct him. The silence of his Christian peers on this issue compared to their criticism of his views on the law (see Galatians) is deafening. It shows where the common ground truly lay.

Thus, it will not do to suggest that the passion and resurrection narratives in the Gospels are largely constructed from the Old Testament. The outline of and some vignettes from these narratives can already be found in Paul's letters in places like 1 Corinthians 11 and 15. It was the startling things that happened to Jesus at the close of his earthly career—his shocking crucifixion and then his equally astonishing resurrection—that caused the earliest Christians to race back to their sacred Scriptures to help them interpret the significance of these events. They did not first find these events in the Old Testament prophecies and then create new narratives out of the old prophecies. This is shown most clearly by the fact that many of the texts used to interpret the key final events of Jesus' life, in their original contexts in the Hebrew Scriptures, would not have suggested such things to a reader who had not heard of Jesus' life, death, and resurrection. I know of no evidence that non-Christian early Jews were looking for a resurrected messiah, and in fact, the evidence that they were looking for a crucified one is also very doubtful.

C. H. Dodd once proposed that the story of Mary Magdalene at the tomb was one of the most self-authenticating stories in all the Gospels. In his view, it had all the elements of the personal testimony of an eyewitness. First, knowing what the tradition said about Mary Magdalene's past (see Luke 8:2), it is hardly credible that the earliest Christians would have made up a story about Jesus appearing first to her. Second, it is not credible that a later Christian hagiographer would have had her suggest that perhaps Jesus' body had been stolen from the tomb. Third, it is not believable that later reverential Christians would have suggested that the first eyewitness mistook Jesus for a gardener. The portrait of Mary and her spiritual perceptiveness is hardly flattering here. Fourth, it is not believable that early Christians would have created the idea that Jesus commissioned Mary to proclaim the Easter message to the Twelve. On this last point we have the clear support of

1 Corinthians 15, where we see that the witness of women to the risen Lord, if not totally eliminated from the official witness list (they might be implied in the reference to Jesus' appearance to the five hundred), is clearly sublimated. It is not believable that early Christians made up stories about women, and particularly Mary Magdalene, as the first and foremost validating witnesses of the risen Lord. This is not credible especially because the writers of these Gospels, like other early Christians, were hoping for more converts. "These things are written in order that you might believe," says the Fourth Evangelist at the end of John 20. A more serious reckoning with these narratives, especially John 20, but also Mark 16, Matthew 28, and to a lesser degree Luke 24, is necessary if we really want to get at the heart of the earliest forms of the stories about that first Easter, and get to the bottom of what happened on that first Easter Sunday morning. I submit that these stories cannot be ignored. It is not convincing to appeal to Mark 16:8 as the original ending for such stories, as that is an argument from silence not substance. In fact, even if we stop at Mark 16:8, the empty tomb and resurrection are clearly proclaimed (cf. 16:7), and the "going before you into Galilee" motif suggests appearances not only in Jerusalem but also in Galilee.[3] Thus, a consistent witness to Jesus' resurrection runs throughout our sources, and this provides prima facie evidence that Jesus' resurrection and appearances provide the key historical middle terms between the life and death of Jesus and the birth of the early church.

The Rise of the Christian Movement

The tradition in various ways and forms suggests that Jesus had promised empowerment for his followers after he departed from this earth. The Holy Spirit is not subject to historical scrutiny directly, but one can talk about the fact that something was empowering these early Christians to witness, and to heal people as Jesus had done. Their historical deeds and words provide evidence that something had transformed and galvanized them.

Luke, as a historian, is the only Gospel writer who places emphasis on the ascension of Jesus into heaven. From a historical point of view, this recounting is meant to make clear that there was a period after which Jesus was not bodily present on earth. This brings closure to his historical career. This also means that from the Lukan point of view, the ap-

3. Portions of the last few paragraphs appear in another form in B. Witherington III, "Resurrection Redux," in *Will the Real Jesus Please Stand Up?* ed. P. Copan (Grand Rapids: Baker, 1998), 129–45.

pearance of the risen Jesus to Saul of Tarsus was from heaven. The Book of Acts is interesting and often puzzling, with much of historical interest for those curious about the earliest days of the Christian movement. It will be helpful to say something at this point about the type of history writing found in Acts and the nature of the book in general.

Illustration 6.2 Chronological Comparison: Paul's Letters and the Book of Acts[4]

Event	Letters	Acts
Paul the persecutor	Gal. 1:13–14	Acts 7:58; 8:1–3
Paul's call/conversion near Damascus	Gal. 1:15–17	Acts 9:1–22 (etc.)
To Arabia	Gal. 1:17b (cf. more visionary experience, 2 Cor. 12:1–10)	
Return to Damascus	Gal. 1:17c (3 years)	
Flight from Damascus	2 Cor. 11:32–33	Acts 9:23–25
First visit to Jerusalem as a Christian	Gal. 1:18–20	Acts 9:26–29
To the regions of Syria and Cilicia	Gal. 1:21–22	Acts 9:30 (Tarsus from Caesarea)
To Antioch	(see Gal. 2:11–14)	Acts 11:25–26
Antioch famine fund/second visit to Jerusalem	Gal. 2:1–10	Acts 11:29–30; 12:25

continued

4. This chart represents my own response to and adaptation of some of the elements in the charts found in T. H. Campbell, "Paul's Missionary Journeys as Reflected in His Letters," *JBL* 74 (1955): 80–87; and J. A. Fitzmyer, "The Pauline Letters and the Lucan Account of Paul's Missionary Journeys," *SBLSP* (1988): 82–89. My basic disagreement with them has to do with the placement and date of Galatians and the parts of the province of Galatia likely addressed in that letter. I suggest that it is probably not a coincidence that the earliest events in the chart are spoken of in Galatians almost without exception, and the next earliest in 1 Thessalonians. Paul's letters are topical, and they tend to refer to events of the recent past. All other things being equal, this points rather strongly to the early date of Galatians as well as of 1 Thessalonians. This chart provides solid evidence that we are likely on the right track in the analysis of Pauline chronology presented in this chapter.

Illustration 6.2—continued

Event	Letters	Acts
First missionary journey	Gal. 4:13–15	Acts 13–14
Return to Antioch	(see Gal. 2:11–14)	Acts 14:26–28
Judaizers to Antioch/Antioch incident	Gal. 2:11–14	Acts 15:1–2
Judaizers to Galatia	(cf. Gal. 1:6–9; 3:1; 4:17–5:12; 6:12–13)	
Paul writes Galatians (from Antioch)	Gal. 6:11	
Paul and Barnabas go up to Jerusalem/third visit		Acts 15:2–29
Return to Antioch/reading of decree		Acts 15:30–35
Second missionary journey with Silas, Timothy		Acts 15:36–18:18
Return to South Galatia (picking up Timothy), passing through Galatian Phrygia, Mysia, Troas (picking up Luke [Acts 16:10]), Philippi (Luke left here)	1 Thess. 2:2	
Amphipolis, Apollonia, Thessalonike	Phil. 4:15–16	Acts 17:1–9
Beroea		Acts 17:10–14
Athens (Timothy and Silas to Thessalonike)	1 Thess. 2:17–3:2	Acts 17:15–34
Paul in Corinth for eighteen months		Acts 18:1–18
Timothy arrives in Corinth, probably with Silas (see 1 Thess. 1:1)	1 Thess. 3:6	Acts 18:5
Paul, Timothy, Silas evangelize Corinth at length	2 Cor. 1:19	
1 and 2 Thessalonians written from Corinth by Paul and Silas		
Paul leaves from Cenchreae		Acts 18:18b
Paul leaves Priscilla and Aquila in Ephesus		Acts 18:19–21

Event	Letters	Acts
Apollos sent to Achaia by Ephesian church and Priscilla and Aquila		Acts 18:17
Paul to Caesarea Maritima		Acts 18:22a
And to Jerusalem?		Acts 18:22b
Return to Antioch for a while		Acts 18:22c
Return to Antioch by way of Jerusalem		Acts 22:22–23a
Third missionary journey		
Galatians instructed about collection	1 Cor. 16:1	
Travels through Galatia and Phrygia		Acts 18:23
Paul in Ephesus	1 Cor. 16:2–8	
Paul in Ephesus for two to three years		Acts 19:1–20:1, 31
Apollos also in Ephesus, urged to go to Corinth	1 Cor. 16:12	
Visit of Chloe, Stephanas, et al. to Paul in Ephesus bringing a letter	1 Cor. 1:11; 7:1; 16:17	
1 Corinthians written from Ephesus		
Timothy sent to Corinth	1 Cor. 4:17; 16:10–11	
Paul in debacle in Ephesus, dragged into theater by rioting mob	1 Cor. 15:32; 2 Cor. 1:8–11	Acts 19:21–41
Paul plans to visit Macedonia, Achaia, Jerusalem	1 Cor. 16:3–8; 2 Cor. 1:15–16	Acts 19:21
Paul's second, painful visit to Corinth	2 Cor. 13:2	
Titus sent to Corinth with letter written in tears	2 Cor. 2:13	
Ministry in Troas	2 Cor 2:12	
Ministry in Macedonia	2 Cor. 2:13; 7:5; 9:2–4	Acts 20:1b

continued

Illustration 6.2—continued

Event	Letters	Acts
Arrival of Titus in Macedonia	2 Cor. 7:6	
2 Corinthians written from Macedonia		
Titus sent ahead to Corinth with 2 Corinthians	2 Cor. 7:16–17	
Paul in Illyricum?	Rom. 15:19	
Paul in Achaia (third visit to Corinth)	Rom. 15:26; 16:1	
Three months in Achaia		Acts 20:2–3
Romans written from Corinth (plans to visit Rome and Spain)		
Paul begins return to Syria via Macedonia		Acts 20:3–6
And Troas		Acts 20:6–12
And Miletus		Acts 20:15–38
And Tyre, Ptolemais, Caesarea		Acts 21:7–14
And Jerusalem		Acts 21:15–23:30
Two-year imprisonment in Caesarea		Acts 23:31–26:32
Journey to Rome		Acts 27:1–28:14
Rome		Acts 28:15–31

A Closer Look: *Acts as a Historical Source*

The Book of Acts chronicles in selective fashion the period of A.D. 30–60/62. It does not seek to give an exhaustive account, nor is it writing about the macrohistory of the period. Rather, it covers what might be called the history of a rising movement—the movement of the followers of Jesus. Luke believes that this movement is a result of divinely initiated social change. Unfortunately, we have no similar chronicle for the last forty years of the first century. Thus, what we have in this book is only about the beginnings of early Christianity.

For those who are students of modern history, the Book of Acts will not look like that sort of history writing. For one thing, one-fourth of the book is given over to summaries of speeches (some 365 verses), most of which the author was not present to hear. One may also wonder why so many things are repeated in Acts when it is a selective narrative (e.g., the threefold telling of Saul's conversion). Why does the narrative stop where it does, offering chapters on Paul's trial but not relating the outcome of the trial in Rome? Why is it that Peter disappears from the narrative in Acts 15 and the rest of the account focuses on Paul? Indeed, some have called this book the Acts of Peter and Paul.

Hellenistic history writing in antiquity was often more like a newspaper today chronicling recent events (note Luke 1:1–4—"the things that have happened among us"). Ancient historiographers in the Greek tradition, when they were writing multiple volumes of a historical monograph, tried to keep the volumes the same size and proportion. Luke's Gospel chronicles 4 B.C.–A.D. 30, while Acts chronicles about the same amount of time. Notice, too, how the last 23 percent of Luke's Gospel presents the events leading to and including Jesus' trial and death, and the last 24 percent of Acts does the same for Paul. The theocentricity of Luke's historical account distinguishes his work from modern historiography but does not set it apart from many ancient ones. The synchronisms in both Luke and Acts (e.g., the reference to Claudius in Acts 18:2) are a clear indication that the author means this to be seen as some sort of historical work, as do the "we" passages, suggesting that the author traveled for a time with Paul. For a historian in the Greek tradition, as Luke was, personal observation and participation in some of the events recorded, as well as traveling and consulting witnesses, were essential aspects of his task. Luke follows the model of Ephorus in that he pursues a generally chronological account but does so on a region-by-region basis, so that there is some overlap. Note that Luke is not an ethnographer, unlike Josephus, who gives the history of one ethnic group, the Jews. Nor is Luke interested in giving equal ink to every year of his account. For example, Acts 1–9 only covers A.D. 30–33, while Luke appears to know very little about the period A.D. 37–46. This imbalance in part reflects the limitations of Luke's sources, and shows that he is not making up the story as he goes along.

According to Acts 1:13–14, after the disappearance of Jesus from the earth several weeks after his resurrection appearances, the Eleven returned to the upper room, where they were joined by some women and Jesus' mother and brothers. Here was the nucleus of the Christian movement at its inception. This was the group that would provide the continuity between the original followers of Jesus (the Jesus movement) and the fledgling Christian movement. It is noteworthy that this group involved members of Jesus' own family, since according to John 7:5, his brothers had not believed in him during his ministry, and according to Mark 3:21, 31–35, none of his family had really understood or followed him. Only Mary is depicted as having some sort of ongoing relationship to Jesus during his ministry and is said to have been there at the cross when he died (cf. John 2, 19).[5] We can only assume that the resurrection appearances of Jesus must have changed the views of Jesus' siblings, and in fact, this is what the reference to an appearance to James the brother of the Lord suggests (1 Cor. 15:7). If the list in 1 Corinthians 15 is in chronological order, then James was one of the last to receive such an appearance.

Thus, the early leadership of the church in Jerusalem was made up of some of Jesus' followers, such as Peter, and some of Jesus' family, such as James. An early letter of Paul tells us that in the early days, something of a triumvirate led the Jerusalem church, and they were called the "pillars" (of the new temple?)—Peter, John, and James the brother of Jesus (Gal. 2:9). But Gal. 2:12 makes clear, as does a text like Acts 15, that the administrative head of the Jerusalem church was James, while Peter seems to have been the chief proclaimer, or evangelist. It is interesting that in Acts 1:13–14, as elsewhere in Acts (2:46; 4:24; 5:12; 8:6; 15:25), a word that Luke uses in describing this early nucleus is "united."

One of the more interesting, and often overlooked, texts in Acts is 1:15–17. Here we learn about the restoration of the Twelve to their full number. Why was this done at all? The clue that helps provide something of an answer is found in the use of the term "lot" or "portion." This seems to echo Num. 18:21–26, which speaks about the "lot" apportioned to the Levites in their ministerial service to Israel. The Twelve were appointed to minister to Israel, and that ministry must go on, sharing the good news with Israel. Symbolically it was important to indicate that there was still a ministry to all of Israel, and it must be remembered that at this point, and apparently before Saul's conversion, there was no focus on a mission to Gentiles. The Pentecost event is about Jews and God-fearers being present in Jerusalem for the feast and hearing the good news, not about the evangelization or conversion

5. On all this, see B. Witherington III, *Women in the Earliest Churches*, SNTSMS 59 (Cambridge: Cambridge University Press, 1988).

of pure pagans. Galatians 2:7–9 states that Peter took the lead in evangelizing Jews (as Acts 2–4 also suggests), but that it was a joint effort of Peter, James, John and others in the Jerusalem church. The team that was recognized as appropriate to go to the Gentiles was Paul and Barnabas and their co-workers. This team did not exist prior to the conversion of Saul of Tarsus in A.D. 33–34. Thus, it is erroneous to see Acts 2 as being about a mission to the Gentiles—at least, in the main it is not about that. Rather, Acts 2 is about beginning to reach the Diaspora Jews through preaching. At this point we need to take a closer look at the speech material in Acts.

A **Closer** Look: *The Speeches in Acts*

The greatest problem for those who wish to argue that Luke is a good historian is the inordinate amount of speech material found in Acts, more than one finds in other ancient historians such as Herodotus, Tacitus, Josephus, Polybius, or Thucydides, though it is fair to say that the speeches in most of these other writers are longer than most of those found in Acts. We have the following speeches in Acts: (1) eight by Peter (Acts 1; 2; 3; 4; 5; 10; 11; 15); (2) two by James (Acts 15; 21); (3) one by Stephen (Acts 7); (4) nine by Paul (Acts 13; 14; 17; 20; 22; 23; 24; 26; 28); and (5) four by non-Christians (Acts 5:35–39; 19:35–40; 24:2–8; 25:14–21, 24–27).

Luke, as I have said, seems to have been following the Greek tradition of history writing, and it is important to note that that tradition did not have a convention of creating fictitious speeches for real historical figures in lieu of actually having data about what they said. Thucydides reminds us that it was hard to retain anything like a verbatim account (in an age before electronic recording devices), but the good historian offered summaries that presented the major points of a discourse (*History of the Peloponnesian War* 1.22.1–2).[6] A brief experiment shows that in Acts we are surely not dealing with more than summaries of speeches, except perhaps in the case of the Stephen speech: it takes only a minute or two to read out loud even the lengthier of these speeches. In actuality they must have been much longer (see Acts 2:40; 20:7–9).

6. See the discussion in B. Witherington III, *The Acts of the Apostles: A Socio-rhetorical Commentary* (Grand Rapids: Eerdmans, 1998), 46–49.

Where could Luke have gotten his information about these speeches? If Luke was a sometime companion of Paul, then of course he could have gotten the Pauline material from talking with Paul, and in a few instances from being present to hear the speeches. But Luke does not claim to have been present for most of the speeches, and so we must assume that he relied on sources—Paul for the Stephen speech, and members of the Jerusalem church for the other early speeches, which data he likely gathered near the end of the 50s while he was in the area during Paul's two-year incarceration in Caesarea Maritima. We must also admit that to some degree Luke has written up this speech material and edited it so that it reflects his own style of writing at various points, though there is enough non-Lukan vocabulary and the like to make clear that he is working with sources, whether oral or written.

When we consider the composition of the earliest group of "Christians" in Jerusalem, it is of course crucial to realize that it is anachronistic to call them by that name, a label that was first applied to a mixed group of Jewish and Gentile followers of Jesus in Antioch at a considerably later date (Acts 11:26). No, these Jerusalem followers of Jesus were all Jews, self-consciously so, and they believed that Jesus was the Messiah. They continued to meet in the temple, continued to keep a kosher table, and, so far as we can tell, continued to practice Judaism in a normal fashion. They did have additional beliefs and practices that other Jews, especially nonmessianic ones, would not have shared, but Acts and Galatians both show that before Paul and Peter wrestled with the issue of unclean foods and unclean persons and there was some sort of resolution of the matter in Jerusalem about A.D. 49–50, the Jerusalem group was a sect of Judaism. It is mistaken to think that before Paul there was any considerable focus on evangelizing Gentiles or any changing of Jewish practices of the followers of Jesus to accommodate a large influx of pagan converts.

What was the social composition of the Jerusalem church?[7] By and large it seems to have mirrored the social fabric of the city itself, which had large disparities between rich and poor, with artisans and craftsmen of various sorts in between. The considerable upper-class group in Jerusalem lived in the upper city (especially aristocrats of the priestly line), and degrees of wealth ranged from those who had moderate-size houses with various luxury items to those who had palatial mansions, probably

7. In the next few paragraphs I am basically following the evidence as presented by D. Fiensy, "The Composition of the Jerusalem Church," in *The Book of Acts in Its Palestinian Setting*, ed. R. Bauckham (Grand Rapids: Eerdmans, 1995), 213–36.

supported by consider-
able estates outside the
city. The evidence of Acts
itself indicates that there
were Jerusalem Christians
who owned land (Acts
4:34–5:1). In addition, there
is Mary, mother of John
Mark, who owned a house
large enough to serve as a
meeting place for the primitive church. She also had
at least one domestic servant, Rhoda (Acts 12:12–
17). An interesting question
is, How did the Galilean
fishermen among the
Twelve make their living
while residing in Jerusalem
during these years, or
rather, were they sup-
ported by others? Perhaps
their families were sending
them money from the fish-
ing business at home, but
we cannot be sure. Also,
widows and other destitute
people were among these
disciples, hence the need

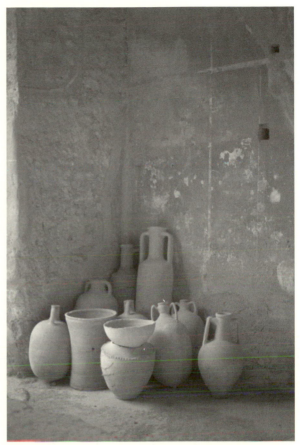

Illustration 6.3 First-century amphorae and water jugs.

for a dole for widows and for a sharing of things in common (cf. Acts 2:44–
45; 4:34; 6:1).

In terms of its cultural mix, the Jerusalem church again reflected
the composition of the city. The city was basically bilingual, with the
spoken languages being Aramaic and Greek. Most Palestinian Jews
spoke Aramaic. Nonetheless, many educated Jews also learned
Greek, especially for business purposes. We should not underestimate the influence of Hellenism on Jerusalem in the early first century. Coins had Greek inscriptions, Palestinian Jews had Greek
names, Jerusalem had a gymnasium and a hippodrome. Perhaps
most importantly, a large number of Greek-speaking Jews came to
Jerusalem to study, such as Saul of Tarsus, not to mention the presence of many Greek-speaking Jewish residents who had their own
Greek-speaking synagogue—the so-called synagogue of the Helle-

nists. Even training in Greco-Roman rhetoric for Jewish teachers in Jerusalem was available.

Even on a conservative estimate, probably 20 percent of the populace normally spoke Greek in public.[8] As M. Hengel suggests, we have to assume the existence of an independent, Jewish-Hellenistic culture in Jerusalem, and Jerusalem was the city in Judea where one was most likely to hear Greek spoken.[9] We must also reckon with the influx of pilgrims during the festival season, many or most of whom spoke Greek. Estimates range from 125,000 to 500,000 pilgrims coming to the major feasts, with the native population of the city being around 60,000. These "tourists" required lodging, and so there had to be pockets of Greek culture in various places in Jerusalem.

The most significant evidence supporting the preceding conclusions is the famous Theodotus inscription, found in the City of David.[10] Theodotus was a synagogue ruler who not only donated a structure for the study of Torah, but also equipped it to house pilgrims, and in addition built ritual baths. This synagogue may be the one referred to in Acts 6:9, called "the synagogue of the freedmen."[11] It is important to keep in mind that the Jerusalem Christians were divided into Hebrews and Hellenists, a language-based distinction, with the latter being Jews who spoke only Greek, and the former speaking Aramaic, with a few having some facility in Greek. But note that the leadership was not so divided at the outset; they only spoke Aramaic, and later recruited some Greek-speakers to help lead.

Something must be said at this point about the family of Jesus and their involvement in the earliest church in Jerusalem. An interesting note in the later, noncanonical *Gospel of Thomas* contains this saying: "The disciples said to Jesus, 'We know that you will depart from us. Who is to be our leader?' Jesus said to them, 'Wherever you are, you are to go to James the righteous, for whose sake heaven and earth came into being'" (*Gos. Thom.* 12). Certainly, James played an important and central role in the earliest days of Christianity, but the ongoing impact and roles of Jesus' family need to be mentioned as well. According to Eusebius and Epiphanius, the first two "bishops" of the church of Jerusalem were relatives of Jesus—James and Simeon. In addition, there is evidence that Jesus' brother Jude (the probable author of the letter by the same name) and his descendants, particularly his grand-

8. See Fiensy, "Jerusalem Church," 230–31.
9. M. Hengel, *The "Hellenization" of Judaea in the First Century after Christ*, trans. J. Bowden (Philadelphia: Trinity, 1989), 9–11.
10. See *CIJ* 2.1404.
11. See Fiensy, "Jerusalem Church," 233.

sons, played important roles in the Christian church in the Holy Land well into the last decade of the first century A.D.[12] It appears that some of them returned to Galilee and exercised Christian influence from that locale, perhaps particularly from Nazareth, but Luke knows little or nothing about this, and so later extrabiblical sources must be relied on to fill in the details. What little evidence we have does not encourage us to think that Galilean Christianity under the family of Jesus, and perhaps some of the Twelve, was any less Jewish than the Jerusalem-centered community.[13] With this cursory introduction to early Jewish Christianity in the Holy Land, we turn now to what is rightly said to be the birthday of the church—Pentecost, as it affected Jesus' followers and those with whom they shared the news.

The Coming of the Spirit

Any study of New Testament history must come to grips with what happened to Jesus' followers at the Feast of Pentecost in A.D. 30, and to those whom they influenced. The Feast of Pentecost was the name in the New Testament era for the Feast of Weeks. Originally, this feast was a harvest feast, but by Philo's time it had come to be associated with the giving of God's word, even in several languages. *Decalogue* 46 reads, "Then from the midst of the fire that streamed from heaven there sounded forth to their utter amazement a voice, for the flame became the articulate speech in the language familiar to the audience" (cf. *b. Šabb.* 88b). In other words, Pentecost was seen as something like what happened at the tower of Babel, only in reverse.

Acts 2:1–2 says that the event began in a house where the disciples were all together, presumably the same locale as mentioned in Acts 1:13–14 and with the same group of participants. This event seems to have begun at a place on Mount Zion called the Cenacle (which became a place for regular Christian worship thereafter)[14] and at some point to have migrated to the temple courts.

In Acts 2:2–4, Luke gropes for words to describe what happened. He says that the sound from heaven was *like* a violent wind. Similarly, the tongues were *like* fire. Divided tongues like fire appeared and rested upon each one present (cf. Luke 3:22). All in the room, not just the lead-

12. See the illuminating discussion by R. Bauckham, *Jude and the Relatives of Jesus in the Early Church* (Edinburgh: Clark, 1990), 45–133.

13. See ibid., 132.

14. See J. Murphy-O'Connor, "The Cenacle and Community: The Background of Acts 2:44–45," in *Scripture and Other Artifacts: Essays on the Bible and Archaeology in Honor of Philip J. King*, ed. M. Coogan et al. (Louisville: Westminster John Knox, 1994), 296–310.

ers, were filled with the Spirit and began to speak in "other tongues." Luke is not trying to give a detailed chronology of individual Christian experience, but rather, to describe the group-empowering event that led to the mission. The event is portrayed along the lines of Old Testament theophanies (Exod. 19:18; 1 Sam. 10:10–11; Ezek. 13:13).

The point of the filling was not conversion per se, but that these followers of Jesus were empowered to speak in "other languages." Now, when Acts 2:4 says "other languages," we need to ask, Other than what? Other than their normal language, or other than human language? What follows Acts 2:4 strongly suggests that the audience was hearing Jesus' followers speak in their own native languages. These speakers were Galileans, yet they were speaking in all sorts of languages other than their native Aramaic. The suggestion that they were drunk probably is prompted by their exuberant praising and exultation, not because they were speaking in angelic speech.

Acts 2:5 suggests that the audience includes Diaspora Jews who were dwelling in Jerusalem, perhaps those who had come to retire and be buried in the Holy City. It is not clear where Luke gets his list of countries indicating the native lands of those present (Acts 2:9–11), but in all of them dwelled some Diaspora Jews. He wishes to indicate that they represent all the countries of the known world, the world of the Mediterranean crescent. The main point is that the Spirit overcomes all barriers, even language barriers, to bring the witness about Christ to the uttermost parts of the earth. The list of nations seems somewhat odd, but makes sense if it is a list in which Jews were known to be present, which of course included Judea. The mention of Romans, both Jews and God-fearers, toward the end of the list in v. 10b is especially apt because it previews where the narrative in Acts and the witnessing are going to end up.

Acts 2:12 indicates that the crowd understood the words but did not grasp the meaning of the event, which leads the narrative into Peter's sermon explaining to them the phenomenon they had just witnessed (Acts 2:14–40). In his speech, Peter first refutes the charge of drunkenness, then accuses certain Jews of the death of Jesus, and finally appeals to the audience to repent and be baptized in Jesus' name for the forgiveness of sins, with the promise that if they do so, they will receive the Holy Spirit. This promised Spirit is said to be for these Jews and their descendants, but also for everyone, which would include Gentiles. Gentiles, however, are not the focus of this narrative. Like Jesus and John the Baptist before him, Peter is calling all Jews to repent and be baptized, indicating their need to start over with God. It is interesting how here, but actually all through Acts, there is a dramatization of what Paul says in Rom. 1:16: the good news of salvation is for all, first for the Jew, then also for the Gentile. This explains Paul's practice of going to the synagogues first as he evangelized city after city.

The Character of the Earliest Church

Luke has chosen to represent the character of the earliest church by a series of summaries followed by illustrative examples. The summary passages are found in Acts 2:42–47; 4:32–37; 5:12–16; and 8:1b–4. Basically, these summaries are about early Christian life in Jerusalem. In the first summary the Christians are said to devote themselves to the teaching of the apostles, sharing of things in common, breaking of bread, and prayer. Probably, these last two elements explain what the author means by *koinōnia*, or the sharing of things in common.[15] This summary makes clear that the earliest days saw no radical departure from Jewish practices, though it is possible that the Christians followed the Essene sect's practices in regard to common property. The situation seems to have been that they were making sure that no one was in need. Property was sold and turned into coin when there was need for funds to feed especially the poor in the community. It is not clear whether the breaking of bread alludes simply to a common meal or whether it refers to the Lord's Supper, but the latter was included in the context of the former in the Corinthian church in the 50s (cf. 1 Corinthians 11).

There were, of course, both inward and outward components to the life of the earliest church, and the outward component was its witness about the risen Jesus. This is what created the growth of the church, but is also what caused or escalated the conflict with non-Christian Jews.

The early speeches of Peter in Acts are filled with quotations and allusions to the Hebrew Scriptures, used apologetically to demonstrate that what happened to and with Jesus was part of God's divine plan all along. They show that the earliest Christians spent considerable time in the Scriptures seeking to understand what had happened to Jesus on that basis. These early speeches try to make the gospel understandable and plausible for a devout Jewish audience. Primitive christological titles like the Righteous One and phrases like "God has made him both Lord and Christ" (Acts 2:36) likely show that Luke is dealing with early

---

15. The word *koinōnia* is probably not best translated "fellowship," because it has a more active sense of participating in common with someone in something, the result of which could be fellowship.

Jewish Christian material, and not simply passing on what he has heard of the gospel from Paul. Also, these early speeches strongly stress the continuity between the historical Jesus of Nazareth and the risen and exalted Christ. Some stress is put on Jewish involvement in the death of Jesus, but the ignorance motif also shows that this is not seen as an unforgivable sin. To the contrary, it is seen as an opportunity to acknowledge mistakes, repent, and receive newness of life.

Acts 3:1–10 typifies the emphasis on the mighty healing deeds of Peter and others. The miracle referred to in Acts 3 has close parallels in its form of telling to the miracle of Jesus recorded in Luke 5:17–26. As a historian, Luke makes a conscious attempt to bring out parallels between the actions of Jesus and of his followers. This demonstrates that God works out salvation history in an orderly fashion.

According to Acts 4, the temple hierarchy and their entourage took exception to the teaching and deeds of the apostles and put them in jail. They then were taken before the high priest and asked by what authority or power they did these things. Note that the reaction of the authorities is amazement at the bravery and knowledge of these unlettered men (i.e., without formal training in the law).[16] The point seems in part to be that Peter and John are cut from the same cloth as Jesus, and have the same dramatic powers of speech and deed. In Acts 4–8 the tensions continue to mount as the opposition rises to the growing Christian movement in Jerusalem, tensions that reach an ugly climax in the martyrdom of Stephen.

Luke has been accused of gilding the lily by presenting utopian summary statements about the life of the early church or by ignoring things like the circumcision crisis that Paul makes so much of in Galatians and elsewhere. There is some truth to these observations, but on the other hand, Luke is presenting a selective account to put the best foot forward of the early church. Yet he does record problems, like the Ananias and Sapphira debacle, and the trouble over the dole for the Greek-speaking Jewish Christian widows (Acts 5–6).

The choosing of the Seven (Acts 6:1–6) is an important event in the life of the early church, not least because it appears that through some of these men came the first mission work outside of Jerusalem and its environs. Acts 6:1 uses an important term, "Hellenists" (cf. 9:29; 11:20). The probable meaning of the term is one who speaks only Greek, or at least who has Greek as the main spoken language. In Acts 6 and 9 it refers to Greek-speaking (Diaspora) Jews who lived in and around Jerusalem. Luke does not use the term to refer to ideological differences

---

16. The term in question, *agrammatoi*, sometimes means "illiterate," but probably not in this case.

with others, such as Aramaic-speaking persons.[17] Nor is there any evidence that the Greek-speaking Jewish Christians were especially singled out for persecution, or that the Aramaic-speaking ones were subject to separate persecution.

A plausible model of what early Jewish Christianity looked like involves converts who ranged from extreme Judaizers to rather antinomian teachers, but that Peter, James, John, Philip, and even Paul held views somewhere between these two radical extremes. James would have been closer in various ways to the Judaizers' views on some issues, including some forms of zeal for the law (Acts 21:17–26), while Paul would be closer to some Gentile Christians and perhaps also some Greek-speaking Jewish Christians on such matters. As we will see, however, Acts 15 suggests that on the fundamental matter of salvation in Christ including Gentiles, there was no major disagreement between James and Paul, which is what Paul himself suggests in Gal. 2:7–9.

In Acts 6:1–7, Luke is making a distinction between the Twelve and the Seven, and the fact that there is a Philip in each group should not be allowed to confuse the issue. These were two different Philips. Notice that the list of the seven includes only men with Greek names. This suggests that only Greek-speaking Christians were assigned to administer the aid to the Greek-speaking widows. Luke knows something about the first two listed, Stephen and Philip, but little or nothing about the rest. Nicolaus is listed as a proselyte from Antioch, which seems to suggest that the other six were born Jews, and may have been from Jerusalem, or at least longtime residents there. What we are being told about here is the diversity of the church almost from its very inception. Though we are told that the Seven are commissioned to wait on tables, so to speak, so as to alleviate the Twelve from such a responsibility, nonetheless, Stephen and Philip serve as the bridge to the next stage of witness and mission—the outreach to Samaria and beyond.

We now take up the story of the demise of Stephen in Acts 6:8–8:3. From a historical point of view, Luke does not see this as an isolated incident, but rather, as the trigger for a series of important events in early Christian history—specifically, the great or general persecution that caused all but the apostles to be scattered throughout Judea and Samaria (Acts 8:1), and the rise of Saul as the lead figure in these persecutions. In essence, the Word of God was driven out of Jerusalem and into Samaria, and the man who was soon to have a major change of life felt driven to pursue these Christians and bring some back for trial in Jerusalem. Thus, we must consider the case of Stephen for a moment.

17. See the discussion in Witherington, *Acts*, 240–47.

Acts 6:8–10 describes Stephen as a wonder worker and a great orator. The venue in which he chose to work was the synagogue of the
Freedmen, which had as some of its members Jews from Asia Minor,
Egypt, and elsewhere in Africa. Stephen, accused of speaking against
the law and against the temple, is brought before the Sanhedrin, like
Peter and John before him. Before we examine his speech, we must
take a closer look at the scholarly debate about synagogues.

A **Closer** Look: *Synagogues in the Early First Century A.D.?*

Scholars have heavily debated the nature of synagogues in the early
first century A.D. Were there purpose-built structures called synagogues,
or were there just meetings in multipurpose buildings and homes? Josephus speaks of a synagogue building in Caesarea Maritima and mentions
another in Syrian Antioch (*J.W.* 2.285–291; 7.43–44). Philo on at least
one occasion also mentions a synagogue building (*Good Person* 81).

The term *synagōgē* is used to refer to a structure being repaired in Be-
renice in Africa in A.D. 56 (SEG 17.16). In addition, the archaeological evidence from Gamala seems compelling proof of a synagogue building in
this locale, complete with adjacent ritual bath and the presence of Jewish

Illustration 6.4 Mosaic floor with the signs of the zodiac from the synagogue at Dura-Europas.

© Editrice Pontificio Istituto Biblico, Roma

iconography in a rosette pattern on the synagogue lintel. Finally, the Theodotus inscription (*CIJ* 2.1404) seems to date from before A.D. 70, since
it was found with a cache of Herodian lamps. Thus, the evidence in Acts
for the existence of purpose-built buildings called synagogues supports
this evidence; or, to put it the other way around, the historical veracity of
Acts on this point is vindicated by this extrabiblical evidence.

Acts 6:11–14 indicates that false witnesses were suborned to say that
Stephen was speaking against the holy place and the law. Stephen's address, the longest speech in Acts, does not seem to address these
charges, or if so, only briefly in regard to the holy place. The speech
should be seen not as law critical or as temple critical, but rather, as
people critical—a radical critique of God's people who down through
the ages have repeatedly rejected God's prophets and messengers. In
essence, this speech brings to a climax the witness to the Jerusalem
Jews, a witness that is rejected, leading to a stoning and to the scatter-
ing of the church.

Acts 8:1–3 allows a plausible conjecture that Saul of Tarsus was the
ringleader of the persecution ("going from house to house"), and that
he had been part of the group that debated Stephen in the synagogue
of the Freedmen (after all, he was from Cilicia [cf. Acts 6:9]). Certainly,
he is the leader of the group heading to Damascus to take captive Jewish Christians who were there. To his remarkable story we now turn, as
we go Saul searching.

Chapter 7

The Roads from Jerusalem

A.D. 33–37

The Itinerancy of Philip

The persecution of the Jerusalem Christians in a sense forced the issue of evangelizing others in the Holy Land. What is interesting about Acts 8:4–40 is that it basically portrays not a mission to other Jews in Galilee but to those on the fringes of Judaism—Samaritans, and proselytes from other countries, such as the Ethiopian eunuch. In both cases the people involved are not completely pagan, and so the efforts of Philip should not be seen as the beginning of a direct mission to Gentiles. Even if Samaritans are thought of as the lost sheep of Israel, the issue would be that it was Judaism they had wandered away from. Nor does the Samaritan mission lead to the Gentile mission. These stories involve a period in the mid-to-late 30s, before the rise of a real Gentile mission.

If we accept that the "we" passages reflect the actual travel of Luke, Acts 21:8–10 tells us that Luke had occasion to encounter Philip when Paul visited Philip. Luke does not see Samaritans as being like Judean Jews or like Galileans (see Luke 17:16–18). They are seen as ethnically different and religiously heterodox. However, Luke clearly has a heart for these people and their salvation and does not wish to stereotype them (see Luke 10:25–37).

The mission work of Philip in Samaria is recounted in Acts 8:4–13, and it is followed by the story of how Peter came behind him to confirm and supplement his work (Acts 8:14–25). Philip is portrayed as proclaiming the good news of God's dominion, which is to say that he is passing on the message of Jesus and of the early church. But who were the Samaritans whom Philip was dealing with?

A **Closer** Look: *The Samaritans*

When the Assyrians invaded and conquered Israel in 722–721 B.C., much changed in the land. Certainly, some mixing of cultures occurred, and it appears in the main that only a minority of Israelite society were taken off into exile after this invasion (27,290, according to the inscriptions of Sargon II [see *ANET* 284–285]). To judge from what we can tell about Samaritan beliefs, they did not seem to reflect a syncretism with Assyrian religion. We should recognize, however, that the Samaritans came to be viewed by Judean Jews as, at best, half-breeds who had significantly intermarried with the pagan Assyrians. In fact, Josephus goes so far as to say that the Samaritans were descendants of colonists settled in the region by the Assyrians (cf. *Ant.* 11.297–347; 2 Kings 17). While this may have been true in a minority of cases, it does not on the whole seem to reflect their actual social condition.

We do know that after the return of Judean Jews from Babylonian exile, something of a rivalry and antipathy developed between the Jews in Samaria and the Jews in Judea, each claiming their holy mountain to be the proper location for the temple (Mount Gerizim in Samaria, Mount Zion in Judea). We learn in Neh. 4:1–2 of opposition from Sanballat (a governor appointed by Darius) and the army of Samaria to the rebuilding of the temple and the walls in Jerusalem (cf. Ezra 4). Probably, the Samaritans did build their own temple sometime around 388

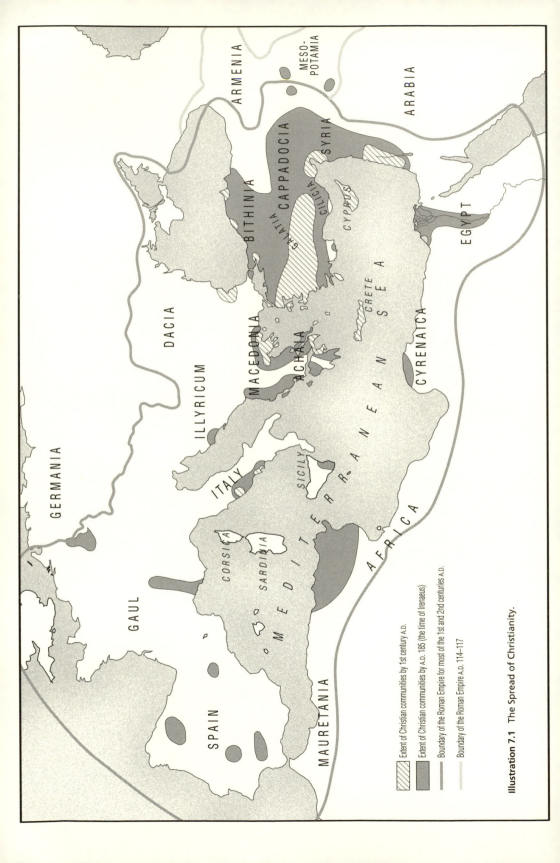

Illustration 7.1 The Spread of Christianity.

Extent of Christian communities by 1st century A.D.

Extent of Christian communities by A.D. 185 (the time of Irenaeus)

Boundary of the Roman Empire for most of the 1st and 2nd centuries A.D.

Boundary of the Roman Empire A.D. 114–117

© Editrice Pontificio Istituto Biblico, Roma

Illustration 7.2   Modern Samaritan holy men with a Samaritan Pentateuch scroll.

B.C., and it was destroyed in 128 B.C. by John Hyrcanus (*Ant*. 13.254–256). Needless to say, this only intensified the animus between Samaritans and Jews.

By the time of the New Testament era, not mere antipathy, but actual racial hatred, characterizes the relationship between Jews and Samaritans. This, of course, makes Jesus' relationships with and teachings about Samaritans all the more remarkable, because probably most Jews did not think there was such a thing as a "Good Samaritan." That phrase would have been an oxymoron to them. Interestingly, Josephus tells us that Samaritans sometimes claimed to be related to Jews when the latter were prospering, but when they were not they disowned them and said they were of a separate race (*Ant*. 9.291).

Something must be said here about Samaritan beliefs. The Samaritan messianic hopes centered on Deut. 18:18, not least because they accepted only the Pentateuch as their sacred Scriptures. They spoke of a *Taheb*, a Restorer, a prophet like Moses, who would come and restore true worship on Mount Gerizim. Thus, it is natural that Samaritans would listen eagerly to a preacher who, like Philip, came proclaiming a messianic figure.[1]

1. The Samaritans, who number a few hundred today, are the only Jewish sect that still offers sacrifices. They celebrate their own Passover on Mount Gerizim, complete with sacrifice, even today.

Philip came performing miracles and proclaiming the good news, and he drew the attention of a man named Simon, later known as Simon Magus. Luke says that Simon practiced magic and claimed to be someone great. Luke's portrait differs from the later, second- and third-century portrayals of Simon as an early broker of esoteric gnostic wisdom. The Samaritans, according to Acts 8:10, listened eagerly to Simon, even saying of him, "This man is the power of God called Great." They listened, according to Luke, because Simon had long amazed them with his magic act. Verse 10 should be contrasted with v. 6, which tells about the reaction to Philip. Close inspection of both texts suggests that we should not see the response in v. 6 as amounting to faith or conversion. Rather, the Samaritans were paying attention in a favorable way. The contrast between the responses to Simon and to Philip comes in v. 12, where the crowd believes Philip, who was preaching about the kingdom and the name of Jesus. After this, they were baptized. Even Simon is said to believe and be baptized (v. 13), but *what* he believed is not made clear. It would appear that he believed that Philip had power and could perform miracles.

The apostles in Jerusalem hear that Samaria has accepted God's word. Peter and John are sent to Samaria to check out the reports—not surprisingly, in light of the usual Jewish opinion of Samaritans. John, son of Zebedee, is really mentioned by Luke only in tandem with Peter (cf., however, Acts 12:2), and it seems clear that Luke knows little about him and his activities. Notice, however, that this same John in Luke 9:54 wishes to call down fire from heaven on a Samaritan village. Peter and John do not invalidate the work of Philip by starting over with the Samaritans; rather, they press forward by praying for the Spirit to fall on them and then laying hands on them.

Here, as elsewhere in Acts, having the Spirit is the sine qua non of being a Christian. Peter and John are able to confirm the work of Philip by the evidence of the Spirit being present among them. Philip is the initiator of the work of salvation in Samaria, and Peter and John are its completers. Luke apparently thought that the Samaritans were not fully Christians until they received the Spirit. Indeed, he believed this about all Christians. There was no such thing as a Christian without the Spirit (cf. Acts 19:1–7, where the disciples of John must start over from scratch and must receive the Spirit to be truly Christian). As for Simon, the evidence suggests that he was never a Christian; he simply recognized that Philip had real power. It seems that from Luke's viewpoint, the Spirit had been withheld in this unique case until the apostles from Jerusalem could authenticate the conversions of Samaritans.

In regard to initiation and conversion, Luke stresses that God is in control. The Spirit comes sometimes with the apostles present, sometimes without (cf. Acts 9:17); sometimes the Spirit comes with the laying on of hands, sometimes without (cf. Acts 2:38); sometimes the Spirit comes near the time of water baptism, sometimes before, sometimes after. In Acts 8:15–17, water baptism precedes the reception of the Spirit, whereas in Acts 10:44–48 it is the converse; and in the case of the Ethiopian eunuch initiation by water and the reception of the Spirit appear to happen virtually simultaneously (Acts 8:35–39). One can only conclude from this that Luke did not see one normative pattern by which initiation and conversion did or needed to happen.

The story of Philip's encounter with the eunuch (Acts 8:26–40) is important on several counts. Luke is following the pattern of the earlier Greek historian, Ephorus, in presenting his evidence by ethnic or geographical group. In the mythological geography of the ancient world, Ethiopia was frequently identified with the ends of the earth (cf. Herodotus *Hist*. 3.25.114; Strabo, *Geography* 1.1.6; 1.2.24; Philostratus, *Life of Apollonius* 6.1). This story may be a foreshadowing of the fulfillment of Jesus' original mandate of universal witnessing (Acts 1:8). One of the major themes of the chronicle in Acts is the universalization of the gospel: it is for all peoples, even those at the ends of the earth (cf. Isa. 52:10).

This story could be seen as being about reaching those beyond the bounds of the Roman Empire. The stress in the eunuch story is on God leading Philip to the eunuch and providentially arranging for the eunuch to be reading a text of Isaiah conducive to evangelism about Jesus—Isaiah 53. The emphasis on this man being an Ethiopian makes it very likely that he was black. Indeed, Ethiopians in antiquity were proverbially thought to be the darkest people on earth. We should stress that there is no evidence from antiquity of widespread prejudice against a particular group of people simply because of their skin color, or a combination of their skin color and distinctive ethnic features (e.g., hair, facial features). On that score, Luke lived in a different world from ours.

Luke in general shows considerable interest in the conversion of people of rather high social status (cf., e.g., Acts 10), and this story is an example of that emphasis. The Ethiopian is the treasurer of Queen Candace, and is castrated. Because of the latter fact, this man would be permanently on the fringes of Judaism because Deut. 23:1 was usually interpreted to exclude eunuchs from God's assembly, though Isa. 56:3–5 promised them full participation in the future. This story may be seen by Luke as a fulfillment of the Isaiah text, and it suggests that he

Alexandria

Alexandria was a city like no other in Egypt. It was, in fact, in many respects the blueprint for the structural renovations made by Augustus and other emperors in Rome. Unlike Athens, Alexandria reached its apogee during the Roman era. It was the crown jewel of the construction projects of Alexander the Great and had not lost any of its luster by the time of the Roman Empire. The Romans, of course, felt it necessary to make their own contribution, building a new suburb of the city called Nicopolis.

Alexandria had been the administrative capital of Egypt under the Ptolemies and remained so during the Roman era. Like other Romanized cities during the empire, it offered copious public entertainment made available to the masses. It was also renowned for its library and university. At one point, Marc Antony, as a gift to Cleopatra, gave the entire royal library of Pergamum to the library at Alexandria. When Athens was sacked by the Roman tyrant Sulla, many philosophers fled to Alexandria, and the city became a major center for philosophical reflection of the Platonic sort. In the Julio-Claudian period, it is probable that Philo, the Jewish writer, was the foremost philosopher from Alexandria. Alexandria was also the hub of medical science and various sorts of scientific endeavors. The famous Galen studied medicine in Alexandria.

Yet the city was not totally refined or cultured; it was also known for its mob. The prefect Petronius was almost stoned to death by this mob, and many Jews had fallen afoul of these thugs on various occasions. The city was a dangerous place, and when Galerius and his wife went to Egypt, she determined never to set foot outside the official residence, and would not admit any of the natives into the residence. The city had an old history of anti-Roman sentiments dating back to the battle of Actium, but after Augustus this tended to be forgotten, and the city became an object of much benefaction.

At the root of many of the disturbances in Alexandria were the major clashes between Jews and Greeks in the city. Alexandria had a very large Jewish population, perhaps the second-largest population of Jews in the empire after Jerusalem. These troubles boiled over in the 30s and 40s, leading to Philo having to go with an embassy before Caligula to try to sort things out. The Greeks in the city were organized in cult groups and guilds, and they sought to put statues of the emperor in the synagogues. Jewish homes were looted and their residents were dragged out, tortured, and killed. Some were burned alive. The animosity between these two groups was acutely palpable. Claudius finally settled the matter by ordering the Jews to stay away from Greek cultural events and to quit trying to Hellenize or to make converts to Judaism; at the same time, Greeks were to leave the Jews alone. This bad blood continued to boil from time to time until the great revolt of A.D. 116–17, when the large Jewish community in Alexandria was virtually wiped out by a pogrom.

The main reason for the flow of patronage to Alexandria was its political and economic significance. Egypt was indeed the breadbasket of the empire, and it was crucial for the emperors to be able to count on the flow of grain to Rome, so to keep its own mob, as well as other citizens, in line. But there were other important things that Alexandria provided to the empire. The city was by far the largest supplier of papyrus to the empire, and also produced glassware that was much in demand, as well as works of art and mosaics. Alexandria was the major exporter of various perfumes and Middle Eastern spices as well, not to mention jewelry of all sorts. The city had considerable wealth as a result of all of these exports. Thus, we may conclude that during the New Testament era, Alexandria was one of the most valuable but also one of the most volatile cities in the empire, one of the most cultured but also one of the most dangerous cities in the empire.

wished to show that Christianity had fewer strictures than Judaism about such matters. The eunuch responds eagerly to Philip's exegesis and is baptized; he then goes joyfully on his way. With the stories in Acts 8, the Gentile mission cannot be far off, but first must come the conversion of the premiere Gentile missionary, a very unlikely candidate for such work named Saul of Tarsus.

Saul's "About-Face"

It has been said often that Saul of Tarsus, after Jesus, is the most important figure to consider when trying to understand the rise of early Christianity. Indeed, some would say that he is even more important than Jesus, since it is sometimes thought that the man from Tarsus was largely responsible for turning a Jewish sect into a world religion through incessant evangelism and missionary work. Therefore, we must consider the historical figure of Saul very closely.

Saul was, of course, a Jew, but the question is, What sort of Jew? Scholars have long debated whether he should be seen primarily as a Hellenized Diaspora Jew or a Palestinian Pharisaic Jew. In a sense, that way of putting the matter is a false dichotomy because, as we have seen earlier in this study, the Holy Land had long since been Hellenized before Saul ever came to Jerusalem. The search for Paul the Jew must begin with his own statements about his Jewishness, particularly 2 Cor. 11:22 and Phil. 3:4–6. In the first text, note that

Paul the follower of Jesus still says "So am I" to others' claims about being a Hebrew, an Israelite, a descendant of Abraham. Clearly, he had not renounced his whole Jewish heritage once he became a follower of Jesus. The term "Hebrew" refers to language and perhaps also to essential ethnic identity. The term "Israelite" has to do with religious allegiance. The reference to the descendants of Abraham indicates ancestry. The implication is that Paul's main identity formation took place in the Holy Land; otherwise, he would not be claiming Hebrew (and/or Aramaic) as an essential identity marker. We know, of course, that Paul related well in writing Greek, and presumably in speaking Greek too, but 2 Cor. 11:22 indicates his essential bilingualism.

The second text, Phil. 3:4–6, reveals a bit more. Paul, in both these passages, engages in a sort of mock boasting, done somewhat tongue in cheek, with the aim of shaming others who take such boasting all too seriously. In other words, both passages are irony laden. Here, Paul claims to have been circumcised on the proper day required in the Scripture. He is, in addition, a Hebrew among Hebrews, speaking the native tongue (see Acts 26:14). Furthermore, he is of the tribe of Benjamin (and named after its most famous progenitor, King Saul). The tribe of Benjamin was noted for being loyal to Judah. Finally, in regard to the righteousness one could gain through obedience to the law, Paul claims to be blameless or faultless. This is not to be confused with a claim to being perfect; the point is that he could not have been charged with any violations of the Mosaic law. We also know, of course, that Paul had been a Pharisee—indeed, a most zealous one. But perhaps here is the place to pause and to deal with the issue of whether Paul spent his formative years in Tarsus or in Jerusalem.

Illustration 7.3   Pauline Chronology[2]

A.D. 5 (+ or - three or four years)	Saul is born in Tarsus in Cilicia of conservative Jewish parents who have Roman citizenship.
A.D. 10 (or a little earlier)	Saul's family moves to Jerusalem while Saul is still quite young.

2. A full discussion of Pauline chronology can be found in B. Witherington III, *The Paul Quest: The Renewed Search for the Jew of Tarsus* (Downers Grove, Ill.: InterVarsity, 1998), 304–31.

A.D. 15–20	Saul begins his studies in Jerusalem with R. Gamaliel, grandson of R. Gamaliel the Elder.
A.D. 30	Jesus is crucified by Pontius Pilate.
A.D. 31–33 (or 34)	Saul persecutes the church in Jerusalem.
A.D. 34 (or 35)	Saul is converted on the road to Damascus and travels on to Damascus.
A.D. 34–37	Paul is in Arabia and Damascus.
A.D. 37	Paul's first visit as a Christian to Jerusalem.
A.D. 37–46	Paul preaches in his home region: results unknown, but possibly a time of great persecution (see 2 Cor. 11:23–29).
A.D. 41–42	Paul's visionary experience and thorn in the flesh (2 Cor. 12:1–10).
A.D. 47 (approx.)	Barnabas finds Paul in Tarsus and brings him to Antioch.
A.D. 48	Paul makes his second visit to Jerusalem (Acts 11=Galatians 2), the famine visit with Barnabas (and Titus). There is a private agreement between Paul and the "pillars" of the Jerusalem church that he and Barnabas would go to the Gentiles, while Peter and others would go to the Jews. Circumcision is not imposed on Titus, and issues of food and fellowship apparently are not resolved at this meeting.
A.D. 48	Paul's first missionary journey, with Barnabas, including a visit to south Galatia, follows his second visit to Jerusalem (Acts 13–14).
A.D. 49	Claudius expels Jews from Rome, leading to the arrival of Priscilla and Aquila in Corinth. Paul and Barnabas return to Antioch. The "men who came from James" visit the church there and the Antioch incident transpires (Gal. 2:11–14).
A.D. 49	Later the same year, Paul discovers that the circumcision party has visited his congregations in Asia Minor and has bewitched some of his converts there. Paul writes Galatians in response to this crisis shortly before going up to Jerusalem for the third time.

continued

Illustration 7.3—continued

A.D. 49 or 50	The apostolic council is held in Jerusalem (Acts 15). Public agreement is reached that Gentile converts do not need to be circumcised but do need to avoid the basic actions that offend Jews, namely, idolatry and immorality, and in particular the sort that transpired in pagan temples. They are not to attend idol feasts in idol temples.
A.D. 50–52	The second missionary journey takes Paul and Silas not only to Asia Minor, but also to Macedonia and Greece. This period of Paul's life is recorded in Acts 15:40–18:23. During this period of time Paul picks up Timothy in Lystra (Acts 16:1) and Luke in Troas (16:10–12). Paul stays in Corinth. He writes 1 and 2 Thessalonians.
A.D. 51	The Gallio incident transpires (Acts 18:12–18).
A.D. 52	Paul returns to Antioch after a brief visit to Jerusalem (Acts 18:22).
A.D. 53	Paul sets out from Antioch to cross Asia Minor for the last time prior to his imprisonment in Rome (Acts 18:23).
A.D. 53–56	Paul is in Ephesus. From there Paul writes his first (currently extant) letter to the Corinthians sometime around A.D. 53 or 54.
A.D. 55	In the spring, Paul makes the so-called painful visit to Corinth from Ephesus (2 Cor. 2:1).
A.D. 55 (or possibly 56)	A relieved Paul writes 2 Corinthians, probably from Philippi or somewhere in Macedonia. Afterward he visits Corinth for three months and then returns to Philippi in time for Passover there.
A.D. 56 or early 57	Paul is again in Corinth, where he writes Romans (see Rom. 16:1–2, 23) in preparation for his planned trip to Rome after a visit to Jerusalem (Rom. 15:25).
A.D. 57	Paul, traveling by boat, sets out for what would be his last trip to Jerusalem. He sails from Philippi to Troas and then on to Miletus (Acts 20:5–15). Paul hurries to be in Jerusalem in time for Pentecost in May of A.D. 57.

A.D. 57–59	Incarceration in Caesarea.
A.D. 59 (fall)	Journey to Rome.
A.D. 60 (spring)	Arrival in Rome.
A.D. 60–62	House arrest in Rome. Production of the Captivity Epistles.
A.D. 62	Release from house arrest. (It also is possible that Paul was executed at this juncture, in which case he did not write the Pastoral Epistles, since they deal with a time subsequent to that of the end of Acts.)
A.D. 62–64	Further missionary travels east, and possibly also west.
A.D. 64–65	Rearrest during Nero's crackdown after the fire in July of 64.
A.D. 65–68?	Imprisonment in Mamertine prison. Production of the Pastoral Epistles, shortly before or after Paul's execution.
A.D. 66–68?	Execution in Rome by beheading. (We owe to *1 Clem.* 5:5–7 the information that Paul was executed during the reign of Nero.)

A Closer Look: *Tarsus or Jerusalem?*

Scholars are divided on whether Saul grew up in Tarsus or Jerusalem. Paul himself does not even say in passing in his letters where he is from. He never mentions Tarsus. Despite a recent dismissal of the idea of Saul growing up in Jerusalem,[3] based on the assumption that Gal. 1:22 makes no sense if Paul grew up in and persecuted Christians in Jerusalem, and the assumption that Paul's fluency in Greek shows that he was a Diaspora Jew, this matter cannot be dealt with so easily. First, M. Hengel and others have shown how greatly Hellenized the city of Jerusalem was in Saul's time, not least in the case of those whose families had moved there from the Diaspora and participated in the synagogue of the Greek-speaking Jews, or "Hellenists," as was likely the case with

3. C. Roetzel, *Paul: The Man and the Myth* (Minneapolis: Fortress, 1999), 12.

Illustration 7.4 Scale model of first-century Jerusalem (pre-A.D. 70).

Saul's family. Second, Galatians 1:22 does not say that Saul was unknown in Jerusalem as a persecutor, but that he was unknown by face
to churches in Judea. This certainly can mean churches outside of
Jerusalem in Judea.[4] Now we must consider the evidence of Acts 22:3–
5. The phrase "born, raised, educated" was a stock way of referring to
one's formative years (cf. Philo, *Life of Moses* 2.1; *Flaccus* 158). If we
compare what is said in Acts 22:3–5 to what is said in Acts 26, the most
natural way to read this evidence is that Saul was raised from an early
age in Jerusalem, not in Tarsus. Acts 23:16 probably provides some cor-
roborating evidence, for it refers to Saul's sister's son. Notice too that
Acts 7:58, where we first hear about Saul, calls him a "youth." In addition, there is no evidence of Pharisees being trained outside the Holy
Land (cf. Phil. 3:5 to Acts 26:5). Acts informs us that Saul was educated
at the feet of Gamaliel (Acts 23:3), which again points us to Jerusalem
as the place where he spent his formative years, and nothing in Paul's
letters contradicts this conclusion. Even his skill in rhetoric could certainly have been acquired in Jerusalem. I suggest that Saul was bilingual, and he chose to use mostly the Septuagint when writing letters to
largely Gentile congregations, for that is the only Bible they could have

4. This interesting point shows that the gospel had spread outside of Jerusalem into
Judea and beyond before A.D. 33–34, when Saul was converted.

read any portions of. This does not necessarily lead to the conclusion that Septuagintal Greek is the only biblical language Paul really knew. Thus, in my view, we must not make too much of the fact that Saul was born in the Diaspora. He himself makes nothing of this fact in his letters.

A fair summary of Saul's pre-Christian life is offered by C. Keener: "As a son in an educated and perhaps aristocratic home . . . , Paul probably began to learn the Law around his fifth year and other Pharisaic traditions around his tenth year, and was sent to pursue training to be able to teach the Law sometime after turning thirteen. . . . Paul's model for zeal may have been Phineas who killed for God . . . and his successors in the Maccabees."[5] Clearly, zeal is a crucial quality that we find in Paul's life both before and after conversion.

The two crucial passages in 2 Corinthians and Philippians show that Paul is happy to still claim that he is a Jew even after becoming a follower of Jesus. He does not renounce that heritage as something bad or wicked. In addition, Paul seems somewhat proud of his past performance as a Pharisaic Jew. He does not seem to have been a guilt-laden person in essence, though clearly he is deeply remorseful for his persecution of Christians (cf. 1 Cor. 15:9; Gal. 1:13, 23; 1 Tim. 1:13). Yet it is clear that something dramatic has surpassed this traditional Jewish influence on his life, indeed, so eclipsed it that in Philippians 3 Paul says that he is prepared to regard that heritage as worthless *in comparison* to what he has gained, namely knowing Christ and obtaining salvation through him.[6]

We must also consider a text like 1 Cor. 9:19–23, where Paul, perhaps surprisingly, says that he becomes the Jew to the Jew and the Gentile to the Gentile. He is talking about accommodating his style of living, eating, dressing, that is, matters of orthopraxy, not his theological or ethical principles. But of course for a Jew, orthopraxy, the way of living one's everyday life, is at the very heart of the matter. Verse 20 of this passage makes clear that in general Paul does not see himself as one under the law, though he can assume that position from time to time for the sake of winning persons to Christ. Keeping the Mosaic law is seen by Paul as optional not obligatory for being a Christian, but he believes that keeping the new law of Christ is obligatory (see Gal. 6:2). Paul seems to have believed that since the Messiah had come and the new creation had begun, new occasions teach new duties.

5. C. Keener, *The IVP Bible Background Commentary: New Testament* (Downers Grove, Ill.: InterVarsity, 1993), 389.

6. On this last section, compare Witherington, *The Paul Quest*, 52–88.

Damascus

Damascus, an important city situated 135 miles north of Jerusalem, lay on the old trade routes from the Babylonian and Persian Empires to Israel. Furthermore, it also lay on the main trade route from Egypt to Mesopotamia. Not surprisingly, then, it became a commercial center. In the New Testament era it was perhaps the leading city in the league of cities called the Decapolis (see Pliny *Natural History* 5.74). We know for a fact that it had a significant Jewish population (*J.W.* 2.559–561), which in part explains Saul's desire to go there and rid the city of the polluting influence of Jewish Christians.

From 64 B.C. Damascus was part of the Roman province of Syria, but it was not the capital of that province (which role Antioch played). The city retained its municipal independence as part of the Decapolis. In general, the Romans tried to leave free cities alone and not alter their administrative structure much. Yet it is clear that others had designs on the city, in particular the Nabatean rulers, including Aretas IV. We read in 2 Cor. 11:32 that King Aretas's ethnarch or governor set a guard on the city of Damascus in order to seize Paul. At the very least, then, Aretas had administrative forces and some soldiers in Damascus at the time this happened. This means that Nabatea had some sort of alliance (a defense alliance?) with Damascus, and it may mean that Aretas had claimed the city for himself, perhaps on the basis of preprovincial connections with the city.

Damascus, Antioch, and Alexandria were very important cities for early Judaism, not just because of the sizable Jewish populations there, but because these cities served as buffers, as it were, between the Gentile and Jewish worlds, and the Jews in those cities were goodwill ambassadors for Judaism to the empire and also to non-Roman pagans. Jews themselves had ancient connections with the city of Damascus, which claimed to be one of the oldest, if not the oldest, city in the world. This city retained a Semitic and Middle Eastern flavor and culture in a way that a city like Antioch did not once the empire began. The Jews of this city were more likely to be natural allies of those in Jerusalem and Judea in a way that would have been less true of the more Hellenized Jews of Alexandria, which was a Greek city with Egyptian and Roman influences.

Galatians 1:13–14 also reveals a bit more to us about Paul as a Jew. For one thing, he was advanced in Judaism beyond most of his fellow Jews. As Saul, he was extremely zealous for the traditions of his ancestors, even to the point of zealously persecuting Christians. Zeal is an essential trademark of Paul's identity both before and after the Damascus road experience. Notice also how Paul contrasts Judaism with the church of God in these verses. Paul has become a sectarian messianic

Jew who stresses more the discontinuity than the continuity with his past.

Herein lies a problem in dealing with the figure of Saul. Should we talk about his conversion on the Damascus road, or should we see what happened to him on that occasion as a call to a new form of ministry but not to a new faith?

Some scholars have pointed to what Paul says in Gal. 1:15 as an indication that he is talking about a call to a new prophetic ministry, for here Paul echoes what Jeremiah says about himself, namely, that he was set apart from birth (Jer. 1:5). Certainly, Paul believes that God has a divine hand in his life from birth, and that he was called by God's grace; but notice that the phrase about being set apart has to do with what was true of Paul from birth, while the phrase "when God . . . was pleased to reveal his Son in me so that I might preach him among the Gentiles" refers to an event at a later time than the setting apart. We need not draw a sharp dichotomy between call and conversion here, for both can be entailed, but we must say that Paul's conversion was from one form of Jewish faith to another. The first focused on the law, while entertaining messianic hopes about the future; the second focused on the person of Jesus Christ, and completely reevaluated the function and purpose of the law. While previously Saul had looked at life through the lens of the law, now he evaluated all things in the light of Christ, crucified and risen. He reevaluated not only Torah, but also temple, territory, and the other pillar beliefs of early Judaism (including the particular form of monotheism he would affirm [see 1 Cor. 8:4–6]). C. K. Barrett puts the matter this way: "This was a radical change of religious direction, and it was accompanied by as radical a change of action: the active persecutor became an even more active preacher and evangelist. If such radical changes do not amount to conversion it is hard to know what would do so."[7]

Luke manages to provide not one, or two, but three separate and different accounts of Saul's conversion in Acts 9, 22, and 26. Obviously, he saw this as one of the most crucial events in early church history. The three accounts serve various purposes in Luke's narrative,[8] and while differing in details, they agree in certain essentials: (1) Saul was authorized by one or more priestly authorities in Jerusalem to do something against Christians, and as the story goes on, it is implied

7. C. K. Barrett, *A Critical and Exegetical Commentary on the Acts of the Apostles*, ICC (Edinburgh: Clark, 1994), 442.
8. On their rhetorical functions in the three different narrative settings, see B. Witherington III, *The Acts of the Apostles: A Socio-rhetorical Commentary* (Grand Rapids: Eerdmans, 1998), 302–20.

that the authorization in Jerusalem to do something against Christians later was clarified to mean against Christians in Damascus; (2) while Saul was traveling to Damascus, he saw a light and heard a voice; (3) the voice said, "Saul, Saul, why do you persecute me?"; (4) Saul answered, "Who are you, sir?" (5) the voice said, "I am Jesus, whom you are persecuting." All three accounts confirm that Saul had an encounter including a real communication from Jesus in the context of a bright light that changed Saul from an anti- to a pro-Christian person. This summary comports quite well with what we find in Galatians 1–2 and 2 Cor. 3:18 and 4:6. In both cases, conversion and call to ministry are juxtaposed. Note that Luke's account stresses that the encounter with Christ was not a purely subjective or internal affair, for Saul's companions were also affected to a lesser degree by the incursion of the divine.

The differences in the three accounts in Acts 9, 22, and 26 show something of how even a careful ancient historian felt free to edit and present his materials in a rhetorically effective manner. This means that where the accounts differ, it is probably wrong to press Luke about the details, especially if he intends only to give a generalized impression by his way of wording things. A good example of that rhetorical freedom is seen in Acts 26:14 where we find the Greek idiom "It hurts you to kick against the goads," meaning that it is fruitless to struggle against God and one's destiny. This proverb is one that an Agrippa or a Festus might appreciate, but is not likely to have emanated from Jesus' lips in Aramaic! It was, after all, not an Aramaic idiom, and Acts 26:14 explicitly says that Jesus spoke to Saul in the native Semitic language. Thus, Luke or his source has inserted this phrase at the appropriate juncture to indicate to a very different audience the meaning of Jesus' words to Saul.

Note that none of the three accounts of Saul's conversion suggests that the conversion experience was spontaneous. Rather, Saul was blinded for three days, and he did not regain his sight or receive the Holy Spirit or baptism until the third day after the Damascus road encounter. In other words, for a brief period, Saul was simply in the dark. The event on the Damascus road began a process of conversion that climaxed when Saul received the Spirit, his sight, and baptism.

Paul explains in Gal. 1:16 that he received a revelation that Jesus was God's Son, accompanied by a revelation that he was to be the messenger of this truth to Gentiles. Bound up in this was the conviction that salvation and a true knowledge of God and his Son came only by grace and through faith. The language that Paul uses elsewhere about conversion in general, a language speaking of what was formerly true and what is now true (cf. Phil. 3:7–8; 1 Cor. 15:9; Gal. 1:10–2:21), indicates that he placed more emphasis on the discontinuity between the past and the Christian present than on the continuity.

A detailed study of conversion in Acts reveals the variety of ways God chooses to act in human lives. Indeed, one could draw that conclusion just by analyzing the differences in the accounts of the conversions of the Samaritans, the Ethiopian eunuch, and Saul as recorded in Acts 8–9. The one thing shared in common by these narratives is not the order of the relationship of initiation (by baptism) and conversion (reception of the Spirit), but rather, the fact of the reception of the Spirit as the distinguishing mark of a converted person.

Beyond the Change—Saul Begins to Pursue His Call

Galatians 1:17 intimates what Acts states clearly: after his conversion Paul spent time in Damascus, where he first learned in more detail about the Christian faith. It became, in a sense, the locus of his first home church. From there he went out on his first missionary venture, into Arabia. The Arabia in question is the one that Saul would have known from his time in Jerusalem, Nabatean Arabia, which actually could be seen from one of the towers of the city of Jerusalem on a clear day (cf. *J.W.* 5.159–160; *Ant.* 5.82). The people whom Paul evangelized there would have been largely non-Jews of Semitic origins. It seems clear that Paul met with considerable resistance there (probably in the capital city of Petra), because he informs us that Aretas, the Nabatean king, was after him in Damascus for something he had done (2 Cor. 11:32–33; cf. Acts 9:25). Bad blood ran between Aretas and the Jews at least since Herod Antipas had dismissed his Nabatean wife for his brother's wife and blood had been shed over this act, which shamed Aretas. After that episode, we can well imagine how Aretas would have reacted to a Jew evangelizing his people. The reference in 2 Corinthians 11 to Aretas and his ethnarch being in Damascus helps us to date Paul's Arabian evangelizing and, indeed, his conversion. It is unlikely that Aretas controlled Damascus before A.D. 37, when Tiberius gave way to Caligula as emperor. This in turn likely means that this episode referred to in 2 Corinthians 11 could not have happened prior to A.D. 37. Paul says in Gal. 1:17–18 that the sum total of his time in Damascus and in Arabia was about three years. This suggests that Paul was converted around A.D. 34–35. This makes good sense in the light of the fact that the church had to have had time to develop outside of Jerusalem and to have reached and formed a notable group of adherents not only in Judea but also beyond in the next great city north, Damascus. We must then conclude that Paul was in Arabia during a part of A.D. 34–37. After being in Arabia, Paul had returned to

Illustration 7.5   The treasury at Petra, the greatest Nabatean city.

Damascus, and only at that juncture, some three years after his conversion, did he first go to Jerusalem and talk to the pillar apostles.[9] Nothing suggests that Paul had any notable success in evangelizing Arabia.

Paul Returns to His Homes—Jerusalem and Tarsus

Somewhere around A.D. 37–38, Paul finally returned to Jerusalem, a changed man visiting a changed city. Pontius Pilate was either no longer the prefect of the province or was just on the way out. Paul, in Galatians 1, emphasizes that he visited with only two of the Jerusalem leaders on this trip, Peter and James, but they are, as Acts bears witness, the most crucial two. Galatians 1:18 adds that Paul spent some fifteen days with Peter, but he does not suggest that this is the total time he spent in Jerusalem, nor does he suggest that he saw no other Christians on this visit. Probably, Acts 9:26–29 summarizes this first visit to Jerusalem. Luke stresses that Barnabas helped introduce Paul to the pillar apostles, and that Paul did some evangelizing in the city, particularly among Greek-speaking Jews. This sparked a violent reaction, and so Paul was sent off to his home region of Cilicia, a fact confirmed by Gal. 1:21. Luke indicates that Paul visited Tarsus in particular.

Unfortunately, we know next to nothing about Paul's time in Cilicia. We have right to suppose that he continued his missionary work, but

9. See the detailed chronological discussions in Witherington, *The Paul Quest*, 304–31.

lacking letters from his hand from this period, we have no reason to suppose that he had any great success. In his letters, Paul passes over the next ten or so years of his life in silence, except that 2 Cor. 12:1–10 reveals that somewhere around A.D. 41–42 he had a notable visionary experience, and some of the travails listed in 2 Cor. 11:23–29 likely transpired during this time period. This in turn suggests that Paul spent time evangelizing in synagogues and paid the price for it. He may also have faced opposition from some fellow Christians of a more Judaizing bent during this time period. Acts only adds to this the fact that Paul spent about a year in Antioch teaching prior to his second trip up to Jerusalem (Acts 11:25–26). We must admit that we are largely in the dark about the period A.D. 37–46 in Paul's life.

The Petrine Passages

It is not at all clear where to date the events that Luke records in Acts 9:32–11:18, but at least some of them could have occurred between A.D. 34 and 37, or more certainly between A.D. 37 and 44. Certainly, if the Cornelius story has a basis in fact, then that event likely happened prior to the agreement spoken of in Galatians 1, which transpired in A.D. 49, and recognized Peter as the apostle to the Jews and Paul the apostle to the Gentiles. In these stories, Peter is presented as a willing healer and a reluctant evangelist of Gentiles. The stories are interesting because of their locale—the coastal plain of the Holy Land, with Peter visiting places like Lydda, Sharon, and Joppa. It would appear that, as in the case of Peter and John following up on the work of Philip in Samaria, Peter here is on some sort of inspection tour of fledgling churches that he did not found. It is natural to think that these congregations were founded by Philip, since Acts 8:40 depicts him evangelizing his way up the coastal plain from Azotus to Caesarea Maritima. Thus, once again his work is being double-checked and confirmed by one of the pillar apostles.

This brings up an important point. When Paul, speaking of a somewhat later time, refers to men who came from James to Antioch (see Gal. 2:11–12) to inspect the situation among the Jewish and Gentile converts in that church, we may assume that this same sort of inspection process was going on. The Jerusalem church, or at least its chief leaders, felt obligated to exercise some sort of supervision and quality control over congregations in outlying areas that were not directly founded by any of the Jerusalem apostles. This sort of role becomes even clearer once the Gentile crisis over circumcision becomes full-blown and must be dealt with, as Acts 15 and Galatians both suggest. It is plausible that the Judaizers who went to Galatia after Paul had planted various churches there were simply acting out of an orientation from and following the example of their leaders in the Jerusalem church, if they were not actually under the direction and guidance of Peter, James, and John in this action. We should not minimize the tensions that arose in early Christianity as the church increasingly became frequented by Gentiles.

We need to keep in mind that the coastal cities in Judea were probably even more Hellenized than Jerusalem itself and had a larger percentage of non-Jews. It is thus possible that a person like Aeneas was a Gentile; and more certainly, it is no surprise that actions in this very Hellenized region led to a more serious raising of the question about Gentiles in the church. Notice that in the Aeneas story in Acts 9:32–35, Peter is not said to touch the man. Perhaps he had been a God-fearer who had already become a Christian, since he is said to be among the "saints" whom Peter went to Lydda to visit. Notice likewise in the story of the raising of Tabitha (Dorcas), that Peter does not touch her while she is dead, but only after she sits up, alive again (Acts 9:36–42). This may reflect a certain scrupulousness on Peter's part about the ritual law, in view of what Acts 10–11 will suggest, but if so, Peter is inconsistent, for Acts 9:43 says that Peter stayed in the house of Simon the tanner in Joppa for some time. Most law-observant Jews saw contact with the carcasses and hides of dead animals as ritually defiling (cf. *m. Ketub.* 7:10; *b. Pesah* 65a). Galatians 2 likewise suggests that Peter could be inconsistent about such ritual matters. Perhaps he had rationalized: staying with an unclean Jew was one thing, but unclean Gentiles were a different matter!

It seems likely that one of the major purposes in Luke's writing of his historical work on the origins of the Christian movement was to show how this movement had universal appeal, crossing ethnic as well as geographical boundaries. Acts 10:1–11:18 then reveals one more step in the direction of full inclusion of Gentiles, although Cornelius is by no means a pure pagan, but rather, a God-fearer. Here is perhaps the best place to discuss this group of Gentiles.

A **Closer** Look: *Synagogue Adherents, God-fearers, and Proselytes*

Scholars have debated at length the existence of a class of Gentiles known as God-fearers, who attended the synagogue and could be distinguished from proselytes. Clearly, the phrase "those who fear God" existed before Luke's time, as can be seen in the Septuagint (2 Chron.

5:6; Ps. 113:19; 117:4; 134:20; Mal. 3:16). The reference in 2 Chron. 5:6 is especially crucial, as it seems to distinguish between Jews and "those who fear [God]" as a second class of people. Also interesting is that the term *prosēlytos* in the Septuagint consistently refers to a non-Israelite, to a foreigner or resident alien who lives in the land (cf. Exod. 20:10; 23:12; Num. 15:13–16).

A comparison of Acts 13:16 to 13:43 suggests that in Acts, at least, the term "proselyte" means the same thing as "God-fearer." Both refer to Gentiles who are synagogue adherents. The term "God-worshiper" (e.g., Acts 16:14; 18:7) seems to refer to the same persons as well. These are Gentiles who are to some degree adherents of early Judaism, but not full-fledged converts to Judaism; otherwise, they would simply be called Jews.

The Lukan significance of these persons is fourfold: (1) they are the bridge between synagogue and church, and between the Jewish and Gentile worlds; (2) they are the ones in the synagogue most likely to become followers of Christ, not least because that might mean they could avoid the social stigma of being circumcised—a real issue in the Greco-Roman world; (3) the interest in them may indicate that Luke or Theophilus or both were once God-fearers; (4) if a God-fearer was of some social status (see Acts 17:4), the conversion of such a person might well threaten to destabilize a particular Diaspora synagogue and its relationships with its fellow residents of a Diaspora city. This would explain the extreme reaction to Paul's preaching in such a locale.[10]

It is a true measure of the importance to Luke of the Cornelius story that, like the conversion story of Paul, he repeats it three times—in Cornelius's case, in quick succession between Acts 10 and Acts 15. Of course, Saul could not be called a typical Jewish convert to Christendom any more than Cornelius could be called a typical Gentile convert. Strictly speaking, since Cornelius was a God-fearer, Peter's approach to him did not represent the inauguration of an evangelistic campaign reaching out to pagans. But Luke believes that the impact of what happened to Saul and Cornelius changed the character of the early church. A crisis for the church was prompted by the direct intervention of God in these two lives that was not resolved (or resolved in part) until the apostolic council in A.D. 49 or 50. Let us consider briefly the visions of Cornelius and Peter and what they are said to have precipitated.

10. See the fuller discussion of this matter in Witherington, *Acts of the Apostles*, 341–44.

The Temple of Dreams

The Egyptian deities were indeed popular throughout the Roman Empire, and so it is no surprise to find a Sarapeion at Thessalonike that was apparently built as early as the third century B.C. The mystery religions had various secretive religious processes and initiation rites about which we have insufficient knowledge. But we do know some things about the process of incubation. In this process, one would sleep in the temple, looking for and expecting some answer or direction from the deity—in this case, Sarapis. What was expected was a vision or dream that gave the needed guidance or answer. It is possible that this process was aided by wine containing some "medicinal" herbs (e.g., myrrh). One would dine and drink in the temple, and then go to sleep hoping for a revelation. The following inscription from the first century A.D. describes what happened when one such seeker came to the temple in Thessalonike:

> It seemed that in his sleep Sarapis was standing beside him and instructing him, upon arrival at Opous to report to Eurynomos the son of Timasitheos that he should receive him (i.e., the god) and his sister Isis; and to give Eurynomos the letter which was under his pillow. Waking up he was amazed at his vision and perplexed about what he should do because of the political hostility which he had towards Eurynomos. But falling asleep again, he had the same dream, and when he awoke he discovered the letter under his pillow, just as was indicated to him. When he returned home he handed over the letter to Eurynomos and reported the god's instructions. Eurynomos took the letter and after hearing what Xenainetos said he was perplexed during the occasion itself, because of the existence of the political hostility between them. . . . But when he read the letter and saw that its contents were consistent with what had been said beforehand by Xenainetos, he accepted Sarapis and Isis. After he provided hospitality (for the gods) in the house of Sosinike, she received them among her household gods and performed the sacrifices for some time. (*NewDocs* 1:30–31)

This story can be compared profitably to the one in Acts 10, which records the visions of Cornelius and Peter that lead to the initiation and conversion of Cornelius. The Thessalonike inscription tells about someone coming to worship new deities, indeed, taking them into the shrine in the home of the household deities and offering them sacrifices after receiving a revelation from Sarapis by means of letter and vision. The implication, as Horsley suggests (p. 31), is the conversion of Eurynomos.

The Romans largely used auxiliary units in Palestine before and after the brief reign of Herod Agrippa I (A.D. 41–44). Cornelius may well have belonged to such an auxiliary unit recruited in Palestine itself, although his name suggests that he is the son of a freedman who in turn was named after P. Cornelius Sulla, the ruler who freed ten thousand slaves in 82 B.C. That he lives with his family, however, suggests that he was a provincial. There is a good chance that he was a centurion attached to the forces stationed in Caesarea Maritima, where the prefect lived. It is important that he is a man of considerable status and rank, and Luke goes out of his way to show that Jesus' followers were not necessarily antagonistic towards Romans, and that even Roman soldiers might find the new religion appealing and worth joining. Yet the portrayal of Cornelius here depicts a man whom a Jew like Peter should automatically find appealing. This is no pagan. Cornelius "has the central qualities that they recognize as true piety."[11] The devoutness of Cornelius is stressed: not only is he devout (shown by his regular prayer and almsgiving), but also all his household feared God (Acts 10:2).

The story hinges not just on two visions but on the providence of God, for it is no accident that as Cornelius's men were approaching Joppa, having been sent to find Peter, Peter had just gone up on the roof to pray and was about to receive a vision of his own. While modern historians would find this a peculiar sort of history writing, ancients would not, for they regularly took into account what they believed was divine as well as human causation in the historical process.

Peter's vision involves a sheet full of creatures, including clean and unclean animals, from the standpoint of ritual purity (cf. Leviticus 11). The story draws an interesting contrast between Peter's apparent disobedience to his heavenly vision and Cornelius's immediate readiness to obey his vision. The problem Peter faced is that any unclean animals in the sheet would, by contamination, make even the clean ones unclean. Thus, Peter rejects the lot as unfit for a Jew to eat. But Peter is instructed that what God had cleansed, no one should call common or profane. Although the vision involves food per se, it has implications for having table fellowship with people normally assumed to be unclean, and for how one should relate to a person whom God has cleansed. Acts 10:22 indicates that Cornelius is upright and well spoken of by Jews, and Peter is directed to go and instruct Cornelius. This goes directly against the grain of early Jewish instructions such as that in *Jub.* 22:16: "Keep yourselves separate from the nations,

---

11. R. Tannehill, *The Narrative Unity of Luke-Acts: A Literary Interpretation,* vol. 2 (Philadelphia.: Fortress, 1990), 133.

and do not eat with them; and do not imitate their rituals, nor associate with them." It takes nothing less than a vision from God to overcome this taboo in Peter's mind. He now believes that he is to call no person ritually unclean.

The focal point of the story is not merely Peter's new insight about ritual purity laws and their inapplicability to humans, but that the coming of the Spirit upon Cornelius indicates divine vindication and validation of the genuineness of the conversion of this God-fearing Gentile. "If God is for them, who can be against them?" is the message of this story. Notice that the reception of the Spirit precedes the baptism of Cornelius and his family. Luke seems unconcerned about the order of initiation and conversion (cf. Acts 8); or better said, as a good historian, he believes that in each case he must report it in the order in which it happened. In the Lukan scheme of things, this story prepares the way for the apostle to the Gentiles to actually approach Gentiles directly as a group, not merely those who happen already to be God-fearers. Both Cornelius and Peter are seen as bridge figures between early Judaism and the future of the church, which lay largely with Gentiles and their evangelization by persons such as Paul. Yet it is fair to say that hard times would come before any significant success among the nations for the gospel.

Chapter 8

Dark Passages

A.D. 37–47

Neither Paul nor his sometime companion Luke has much to say about the period A.D. 37–46. We must fill in the gaps from other sources of information and offer some suggestions as to what was happening among Christians during this period. We know that Pilate was replaced in A.D. 36 by an otherwise unknown man named Marcellus. Vitellius, the Syrian legate, was a sensible man, and he sought to calm the Jewish anger and fear that had been building up because of Pilate's various misdeeds. For example, he himself went up to Jerusalem during Passover and was well received, so Josephus says (*Ant*. 18.90–95). During this visit he remitted all taxes on agricultural products, and he restored to the high priest control of the vestments. He also removed Caiaphas as high priest and replaced him with Jonathan, another son of Annas. This arrangement proved untenable, and Jonathan was quickly replaced with his brother Theophilus (*Ant*. 18.120–123). But what of the imperial situation?

The Julio-Claudians after Tiberius—A.D. 37–46

After Tiberius having been an absentee emperor for so long, se-
cluded for years on Capri until his demise, the rise of Gaius in A.D. 37
(nicknamed Caligula, "Little Boot," due to his size and the boots he
wore while involved with the military) was widely hailed throughout
the empire. Even Philo, who in due course was to have great anxiety
about this emperor, says that for the first seven months of his reign,
Gaius Caligula approached matters in a high-minded and moderate
way (*Embassy* 13). Philo later adds that the Jews of the Syrian province
were the first to rejoice at the rise of Caligula, and the temple in Jerusalem was the first one to offer sacrifices on his behalf (*Embassy* 231–
232). This initial enthusiasm can be attributed to two factors. First, the
anti-Semitism of Sejanus, Tiberius's right-hand man, had offended
Jews everywhere. His demise, along with his master's, was welcome
news. Second, Caligula was the son of the very popular Germanicus,
whose untimely death had been widely mourned in the empire. There
was perhaps hope that Caligula would be as good a man as his father.
But the truth is that Caligula was not mentally well. He imagined himself really to be a god during his human lifetime, not merely after his
death, and he gradually acted more and more on this belief. As a god,
he felt that he could ignore the advice and guidance of others and exercise divine powers directly (*Ant.* 18.256). This was to prove disastrous
in various ways and for many of Caligula's subjects.

The first outrage for Jews came when Alexandrian Jews refused to
worship Caligula as a god, something Caligula and his emissaries were
strongly pushing for throughout the empire. This refusal led to an anti-
Jewish campaign by the governor of Egypt, Flaccus, who no doubt
wanted to ingratiate himself with the anti-Semitic emperor. Philo reports that an increasingly horrible situation developed in Alexandria.
Images of the emperor were forcibly installed in the synagogues there.
Then Jews were deprived of their citizenship rights. Finally, Jewish
property was plundered, as if Jews were foreign enemies of Alexandria
(*Flaccus* 40–57; *Ant.* 18.257–260).

But it was not just Jews in Egypt who refused to worship Caligula.
In A.D. 39–40 in Jamnia, when non-Jews set up an altar to the emperor,
it was immediately torn down by Jewish residents of the area. This led
to the infamous attempt by Caligula to have his statue installed in the
temple in Jerusalem (cf. the accounts in Philo, *Embassy* 188, 198–348;
Josephus, *Ant.* 18.261–309; *J.W.* 2.184–203). In fact, Caligula wanted to
go further. He ordered the new Syrian legate, Petronius, to turn the
temple in Jerusalem into a shrine for the emperor cult. He was to build

Illustration 8.1 Image of Emperor Claudius on a Roman coin and the obverse of the Claudius coin.

a statue of Caligula, escort it by two Roman legions to Jerusalem, and place it in the temple there.

But Petronius was a wiser man than his emperor, and he knew well what an uproar this would cause in the region. Philo even says that Petronius had done his homework, studying Judaism prior to coming to the region (*Embassy* 245). Thus, when met with a huge outcry by Jews in Ptolemais and in Tiberias, he initially told the artisans to work slowly on the statue, stalling for time; and when lobbied against the statue by Aristobulus, the brother of King Agrippa, and other Jewish leaders, he eventually wrote to Caligula explaining that the statue would be a disastrous thing, probably leading to a loss of all the crop revenues and to a revolt. Caligula responded by rejecting this plea.

As it happened, Agrippa I, who had been educated in Rome, was a longtime friend of Caligula. He appealed in writing to his old friend not to erect the statue. Caligula then dropped this project, but insisted that the Jews must be tolerant of the imperial cult, and so he ordered altars to be built for that cult outside Jerusalem.[1] But Philo reports that the matter did not end there, for according to *Embassy* 337–338, Caligula commissioned a statue to take with him as he himself headed east to march down the coast of Israel and on to Egypt. Mercifully, from a

1. G. Theissen makes the interesting speculation that the Markan apocalyptic discourse was originally written up during the Caligula crisis, and that Mark 13:14 reflects this (*The Gospels in Context: Social and Political History in the Synoptic Tradition*, trans. L. Maloney [Minneapolis: Fortress, 1991], 125–65). This theory probably should be rejected because in fact the statue never got anywhere close to Jerusalem. Nevertheless, Theissen may well be right that this part of Mark's material had a written form as early as the 40s.

Illustration 8.2 Model of first-century Rome showing the Colosseum and the Circus Maximus.

Jewish point of view, before this could transpire, the emperor was assassinated on January 24, A.D. 41.

The next Julio-Claudian emperor was Claudius, who ruled from A.D. 41 to 54. On the whole, he turned out to be a better ruler than either of his two immediate predecessors. One of the first actions of Claudius as emperor was to make Herod Agrippa I the monarch over all of the Holy Land, reverting to the situation that existed during the time of his grandfather Herod the Great.

On the surface, Claudius was a highly unlikely candidate to rule the empire. Both Augustus and Tiberius had kept him out of the public eye, apparently due to his unusual mannerisms or lack of social graces, which made him the butt of many jokes. One speculation is that Claudius stuttered. Yet whatever may have been true about Claudius's physical maladies or poor self-presentation, the man had a good sharp mind, and he made many wise decisions. For example, he courted the senate and showed it respect, as had Augustus, which was a refreshing change after Tiberius's and Caligula's adversarial relationships with that body. Claudius also was most careful to cultivate a good relationship with the army, and unlike Caligula, he actually went on military campaign briefly, being present at the final defeat of the Britons in A.D. 43. He thus established Britannia as a new province, something he accomplished for Thrace and Lycia as well.

Claudius's efforts to set up a civil service of sorts, chiefly staffed by freedmen, was seen as an affront by the upper classes, but Claudius felt that it would improve the efficiency of the government, and in this he was likely right. His reestablishment of the office of censor also raised the hackles of the patricians, for it meant that he had power through the censor to add or remove members of the senate. The net effect of Claudius's actions was the further centralization of power in the hands of the emperor and his entourage.[2]

Lest we think that Claudius was more temperate and understanding in his relationship to Jews than all his ruling predecessors, the record shows that he manifested some of the same sort of anti-Semitism that was common among Romans. For example, in A.D. 41 Claudius became alarmed at the ever growing multitude of Jews in Rome and how they were attracting followers from among the Romans, and so, according to Dio Cassius, he forbade them to hold open meetings, while not prohibiting them from continuing their traditional mode of living (*Roman History* 60.6.6).

Like his predecessor Caligula, Claudius had to deal with the turmoil in Alexandria between Jews and the other city residents. Recall that two delegations of Jews (one led by Philo) went before Caligula in A.D. 39–40 seeking relief from persecution. No decision was rendered by Caligula, as he was assassinated. Claudius likewise received two delegations trying to resolve this matter peaceably, which resulted in a famous edict by Claudius issued in the summer of A.D. 41. In this edict he did not rule on any past actions but warned both sides against any future actions that could arouse the ire of the emperor. The ruling included the requirement that Jewish customs were to be respected, that Jews were not to be ghettoized in one part of Alexandria, and finally, that Jews were not to infiltrate the Greek games. In short, Jews were to be allowed to be Jews and citizens, but they should not seek to be Hellenes. The point was to keep Jews within certain bounds while giving them freedom to be themselves. Claudius, most definitely a philhellene himself, did not want that tradition polluted or diluted by Jewish influence.[3] I will say more about his later banishment of Jews from Rome in the next chapter in discussing the events of A.D. 46–50. For now, it is sufficient to say that we must not misjudge Claudius's views of Jews on

2. See L. Grabbe, *Judaism from Cyrus to Hadrian*, vol. 2 (Minneapolis: Fortress, 1992), 434–35.

3. I have argued elsewhere that there is no good reason to collapse actions taken by Claudius in A.D. 41 and 49 in regard to Jews into one set of actions, as J. Murphy-O'Connor and others have done. See B. Witherington, *The Paul Quest: The Renewed Search for the Jew of Tarsus* (Downers Grove, Ill.: InterVarsity, 1998), 311–14.

the basis of his appointment of Herod Agrippa I to rule Judea and Galilee in A.D. 41. This was a matter of personal friendship, and, as we will see, in A.D. 44 Claudius just as quickly abolished the Jewish state and reestablished the direct rule of Rome in Judea.

The Gripping Tale of Herod Agrippa I—A.D. 41–44

Agrippa I is an interesting example of another very Hellenized Jewish ruler. Born in about 10 B.C. (*Ant.* 19.350), he was sent to Rome at an early age for his education.[4] Agrippa was both a Hasmonean and a Herodian by heredity. His mother was the famous beauty Bernice, whom the later emperor Titus became enamored with. She accompanied Agrippa to Rome. Agrippa was noted for periods of poverty and plenty in his life, due in large measure to his lavish lifestyle and spending habits. A good friend of Caligula, he once was thrown in jail for publicly expressing the hope that Caligula would succeed Tiberius, while Tiberius was still alive. Once Caligula took the throne, he released Agrippa from jail and gave him the territory previously supervised by Herod Philip, and also gave him the right to the title "King of the Jews."

Agrippa returned in triumph to Palestine in A.D. 38 by way of Alexandria, which provoked near riots there, according to Philo (*Flaccus* 25–35). Apparently, having a Jewish king in town was too much for some anti-Semites to bear. Jealousy arose on the part of Herodias, Antipas's wife, about this title that Agrippa had been given, which led her to prompt her husband to act in a fashion that led to his demise. Caligula deposed Antipas and gave his territory to Agrippa I as well.

If we wonder how Agrippa I managed to obtain the rulership of Judea too, it seems to have been a matter of reciprocity or payback. Recall that Agrippa was in Rome during the Caligula statue debacle, and he was the one who persuaded Caligula to back down from his demand to have his statue placed in the temple in Jerusalem. He was apparently a skilled diplomat, for he was also one of those who helped convince both Claudius and the senate to accept Claudius as emperor. In gratitude, Claudius bestowed Judea on Agrippa I (*Ant.* 19.274–275, 362). Thus it was that Agrippa returned to the Holy Land with great power and status, being both friend of Caesar and king of the Jews. His clout led to edicts by Claudius restoring the civil rights of Jews in Alexandria and throughout the empire (*Ant.* 19.279–288).

---

4. It is interesting to contrast Agrippa's case with that of Saul. The latter was moved to Jerusalem to receive his education, which says much about the difference of orientation between Saul's parents and Agrippa's parents when it came to which set of cultural traditions they wanted their child to focus on.

It is interesting that Josephus speaks in glowing terms about the piety and Jewishness of Agrippa (*Ant*. 19.330–331). We may take this to be apologetical to some extent, but it would be wrong to see it as not somewhat grounded in the truth. When Agrippa first returned to the Holy Land, he went up to Jerusalem, offered sacrifice, presented the temple with a gold chain given him by Caligula, and enforced the vows of some Nazarites (*Ant*. 19.292–294; cf. Paul's behavior in Acts 21:18–26). At the very least, Agrippa wished to appear to be a good Jew. Jerusalem seems to have received Agrippa warmly when he returned to the land, and as a result, he remitted the property tax of all houses in that city (*Ant*. 19.299).

Yet there is also the other, Hellenized side of Agrippa, shown by his minting of coins with images of the emperors on them, as well as images of a pagan temple and a goddess. He had statues of his own daughters set up in Caesarea Maritima and at Sebaste, the Samaritan capital (*Ant*. 19.357). Like his grandfather, Agrippa played the grand benefactor, bestowing on the city of Berytus (Beirut) a theater and an amphitheater as well as public baths (*Ant*. 19.335). There is also the famous episode, said to have ended his life, when he appeared in the theater at Caesarea in a woven silver garment that reflected the sunlight and he was acclaimed a god, which acclamation he did not repudiate (cf. *Ant*. 19.343–350 and Acts 12:20–23).[5]

Several actions of Agrippa raised the eyebrows of the emperor. For example, he attempted to build a substantial wall on the north side of Jerusalem, which would make the city far less vulnerable to attack (the north being the one side with no deep valley protecting the city). The legate in Syria got wind of this, reported it to Rome, and Claudius ordered the work stopped. Agrippa appears not to have protested this decision (*Ant*. 19.326–327; *J.W.* 2.218; 5.152). Agrippa was to die deep in debt at the age of fifty-four, and the realm passed into Roman hands again for direct rule. All in all, Agrippa seems to have been a slightly more Jewish Herodian than his grandfather, but clearly, he sought to be recognized as a Hellenized ruler once he was given the status of king by Claudius.

Christians under the Rule of Agrippa—A.D. 41–44

One could debate whether Jewish Christians in Jerusalem and the Holy Land were better off under prefects or under Herod Agrippa. On

5. We may also wonder why it was that in a little over three years, Agrippa put four different priests into the office of high priest. During the long reign of his grandfather there had been only five.

the whole, it appears they fared a bit better under direct Roman rule, at least before the Jewish wars in the 60s. In part this was probably because to the Romans, Jewish Christians were indistinguishable from other Jews, but to Agrippa, there was a recognizable difference, and the tolerance of that difference might upset the status quo.

Luke tells the story in Acts 12 as a continuation of the theme of Jewish Christians being under persecution, but it also may be given in part to explain why Peter moved on from Jerusalem and James was left as the central focus of the Jerusalem church. The chapter begins by stressing that Agrippa laid violent hands on some Christians. This seems likely to have transpired well into Agrippa's reign, not when he first came to power and was still assessing the situation. We must note that Agrippa apparently went after only the Christian leaders, in this case, James the son of Zebedee and Peter. Agrippa perhaps was trying to curry favor with his Jewish constituency by these actions, but whatever the reason, we are told explicitly that he executed James, and he likely would have executed Peter had he not escaped from prison.[6] Notice that James is executed by a Roman means, beheading, again reflecting the Greco-Roman orientation of Agrippa.

Apparently, Agrippa was encouraged by the positive response to James's execution and thus went after Peter as well during the Feast of Unleavened Bread. Since this festival began on the eve of the Passover (in the spring), and since Josephus says that Agrippa died after celebrating Claudius's birthday (August 1), if there was a close connection in time between the capture of Peter and the death of Agrippa, we may surmise that Peter's jailing happened in the spring of A.D. 44. Acts 12:4 indicates that Agrippa relied on Roman troops during his reign, and apparently, Peter would have been guarded by four squads of four men during the various watches of the night. That Agrippa planned to bring Peter "out to the people" suggests a formal and public Roman trial and shaming. According to 12:6, divine intervention came at the last possible moment before the morning of Peter's trial. What follows, however, is an account of how Peter will no longer be the leading figure in the Jerusalem church, but rather, James will be. But the very fact that Peter's report must go to James especially shows that James already had prominent status in the early church. Apparently, Peter will be in Jerusalem only occasionally hereafter.

Acts 12:17b has mystified many, for it says simply that Peter went to another place. Some have conjectured that this means Rome, but Paul, writing Romans in the 50s, still knows nothing about Peter being in

6. According to Josephus (*Ant.* 20.197–203), the high priest Annas executed James. Agrippa deposed him for this action.

Rome, much less about his founding the church there (see Rom. 15:20). The point seems to be that Peter will be out of the range of Agrippa's clutches.

Acts 12:20–23 recounts the demise of Agrippa. Luke's account comports in the main with that of Josephus. Luke adds some substantial details not included by Josephus—for example, that an embassy from Tyre and Sidon had come to appeal to Agrippa for reconciliation and aid, and this is what prompted his public display. He had donned his robes and come to rule on their request. Luke does not provide the content of Agrippa's public address, only that the crowd who heard it said that they were listening to the voice of a god not a man (cf. Acts 12:22 to *Ant.* 19.344–345). Luke and Josephus agree that it was just after this that Agrippa was stricken, and that the cause was his failure to give God the glory, or as Josephus puts it, his failure to rebuke the crowd and reject the impious remark (*Ant.* 19.346). Josephus says that Agrippa developed severe stomach pains, while Luke the physician is more specific, saying that worms felled him.

Gerd Theissen suggests that the passion narrative found in various forms in the Gospels first took shape during the period of persecutions while Herod Agrippa was ruling. "Those were years when the Passion tradition's narrating community lived in fear. At that time, it is understandable if the names of the inner circle were given protection by anonymity in order that no negative consequences should ensue from their conflicts with authorities. In this period, the community could recognize its own fate in that of Jesus."[7] This conclusion is quite plausible and reminds us that certain social situations and crises prompted the church to put its sacred traditions in writing. If it is believable that Mark's Gospel was written during the dark days at the end of the Jewish war, when Christians in Rome had fresh in their minds the recent persecutions of Nero, it is plausible that the passion narrative was first put into writing under similar conditions of persecution.

Except for cameo appearances in Acts 15, Peter disappears from the Lukan radar screen. From Paul we learn of Peter being in Antioch sometime after A.D. 44 (Galatians 1–2; perhaps sometime during 46–48), and we may possibly deduce from 1 Cor. 1:12 and 9:5 that at some juncture Peter had been in Corinth in the early 50s. Otherwise, we lose track of Peter. The Book of 1 Peter perhaps gives us some clues that Peter was later in Rome (5:13). It is also interesting that 1 Pet. 1:1 indicates Peter is addressing Christians in Pontus, Asia, Galatia, Bithynia, and Cappadocia. This may suggest a mission of Peter in what is now western Turkey. But we must leave speculation about what happened

---

7. G. Theissen, *Gospels in Context*, 198.

to Peter until later in our study. For now, we turn to the one who after Acts 12 is the central figure in Jerusalem—James the brother of Jesus.

James the Just

The "first Christian community that gathered in Jerusalem was made up of people who, at least in part, had moved there from other places. In their case, the place of origin was more significant than the name of the father. If we include the fact that the first Christians often joined the followers of Jesus after making a radical break with their parents and leaving the family home (cf. Matt. 8:20–21), it is plausible that fathers became less important as points of identification. People were identified by their fathers in the larger society, but not in the Christian community, for the community is the *familia dei*, which re- places the earthly family."[8] While this observation is basically correct, the role of James in the early church reminds us that family connec- tions were not unimportant.

Up to Acts 11:1, the apostles are presented as the leaders of the Jerusalem Christian community (cf. 2:42–43; 4:33–37; 5:1–2, 18, 29, 40; 6:6; 8:1, 14; 9:27; 11:1), with Peter being the preeminent figure. There- after, the leadership group seems essentially to consist of James the brother of Jesus and a group called the elders (11:30). Our interest here is James.

Perhaps the essential place to begin is with the remark in John 7:5, which says that at that point, the brothers of Jesus did not believe in him.[9] This would include James. But at Acts 1:14, the brothers of Jesus are present with the Twelve at the founding of the church. This volte- face, at least in the case of James, is best explained by reference to 1 Cor. 15:7a, which says that the resurrected Jesus appeared to James. From a Pauline point of view, this would constitute James as one of, or at least on par with, the apostles. He had seen the risen Lord and was changed irrevocably by that experience. Galatians 1:18–19 and 2:9 con- firm that he was one of the pillars of the Jerusalem church, along with Peter and John.

Acts 12:17 supplies the first direct reference to James by name in Luke's historical monograph. That word needs to be left with him about Peter's status indicates his leadership position. R. Bauckham suggests that Agrippa's persecution led not only to the flight of Peter

8. Ibid., 180.
9. In my view, James was an actual brother of Jesus, the eldest of the family after Jesus (see Mark 6:3), and not merely a cousin. For the debate on this issue, see B. With- erington III, *Women in the Ministry of Jesus*, SNTSMS 51 (Cambridge: Cambridge Uni- versity Press, 1984), 89–92.

and the death of one of the sons of Zebedee, but also to the dispersal of others among the apostles still in Jerusalem. James then would have stepped into a power vacuum.[10] This is plausible.[11]

What role, then, must James have played during this time? If indeed the Jerusalem church had the status of mother church, sponsoring and inspecting other churches that were planted, James's role must have been a significant one indeed. If we read between the lines in Galatians 1–2, it seems clear that Paul, writing in A.D. 49, recognizes that James has considerable status and power, such that if he did not recognize Paul's gospel and mission, Paul might be "running in vain." This standing of James existed before Paul ever visited Jerusalem, and seems already to have been the case in some sense as early as A.D. 37–38, when Paul first went up to Jerusalem, or why else mention specifically that he had seen James the Lord's brother on this occasion? The reference to Paul's second visit to Jerusalem in Gal. 2:9 implies that James is now preeminent in Jerusalem, for whereas when Paul refers to the first visit in Gal. 1:18, he speaks of visiting with Peter for fifteen days but only seeing James, in Gal. 2:9 he mentions James first among the pillars, and later he refers to "men who came from James." This second Jerusalem meeting transpired in A.D. 48, before the first missionary journey.

What sort of Jewish Christian was James? The one reference of relevance in Josephus (*Ant.* 20.197–200) indicates James's central importance in the early Christian movement, but also that he was an observant Jew. It also informs us of how he met his untimely demise, probably in A.D. 62. But should we then conclude, as various scholars have done, that in essence James should be seen as the leader of the Judaizers, or at least one who agreed with their opinion that Gentiles must first become Jews in order to be full-fledged Christians? The evidence as we have it in Acts and Paul does not support this conclusion. I will discuss Acts 15 and James's speech and decision in the next chapter, but here it is in order to point out that James appears to be a mediating figure whose views stand somewhere between those of Paul and those of the Judaizers.

Some possible support for this mediatorial role can be found in the document attributed to James that found its way into the New Testament canon. In my view, the Book of James reflects a situation after the successful Pauline mission to Gentiles has begun in earnest, which is

10. R. Bauckham, "James and the Jerusalem Church," in *The Book of Acts in Its Palestinian Setting* (Grand Rapids: Eerdmans, 1995), 440.

11. Could the apostles have seen Agrippa, "King of the Jews," as the abomination that makes desolation and thus took his action against James the son of Zebedee as a sign that they should flee (cf. Mark 13:14)?

to say, after A.D. 46, and after the misunderstanding of Paul's gospel of salvation by grace through faith had developed. This document, then, could have been written sometime in the early to mid 50s.[12] What James 2 shows, however, is that the author, while not at all wishing to deny the notion of salvation through faith, stresses that real faith works, or to put it another way, that the fruit of real faith is good deeds—something that Paul would have agreed with wholeheartedly. Yet James uses Abraham as an example of righteous deeds, while Paul uses him as an example of justifying faith. Nothing in the encyclical that we call the Book of James suggests that James advocated imposing the Jewish law on Gentiles. Yet clearly, the focus in this document addressed to Jewish Christians outside Israel is orthopraxy not orthodoxy, including the ways James draws on the Jesus tradition found in the Sermon on the Mount.[13] This focus on ethics comports with the depiction of James in Acts 15.[14] In other words, James was closer to the focus of early Judaism by way of the continual emphasis on orthopraxy than Paul was.

The series of events that led to Paul's second visit with James and the pillars in Jerusalem involved not only a human endeavor (the first missionary journey by Paul and Barnabas), but also a natural occurrence, a food shortage caused by drought. This drought, which caused a grain shortage in Egypt, affected the Holy Land as well. We must look at this series of events in some detail.

Antioch, Agabus, and the Apostle of Famine Relief

Syrian Antioch was a great city. In fact, Josephus says that it was the third greatest city in the empire, after Rome and Alexandria (*J.W.* 3.29). We may suspect that Antioch, after Damascus and Jerusalem, was the third major city to become a center for the growing early Christian movement, before there ever was a Pauline mission. Antioch was a large commercial city located on the Orontes River. It was the Roman provincial capital for Syria, with a population in the mid-first century of about a half million people, much larger than either Jerusalem or Damascus. The city had close ties with the Herodians and had received benefactions from them. In addition, the city had a large Jewish popu-

12. See R. Bauckham, *James: Wisdom of James, Disciple of Jesus the Sage*, New Testament Readings, (London: Routledge, 1999), 11–28.

13. See B. Witherington III, *Jesus the Sage: The Pilgrimage of Wisdom* (Minneapolis: Fortress, 1994), 211–19.

14. For the most thorough treatment of sources on James, see J. Painter, *Just James: The Brother of Jesus in History and Tradition*, Personalities of the New Testament (Minneapolis: Fortress, 1999).

Antioch

While the Ephesians would have disagreed, Josephus calls Antioch "third among the cities of the Roman world" (*J.W.* 3.29). Clearly, it was of great importance for both Jews and Christians. For the latter, it was to become the first major cosmopolitan city outside Jerusalem and the Holy Land where Christianity established itself as a force to be reckoned with and as an entity that could be distinguished from Judaism.

Antioch was located on the Orontes River, and was some eighteen miles from the Mediterranean Sea, with its seaport being Seleucia Pieria. The city was an important governmental and commercial center, and also was near to Daphne, an important religious center connected with Artemis and Apollo.

By the mid-first century, Antioch was a city of perhaps a half million people. Its strategic importance was recognized by Rome, and so it was made the Roman capital for the province of Syria, where the legate resided. On its coins it called itself "Antioch, metropolis, sacred, and inviolable, autonomous, and sovereign, and the capital of the East." The city had grown and developed enormously since its founding circa 300 B.C. by Seleucus I, who named it after his father, Antiochus. Several cities had Antioch as part of their name, but this one was the most important, and is not to be confused with another city that Paul visited in the Galatian province, Pisidian Antioch.

In the first century A.D., a well-established Jewish colony existed in Antioch, and Josephus cites an abundance of proselytes to Judaism there (*J.W.* 7.45; cf. Acts 6:5, which speaks of "Nicolaus, a proselyte of Antioch"). This city was the beneficiary of all kinds of patronage, including patronage from Herod the Great, who had its main street paved and lined with columns along both sides. The connection between the Herod family and Antioch may explain how Manaen, a member of the court of Herod the tetrarch, came to be a prominent teacher and/or prophet in this city. Presumably, he originally was one of Herod's retainers in Antioch. For an evangelistic religion this city was especially important, as it served as the gateway to the east if one was coming from the west, and as the gateway to the west if one was traveling overland through the land mass we call Turkey. It is no accident that Paul's missionary journeys tended to begin and end in Antioch.

lation, and Josephus informs us that there were also many proselytes to Judaism there (*J.W.* 7:45). For Jewish Christians fleeing persecution in Jerusalem, Antioch was a natural place to go to. In fact, Acts 11:20 says that it was Jewish Christians, originally from Cyprus and Cyrene, who began the mission to Antioch, which included approaching both Jews and Gentiles. The considerable success of the witness to Gentiles is probably why Jesus' followers were first called *Christianoi* in this city (Acts 11:26), for this term, which means "adherents of Christ," suggests a group of people who could be naturally distinguished from both Jews and pagans.[15]

As with other missions not begun by one of the Twelve, an emissary was apparently sent from the Jerusalem church—in this case, Barnabas—to validate the authenticity of the Christian work done in Antioch (Acts 11:22). This was a natural choice because Barnabas was from Cyprus (Acts 4:36). Barnabas, seeing a further opportunity, heads west to Tarsus to find Paul to help with the work in Antioch (Acts 11:25). Acts 9:27 perhaps suggests that Barnabas had recognized Paul's abilities when he observed him preaching in Damascus. But before Paul came to Antioch and taught there for an entire year with Barnabas, an event was already transpiring that would shape the course of Paul's later missionary work.

Recall that Egypt was the breadbasket of the Roman Empire. A famine in Egypt meant food shortages elsewhere in the empire. Obviously, this drove up the price of grain, which most affected the poor. There is considerable evidence of poverty and food shortages being an ongoing problem for the Jerusalem church, as we have already seen in Acts 6 (cf. 2:45; 4:32). In short, a drought or famine in Egypt would affect the poor in Judea.

We have good evidence of an unusually high Nile inundation during the reign of Claudius, indeed, what amounted to a "one-hundred-year flood" in A.D. 45. This flooded the grain fields, causing a very late, very poor harvest. By the fall of A.D. 45, the grain price had jumped to more than twice that of its recorded price at any other time in the first century A.D. The year A.D. 46 was to be horrible for those having to buy grain to make the ration of bread needed to survive another day. Because of grain hoarding by the more well-to-do, the problem stretched on, into A.D. 47 in all likelihood. Josephus refers to the great famine that occurred in Judea during the reign of the procurator Tiberius Alexander, which places the event in A.D. 46–48.[16] It is possible that another matter further aggravated this already severe situation in Judea: the sabbatical year, when many would abstain from planting, apparently occurred in A.D. 47–48.

---

15. It is of some importance in dealing with the date in Acts 18 that this term could also be spelled *Chrestianoi*, just as *Christus* could be rendered *Chrestus* by the less than precise.

16. The term "procurator" is used here advisedly. After Herod Agrippa I's death in A.D. 44, Claudius made "procurator," rather than "prefect," the term to be used for the governor in the region.

Thus, the general food crisis became an early-church crisis that required one part of the church to help another, and so strengthened the social networks between Christians in Antioch and in Jerusalem. Acts 11:28 relates that Agabus came from Jerusalem to Antioch, stood up in the assembly there, and predicted a famine that would affect the whole of the inhabited world, which probably means the Roman Empire.[17] Agabus's prophecy, which seems to have been given at some point during A.D. 46 or perhaps a little earlier, led to the decision by Christians there to deliver aid to the Christians in Judea, aid raised by taking up a voluntary collection, delivered by Paul and Barnabas to Jerusalem.

Acts 11:29–30 should be linked to the brief note in 12:25, which is best rendered "Barnabas and Paul returned, having completed their mission unto Jerusalem, and brought with them John, whose other name is Mark."[18] In my view, Luke in these two texts is speaking about the same visit to Jerusalem that Paul refers to in Gal. 2:1–10, a visit undertaken to deliver the famine relief but in the process made further profitable by a private meeting between Paul and the Jerusalem church pillars. In this meeting, Paul was able to lay out his gospel to them and receive the right hand of fellowship and an endorsement as the apostle to the Gentiles, while the pillars (including James) would concentrate on evangelizing Jews. Galatians 2:10 should be translated "They wanted us to continue to remember the poor," implying that they had already begun doing so by this visit, which seems to have transpired in the early part of A.D. 48.[19] Little did these Christians realize at the time what a crisis for their movement would be provoked by the growing Gentile population in the church in Antioch. Paul and his gospel were about to undergo trial by fire. To this crisis we turn in the next chapter.

17. See B. Witherington III, *The Acts of the Apostles: A Socio-rhetorical Commentary* (Grand Rapids: Eerdmans, 1998), 370–75.

18. Textual variants in the ancient manuscripts leave this verse open to other translations.

19. Remember that partial years would be counted as full years by ancient ways of reckoning, and so when Paul says that fourteen years lapsed between the first and second visits to Jerusalem, it may actually have been a little over twelve.

Chapter 9

The Gentile Mission and the Jerusalem Council

A.D. 48–49

The Apostles of Antioch

Acts 13–14 presents a picture of what has been called the first Pauline missionary journey. The journey starts and ends in Antioch, and if Luke is to be believed, it is the Antioch church that sends out Paul and Barnabas on this trip, not the Jerusalem church. The trip involved a visit to Barnabas's native land Cyprus, as well as a trip to the southern coastal region of Asia Minor with stops at Pisidian Antioch, Iconium, Lystra, and Derbe, not once but twice. Acts 14 is the only place in that book where we find Paul and Barnabas being called apostles, and there is some debate as to what it means even there. We must consider this missionary venture, undertaken probably in A.D. 48.

The narrative in Acts 13 begins with a list of prophets and teachers in Antioch, and Paul and Barnabas frame the list. Since these two have already been depicted as teachers there (11:26), and since Paul will be portrayed as a prophet in 13:9–11, it is perhaps unnecessary to ask which were prophets and which were teachers. In Paul's case, at least, he was both. It is wholly plausible historically that a church with a significant number of Gentile converts would be the first to be concerned with reaching out to Gentiles with the gospel in some sort of intentional rather than haphazard fashion. In view of the way the matter is couched, this venture appears to have been of limited duration, but of course if the venture was successful, there would be ongoing work to do in the mission field. The use of the term *apostoloi* in 14:4 and 14 seems to indicate that Paul and Barnabas are being viewed as agents/ apostles of the Antioch church (cf. 2 Cor. 8:23), not apostles with a capital *A*.[1] The laying on of hands in 13:3 indicates that these two men were set aside for a particular task, but also indicates the recognition and endorsement by these church leaders of the call of God on their lives.

Cyprus was but sixty miles off the coast of Asia Minor. I. H. Marshall's assessment of Paul's missionary trips needs to be kept in mind as we consider his efforts.

> Paul's missionary work [during] this period has the best claim to being called a "missionary journey" as is customary on Bible maps. The later periods were much more devoted to extended activity in significant key cities of the ancient world, and we gain a false picture of Paul's strategy if we think of him as rushing rapidly on missionary *journeys* from one place to the next, leaving small groups of half-taught converts behind him; it was his general policy to remain in one place until he established the firm foundation of a Christian community, or until he was forced to move by circumstances beyond his control.[2]

In fact, it appears that after this first missionary trip, Paul focused on an urban strategy, concentrating on significant and major cities like Ephesus and Corinth and Philippi. These were cities on major Roman roads, or were capital cities, and/or Roman colony cities. The strategy that Barnabas and Saul pursue on this trip sets the pattern for later

---

1. See the discussion in B. Witherington III, *The Acts of the Apostles: A Socio-rhetorical Commentary* (Grand Rapids: Eerdmans, 1998), 393–94.

2. I. H. Marshall, *The Acts of the Apostles*, TNTC (Grand Rapids: Eerdmans, 1980), 137.

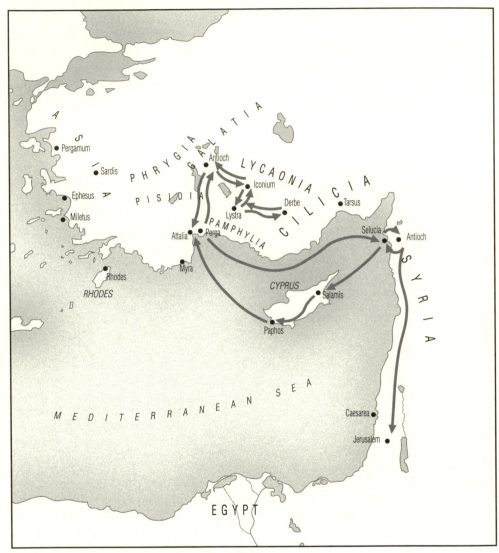

Illustration 9.1 Paul's First Missionary Journey, A.D. 46–48.

trips. This involves sharing the gospel first with Jews (and God-fearers) and also with Gentiles, which means going to synagogues or Jewish meetings first in each locale. It is a misreading of the evidence of Acts to suggest that a rejection by Jews in a particular locale ever causes a permanent decision to approach only Gentiles thereafter. Indeed, in Acts 28 we still find Paul addressing Jews and even Jewish synagogue leaders, sharing the gospel with them (cf. 13:14; 14:1; 17:1, 10, 17; 18:4,

19; 19:8). It is sometimes alleged that this portrait of Paul going first to synagogues in each locale is not well grounded in historical fact, but Paul's own letters suggest that he likely did so. First, Paul enunciates the principle in Rom. 1:16. Second, Paul states first that he became the Jew to the Jew to win some (1 Cor. 9:20–21). Third, Paul reports having received disciplinary whipping from the synagogue on multiple occasions (2 Cor. 11:24), and we may assume that there were other occasions when he was simply expelled. Fourth, Paul says that he has been endangered by his own fellow Jews (2 Cor. 11:26), but how so if he had never darkened the door of a synagogue or threatened their status quo? Fifth, a letter like Galatians (in my view, Paul's earliest letter) makes very evident that Paul's converts are seriously considering circumcision and keeping the whole Mosaic law. Surely, it is easier to believe that some of these converts were already God-fearers and had great reverence for the Mosaic law before they ever became Christians. In short, Paul's letters are not at odds with the portrait of Paul found in Acts on this matter.[3]

Acts 13:5 says that John Mark is with Paul and Barnabas on this trip, at least initially, as a subordinate helper, though Luke does not specify what sort of help he was to render. After the visit to Cyprus, when a decision was made to continue the venture into the mainland of Asia Minor, 13:13 recounts that John Mark "left them," having decided to return to Jerusalem. Luke suggests in 15:37–39 that John Mark was guilty of having "deserted them" on that particular venture, though he does go with Barnabas on another venture later—but then, he was a relative of Barnabas (see Col. 4:10).

We are not told the outcome of the evangelizing of Salamis on Cyprus, but some success seems to have come on the other end of the island at the new capital of Paphos. Here the proconsul resided, and here Paul and Barnabas encountered a Jewish false prophet named Bar-Jesus (Acts 13:6). He is further described as a "magician" or diviner, perhaps attempting to tell the future through necromancy or astrology. What is important to Luke about this encounter, especially in light of the earlier similar encounter between Peter and Simon Magus in Acts 8, is that Christianity is distinguished from and indeed is deadly to the practice of magic (cf. Acts 19:13–20).

3. This is not to deny the existence of some salient differences between Luke's portrait of Paul and the one gathered from the letters. For example, Luke does not present Paul as a letter writer, nor does he stress his apostolicity; on the other hand, the letters say nothing directly about Paul being a Roman citizen. On these differing portraits and whether they are reconcilable, see the excursus in Witherington, *Acts of the Apostles*, 430–38.

Luke portrays a Christian movement that is in competition for followers not merely with the magical arts, but with Judaism, and indeed with various traditional pagan deities and popular forms of religion (cf. Acts 14:8–18; 17:16–33; 19:23–41). This suggests that Luke and other early Christians were more concerned with these sorts of competitors than with the Roman overlay of gods or even with the emperor cult.[4] Christianity arose during a time of enormous interest on the part of many pagans in eastern religions—Judaism, the Jesus movement, mystery religions from Egypt, Persian astrological practices, and so on. Christianity had an advantage over Judaism in this competition at least in this respect: it did not require Gentiles to perform circumcision, a ritual their fellow Gentiles would see as shameful.

The encounter with the proconsul Sergius Paulus (Acts 13:7) is significant on several counts.[5] Wayne Meeks has made the intriguing suggestion that Paul was connected to this man as a freedman of the same gens.[6] The question is, Which member of the Pauli gens is this Sergius Paulus? We know that this family had extensive property in the region of Pisidian Antioch.[7] We also know that apparently this same man was one of the curators of the Tiber during Claudius's reign (CIL VI.31545). Another inscription clearly also places the Pauli on Cyprus (IG III.930). Luke tells us that Sergius Paulus was an intelligent man and was prepared to listen to the apostles, perhaps because they would have appeared to him as interesting traveling philosophers or rhetors.

At Acts 13:9 we hear for the first time about Saul being called Paul. This does not amount to a change of name, but the identification of an alternative name. Luke's way of putting the matter probably rules out the suggestion that Saul was being opportunistic and simply adopting his listener's name in order to identify with and perhaps win the man as a convert. A better suggestion is that Luke has introduced the name here because now Paul will be dealing with Gentiles and accordingly will want to use his Roman name in doing so. Notice that the alternative name does not arise at the point in the narrative about Saul's conversion but at the point of the actual outreach to Gentiles. Probably, Paulus was the apostle's cognomen, for a Roman had three names—the praenomen, the nomen, and the cognomen (e.g., Gaius Julius Caesar).

---

4. Or is it rather that Luke is on tiptoe as the emperor cult became increasingly popular during the first century, and he does not wish to risk raising the ire of Roman authorities as Christianity keeps gaining ground with Gentiles of all kinds?

5. If Luke was a sometime companion of Paul, there is no reason to doubt the authenticity of this encounter, for Luke could have learned of it from Paul himself.

6. W. A. Meeks, *The First Urban Christians: The Social World of the Apostle Paul* (New Haven: Yale University Press, 1983), 218 n. 68.

7. See Witherington, *Acts of the Apostles*, 399.

Alternatively, Paulus could have been either a praenomen or even a nickname, for *paulus* in Latin means "little."[8] After Paul wins the show-down with Bar-Jesus, Sergius Paulus is "astonished" (13:12), not at the darkness that envelops Bar-Jesus, but at the teaching of the Lord. The proconsul then responds positively to the message, but Luke does not suggest that he became a Christian. The key verb, *episteusen*, probably means "he began to believe," which is to say that he was open and fa-vorably disposed to the message. Luke is eager to point out that per-sons of high social status and even Roman officials could find this new faith enticing and attractive.

It is possible, even plausible, that Paul and Barnabas next went to Pi-sidian Antioch (not the most obvious choice for a next stop) because the proconsul had connections there and suggested this destination. It is even possible that Sergius Paulus wrote a letter of introduction for the apostles to members of his family there. This would explain the oth-erwise surprising next stop on the preaching tour.[9] In any event, Luke is presenting Paul as being comfortable in the circles of high status and power right from the beginning of his missionary career.

Pisidian Antioch was in the Roman province of Galatia in Paul's day and in the region known as Phrygia, and so was called Phrygian Galatia (so Acts 16:6). It is perfectly plausible that the persons whom Paul ad-dresses in his letter to the Galatians are in places like Pisidian Antioch and Iconium. The city was a Roman colony city and was the civil and administrative capital of the region. It had a large Gentile population and also a significant Jewish community of long standing.[10] We have here one of three representative speeches of the Pauline mission. Luke apparently decided to present Theophilus with a sample of a speech to Jews in a synagogue (13:16–41), a sample of a speech to pagans in Ath-ens (17:22–31), and a sample of a speech to Christians at Miletus (20:17–35). Paul is being portrayed as a speaker effective with either Jewish or Gentile audiences, though also a speaker who engendered enormous opposition.

The message in Acts 13 draws on texts such as Deut. 4:25–46, 2 Sam. 7:6–16, and 1 Sam. 13:14. Jews and God-fearers are addressed (v. 16; cf. v. 43, where Jews and devout proselytes are referred to). The sermon begins with a focus on Jewish election and the formative exodus-Sinai

8. For more on this matter, see B. Witherington III, *Conflict and Community in Corinth: A Socio-rhetorical Commentary on 1 and 2 Corinthians* (Grand Rapids: Eerd-mans, 1994), 5 n. 12.

9. On this suggestion, see R. L. Fox, *Pagans and Christians* (New York: Knopf, 1987), 293–94.

10. Jews had been brought to the region during the Seleucid period.

events, but by v. 26 it becomes clear that the message of salvation is for both Israelites and those who fear God in their midst. Jesus' death is portrayed as an injustice, something that happened despite the fact that his fellow Jews could find no good reason to condemn him, but nonetheless something done in ignorance. Verse 29 indicates that what was done to Jesus was foretold in the Scriptures and was a part of God's plan. Likewise, Jesus' resurrection and appearances to various Galilean disciples was part of the divine plan. The promises in the psalms about not letting God's Holy One see corruption applied to Jesus (Ps. 16:10). Verse 39 makes an interesting and important point: Jesus' death atones for sins that the Mosaic provisions did not atone for. Sin offerings in the Old Testament were to expiate inadvertent sins, but no such sin offering could expiate deliberate sins, sins committed high-handedly. The language of justification and faith here certainly sounds a Pauline note. Lacking samples in Paul's letters of his missionary preaching, we have no reason to reject the possibility that this is a useful summary of the kind of salvation-historical message Paul might have offered to such a predominantly Jewish audience. Certainly, nothing about the speech is un-Pauline. Notice that Paul was asked to come and speak again the following Sabbath.

On the second Sabbath, Jewish opposition arose to Paul's message, apparently because he had attracted a large Gentile audience from the city (Acts 13:44–45). Rhetoricians, or public speakers, were a chief form of entertainment in antiquity, and it is plausible that many would turn out in a provincial town to hear such a controversial speaker who sought to address all the people of the city. Verse 46 indicates the missionary principle by which Paul operates: the message must be brought first to the Jews, and if they reject it, Paul will turn to the Gentiles. In Pisidian Antioch, this meant that he would turn to Gentiles once he was no longer welcome in the synagogue. It did not signal a refusal to approach Jews in another city, nor did offering salvation first to the Jews mean that Paul would bypass Gentiles if the first audience largely accepted the good news. Notice that Paul's opponents enlist devout women of high standing and leading men to get Paul and Barnabas run out of town. High-status God-fearers provided the link with the Greco-Roman pagans that provided stability and protection to the Jewish community. If the former were lost to the community by conversion to Christianity, then the native anti-Semitism might take over. In short, the Christian message was seen as a threat to the well-being of the Jewish community in a largely Gentile city.

Having shaken Antioch's dust off their feet, Paul and Barnabas moved on some ninety miles south and east on the Via Sebaste to Ico-

Illustration 9.2 A street in Jerash, one of the cities of the Decapolis built in the Greco-Roman pattern.

nium, the easternmost city of Phrygia.[11] The emperor Claudius had given the city the privilege of calling itself Claudiconium. Acts 14:1 relates that Paul and Barnabas's experience was the same in Iconium as in Pisidian Antioch: they began with the synagogue, and some responded in faith while others rejected the message. Again, it was Gentiles who responded positively to the message, with the result that a city was divided about these two missionaries and their message. Verse 3 says that the Lord confirmed the message by means of miracles.

Acts 14:4 contains the only reference to Paul as an apostle in Acts (with the possible exception of v. 14). Here the term seems to mean a missionary agent of the church in Antioch, like the usage in 2 Cor. 8:23, for elsewhere Luke reserves this term for the Twelve, referring to those who had traveled with Jesus during his ministry and had seen him alive after Easter. In other words, unlike Paul, Luke does not use the term "apostle" to refer to someone who has seen and been commissioned by the risen Lord but was not necessarily a companion of the earthly Jesus. This difference in the use of terminology is important and probably reveals why various early Christians did not recognize Paul to be an apostle. He had never been a companion of the earthly Jesus. To the contrary, he had opposed the Jesus movement with zeal. First Corin-

11. Notice the later reflections on this missionary trip in 2 Tim. 3:11.

thians 9:1–6 manifests that Paul operated under a cloud of suspicion about his apostolic status (as does Galatians and 2 Corinthians; cf. Philippians 3 on his Jewish status). He was frequently having to defend that status even to his own Christian converts. This reflects clearly how controversial a figure Paul was in early Christendom. For Luke, apparently, Paul's missionary work on the first journey was a response to the commissioning of the church in Antioch, while the later work did not involve Paul being an "agent" of that church, but rather, was of a more independent nature.

Notice that Paul and Barnabas stayed in a city until forced to leave. The next city they visited was an important Roman colony city, Lystra, which, like Derbe, was in the region of Lycaonia (Acts 14:5–7). The story of the visit to Lystra requires as background knowledge the famous story in Ovid, *Metamorphoses* 8:626–725, about the visit of two gods (Zeus and Hermes) incognito to the city, who were not received as hospitably as they should have been, with the result that Lystra missed out on various blessings. The city, of course, did not want to repeat that mistake; thus, when Paul appeared in the city as a herald, a messenger of God, and performed a miracle, the crowds assumed that Paul and Barnabas were indeed Hermes and Zeus.[12] Because neither Paul nor Barnabas knew the local Lycaonian language, things got out of hand quickly, and even reached the point where a priest of Zeus was preparing to offer a sacrifice to Paul and Barnabas! This, of course, the missionaries rejected, but even Paul's further speech disclaiming their divinity did not dampen the crowd's enthusiasm. What changed the whole tenor of things was the arrival of Jews from Pisidian Antioch and Iconium who won the crowd over. In due course, Paul had been stoned, dragged outside the city, and left for dead. Through what seems to have been the laying on of hands, Paul recovered, and he and Barnabas then moved on to Derbe, some fifty to sixty miles farther on, but still within the Galatian province (Acts 14:20).

In Derbe, once again converts were made, then the missionaries retraced their steps through the cities they had already visited, strengthening their converts. Luke wants to make clear that persecution is what caused the missionaries to leave a city prematurely, and not that they were simply interested in doing a preaching tour leaving a number of half-converted new Christians in their wake. Indeed, as we will see, Paul continued the care of these Galatian converts by writing them a letter from Antioch sometime after he had returned to that city. As R. Tannehill has aptly remarked,

12. See the full treatment of this remarkable story in Witherington, *Acts of the Apostles*, 421–26.

Acts 13–14 presents a representative picture of Paul's mission and includes many themes that we will encounter again. He preaches first in the Jewish synagogue but turns to Gentiles when the synagogue preaching is no longer possible. He announces the one God to Gentiles who have no contact with Jewish monotheism. He repeatedly encounters persecution and moves on when necessary, but he does not abandon the mission. He works signs and wonders. He strengthens the new churches. In this mission Paul is fulfilling the Lord's prophecy that he would "bear my name before Gentiles and kings and sons of Israel" and "must suffer for my name" (9:15–16).[13]

Explosion in Antioch

When Paul and Barnabas returned to Antioch, they reported about their adventures and misadventures and stayed in Antioch for a good while (Acts 14:26–28). But reports of what Paul and Barnabas had been doing must have reached Jerusalem before they ever got back to Antioch, through John Mark (cf. 13:13). It is thus not altogether surprising to hear in Galatians about the following occurrences: Peter came to Antioch, presumably to inspect things as he had done in Samaria and elsewhere before, and even shared in table fellowship with Gentile Christians—that is, until men representing James, called the circumcision party, came to Antioch, and Peter drew back from such table fellowship. Paul opposed Peter on this matter in public but seems to have lost the argument, as he does not relate the outcome (see Gal. 2:11–14); and even worse, all the other Jewish Christians in Antioch, including even Barnabas, withdrew from having table fellowship with the Gentile Christians, thus dividing the Christian community into two parts. But this is not all, because some person or persons had come to Galatia after Paul and had been persuading the Galatians to submit to circumcision and the Mosaic law in order to become full-fledged Christians (Gal. 3:1–3). Paul may not have known exactly who his adversaries were in Galatia, but the allegory in Gal. 4:21–31 suggests that he thought they came from Jerusalem, and made much of their connection with the mother church and the Holy City. Perhaps, the men from James continued on from Antioch to check up on Paul's work in Galatia. In short, we have a full-fledged crisis on the mission field in A.D. 48, precipitated in part by what was happening in Antioch (table fellowship between Jewish and Gentile Christians) and in part by what was happening in Galatia.

13. R. Tannehill, *The Narrative Unity of Luke-Acts: A Literary Interpretation*, vol. 2 (Philadelphia: Fortress, 1990), 182.

Paul responds to the crisis by writing the fiery letter that we know as Galatians, probably early in A.D. 49, in which he expends no little energy and argument to persuade the Galatians not to submit to circumcision and the law. This letter is the earliest extant Christian document, and it shows the volatility and difficulties of the fledgling church as it tried to find a *via vivendi* for Jewish and Gentile Christians who were part of the same Christian congregations in one city or another in the empire. In my view, the letter was written shortly before Paul and others went up to Jerusalem for the third time to resolve these matters. Before turning to the Jerusalem council spoken of in Acts 15, we consider for a moment this earliest piece of Christian literature.

The Rhetoric of Rejection—Galatians

Paul lived in an age when letter writing was becoming a popular means of communication across distances, and indeed was becoming more viable because of the system of Roman roads being constructed all over the empire. Paul's letters usually were public communications, by which I mean that they were not written to private individuals but to congregations. Even the letter to Philemon was meant to be read aloud before the congregation that met in Philemon's house. Paul operated in a largely oral culture, and his letters mainly were surrogates for oral communication. Colossians 4:16 and other pertinent texts make evident that Paul's letters would be read aloud as part of a congregational gathering (cf. Gal. 6:11). The literacy rate in antiquity was nowhere close to what it is in most countries today. Even a liberal estimate would suggest that no more than 20 percent of the general populace in Paul's day could read and write. This being the case, letters had to be read aloud if the whole congregation was to benefit. Letters were regarded as inadequate substitutes for face-to-face communication, and Paul clearly shares that opinion (cf. Rom. 15:14–33; 1 Cor. 4:14–21; 1 Thess. 2:17–3:13; Gal. 4:12–20).

The customary form of an ancient letter had the following components: (1) the name of the writer; (2) the name of the addressee; (3) a greeting; (4) the body of the letter—including a thanksgiving or wish prayer, an introductory formula, the substance of the letter, and possibly a concluding travelogue; (5) ethical or practical advice; (6) a conclusion with final greetings, benediction, and sometimes a description of how the letter was or came to be written. One or another of these elements could be omitted, and in fact, Galatians lacks the thanksgiving prayer that we find in some form in all Paul's other letters. We are right to conclude from this that Paul was extremely angry and could not think of anything to be thankful about. The fourth and fifth elements

A Mundane Missive

Personal letters in antiquity were often written on any sort of surface that would take the ink, including on bits of pottery called *ostraka*. The following letter, perhaps to a soldier from his wife or possibly his sister in the second century A.D., gives us a window on the daily life of ordinary people: "Sentis to Proklos her brother, greetings. You did well, brother, giving the two liquid measuring devices to Anchoubis. And write to me about the fare, and I shall send it to you immediately. I did not send you meat, brother, lest I 'bid you adieu.' Finally, I ask you, sir, respect me and come with the Ethiopian. Let us rejoice. Farewell. So do not do otherwise, but if you love me come . . . let us rejoice." The letter is interesting in several respects. The reference to meat that could be spoiled and cause death is important. Ordinarily, the ancients, unless they were very wealthy, ate meat only on special occasions right after a temple sacrifice. There were no good means of refrigeration, so meat had to be cooked and eaten very shortly after the animal was killed. The term *kolophōnia* I have translated "liquid measure devices," as it refers to measures used particularly with wine. Wine, of course, was the staple drink of the entire region throughout the New Testament era, and perhaps Proklos's wife is running the family business and needs the measuring devices as she sells wine in portions smaller than an amphora would contain. Finally, the reference to the Ethiopian would seem to indicate a slave or possibly a traveling companion. (*NewDocs* 1:58)

normally are found in Paul's letters but are rare in secular letters, except in some of the more philosophical ones. Most ancient letters were short and to the point, and were almost always occasional documents, that is, texts written in response to some particular situation. This is true of Paul's letters, with the possible exception of Ephesians, which may be a homily or circular letter.

Paul, like other ancient letter writers, used a secretary (see Rom. 16:22), as is clearly witnessed by references to his taking up the pen near the end of a document to write a note in his own hand (1 Cor. 16:21; Gal. 6:11; 2 Thess. 3:17). This raises the question of how much freedom Paul accorded his secretaries in the composition of a letter. Did he dictate word for word, or did he just give the sense of things and leave the composition to the scribe? In the case of a document like 1 Thessalonians (the second-earliest letter we have from Paul), it appears that we must speak of joint composition by Paul, Silas (Silvanus), and Timothy. Second Thessalonians 3:17 claims that Paul signed all his letters (likely reviewing the document first). If this was his usual procedure, then it may not matter much whether we have Paul's words

verbatim in the letter. But in fact, the evidence on the whole suggests that Paul not only used fellow Christians and co-workers to help in the composition of his letters, but also that he often did dictate texts verbatim, which was the normal way of handling the matter in antiquity when using a scribe. This would explain why we have some sentence fragments in Paul's letters: the scribe could not keep up. We may assume that Paul saw these letters as being too important to be written without his close supervision of their content.

Paul's letters must be seen as part of a larger ongoing conversation with his converts and co-workers that also involved oral communication through messengers as well as face-to-face discussions. Paul was, of course, a pastor, and his letters are pastoral in nature, trying to help a congregation either overcome problems or make progress in a direction they were already heading in. Clearly enough, Galatians is a problem-solving letter, full of exclamation points and stern warnings.[14] We also need to be aware that Paul's letters, as surrogates for oral communication, to a large extent take the forms of ancient speeches. In other words, Paul draws on the art of persuasion in its ancient form to convict, convince, and convert his audiences to his point of view. This art of persuasion is known as rhetoric.

A Closer Look: *The Ancient Art of Rhetoric*

Paul and his contemporaries lived in a rhetoric-saturated culture. Early in the first century A.D., rhetoric became the main discipline in Greco-Roman higher education.[15] Eloquence, or the ability to persuade, was seen as one of the main cultural goals of Paul's world. Thus, training in rhetoric was seen as essential, indeed, as the capstone of a liberal education. Rhetoricians were found in all the great cities of the empire, including Jerusalem, and a famous orator could gain considerable wealth, especially through exercising the trade in the law courts. Rhetoricians also were in demand to train young men in the art of persuasion. Paul seems to have obtained these skills in Jerusalem while acquiring the rest of his education.

There were three main species of rhetoric: deliberative, forensic, and epideictic. Each had its own use and purposes. Deliberative rhetoric was

14. On this letter, see B. Witherington III, *Grace in Galatia: A Commentary on St. Paul's Letter to the Galatians* (Grand Rapids: Eerdmans, 1998).
15. See the fuller discussion of this matter in Witherington, *Conflict and Community*, 40–48.

the rhetoric of the assembly (*ekklēsia*) or of the ambassador, and was used to persuade someone or a group of people about the proper course for future action. It considered issues of what would be beneficial or harmful to do. This is the sort of rhetoric we find in letters like Galatians and 1 Corinthians, where Paul is trying to correct problems and help his converts avoid making bad choices in the near future. Forensic rhetoric, which we find, for example, in 2 Corinthians 10–13, was the rhetoric of attack and defense, the rhetoric of the law court, and its focus was on the past, on something someone said or did. Epideictic rhetoric was the rhetoric of praise and blame, and focused on the present. This sort of oratory was often heard at a funeral or in public speeches where someone was being lauded or lambasted. By far the most common form of rhetoric in Paul's day was forensic rhetoric, the rhetoric of the law court. But of course passion and anger could be expressed in any of the three forms of rhetoric, and it is a mistake to judge the rhetorical species of a speech on the basis of its tone. For example, the substantial pathos and emotional material in Galatians does not make it a piece of forensic rhetoric.

There were, in a sense, two approaches to rhetoric: learning how to speak eloquently, or learning how to persuade. The latter was a more serious-minded and substantive approach, and this is the sort of rhetoric we find in the New Testament. It is never merely an exercise in verbal gymnastics, or the use of rhetoric just for display or entertainment.

Rhetoricians understood that one must appeal to both the mind and the heart to effectively communicate. Thus, a good speech must involve both *logos* and *pathos*. Generally speaking, the emotions are addressed at the beginning and near the end of the speech. The less profound emotions are dealt with early in the speech (in the *exordium*), when the orator seeks to gain the good graces of the audience and make them willing to listen to the discourse. This was called establishing *ethos*, the speaker's rapport with the audience. The deeper emotions, such as anger and love, would be appealed to at the end of a speech in the summing up (called the *peroratio*). In between came a series of arguments, usually arranged in order of strength. A speech always had a thesis statement, called a *propositio*, supported by the arguments. For example, 1 Cor. 1:10 is the thesis statement for that piece of deliberative rhetoric, and it makes clear that Paul is arguing for concord and unity in a fractured and contentious congregation. In Galatians, 2:15–21 is the thesis statement in which Paul makes very clear that it is by the faithful-

ness of Christ and not by works of the law that one has right standing
with God and full membership in the body of Christ.

The real cash value of rhetorical analysis of Paul's various letters is
that it lets us know what his aims were, his main purposes and goals in
writing this or that letter. It also helps us avoid over- or undervaluing
particular aspects of his case. If we fail to recognize when Paul is being
ironic or sarcastic, or is speaking tongue in cheek, we will mistake the
force of his words.

Clearly, things had reached the boiling point in Antioch and elsewhere, and the issue of the Gentile mission and the proper relationship
between Jewish and Gentile converts had to be sorted out. Paul was adamant in Galatians that there could be no compromise on the heart of
the Gospel, which is to say that one could be redeemed quite apart
from the observance of the Mosaic law. Salvation was by grace through
faith in the crucified and risen Jesus. On this point, Paul was prepared
to be resolute for the sake of his Gentile converts. But how, then, could
things be sorted out when there were Judaizing Christians who took
just the opposite point of view?

There was also the issue of how to deal with non-Christian Jews, or
better said, how to approach Jews without immediately offering offense to them and their sacred practices. It must never be forgotten that
Christianity was a missionary religion, and thus had to be concerned
with how it came across to outsiders, whether Jews or pagans. We must
now consider the great council spoken of in Acts 15.

A Council of Hope—Acts 15

From any vantage point, A.D. 49 was a tumultuous year for early
Christians. The emperor Claudius issued an edict expelling Jews, thus
also Jewish Christians, from Rome (Acts 18:2). This affected some
who were to be prominent early Christian missionaries, such as
Aquila and Priscilla. This action no doubt sent shock waves through
the empire and would have had the net effect of making Jews everywhere all the more protective of their status and ancestral traditions.[16] In other words, it upped the volatility of the situation that
evangelizing Christians faced if they approached the synagogues in
the empire. The Jerusalem church quite rightly was concerned that
Jews would be unapproachable if they thought that the followers of
Jesus were not expecting their converts to respect the basic tenants of

16. On this, see Witherington, *Acts of the Apostles*, 539–44.

the Mosaic law. How could this matter be adjudicated without compromising the gospel of salvation by grace through faith? Into this tense environment came Paul, Barnabas, James, Peter, and a variety of other early Christian leaders, meeting in the most volatile of all Jewish locations, Jerusalem.

It is no exaggeration to say that Acts 15 is the most crucial chapter in the whole book. Luke understands that there had to be a conclusion about what constituted the people of God and what the basis was for their relationship to God. How could the Jew/Gentile divide be bridged so that both groups could be included in God's people on equal footing and fellowship could be had between these two groups of Christians so the church could remain one?[17] While Luke no doubt omitted discussing some of the early Christian controversies, he could not omit the discussion of this matter.

Scholars have debated at length whether Acts 15 discusses the same meeting as that described in Galatians 2. I strongly believe this is not so, and that instead, Galatians 2 refers to the same meeting as that described in brief in Acts 11:27–30.[18] In my view, had there already been a decree from the Jerusalem church that did not require Gentiles to be circumcised in order to be Christians, Paul simply could have appealed to it in his letter to the Galatians, and that would have settled the matter. The silence of Galatians is deafening on this matter, and it strongly suggests that Galatians was written prior to such a council and decree being issued. This means in turn that we should not look for traces of the decree before Paul's letters written after the *second* missionary journey, which followed the Jerusalem council.[19]

We should note at the outset that the meeting described in Acts 15 dealt both with circumcision and table fellowship between Jews and Gentiles, at least in one sense of the term. Unlike the meeting described in Galatians 2 and Acts 11, the Jerusalem council of Acts 15 is a public meeting involving a variety of persons and views. Notice, however, that in the private meeting referred to in Galatians 2 and Acts 11, Paul had already gotten, from the pillar apostles at least, an agreement in principle about his apostolic mission to the Gentiles, and about the nonrequirement of circumcision, as the case

17. This must have been an especially pressing issue for Luke, with his emphasis on the universalism of the gospel message. His social premise had to be not "one emperor, one empire" but rather, one God, one redeemed people gathered out of the many ethnic groups.

18. See Witherington, *Acts of the Apostles*, 440–43.

19. Noting that we have only one letter dealing with those converted on the first missionary journey, Galatians.

of Titus illustrated.[20] But clearly, there were those in Jerusalem who opposed Paul's activities on the first missionary journey, especially if they were undertaken on the basis on which Paul did undertake them—no requirement of circumcision and submission to the law of Moses. Paul was not going to require Gentiles to become Jews in order to be Christians.

The narrative in Acts 15 records not one event but a series of events in chronological order, and Luke does not make clear the time intervals in between—for example, the dispute in Antioch and the meeting in Jerusalem. Luke seems to be following an Antiochene source for the account of this event, for it mentions Barnabas first when he and Paul are mentioned together at 15:12 and 25, and Paul's contribution to the discussion is barely mentioned at all. In other words, this meeting seems very different from the one described in Galatians 2 as far as Paul's role is concerned.

At Acts 15:1 we hear of a group of Christians who came down from Jerusalem to Antioch and were teaching, "Unless you are circumcised according to the Mosaic custom, you cannot be saved." This is an extreme view, which says not merely that circumcision is necessary for Christians, but that without it, one cannot be saved. This is indeed precisely the view that Paul is combating in Gal. 2:15–21 and 6:15–16, and elsewhere in that letter. Thus there is good reason to think that Luke is referring to the same group that came from Jerusalem to Antioch and then went on to Galatia. Presumably, they are also the same as the ones whom Paul calls "false brothers" in Galatians 2. Acts 15:2 says that Paul and Barnabas had "no small debate" with these Jewish Christians from Jerusalem, and this produced a conflict. Paul and Barnabas are appointed as representatives of the Antioch church to go up to Jerusalem and resolve the matter. The Antioch church is requesting a ruling from the mother church, and Acts 15 portrays the outcome in a fashion that

20. But notice also how Paul puts the matter in Galatians 2. Titus was not *compelled* to be circumcised. This indicates that there was still strong sentiment among the pillars at that time that circumcision was important, even if it should not be forced upon unwilling Gentiles. Paul also says that false brothers slipped into the private meeting and caused debate and trouble, leading to a vigorous defense by Paul of his gospel. Notice too that Paul only says that the pillars recognized his legitimacy; he does not say that the others in Jerusalem did. Nothing in Galatians 2 suggests that a ruling was made on whether Gentiles should be circumcised, perhaps voluntarily, or on the issue of table fellowship. What was settled at Paul's second visit to Jerusalem was that his mission to the Gentiles was seen as legitimate and should continue. The specifics of how those Gentiles would be integrated into a Jewish sect was by no means settled then. One definitely gets the impression that Paul is running against a stiff wind when he writes Galatians, still fearing that he could be running in vain.

accords with this portrayal. The decree is sent to Antioch and to the churches in its region (15:23).

The journey from Antioch to Jerusalem was a good 250 miles, and other Christians from Antioch accompany Paul and Barnabas along the way. Acts 15:4 indicates that the Jerusalem leadership, both apostles and elders, as well as the Jerusalem church itself, welcomed this delegation. The delegation gives a report about the conversions at Antioch (and perhaps elsewhere), and this prompts the response mentioned in v. 5 of Pharisaic Jewish Christians, who say that Gentiles must be circumcised and ordered to keep the law of Moses, which is to say that they must be treated like proselytes to Judaism. Of course, most if not all of these early Jewish Christians saw themselves as representing true messianic Judaism, not a new religion.

The demand of the Pharisaic Jewish Christians produced much debate, and finally prompted a speech by Peter. This is perhaps the most Pauline sounding of all Peter's speeches, but we must remember that Paul had more than once consulted with Peter in Jerusalem about his gospel and had argued about it with Peter in Antioch, and perhaps, we are to think, convinced him of its correctness. Peter himself, remember, previously had been called on the carpet over the Cornelius episode and had had to answer for his conduct to the circumcised believers (Acts 11:2–3). Considerable time had passed since the Cornelius episode, and so a reminder of the early days when this issue first arose was in order. In Peter's view, as 15:8–9 states, the Gentiles' reception of the Spirit before the law had been kept and before baptism had been administered showed how God had testified directly on the matter of receiving Gentiles into the church and on what basis.[21] Peter's conclusion is that if God accepts them without obedience to the law, how can the church require it of them? Furthermore, Paul tells us that Peter for some time had been living like a Gentile (Gal. 2:14), and held back from table fellowship with Gentiles only after being pressured by Jewish Christians from Jerusalem. Clearly, the notion of a Judaizing Peter is a myth.

Acts 15:12 mentions only very briefly the report of Paul and Barnabas about the miracles that happened among the Gentiles as they were being converted, and this can be seen as seconding Peter's point about the Holy Spirit and the Gentiles. Notice that Luke does not recount the debate between the various factions in Jerusalem but concentrates on the speeches of Peter and James, those who made the decisive difference in a positive way.

---

21. It is striking how similar Peter's argument here is to what Paul says in Gal. 3:2 in his very first argument.

Illustration 9.3 Roman male offering a sacrifice.

The speech of James (Acts 15:13–21) and what follows it make perfectly clear that James is seen as the ultimate authority figure in this entire discussion who can give a ruling that would settle the matter. The essence of James's homily is that the eschatological restoration of the "tent of David" (i.e., the Jewish people) was intended to cause the Gentiles to seek God, as the text of Amos 9:11–12 is thought to show. Therefore, the witness of Peter about the Gentiles must be accepted and validated by the church as a whole.

Yet there is still the concern about the effect on non-Christian Jews in Diaspora synagogues if it is learned that Gentile converts to the Jesus movement are not required to be circumcised and keep the Mosaic law. The decree that follows in 15:20 and 29 (and in 21:25) seeks to address this problem. Textual problems cloud the earliest form of the decree that Luke originally conveyed, but probably it involved a prohibition of four things: *eidōlothyton*, blood, things strangled, and *porneia*. Traditionally, scholars have taken this to mean that James was imposing a modicum of food laws and a general prohibition of sexual immorality. But what needs to be asked about the decree is this: Where might one find all four of these things in one venue? The answer is, in a pagan temple.

Obviously, the heart of the Mosaic law was the Ten Commandments, and at the heart of those commandments was a prohibition of idolatry and immorality. In my view, the term *eidōlothyton*, which literally means "idol stuff" or "something dedicated and sacrificed to an idol" (in this case, an animal or meat) connotes meat eaten in the presence

Banquets in Antiquity

In antiquity, the main public restaurants suitable for those of higher social status to dine in were not the *tabernae* (taverns), which were frequented by the lower social orders, but rather, the temples. In 1 Corinthians 8–10 Paul deals with the problem that some of his higher-status Corinthian converts continue to attend feasts in pagan temples, which involved dining with the god itself. Sometimes the statue of the god even would be placed on a separate couch as if the god were dining with the feasters, and of course, a prayer would be offered to this god before eating.

How did one get to attend such a banquet in a temple? The following second- or third-century A.D. inscription provides an answer: "Nikephoros asks you to dine at a banquet of the lord Sarapis in the Birth-House on the 23rd, from the ninth hour." And another similar inscription reads, "The god calls you to a banquet being held in the Thoereion tomorrow from the ninth hour." (*NewDocs* 1:5)

First, we notice that the beginning of the dining is at three o'clock in the afternoon, and attendance is by invitation only. These meals were not public affairs, unlike some that were held as part of city festivals. Such banquets in the Greco-Roman style were extended affairs that went on for hours, and usually included an after-dinner speaker at the *symposion*, or drinking party, which followed the meal.

The religious character of these meals must not be overlooked. The meal is in a temple, and in the second inscription it is actually the god who is inviting a person to dinner. The procedure was that a sacrifice was made to the god, and then the god was given its portion (sometimes as a burnt offering) and the rest dispensed to the guests reclining on couches. Meat was a fairly expensive commodity in antiquity, and the ordinary person seldom ate it, one of those rare occasions being at a city festival. The dining rooms that have been uncovered at Corinth suggest that such meals would not involve a large number of people, for the dining rooms would hold only seven to ten people reclining on couches. This was a function for the elite of society, and a select group of them at most.

of the idol, where the act of dedication actually took place. It is the negative counterpart to the term *Korban*, which referred to something dedicated to the temple in Jerusalem. Early Jews believed that the place where one would find meat offered to idols, blood, things strangled, and sexual immorality was a pagan temple (2 Macc. 6:4–5). In essence, James is arguing what Paul later would argue in 1 Corinthians 8–10: Christian converts, even Gentile ones, must stay away from pagan temples. The break with pagan religion and its practices must be absolute.

This is what would be an impressive witness to monotheistic Jews in the Diaspora synagogues. Also remember that early Christians did not often eat meat. The place where meat most frequently would be found and consumed by an ordinary person was at a meal in a temple, whether a Jewish one or a pagan one. The associations of eating idol meat with being in a temple would be clear in the mind of the ancients. Thus, at the end of the day, it does not appear that James is imposing Jewish food laws on Gentiles so much as he is urging them to break completely with all that went on in pagan temples, including sacred prostitution, which is what the term *porneia* often refers to. In Acts 15:20, James speaks of avoiding the pollutions of idols, which would have been understood as a warning against going to a pagan temple.[22]

The council was concluded not by the ruling of James, but by the writing of an official letter from James and the elders and the apostles in Jerusalem to the churches in Antioch and elsewhere in Syria and Cilicia. The transcript is found in Acts 15:23–29, and it has the proper form of an official document. Verse 24 relates that those who went out and disturbed the churches in Antioch and elsewhere had no instructions from the Jerusalem church to do so. Verse 25 indicates that delegates would be sent with Paul and Barnabas from the Jerusalem church, presumably to offer oral confirmation of the authenticity of the decree. The form of the letter shows the Jerusalem church making every effort to communicate in a form that Greek-speaking Christians in Antioch would recognize as authoritative. The letter is well received in Antioch, not surprisingly, and the net effect of what happened in Jerusalem is that Paul's independent mission to the Gentiles without the imposition of circumcision or food laws is legitimated before he even undertakes the second missionary journey. A great turning point in church history had transpired, and the church survived intact, but this did not mean a future without troubles of various sorts, including troubles with Judaizers. What it did mean was that James and the pillars stood with Paul in the Gentile mission, with James being a bridge figure between the Pharisaic Christians in Jerusalem and Paul.

22. See Witherington, *Acts of the Apostles*, 460–67.

Chapter 10

Good News Heading West

A.D. 50–52

The Aftermath of the Decree

The official decision of the Jerusalem council had been made, but this did not mean that everyone accepted the outcome. Indeed, to judge by Paul's subsequent letters (see especially 2 Corinthians 10–13), some in the church never would accept a law-free offer of salvation to the Gentiles. When Paul says in 2 Cor. 12:26 that he has been endangered not only by Jews and Gentiles but also by "false believers," we must take this seriously. He may or may not be referring to the "false brothers" in Jerusalem whom he mentions in Gal. 2:4. But in any case, what is important to recognize is that the opposition to Paul and his ministry, while possibly stemming from the Pharisaic Christian group within the Jerusalem church, did not come from any of the pillar apostles,

249

which is to say, the major leaders of early Christendom. Yet opposition there was, even violent opposition from within the church. Paul was the kind of person who aroused strong feelings, negative and positive.

Paul's résumé, which included being stoned, beaten with rods (Roman punishment), receiving thirty-nine lashes (a Jewish disciplinary procedure), imprisoned, shipwrecked, and in constant danger from a variety of persons, manifests how controversial a figure Paul was. It is doubtful that anyone would hire him as a minister today, with that sort of track record. Yet there is a sense in which, humanly speaking, if Paul had not done what he did to evangelize the empire, the church even today might not have the predominantly Gentile character that it in fact came to have in the middle of the first century and has had ever since. It behooves us, then, to examine closely Paul's actions in the period A.D. 50–52, for this seems to be the period in which he saw his greatest success as a missionary, to judge from the fact that most of his extant correspondence is written to churches founded during this time.

First, a word of caution is in order. We are captives to the sources we have. Undoubtedly, there were many other missionaries and missionary efforts of which we know little or nothing because we lack sources. We must not assume that Paul alone, or even Paul and his co-workers, was solely responsible for the evangelizing of the Gentile Roman world. This becomes especially clear when we read Romans 16 comparing it to Acts 28 and discover the presence of many Christians in Rome before Paul visited the Eternal City, and indeed, before he wrote Romans in the 50s. We also must avoid the mistake of thinking that no evangelizing occurred in the eastern parts of the empire that Paul never visited, for clearly it did, especially in places like Egypt, and in cities ranging from Pella to Palmyra. We simply do not have any significant first-century evidence about such efforts.[1]

The Second Effort

Acts 15:36–18:23 provides the only somewhat full record of what happened in church history during the period A.D. 50–52. There is a sense in which, after the Jerusalem council, Luke compresses the whole of the church's missionary work into the story of the Pauline mission, for Peter and the others basically disappear from Luke's radar screen except when they interact with Paul (see Acts 21).

1. The evidence from the second and third centuries confirms that such efforts were ongoing even in the first century A.D., but our records of them postdate the period we are focusing on, and all such later reports, including those of Eusebius the church historian, must be critically sifted. In this study we must limit ourselves to first-century evidence.

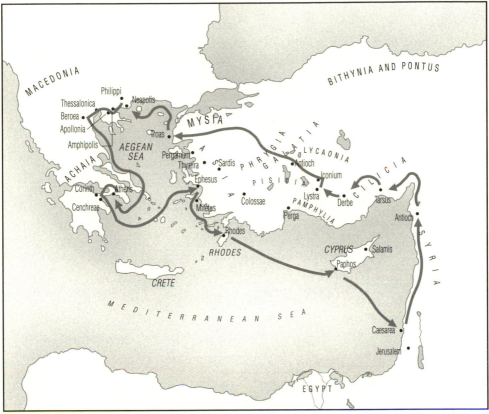

Illustration 10.1 Paul's Second Missionary Journey, A.D. 49–52.

After some time in Antioch, Paul proposed to Barnabas that they make a return visit to every city where they had previously preached God's word on their first mission venture, presumably including the cities of Cyprus, to see how the new converts were doing.[2] Clearly, Paul had no qualms about working with Barnabas again, nor did Barnabas oppose this plan. But 15:38 tells us that Barnabas wanted to take John Mark along, but Paul strongly opposed this idea because John Mark previously had turned back from a mission (13:13). Luke appears to side with Paul in this matter, because he calls Mark's turning back a form of apostasy or desertion of ministerial work. The dispute became so heated that Paul and Barnabas parted company, and Barnabas is never mentioned again in Acts after 15:39. Barnabas sailed off to Cy-

2. Notice that at least initially, nothing is said about venturing into unevangelized new territory.

prus with John Mark, and Paul summoned Silas to accompany him, presumably sending for him in Jerusalem (15:40).

The choice of Silas (or Silvanus, his Latin name) was an excellent one, for he could represent the Jerusalem church and make clear that Paul was not at odds with its leaders. He also could interpret the decree (see Acts 16:4), which was crucial to the ongoing Pauline mission. If we jump ahead briefly and note texts like 1 Thess. 1:1, 2 Thess. 1:1, and 2 Cor. 1:19, we can say that Silas was not only an excellent co-worker, but probably even a co-author of Paul's correspondence to Thessalonike. In addition, Acts 16:37–38 reveals that he likely was also a Roman citizen, which would prove invaluable in Roman colony cities like Philippi and Corinth.

The first task was to go through the churches of Syria and Cilicia and strengthen them on the way overland to the province of Galatia. The overland route allowed Paul to pass through his own native region, but it also meant that he had to go through some rugged territory, passing through the Cilician gates to reach Derbe (see illustration 10.1).

We hear nothing about the outcome of the visit to Derbe, but when Paul reached Lystra, according to Acts 16:1–3, he picked up a new companion for the journey, Timothy. Timothy's mother was a Jewish Christian, but his father was a Greek. He had the endorsement of Christians in both Lystra and Iconium. We are told that Paul circumcised Timothy because of the Jews who lived in the area, presumably because Paul wanted to continue to visit synagogues and evangelize in that setting in the Galatian province, and Luke explains that the people of the region knew that Timothy's father was a Greek. In other words, they did not see him as a Jew, which would cause various problems if Paul brought him into synagogues as a co-laborer proclaiming a Jewish messiah.[3]

First Corinthians 4:17 seems to confirm that Timothy had been converted by Paul on his first missionary journey, since there he is called Paul's spiritual child. Various scholars have balked, however, at the notion that Paul really circumcised Timothy. But we must remember that unlike Titus, who was simply a Gentile, Timothy was half Jewish by birth. Furthermore, there is no evidence that Paul objected to Jewish Christians practicing their religion as long as it was not a cause for breaking fellowship with Gentile Christians or requiring Gentiles to become Jews in order to be Christians. Paul himself

---

3. It is significant that *m. Qidd.* 3:12 says that a Jewish woman who is married to a non-Jew and has a baby should assume that the child has her status as a Jew. This ruling seems to go back to the first century A.D., and explains in part Paul's assumptions and behavior, whatever the townsfolk would have assumed about Timothy.

says that he was happy to be the Jew to the Jew (1 Cor. 9:20). The problem was, of course, with the Judaizers, as is well stated in Acts 15:1. They believed that circumcision law observance was necessary for the salvation of anyone, Jew or Gentile. In the Lukan scheme of things, Acts 16:1–3 anticipates 21:21 and makes clear that Paul was not insisting that Jews forsake Moses' law; in particular, he was not arguing that they cease circumcising their sons. Paul's basic attitude as a Christian about circumcision is expressed in 1 Cor. 7:18–19: he does not see it as a bad thing, but neither does he think that the act has any salvific weight.

Thus, Luke says that Paul went through the Galatian churches proclaiming the decree and strengthening the converts. The decree, far from dividing the church, helped unite it, for it made clear what was necessary for Gentiles: avoid idolatry and immorality, particularly as found in pagan religion and pagan temples. The evidence of 1 Corinthians suggests that Paul also proclaimed and carried out the decree in the new churches he founded in Macedonia and Greece.

Acts 16:6–10 indicates that Paul intended to pass through Galatia and then head basically due west into the province of Asia, presumably heading eventually for Ephesus. However, Luke says that God, not once but twice, corrected Paul's course, and he went northwest to Troas. Some controversy lingers about the meaning of 16:6, but the most natural way to read the phrase (cf. 18:23) is "the Phrygian and Galatian region," referring to one region not two. Phrygian Galatia was distinguished from Asian Galatia when one was dealing with regions in a province. In general, Luke uses ethnic and regional designations, while Paul in his letters uses provincial designations. This is perhaps in part because Luke was from Asia and grew up in the region before the Roman Empire took control of it.

The most natural reason to go to Troas was to book passage to Macedonia. This suggests that Paul's vision of the Macedonian man had confirmed an intention already extant in the mind of Paul. But on the other hand, Troas was a significant city in its own right, a Roman colony city (called Alexandria Troas). We may deduce from 2 Cor. 2:12–13, 2 Tim. 4:13, and perhaps Acts 20:6–12 that a Christian community was founded in this town, and the first of these references hints that it was founded by Paul.

At Acts 16:10 appears the first use of the word "we" that signals the famous "we" passages in Acts. Who is included in this "we"? Certainly, it includes Paul, Silas, and Timothy, but is there someone else? We must consider this much controverted issue in some depth.

⊞ A **Closer** Look: *The "We" Passages*

Ancient historians who stood in the Greek tradition committed themselves to research, consultation of witnesses, and in general, the use of sources. The "we" passage source in Acts is found in Acts 16:10–17; 20:5–15; 21:1–18; 27:1–28:16. We have clear enough evidence that some ancients did keep diaries of their travels, complete with itinerary and the use of the first-person pronoun.[4] There is, then, no reason that one of Paul's companions might not have done so. Also, if we evaluate Luke-Acts as a whole, we discover that the author is not an intrusive author—that is, he seldom interjects personal or parenthetical comments into the narrative. The likelihood that Luke would have artificially created and interjected these "we" passages into the narrative seems slim, especially because these passages do not claim that the author was present at many of the very important moments in Paul's life. Indeed, they suggest only that the author was a sometime companion of Paul during his second missionary journey and occasionally thereafter. Why would a writer invent the notion that he was present on a sea journey from Troas to Macedonia, one of the least consequential things he could validate about Paul's travels?

Some collateral support for the notion that the "we" passages in Acts 16 and following refer to the author is in Luke 1:3 and Acts 1:1, where the presence of an authorial "I" shows that he is not afraid to refer to himself in his narrative where it is warranted. Indeed, I submit that Luke 1:1–4 makes a claim of placing the author in contact with various eyewitnesses and proclaimers of the Word; in other words, he is in contact with the first generation of Christians. But notice then that the "we" passages do not suggest that the author had a major role himself as an eyewitness of the events he records. Indeed, these passages make clear that he was present for only a distinct minority of them beginning in the middle of the century. Luke-Acts is in general a work written in the third person, and so we must take very careful note when the author appears to refer to himself in the account.

There is a difficulty in arguing that the author of Luke-Acts was using someone else's eyewitness diary about Paul's travels. It is unlikely that Luke would have used such a source without identifying where it came from and yet at the same time gradually making clear that none of the

4. See B. Witherington III, *The Acts of the Apostles: A Socio-rhetorical Commentary* (Grand Rapids: Eerdmans, 1998), 481 n. 44.

named persons on the trip—Paul, Silas, Timothy—could possibly be the author of the account. The general style and vocabulary of these "we" passages is perfectly consistent with the style and syntax and vocabulary found in the rest of Acts. There are no telltale signs that the book was likely to be by another author.[5]

We may conclude that the author does not want to make too much of his participation in the events he is recording, especially since mainly he seems to be an observer and recorder of events rather than a major actor in the drama. Thus, he quietly and without announcement includes the "we" passages, because as a Greek historian, it was an important part of his tradition to indicate authorial participation in some of the events that were narrated. That he claims to have been present only during some of the second and more of the third missionary journeys raises no suspicions that he is claiming more than he ought to.

Joseph Fitzmyer puts the matter well:

> If one takes the We-sections at face value—and does not overinterpret them . . . one could still admit that Luke was a companion or fellow worker of Paul, without having been with him inseparably. . . . Luke was not with Paul during the major part of his missionary activity, or during the part when Paul's most important letters were being written. . . . Luke was not on the scene when Paul was facing the major crises in his evangelization of the eastern Mediterranean world, e.g., the Judaizing problem, the struggle with the factions in Corinth or the questions that arose in Thessalonica. Luke would not have been with Paul when he was formulating the essence of his theology or wrestling with the meaning of the gospel. This would explain why there is such a difference between the Paul of Acts and the Paul of the letters.[6]

But to this I would add that what we see in Acts is largely the public missionary face of Paul, while in the letters we behold the more private, pastoral face of Paul. The two are not incompatible, even though the portraits that result from the two sources have differences of emphases.

Often, much is made of Paul having crossed over into Europe when he reached Macedonia, but that is an entirely anachronistic way of put-

---

5. In any case, a careful investigation of Lukan editorial technique in his handling of Mark shows that he tends to present his sources in his own style anyway.

6. J. Fitzmyer, *The Gospel according to Luke I–IX*, AB 28 (Garden City, N.Y.: Doubleday, 1981), 48, 51.

Itinerant Doctors in Antiquity

In my view, Luke was an itinerant physician who plied his trade in places like Troas and Philippi, which is where he came to know and then to travel with Paul, who himself needed from time to time the services of a physician. We now have inscriptional evidence of such doctors in this era in the Roman Empire. From Nicaea, in territory that Paul likely traversed, comes this epitaph: "Fire burned the flesh, but here are the bones of Hedys the doctor who saw many a land and the currents of the ocean and the bounds of the continent of Europe and Libya and Great Asia. And in this way everything has come to a wretched end, and Hedys had no children at all. Hedys the elder, 55 years." (*NewDocs* 2:19)

Horsley is right to relate this example to the case of Luke the physician. Many advantages accrued from having such a skilled itinerant write the history of early Christianity, not the least of which is that wherever he went, he could support himself and gather information rather unobtrusively while practicing his trade. Understandably, doctors were in great demand in the New Testament era.

ting things. The idea that Macedonia belonged to a different continent from Asia never would have crossed the minds of the ancients. They would have seen them simply as two provinces of the Roman Empire very closely bound together by language and political organization. If there was a divide at all, it would be between the Greek- and the Latin-speaking provinces farther west.

What we notice immediately once the "we" sections begin is that the accounts become more circumstantial and lively, as we would expect when dealing with an eyewitness report. There is more dialogue and description and less dependence on set speeches. Notably, in all the sea voyage portions of the "we" sections, Luke gives very specific port-to-port descriptions of the voyage, complete with specific mention of the time it took, and usually even a description of the weather conditions. We also notice that Luke is quite concerned with the honor rating of the city of Philippi, and so here is the point where it will be useful to explain my thoughts regarding the author of Acts.

The author of Acts is probably a Gentile, but had been a God-fearer before becoming a Christian. His Bible is the Septuagint, and he is most definitely literate, even to some degree learned. There is no good reason to dispute that the author was a physician, nor that he was a sometime companion of Paul (see Col. 4:14). In my view, he was probably an itinerant physician before he ever met Paul, accustomed to the road, and working not only in Philippi but also in Troas and perhaps elsewhere as well. But it would appear that Philippi is his home city, which makes it possible, though unprovable, that Luke is the one referred to in Phil. 4:3. It is certain, however, that Philippi had a famous school of medicine, with graduates practicing their trade throughout the empire. Luke may have been one such graduate.

The crossing of the Hellespont by Luke, Paul, and the rest leads them to Neapolis, the port city for Philippi, which was some ten miles distant. Philippi was an important Roman colony city, and in fact the only one so described by Luke (Acts 16:12). Over 80 percent of the inscriptions from this city are in Latin. Roman citizenship was highly prized in such a place, and the city was run on the basis of Roman jurisprudence—two factors not unimportant as the story of Paul's visit to the city develops. This city had added importance because Augustus, after defeating Antony here in 31 B.C., had made the city in effect legally an Italian city, and it became a place where Roman soldiers retired. This was the highest honor a city could have, and it meant exemption from land as well as poll taxes. The city was Greco-Roman in character, and there is no reason to envision any significant Jewish presence there, as is shown by the lack of a synagogue in the middle of the century. Luke calls Philippi "a first [i.e., leading] city of that portion of Macedonia." This is not a political assessment, but a statement about the city's honor rating and importance in Luke's eyes. Since Luke does this for no other city except his hero Paul's hometown of Tarsus (see 21:39), we may plausibly conjecture that this reflects Luke's personal pride in his hometown.

Acts 16:12 says that "we" stayed in Philippi for some days, and it is noteworthy that Luke devotes the balance of this chapter to what transpired when Paul and his co-workers were in the city. Clearly, Luke sees this as an important juncture in Paul's missionary work. Following his usual procedure, Paul looked for a group of Jews to begin his work with, but found only a few meeting, apparently next to the river Gangites, on the Sabbath. This suggests very few Jews present in the city, and those who were there not having much social status, or else they would have met within the city. On the other hand, it may be in light of the expulsion of Jews from Rome in A.D. 49 that Jews in Philippi were seeking to maintain a low profile in a Roman colony city.

Paul sits down in the posture of a teacher to address a Jewish group, apparently composed mostly of women, at a place of prayer. Presumably, they had gathered not only to recite the Shema and read from the Law and Prophets, but also to hear from a teacher and receive a benediction.

Philippi

Philippi was an important Roman colony city that lay on the main east-west Roman road across northern Greece, the Via Egnatia, which connected Rome with the eastern provinces. Philippi could not really be called a port city, since its port, Neapolis, was some ten miles away.

The city was originally built and fortified by Philip of Macedon in about 358 B.C., and, of course, he named the city after himself. The city prospered not only because it was originally an administrative center for Philip's empire, but also because it sat in a region of fertile land and active mines, including gold mines. Even the capital city of the district, Amphipolis (so named in 167 B.C.), was not to be as influential, famous, or prosperous as Philippi. This may well be one reason why Luke calls it the "first city" of the district.

After A.D. 44, the city was in a senatorial province, which meant that it was governed by a proconsul, whose administrative seat was in Thessalonike. Thus, the supreme authority to whom a Philippian could appeal was in another city, perhaps an important detail in light of Paul's encounter with Roman officials in Philippi. This city was thoroughly Romanized, unlike some of the colony cities Paul visited. For example, 80 percent of the period inscriptions in Philippi are in Latin, compared to 40 percent in Pisidian Antioch. The city that Luke and Paul knew was run on Roman principles, and its Hellenistic heritage was a secondary cultural factor.

Philippi gained further fame when it became the site of a famous battle in 31 B.C. Marc Antony was defeated there by Octavian, who then made the city into a Roman colony, settling some of his soldiers there. He even gave the city the *ius italicum*, which meant that in every legal respect it was an Italian city, only transplanted to northern Greece. This was the highest honor that could be bestowed on a provincial city. The benefits of such a status included exemption from poll taxes and land taxes. In addition, the colonists could buy or sell land and engage in civil lawsuits. In short, Philippi was Rome in microcosm.

Acts 16:14 introduces Lydia, a seller of purple cloth, from the city of Thyatira. That Lydia is called by her personal name suggests that she is of Greek extraction and is a person of some social status and standing. Also, Lydia has both a house and servants, indicating a person of some means. But we could have guessed this from her trade. Dealing in royal purple (the murex dye) was an imperial monopoly; indeed those who traded it were members of Caesar's household. In short, whether or not Lydia was of Caesar's household, she was a person of some social significance who could provide a venue for a house church.

Sellers of Royal Purple Cloth

Acts 16 tells the story of Lydia, a seller of purple cloth. The evidence suggests that there was an imperial monopoly on the murex dye and its use on cloth, a monopoly that dates back at least to the time of Nero (see *NewDocs* 2:28). It is possible but unprovable that Lydia was a member of the "household of Caesar" (cf. Phil. 4:22) who had been authorized to practice her trade in the Roman colony city of Philippi. More clearly, we have inscriptional evidence of imperial dyeworks and dyeworkers. It reads, "Lord . . . spare the marble tomb of the catechumens, reserved for Theoktistos, purple-dyer of the imperial dye-works." (*NewDocs* 2:26)

This is a reference from the Christian era to a Christian involved in this trade, and perhaps it can be said that Lydia was the first such to do so. Important for our purposes is that Lydia is a person of some social status, as she has servants and a household where the apostles could stay. Her potentially lucrative source of income was the purple cloth so much in demand during the first century A.D.

Luke on various occasions in his work wishes to stress that Christianity was for the up and in, as much as it was for the down and out, and socially elite persons like Theophilus should see that the gospel was for them as much as for anyone else.

The conversion of Lydia is described simply in Acts 16:14 in terms of the Lord opening her heart to hear Paul's message. Verse 15 says that she and her household were baptized immediately, and then Paul and his co-workers accepted her offer of hospitality. To refuse hospitality in ancient times was considered a slap in the face, and so Lydia prevailed upon the missionaries.

Acts 16:16 suggests that Paul and his colleagues stayed for some time in the city. When they were going once more on the Sabbath down to the river, Paul met a slave girl who had a "Python spirit," meaning that she was inspired by Apollo, the Python deity consulted often through the oracle at Delphi. Luke sees this as a case of possession by an evil spirit, which required exorcism. Here, as in the case of Simon Magus and as in Acts 19:11–41, Luke sees a close connection between magic, pagan or false religion, and the profit motive of humans. The girl had been a very profitable fortune teller, lining the pockets of her owners. Note that the girl's proclamation in v. 17 probably should not be seen as a true confession, for the phrase "the most high god" implies the existence of other deities, and in a religiously pluralistic setting, to say that Paul and his co-workers were proclaiming "a way of salvation"

The Most High God

From the imperial period in the Phrygian region that Paul visited comes an interesting inscription found on a small altar: "With good fortune, Aurally Tattoos, spouse of Onesimos the blacksmith, set up (this monument) along with her spouse Onesimos, to the most high god, at their own expense." (*NewDocs* 1:25)

The reference to the most high god reflects the existence of a pantheon of deities dominated indeed by a supreme deity, Zeus or Jupiter. The society of gods was viewed as hierarchical and stratified, just like human society. At Acts 16:17, Paul and Silas are announced as "servants of the most high god," which is not a monotheistic remark, but simply a recognition that they serve a very powerful deity, perhaps indeed the most powerful one.

did not mean that they were proclaiming *the* way of salvation. Paul is rightly disturbed by the girl's pronouncement, for it not only leaves a false impression, but also comes from a dubious source. For example, to a pagan, the word "salvation" would usually connote rescue or healing or the like, not eternal salvation. Fed up after days of being followed by this girl, Paul commanded the spirit within her to come out. Naturally, the owners were furious and dragged Paul and Silas before the authorities seeking, if not compensation, at least revenge.

Since the slave owners were persons of some means, the authorities took very seriously their complaint. The magistrates stripped Paul and Silas and had them beaten with Roman rods. Following this severe flogging, they were thrown into jail. Nothing in 16:19–24 suggests that the apostles had an opportunity to defend themselves, and clearly the authorities did not know that the two men under arrest were Roman citizens. In fact, it is not until the jailer makes clear after the liberating earthquake that Paul and Silas are free to go that Paul reveals their status. He refuses to be secretly discharged, because he and Silas are uncondemned Roman citizens. According to Roman law, binding or beating a Roman citizen without trial was prohibited, and officials in a city under Roman law could lose their jobs for doing so. Thus, the alarm of the officials mentioned in v. 38 is understandable, as is the apology that follows in v. 39. Paul had occasion slightly later, writing from Corinth to the Thessalonians, to speak of the suffering and shameful mistreatment he endured in Philippi (1 Thess. 2:2). But why had Paul not made known his Roman citizenship before he underwent his ordeal? We must consider this matter more closely for a moment.

A **Closer** Look: *Paul the Roman Citizen (Part 1)*

There is clear evidence from before the middle of the first century A.D. that Jews could indeed be Roman citizens (see *NewDocs* 4:111). Yet in the year A.D. 49, Jews definitely were out of favor with the imperium, and the slave owners had accused Paul and Silas of being Jews (Acts 16:20–21), something they could not deny. Under these circumstances, perhaps there was not time to make a proper presentation of citizenship claims, which likely would have involved producing the *testatio*, a certified private copy of evidence of a person's birth and citizenship inscribed in wax on a wooden diptych. We may be sure that a proper presentation would have been important since it was a rarity for Jews to be Roman citizens.

Paul does not use his citizenship to escape punishment, but rather, to force a restoration of his honor and good name. This was important since Paul no doubt wanted to return to the city and revisit his converts there. Also, Paul did not want the reception of the gospel to stand or fall on the basis of his high status as a Roman citizen, which explains why he did not mention it prior to the event jeopardizing the future gospel work in Philippi. In other words, Paul used his Roman citizenship, just as he did his Jewish pedigree, in a prudential manner when it could help advance the gospel or forestall its hindering. Paul really

Illustration 10.2   The dais in the Roman senate.

believed in an eternal commonwealth of which Christians were already citizens (Phil. 3:20), and that the form of this world and its institutions were passing away (1 Cor. 7:29–31). Thus, he was perfectly prepared to sit lightly with the status markers of this world, using them only when necessary to advance the gospel, not merely when it was personally advantageous.

Acts 17:1 narrates a considerable journey along the Via Egnatia some one hundred miles to Thessalonike. Thessalonike was the capital of the Roman province of Macedonia and was a free city, not a Roman colony city. It minted its own coins and had its own form of government, namely, ruling politarchs. The city had very close ties with Rome and the emperor, including having a shrine for the emperor cult. This meant that though in principle the city was free, in practice it was caught in the web of imperial patronage and very sensitive to anything—including an eastern superstition—that might threaten that "favored city" status.

Paul followed his regular custom by going first to the synagogue. Paul did not wish to rely on the patronage of his fellow Jews, so he and Silas practiced the tentmaking trade while there (cf. 1 Thess. 2:9). In addition, they received some support from the grateful and generous converts in Philippi (Phil. 4:16). The account suggests that Paul, Silas, and Timothy stayed in the city for some weeks or months (Acts 17:2 says that they were in the synagogue for three consecutive Sabbaths). The preaching in this location was quite successful, for many Jews and high-status Greek women and men were converted. This aroused the anger of the unconverted Jews, and once again Paul and Silas were in hot water as complaints were lodged with the politarchs. The complaints are that these missionaries are upsetting the *stasis*, or stability and status quo, of things in the empire, and that they are acting contrary to the decrees of the emperor by proclaiming another king, Jesus.

These charges ring true. Paul had come to this Thessalonike urging Gentiles to turn from idols, worship the one true God, and recognize his Son (1 Thess. 1:9). Also, while the emperor had offered peace and security, Paul proclaimed the parousia, and that God's judgment would fall on unprepared human beings (1 Thess. 5:3; cf. 2 Thess. 1:5–2:12). There indeed had been an imperial decree banning the prediction of the coming of a new king and kingdom in the cities of the empire (first issued by Tiberius in A.D. 16). Paul could be said to fall afoul of this ban. Clearly, the officials took the matter seriously, and they banished Paul and Silas from returning to the city during the rule of these particular

Thessalonike

The capital of the Macedonian province was Thessalonike. Because of its support of Octavian in the struggle with Antony, Thessalonike had been made a free city in 42 B.C. and was not turned into a Roman colony city. This meant that it minted its own coins, both imperial and local, and had its own form of government, involving politarchs. There were five such officials at a time, and their rulings were valid only as long as they held office. This is of no small importance to Paul's case, because it meant that although he was banned from the city by a politarch, he could return there once that official was out of office.

Thessalonike may have been a free city officially, but like other such cities, it was caught up in the patronage and reciprocity network of the emperor. It sought to maintain close relationships with Rome and its ruler right from the start of the Roman Empire. Note, for example, the coins minted in Thessalonike before the time of Christ displaying the head of Julius Caesar and bearing an inscription indicating that he was a god. When Augustus comes to power, the image of Zeus on the coins is replaced, judiciously, by that of Augustus as a god. This practice reflects that Thessalonike is showing its gratitude for the benefactions of the ruler by responding with celebratory coins. There was a growing imperial eschatology in the city, with the emperor seen as the universal savior whose benefactions need to be proclaimed as good news throughout the region. Local officials were expected to enforce loyalty to Caesar in order to maintain the flow of benefactions to the city.

Like other major cities in the Diaspora, especially the free cities, Thessalonike had a significant population of Jews, and there is evidence from a second-century A.D. inscription of a synagogue. We must remember that during the reign of Claudius, with the expulsion of Jews from Rome in A.D. 49, cities like Thessalonike—the first major city east of Rome on the Via Egnatia—would find themselves with refugees from Rome. Their presence in Thessalonike would further underline the tenuousness of the position of Jews in the empire. Therefore, anything that might cause the politarchs to take notice in a negative way of the Jewish community existing in a pagan capital city was not good. Thessalonike, like Ephesus, another free city, depended too much on royal patronage to allow disturbances caused by minorities to last long. The polemic in 1 Thess. 2:14–16 is but the reaction to and residue of the strong reaction of marginalized Jews to the proclamation of the gospel in the Thessalonike synagogue. They wished to maintain their current status in the city without official interference or reprisals.

politarchs (Paul likely alludes to this in 1 Thess. 2:14–18). It is noteworthy that the ruling apparently did not include Timothy, since he was
not accused by the Jews. Acts 17:10 indicates that Paul and Silas quietly went off to Beroea under cover of night.

Beroea was some fifty miles south and west of Thessalonike, and it
was one of the capitals of the Macedonian region, also ruled by politarchs. Acts 17:11–12 indicates that the gospel was well received by the
Jews there, and many believed, as did some Greek women and men of
high standing. As had transpired previously in Lystra, Jews from Thessalonike heard of what was happening in Beroea and came to stir up a
crowd against Paul. But the Beroean Christians acted quickly and sent
Paul south, with Silas and Timothy staying behind to strengthen the
church there, with plans to rejoin Paul in Athens (Acts 17:14–16; cf.
1 Thess. 3:1–2). It appears from 1 Thess. 3:2 that they did rejoin in Athens, at which point Paul sent them back to strengthen things in Thessalonike and Philippi, while he went on to Corinth. They were to rejoin
him there later (cf. 1 Thess. 3:6 to Acts 18:5). But how would Paul fare
alone in a city that was the center of pagan philosophy and all things
Greek? How would he relate the gospel to pagans who were not part of
a synagogue? We must consider Paul's time in Athens.

Jerusalem Meets Athens

Paul's time in Athens may not have been extensive, but clearly enough,
it was intensive. Here in Acts 17, Luke presents the fullest example of what
Paul's missionary preaching would have looked like when delivered to a
pagan audience of some philosophical sophistication. The speech in Acts
17:22–31 should be compared to the briefer but similar one found in
14:15–17. The essence of Paul's message here, which draws on certain
Greek philosophical notions but places them into a very Jewish framework, is that it was God's plan all along to make from one human being
the various nations of humans and to establish their boundaries, but it is
also God's plan to unite all these different peoples into one people of God
through Christ. Those who reject this good news must face the coming
final judgment also brought to the world by Christ. An interesting inter-
play occurs between the speech and the narrative about Paul's visit to Athens, as the speech builds on Paul's encounters with the Stoics and Epicureans, and also to a real extent on Paul's great irritation with the forest of
idols and pagan temples and altars he came across in Athens.[7]

7. The next place that Paul visited after Athens was Corinth, and to judge from 1 Corinthians 8–10, the issue of idols and temples and the like was still exercising him as a serious problem in Achaia.

Athens

Like Ephesus and Antioch, Athens was a free city, not a Roman colony city, in the middle of the first century A.D. Clearly, as a city of political importance, Athens had passed its prime. It was not even the capital of its own province, Achaia, that role falling to Corinth. In size as well, Athens seems to have dwindled since its prime in the golden age before Alexander. Athens may have had as few as five to ten thousand voting citizens in Paul's day, with perhaps a total population of no more than fifty thousand. Nor was Athens as important a port city (its port was Piraeus) or commercial center as Corinth. Furthermore, it was not the locale for the famous Greek games, which were held at Olympia, Isthmia (near Corinth), and Nemia.

The reason Pliny the elder says of Athens, "Her celebrity is more than ample" (*Natural History* 4.24) was, of course, because of its reputation as the birthplace of Greek philosophy and its continued reputation as an academic center of some note. Yet outsiders perceived Athens as trading on the glories of its past, and being a place full of intellectually arrogant people and those who liked to bandy about the popular ideas and topics of the day. Luke was not alone in this opinion (cf. Acts 17:21; Thucydides, *History* 3.38.5; Demosthenes, *Philippic* 1.10). In truth, both Alexandria and Tarsus, not to mention Rome, may have been more academically high-powered places than Athens in Paul's day.

Then, too, Athens had become something of a museum of Greek culture, especially intellectual and religious culture, though its literary culture was nurtured there as well. Every religion imaginable wished to have statues of its gods erected in this ethereal place, especially upon the famous Acropolis. By Paul's day, so many temples and statues of gods ancient and modern crowded the Acropolis that one could speak of a forest of shrines. Also, according to Pausanias, altars to unknown gods were erected to make sure that one was not on the bad side of some deity whose name was unknown (*Description of Greece* 1.1.4). Besides the Parthenon, dedicated to the protector of the city, Athena, there were also the

The Athens of Paul's visit was a free city but one in some decline, trading on its glorious past. It had passed its time of greatest political import; Corinth was now its political and economic superior. The city's claim to house the empire's leading university probably was void, and its voting population seems to have dwindled down to a mere five to ten thousand citizens.

As was his wont, Paul went first to the synagogue and reasoned with the people there. He also dialogued in the agora with whomever would talk to him (Acts 17:16–17).

temple of Nike, the god of victory, and the famous Erecthion, with its beautiful Porch of the Maidens. Of more recent vintage were the statues on the Acropolis to Augustus, Tiberius, Germanicus, and Drusus. The altar to an unknown god is important for Paul because the God he worshiped was not to be called by name; hence, the connection was natural for him as a starting point for his discourse before the Areopagus.

Athens was dominated by its Acropolis, but much of daily life took place in the Stoa, especially the Stoa Basileios, which was adjacent to the agora and in the shadow of the Acropolis. Here, one could encounter Cynics, Stoics, and Epicureans, as well as rhetors, hawkers of all sorts of goods, businesses and their propietors, and politicians. Apparently, the Areopagite council met in this Stoa, and deliberated various issues pertinent to the life and well-being of Athens, especially including religious issues. This in turn means that the small hill of marble named Ares' Hill just below the Acropolis, while likely the locale of some court in antiquity, probably was not the site of Paul's hearing before the council.

Epicureans and Stoics both engaged Paul in lively debate. The Epicureans based their philosophical and ethical worldview on the materialistic atomic theory of Democritus. The gods themselves were seen as part of the material realm, and pleasure was seen as the chief end in life.[8] The highest pleasures, however, were not seen as the physical ones, but rather, the pleasures of the mind—in particular, the pleasure of being free from passions and superstitions was highly prized. Their motto was "Nothing to fear in [the] gods, nothing to feel in death." The Stoics, apparently, were more popular during this era than the Epicureans. Their name came from the place where they met on the northwest side of the agora in Athens—the Stoa Poikile. Basically, the Stoics were pantheists, believing in a divine rational ordering principle in all things and all beings. God was the soul, and the material universe was God's body. Like the Epicureans, the Stoics were materialists, for they believed that even God and the human soul were made up of highly refined matter. The goal of life was to live in accord with the rational ordering principle in everything. The Epicureans and Stoics both emphasized the rational over the emotions, and saw self-sufficiency, or autonomy (*autarkeia*), as the highest good.

Acts 17:18 indicates that the philosophers were not all that impressed with Paul's arguments. They called him a "babbler," suggesting that he merely was serving up sound bites of real philosophy (the ad-

8. Though part of the material realm, the gods were believed to be far removed from the human realm and to take no real interest in it.

Areopagus as a Council, Not a Site

A fragmentary catalog from Athens, dating possibly to A.D. 61–62, makes mention of a herald of the Areopagus (*IG* 2.1723). This makes clear that the reference is not to the location ("Ares' Hill"), but to an assembly, which comports with the usage in Acts 17. It appears that the Areopagus was the governing body of the polis in all matters, including financial, judicial, and religious. It is thus quite possible that Paul was on trial before the Areopagus for introducing foreign deities into the city. (*NewDocs* 1:82)

jective *spermologos* means "picking up seeds," and thus is used of someone who picks up little snippets of knowledge like a bird picking up small seeds). But the second complaint, that Paul was a proclaimer of foreign deities, is a politically dangerous allegation, for it is the one that led to the demise of Socrates (see Plato, *Apology of Socrates* 24B-C). The use of the plural "divinities" is explained by Luke as due to Paul's proclamation of Jesus and *anastasis* ("resurrection"). This was assumed to refer to another deity, perhaps even a male/female pair of deities (Jesus and Anastasia). Remember that resurrection was not a notion native to the Greek philosophical lexicon. They believed in immortality of the soul, not resurrection of the body.

Paul is taken to the Areopagus, here probably meaning the council rather than the hill, or perhaps both. In Paul's time this council apparently met in the Stoa Basileios and not on Ares' Hill, which probably was the original meeting site. Among other duties, this council had to maintain order and review religious customs. Luke's aside about the Athenians in Acts 17:21 is interesting: he calls them dilettantes, always spending their time gossiping about or longing to hear something new. The problem for Paul was that at the heart of his message were ideas that Greeks would have great difficulty in accepting: the resurrection of a human being and the judgment of the world by the one true God. The essence of what he will say comports with the summary of his basic message found in 1 Thess. 1:9–10, that letter written not long after Paul was in Athens. Gentiles must turn from idolatry to serve the one true God, and await God's Son from heaven, whom he raised from the dead and who rescues the righteous from the wrath to come. This also comports well with the essence of the apostolic decree of Acts 15.

Paul's speech also denies that he was introducing new deities into Athens. Rather, he was proclaiming a deity that Athens had been honoring unawares through their altars to an unknown god. Evidence from Pausanias (*Description of Greece* 1.1.4) shows altars for unknown gods, and inscriptional evidence reveals an altar to a hero of unknown name (*IG* 2.1546, 1547). We need to recognize that Paul is not just grasping after straws here, because for a pagan, the Jews' God, who could not be named or imaged, certainly was the most unknown God. Paul tries to strike a balance in this speech between making contact with the audience and critiquing their idolatry. He is arguing that the Athenians have an inkling that the true God exists, but they are not properly acknowledging him. This idea is similar to that in Rom. 1:20–23. But the point is, having ignored the true God, they are groping around in the dark to find him, but will not do so without the proclamation of God's revelation to them.

I have treated the details of this much controverted apologetical sermon elsewhere.[9] The central point to note here is that Paul was not punished for his evangelistic work, and in fact, this speech produced some converts, including at least one member of the Areopagus council named Dionysius, as well as at least one woman named Damaris (Acts 17:34). Nevertheless, there is no evidence of an ongoing, vital Christian community there. Notice that in 1 Cor. 16:15, Paul refers to Stephanas and his household being the first real Christian household in Achaia.[10] Paul moved on to Corinth from Athens, where one of his most fruitful but frustrating church-planting exercises was to take place.

Conflict and Concord in Corinth

It is fair to say that the Roman citizen Paul had as part of his missionary strategy not only hitting the major urban areas, but also focusing on Roman colony cities like Philippi and Corinth. It is probably not an accident that by and large he had his greatest successes in such cities. Roman Corinth in the A.D. 50s was well on the way to becoming the largest, most prosperous city in Greece. The city was rebuilt in 44 B.C. on the orders of Julius Caesar as a Roman colony city, and its architecture, law, and official Latin language all reflected Roman dominance. Corinth was in most ways the best possible city in Greece for making contact with all sorts of people, since it was the crossroads of the sea trade, having ports facing both east and west, and in addition was the center for the Isthmian games, the slave trade, and other kinds of economic ventures such as the casting of objects in bronze. Reli-

9. See Witherington, *Acts of the Apostles*, 520–32.
10. Nevertheless, we should not necessarily take 1 Cor. 2:1–4 as evidence that Paul was renouncing the sort of apologetical and philosophical missionary preaching we find in Acts 17. He is speaking to the Corinthians and telling them what he resolved to say to them.

giously, the city was pluralistic and included the
traditional Greek gods,
especially Aphrodite and
Apollo, and the imperial
cult. Corinth was also
the home of a significant
and long-standing Jew-
ish colony.

The points of conver-
gence between Paul's Corinthian correspondence and
the brief account in Acts 18
are more than sufficient to
show that Luke knows
what he is talking about,
but the paucity of mate-
rial probably means that
he had not read that cor-
respondence. Both sources
mention Priscilla and
Aquila, Paul's earning his
living by practicing a
trade, the conversion and
baptism of Crispus (Acts
18:18; 1 Cor. 1:14), Timothy's involvement in the
ministry there (Acts 18:5;
1 Cor. 4:17; 16:10–11),
and possibly the reference
to Sosthenes (Acts 18:17; 1 Cor. 1:1).

Illustration 10.3 View of the Acro-Corinth from the ancient temple in the center of the city.

The narrative of Acts 18 is structured around a pronouncement by
Paul (v. 6), one by the Lord (vv. 9–10), and one by the Roman ruler stationed there, Gallio (vv. 14–15).

Aquila and Priscilla had preceded Paul to Corinth, having come because of the expulsion of Jews from Rome. These two were to become
essential ministry partners for Paul (Acts 18:18, 26; Rom. 16:3; 2 Tim.
4:19), working with him in Corinth and Ephesus, and perhaps elsewhere as well. The narrative suggests that this couple were already
Christians when they came to Corinth, or else we would have expected
their conversion to be mentioned in Acts or in the Corinthian correspondence. Verse 3 informs us that their trade, like Paul's, was tentmaking, a very appropriate trade to practice in a city that would have

Illustration 10.4 A shop in Corinth, perhaps similar to the one where Paul made tents.

lots of visitors for the biannual games (which Paul attended at least once). Paul's practicing of a trade was strategic in that it gave him a venue in the marketplace to reach people and it let him be independent from the entangling alliances involved in the patronage system, but it came with a cost, namely, that upper-class Romans would have seen him as a person of lesser status.

Luke says that Paul was in Corinth for a year and a half, which reminds us that it was not his plan simply to evangelize cities in a matter of days and then leave them quickly behind. Acts 18:4 recounts that Paul visited the synagogue and proclaimed his message there. Once he was rejoined by Timothy and Silas (cf. 2 Cor. 11:9; Phil. 4:14–15), he was able to devote his full time to such preaching, since they had come with some financial support for Paul. Paul's message in the synagogue, that the Messiah was Jesus, prompted sharp opposition as well as some positive response. Acts 18:6 indicates that Paul would go with "plan B," turning to the Gentiles in that locale, since he had been rejected in the Jewish synagogue. Again we must stress that this plan did not involve turning away from Jews and the synagogue in the next city that he would evangelize. Matters undoubtedly became awkward and difficult when Paul simply went next door to the house of one Titius Justus, who had been a devout Gentile God-fearer and now was a Christian. Even

Corinth

It is fair to say that from an evangelistic or missionary point of view, the two most important cities Paul visited were Corinth and Ephesus; and not coincidentally, they were the cities that, according to Acts, Paul spent more time in than any others. The Corinth that Paul and other Christians encountered in the middle of the first century was a Roman colony city, the most prosperous in Greece and well on the way to being the largest city in Greece, if it was not already so. The Romans had destroyed the classical city in 146 B.C., and shortly before his death in 44 B.C., Julius Caesar had ordered the city to be rebuilt on a Roman plan so that various retired Roman soldiers could be settled there, forming a Roman colony. The architecture, law, and official language (Latin) all reflect the thoroughly Roman character of the city in Paul's day.

Corinth's prosperity in large measure was owed to its two ports, one facing east and one facing west, with only a narrow isthmus (two miles wide) separating the two. In fact, the normal operating procedure was to drag boats, if small, from one side of the isthmus to the other on sledges. Failing that, larger boats usually would offload their cargo on one side of the isthmus and then reload it on another boat on the other side. This practice sought to avoid the trip around the southern cape of Greece, which could be quite treacherous. Corinth then had all the benefits, but also all of the drawbacks, of a major port city. Many people were coming and going, and many who had traveled a long way were looking for some rest, recreation, and entertainment. In addition to being the jumping-off point for travelers going either east or west in the Mediterranean, Corinth was the link between northern and southern Greece for those traveling overland.

To this we may add another reason for Corinth's prosperity. It was the major sponsor for the nearby Isthmian games, a biannual set of games only slightly less famous than the Olympic games. Even an emperor like Nero came to compete in these games. This, of course, created a situation in which many people were looking for temporary shelter, something Paul, Priscilla, and Aquila could help provide through making tents.

Religiously, the city was pluralistic, hosting famous older temples to Apollo (in the city center) and to Aphrodite (on top of the Acrocorinth, the mountain that towered over the city). In addition to this was a well-known healing shrine of the god Asclepius, where people came to get well in part by soaking in the medicinal spring water. We also must note the overlay of Roman culture, which included a temple for the cult of the emperor. In this same city was a well-established Jewish colony, many of whose ancestors originally had been brought to the city as slaves to help rebuild it.

Here, Paul could stay and the world would come to him. He would have occasion to meet people of many sorts of social statuses and ethnic extractions. With so many people transient or new, Corinth was the perfect place to make converts. In short, this city was an ideal locale for an evangelistic religion to imbed itself into the Greco-Roman culture.

worse, from a Jewish point of view, the synagogue ruler Crispus and his whole household became Christian (Acts 18:8; cf. 1 Cor. 1:14–16).

The event mentioned in Acts 18:12, then, comes as no surprise. Non-Christian Jews bring Paul before the proconsul Gallio. Gallio we know well from extrabiblical sources. He was the brother of the famous Stoic philosopher Seneca. Gallio came from his native Spain to Rome during the reign of Claudius and was adopted by the famous rhetorician Lucius Junius Gallio, whose name he took. On the positive side, he was said to be witty (Dio Cassius, *Roman History* 61.35), and his brother says that he was a very pleasant person (*Quaestiones Naturales* 4a); on the negative side, like his brother, he was anti-Semitic. Seneca also says that Gallio had to leave his province prematurely due to a fever (*Epistulae Morales* 104.1). We know that Gallio was no longer proconsul in Corinth by May of A.D. 52, and that he lasted less than two years, the regular tenure for that post. We also know that such officials were usually sent out from Rome in April of a given year. This means that he came to Corinth not later than May of A.D. 51. Clearly, Paul appeared before Gallio after having been in the city for some time, during A.D. 50–51. Gallio, however, saw no real crime involved, only a Jewish family squabble, a dispute about words and names and Jewish law (18:15). Thus, he dismissed the case, saying that he did not wish to be the judge of such a matter. Notice that Gallio is not interested in hearing from Paul on the legitimacy of his undertakings (18:14). This implies that Gallio was not prepared to see Christianity as a *superstitio* unconnected with Judaism. This was a good thing for Corinthian Christians.

At some juncture during his stay in Corinth, Paul wrote to the Thessalonian Christians. There is a good deal of debate about the authenticity of 2 Thessalonians, but many scholars still think that it was written by Paul, and some even think that it was penned prior to 1 Thessalonians and prompted the issues Paul has to deal with in 1 Thessalonians 4–5. First Thessalonians is filled with references to suffering, persecution, endurance, and the like. Paul definitely is writing to Christians under pressure, and he is anxious about their well-being (cf. 2 Thess. 1:6 and 1 Thessalonians 2).[11] It is clear from the first letter that Paul had taught the Thessalonians about matters eschatological, but insufficiently, as misunderstandings remained. He wanted to make clear that they should always be prepared for the coming of Christ, even though the time of that event was unknown (Christ would come at an unexpected time, "like a thief in the night"). He also seems to have con-

11. Perhaps 1 Thess. 2:15–16 provides a clue for the date of this letter. The expulsion of Jews from Rome in A.D. 49 might be in view here, or at least the shock waves created by that expulsion, which may have led to spates of anti-Semitic activity in various places.

veyed the notion that his converts were already suffering the messianic woes. Eschatological fervency had led to lethargy on the part of some. Yet Paul did not want to dampen the spiritual enthusiasm of the group, and certainly did not want them to despise prophetic or other kinds of revelatory speech. Thus, a certain balance is struck in this correspondence between wanting to keep their eschatological fervency in check without wishing to quench the Spirit who gave them courage to endure and hope that Christ would come and deal with their persecutors.

According to Acts 18:18, Paul stayed on in Corinth for a while after the trial, perhaps until the sailing season in the spring of A.D. 52. He sailed with Aquila and Priscilla to the east, heading ultimately to Syria. Verses 19–21 indicate that Ephesus was the first port of call, and that Paul left Aquila and Priscilla there, presumably to lay the groundwork for future missionary efforts. Verse 22 relates that the sea voyage that set out from Ephesus landed at Caesarea Maritima. From there, Paul went up briefly to Jerusalem, reporting to the church there. He did not stay long there, going back to Antioch, and then once more on to the west through the Cilician Gates, visiting the Galatian churches and heading for Ephesus. Thus, while we may divide the ministry of Paul up into missionary journeys, for him it was a matter of continuous activity on behalf of the Lord until and even after he was made a prisoner of Rome.

Chapter 11

The Expansion of the Enterprise

A.D. 53–57

Dark Clouds over Judea and the Last of the Julio-Claudians

The Jerusalem that Paul returned to after his second missionary journey was a city in turmoil. To understand why, we must consider briefly the succession of procurators who served the province of Judea in the A.D. 40s and 50s. After the death of Herod Agrippa, Cuspus Fadus governed from 44 to 46. His first undertaking was to punish the cities of Sebaste and Caesarea for the insults that their inhabitants directed at Herod Agrippa and his family after he died. Fadus was also commissioned to send the soldiers recruited from those two cities out of the region and replace them with regular Roman legions from Syria. Such an action was a clear sign that things were getting worse in Judea, but the auxiliaries from the region appealed to Claudius to allow them to stay there, and it was permitted. Clearly, Josephus thinks that this was a big mistake and was one of the causes of the Jewish war breaking out in the 60s (*Ant*. 19.356–365). "Soldiers recruited from outside the area probably would have done a better job in policing the area than locals with their vested interests, local loyalties, and regional commitments and animosities."[1]

Perhaps the first major mistake that Fadus made was to decide that the high priest's vestments should be returned to Roman control (*Ant*. 20.6). Things got so heated over this move that Longinus, the legate of Syria, put in an appearance with troops in Jerusalem. However, through Herod Agrippa II the Jews made an appeal to Claudius about this matter, and surprisingly, Claudius, perhaps due to his personal friendship with the Agrippa family, sided with the Jews against Fadus. In fact, Claudius was to allow Herod of Chalcis to have the right to be in charge of the temple, the selection of high priests, and the holy vessels and vestments (*Ant*. 20.7–16).

Another episode of consequence during the reign of Fadus was his dealings with the prophetic figure Theudas (*Ant*. 20.97–98; Acts 5:36). Theudas was certainly not a mere bandit. He gathered a crowd at the Jordan River and claimed that, prophetlike, he would part the waters and lead them across. Fadus sent soldiers out to stop the procession to the Jordan, violence broke out, and Theudas was captured; but interestingly, he was beheaded, not crucified like Jesus. Hayes and Mandell speculate that this is because of how the Jesus sect was claiming to have a martyr king. Beheading was not seen as a shameful way to die in the same way that crucifixion was, and so perhaps Fadus chose it hoping to avoid having another messianic martyr on his hands.[2]

The next procurator was a nephew of the famous Jewish philosopher Philo. His name was Tiberius Alexander, and he came from a wealthy Alexandrian family, but unlike his uncle, he had repudiated his Jewish faith (*Ant*. 20.100–104). In some ways he was a wise choice for procurator of Judea, since he knew and understood Jewish ways very well. But unfortunately for him, Judea suffered a severe famine during his tenure of A.D. 46–48. He found some relief, especially with the help of Queen Helena of Adiabene, a recent convert to Judaism (cf. *Ant*. 20.17–96; Acts 11:28–30). It is interesting that Josephus really does not criticize Tiberius Alexander, though he does mention that he crucified two of the sons of Judas the Galilean who had led the census revolt in A.D. 6 (*Ant* 20.102). This reminds us that we must take seriously the fact

---

1. J. Hayes and S. Mandell, *The Jewish People in Classical Antiquity: From Alexander to Bar Kochba* (Louisville: Westminster John Knox), 166.
2. Ibid., 171.

that there was an ongoing revolutionary faction in Judea and Galilee, apparently chiefly associated with this one family. Preparations for what happened in A.D. 66 when the Jewish war broke out had been going on for a very long time. During Tiberius's procuratorship, Herod of Chalcis died and Claudius replaced him with Herod Agrippa II. He was allowed to oversee the high priest's office and to choose the candidate for the post.

If Tiberius Alexander seemed a rather able governor, the same could not be said for his successor, Cumanus, who ruled during the period A.D. 48–52. His reign involved one upheaval after another. At Passover (in A.D. 49 or 50, near the time of the Jerusalem council), a Roman soldier standing on the temple portico exposed himself to the crowd. A riot ensued in which, according to Josephus, Cumanus's troops slaughtered thousands of Jewish pilgrims (*Ant.* 20.105–112; *J.W.* 2.223–227). A second episode began when one of the emperor's slaves was robbed on a public road. When the perpetrator could not be found, Cumanus had villages near the locale of the theft sacked, during which one soldier found a copy of the Torah, and ripped and burned it. While Cumanus certainly was anti-Semitic, he recognized the danger in this particular act, and to prevent all-out war, he executed the soldier who committed the sacrilege (*Ant.* 20.113–117; *J.W.* 2.228–231). Toward the end of his tenure, there was an eruption of hostilities between Jews and Samaritans. A Galilean on pilgrimage to Jerusalem was killed in Samaria. Cumanus did not respond to this provocation, and so Judeans and Galileans banded together to execute summary justice. The Samaritan villages near Shechem were attacked and many innocent Samaritans were killed. Now, Cumanus responded, and the bloodshed escalated until Quadratus, the legate of Syria, brought troops and intervened after an appeal from the Samaritans. Tacitus says that but for Quadratus's intervention there would have already been a Jewish war in A.D. 51–52 (*Annals* 12.54.3). Quadratus held two hearings and eventually executed some Jews and some Samaritans. In due course, he felt it necessary to send the high priests and other Jewish leaders to Rome in chains, along with Cumanus and Samaritan high officials. Agrippa II, who was in Rome, intervened on behalf of the Jews, Claudius sided with him, and the Samaritan leaders were executed and Cumanus was exiled (*J.W.* 2.232–246).

The next Judean procurator had a very long tenure indeed, from A.D. 52 to 58 or 59. His name was Felix, and he was requested by Jonathan the high priest while pleading the Jews' case before Claudius. Felix was noted for having had three famous wives in succession (see Suetonius, *Divus Claudius* 28), one of whom was Drusilla, a Jewish

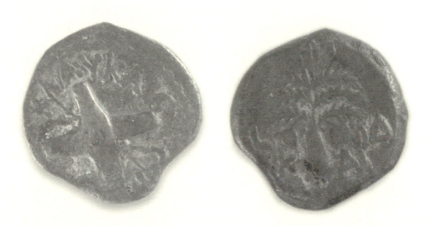

Illustration 11.1 Roman coin minted by the procurator Felix while Claudius was still Emperor (note Roman fiscus), and the obverse of the Felix coin with fruit-bearing tree (note the absence of a human image).

princess, the sister of Herod Agrippa I (*Ant.* 20.139–144; Acts 24:24). Drusilla had divorced the king of Emesa in order to marry Felix in A.D. 54. This act, of course, would be seen by law-observant Jews as a violation of Jewish marital customs and laws. I will say more about Felix when we discuss Paul's trial in Caesarea. For now, let us note that Felix had to deal with the reality of another power in the region who kept being given more and more territory north of Judea by both Claudius and then Nero: Agrippa II.

Josephus's chronicling of the violence of Felix's procuratorship reads like a story about a reign of terror. Felix was always executing one zealot or another (*Ant.* 20.161). He seems to have made it his personal mission to root out and execute bandits and messianic figures— for example, Eleazar, the leader of a revolutionary group, who had been active for more than twenty years (*Ant.* 20.121, 161; *J.W.* 2.253). It was during Felix's brutal rule that the dagger men (*sicarii*) seem to have come to prominence. They were hit men famous for their "walk-by knifings" in the streets of Jerusalem. One of their earliest victims was the high priest himself, Jonathan, presumably because he was pro-Roman (*Ant.* 20.163).

Also during Felix's reign, an Egyptian Jew, claiming to be a messianic liberator, rallied a group of his Jewish followers, numbering in the thousands, with the promise that he would destroy the walls of Jerusalem with a shout from the Mount of Olives (*Ant.* 20.169–172; *J.W.* 2.261–263). Although Felix sent out his troops against this group, the Egyptian escaped, which explains how later during the reign of Felix,

Paul could be mistaken for him (Acts 21:37–38). Much more could be said along these lines, but this amply conveys the volatility of the situation in Jerusalem when Paul visited there A.D. 52 and then again in A.D. 57 or 58. Suffice it to say that the church in Jerusalem must have been under severe pressure to appear to be truly Jewish during this entire period of time. It appears to be during this period in the 50s that James wrote his famous homily, and another brother of Jesus, Jude, wrote in a more apocalyptic vein his brief letter.

While many Jews may have thought that in most respects there could not have been a worse emperor than Claudius as far as justice and fairness to the Jews were concerned, they had not reckoned on Claudius being followed by someone like Nero. If Claudius was anti-Semitic, Nero was that and much more, especially after his advisors, Seneca and Burrus, were no longer around to keep him in check.

Claudius was dispatched in A.D. 54 by family machinations. More specifically, he was killed by his niece/wife, Agrippina, who had been married to him since A.D. 49 and wanted to advance her own son Nero to the throne, even though he was only sixteen. She managed this by poisoning Claudius's favorite dish, mushrooms. Apparently she also instigated the poisoning of Britannicus, Claudius's own son, by early A.D. 55.

By the usual standards of imperial moral corruption and degradation, Nero's first five years of rule appeared relatively moderate. This was the period of time when he was most significantly under the influence of Seneca. During this time, the senate seems to have been allowed more power than during the reign of Claudius, and Nero had discontinued the practice of private treason trials of prominent men.[3] He also allowed the Jews to return to Rome in the year of his accession. But all pretense to morality and fair government clearly was laid aside in A.D. 59 when he killed his own mother because of her continual interference in his affairs and took power more directly into his own hands. Apparently, Agrippina had planned on co-rulership with her son (cf. *Sib. Or.* 4:119–21). I will say more about Nero in the next chapter in discussing the late 50s and early 60s A.D. Here it may be said that although the emperor Nero was not the major problem for Jews and Christians in the 50s, the procurators often were another story.

3. See the discussion in M. T. Griffin, *Nero: The End of a Dynasty* (New Haven: Yale University Press, 1985), 50–66.

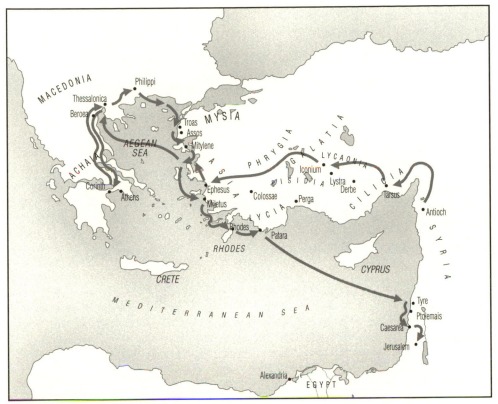

Illustration 11.2 Paul's Third Missionary Journey, A.D. 53–57.

The Ephesian Ministry

The end of Acts 18 relates how Paul once more visited Jerusalem and Antioch, then went through the Galatian churches strengthening them, and then on to Ephesus. In this material Luke is intimating that Paul felt the need to be accountable, for he did not see himself as founding a separate Pauline church. Indeed, one of his great concerns was the unity of Gentiles and Jews throughout the church, and in particular, the unity of his largely Gentile churches with the church in Jerusalem. Furthermore, the motif of the disciples being strengthened in Galatia indicates not only that Paul was concerned with more than just conversions, but also that he intended to finish one church-planting process before totally moving on further west. The commitment to strengthening already founded churches is manifest not only in Paul's letters to these congregations, but also in the fact that once Paul leaves Ephesus after a long stay there, intending to go to Jerusalem, he goes by way of

Ephesus

Ephesus, after Corinth, is the city we are best informed about, on the basis of literary and archaeological data.[1] Ephesus was a free city of perhaps 250,000 (in Paul's day), and therefore a very different type of city than Corinth or Philippi, which were Roman colony cities. Ephesus was the third-largest city in the empire, after Rome and Alexandria. Like most large cities in the empire, Ephesus was cosmopolitan, but it retained its strong Greek flavor, while having large Roman and Jewish populations. Josephus speaks of the major Jewish colony in this city (*Ant*. 14.225–227; 16.162–168, 172–173). It is likely that, as in the case of Corinth, many of these Jews originally were brought to this city as slaves to serve various functions, including to work as various sorts of artisans.

Ephesus had been "bequeathed" to the Romans by King Attalus III in 133 B.C. Because Asia was a senatorial province, the emperors usually stayed out of its business—except, of course, financially strapped ones like Domitian. Asia was in most ways the most wealthy and resource-rich of the provinces, and most emperors realized that they needed to milk that cow carefully in order for the flow of resources and revenues to keep coming.

The city held a strategic location of inestimable importance. In terms of both land and sea routes, Ephesus was key. This is why the emperor's college of messengers was based in this city. Ephesus was the communications hub for almost every part of Asia. This may help explain why Paul spent nearly three years there, as he was in the communication business in a major way. It also may explain Revelation 1–2, which lists seven churches all on the main road out of Ephesus. The founding church would have been in Ephesus, and its satellites or church plants on major roads out of that city.

Ephesus lay near the mouth of the river Cayster and had been for many centuries a major port city, but by the first century A.D., the harbor required constant dredging due to the silt. It is fair to say that by the middle of the first century, the city's importance as a port was waning. From an economic standpoint, this made it all the more crucial that Ephesus's religious-tourist trade, involving the world-famous temple of Artemis, succeed. That temple was one of the seven wonders of the ancient world, a fact obscured today by its remains—a single stone column standing on marshy ground.

1. For a helpful introduction on this city, see P. Trebilco, "Asia," in *The Book of Acts in Its Graeco-Roman Setting*, ed. D. Gill and C. Gempf (Grand Rapids: Eerdmans, 1994), 291–362.

the Greek regions in Macedonia and Achaia, where he had founded churches, to strengthen them before moving on (see Acts 19:21; 20:1–3). No doubt, Luke has schematized the three missionary journeys, which always begin in Antioch and end either there or in Jerusalem, and each of which contains one major speech. But we should not doubt that Paul did his best to proceed in an orderly fashion in his work, both in planting congregations and in nurturing and guiding them thereafter. Clearly he highly prized personal, face-to-face contact with his converts.

At Acts 18:24 the narrative turns to Ephesus, a city that Paul had wanted to reach at the end of the second missionary journey but had managed only to visit briefly on that occasion. The importance of Ephesus for the Pauline mission should not be underestimated. It turns out to be the place where he spent the longest time working, and indeed, it was the last place where he worked at length as a free man. In fact, it is not appropriate to call Acts 18:24–21:26 the chronicling of a journey. Acts 19:10 makes that impossible: Paul was in Ephesus for over two years. This entire section focuses on Ephesus and its environs.

Clearly, Ephesus, after Corinth, is the most important city that Paul evangelized. It was the center of all culture and commerce in western Asia (see sidebar on Ephesus). But by Paul's day, the city's economic importance was beginning to wane, and this made the tourist trade to the temple of Artemis all the more crucial to Ephesus's economy. This, plus the presence of a large Jewish colony in the city, forms the background for reading Paul's actions that affected the temple trade.

Acts 18:24–28 introduces the figure named Apollos. He is an Alexandrian Jewish Christian who apparently had also had contact with the followers of John the Baptist. It has been suggested that he may have been a pupil of Philo, which certainly is chronologically possible. This suggestion might add some further weight to the old conjecture that Apollos was the author of the Book of Hebrews, for that document certainly has some rhetorical, philosophical, and religious resonances with what we find in Philo. Luke stresses that Apollos is an eloquent man, which likely means he was rhetorically adept.

Besides being gifted with words, Apollos was quite literally "boiling over in the Spirit" (Acts 18:25), which in light of Rom. 12:11 probably means more than being an enthusiastic or charismatic figure. Apollos was full of the Holy Spirit, and thus he taught accurately the things concerning Jesus. But there was a gap in his Christian knowledge: he did not know about Christian baptism, but only about John's similar rite.[4] But Apollos had been instructed in the way of the

4. The case of Apollos reminds us that early Christian history has many incongruities, and later correlations or regulations about water and Spirit baptisms did not apply during this era.

Illustration 11.3 A Gentile woman with a headcovering.

Lord, which in the light of 18:28 would seem to include being instructed in how to show from the Hebrew Scriptures that the Messiah was Jesus. He was powerful in the use of these Scriptures for apologetical purposes (18:24).

In regard to his one deficiency, his ignorance of Christian baptism, Apollos receives instruction from Paul's co-workers Priscilla and Aquila. It is both interesting and important that Luke sprinkles references to the significant roles women played in early Christianity throughout Acts.[5] They are depicted as teachers, prophets (the daughters of Philip), hosts of house churches (Lydia and John Mark's mother), and providers of patronage and practical help (Tabitha). This general impression is confirmed by even more references in Paul's letters to the roles of women. It is fair to say that Christianity offered women, especially Jewish women, opportunities to serve important religious functions that they might not in other religions. This might explain why so many of them became Christians.

Why is it that Luke records Priscilla and Aquila teaching, but not baptizing, Apollos? Did they think it unnecessary, since he had the Spirit already? Did they see John's baptism as sufficient and valid? It is intriguing that we are never told that the original Twelve received Christian baptism. Even more intriguing is that Paul, frustrated with

5. For a detailed discussion of this matter, see B. Witherington III, *Women in the Earliest Churches*, SNTSMS 59 (Cambridge: Cambridge University Press, 1988).

the Corinthians' ways, says that he is glad he did not baptize more of them (1 Cor. 1:14–17). All of this cautions against reading later assumptions about the cruciality of Christian baptism back into the earliest period.

According to Acts 18:27–28, Apollos needed and obtained a letter of reference from the church at Ephesus in order to do evangelistic work in the province of Achaia. The letter was needed because there was already a church there, founded by Paul. We have clear evidence here and in 1 Corinthians 1–4 that Apollos did go to Corinth and elsewhere and watered the ground that Paul had previously planted. But also, it may be that Apollos unwittingly caused problems for Paul. Baptism, pneumaticism, and rhetorical excellence were all of great interest to the Corinthians, and it is possible that Apollos took an approach to things that led the Corinthians to critique Paul as a less able rhetor and a less pneumatic person. This also may explain why in 1 Cor. 16:12, Paul says that Apollos, who is with him in Ephesus, is not coming back just yet to visit with the Corinthians.[6] Paul then has to stress in 1 Corinthians 1–4 that Paul and Apollos are not engaged in an honor challenge, but rather, are working together.

Acts 18:24–28 must be contrasted with Acts 19:1–7. The two stories have been juxtaposed by Luke because both deal with those who know or have experienced John's baptism. This latter story reminds us that there was an ongoing Baptist movement even some twenty-plus years after John's beheading.[7] The first century A.D. was a time of great fervor and ferment in early Judaism, with many prophetic figures and various reform movements. It is not surprising, since the essence of religion in the Greco-Roman world was ritual, that Luke felt it important to distinguish between the Baptist movement and the Jesus movement, not least because they had in common a baptismal ritual of initiation.

Paul arrived in Ephesus shortly after Apollos left, having traveled through the interior of Asia to get there. There has been considerable debate among scholars as to what sort of "disciples" Paul is said to have found in Acts 19:1. Probably, they were disciples of John, not of Jesus, since they know only John's baptism, and, more critically, they have never even heard that the Holy Spirit was now manifest or poured out.[8]

---

6. See the discussion in B. Witherington III, *Conflict and Community in Corinth: A Socio-rhetorical Commentary on 1 and 2 Corinthians* (Grand Rapids: Eerdmans, 1994), 83–89.

7. Indeed, there is evidence that this movement continued on well into the fourth century A.D. See B. Witherington III, *The Acts of the Apostles: A Socio-rhetorical Commentary* (Grand Rapids: Eerdmans, 1998), 569, and the references there.

8. Less likely is the translation "We have never heard there is a Holy Spirit." It is improbable that Jews would make a claim of total ignorance of the existence of God's Spirit.

Illustration 11.4 The famous theater in Ephesus.

For Luke, receiving the Spirit is the sine qua non of being a Christian, and so we may be rather sure that he is not talking about Christians here. This is also why they must go through the whole initiation and conversion process—unlike Apollos—before they can be considered Christians. Here we see the sequence water baptism, reception of the Spirit after the laying on of hands, and confirmation of such reception through the evidence of speaking in tongues and prophesying. This is the only text in the New Testament that speaks of rebaptism, and clearly, the author believes that he is not talking about two acts of Christian baptism. John's baptism of repentance was valid, even valuable, but it was not Christian baptism.

The further we read into Acts 19 and 20, the clearer it becomes that Luke is using this material to portray the climax of Paul's ministry in the east as a free man. In Ephesus he has the longest stable period in a city without expulsion of any of the cities he visited (except, of course, Antioch). Here he is able to fully carry out a witness to both Jews and Gentiles (cf. 22:15). Luke's agenda here is to present a paradigm of what a universalistic Christian mission ought to look like. The Ephesian ministry, however, later will come back to haunt Paul because it is Jews from Asia, thinking that Paul had brought an Ephesian Gentile Christian into the temple, who cause the riot that leads to his arrest and detainment in Caesarea for two years (21:27–29; cf. 24:19). It is clear enough that Paul had opposition in Ephesus (cf. Acts 19:23–41; 1 Cor. 15:32; 16:9), but did it consummate in an Ephesian imprisonment, something that Acts does not suggest? We must consider this matter more closely.

A **Closer** Look: *An Ephesian Imprisonment?*

Of late, some scholars have revived the suggestion that Paul was imprisoned in Ephesus for some time, and from there wrote various letters, such as Philippians and Philemon (and possibly Colossians and Ephesians). This is largely an argument from silence not from evidence, for neither Paul's letters nor Acts say that Paul was imprisoned in Ephesus. What, then, is the indirect historical evidence thought to lead to such a conclusion?

First, there is 1 Cor. 15:32, which sometimes has been taken literally. The verse is thought to imply arrest, incarceration, and combat with wild beasts in the Ephesian arena. Even if this verse is taken at face value, it would have to refer to an imprisonment before 1 Corinthians was written, and clearly enough, Paul is a free man when he writes this letter. Few scholars have been prepared to advance a case that Paul wrote Philippians, Philemon, and perhaps the other captivity epistles before 1 Corinthians, that is, before about A.D. 53 or 54. But in fact there is a good reason to take 1 Cor. 15:32 in a metaphorical sense. Notice that the phrase in question is prefaced by *kata anthrōpon*, which likely means "as they say," an appropriate preface to a metaphorical remark. Also, there is plenty of external evidence to suggest that this is a metaphorical phrase (see Ign. *Rom.* 5:1; Appian, *Civil Wars* 2.61; Philo, *Life of Moses* 1.43–44; Plutarch, *De virtute morali* 439). This phrase refers to the struggles a sage has with opposition or opponents, not to actual imprisonment or combat with beasts in an arena. It is, however, quite understandable how Paul might use this phrase to describe the event chronicled in Acts 19:23–41, even though he was not personally present on that occasion. The ruckus was about Paul and his preaching and was raised by his opponents there; and the Ephesians indeed were acting like wild beasts and had to be pacified by officials.

Sometimes 2 Cor. 1:8–10 is brought into the discussion. This text shows that Paul suffered some sort of severe affliction or persecution in the Asian province that brought him near death. He could indeed be referring to the riot in the theater in Ephesus, but Paul does not speak of imprisonment or any official action taken against him by authorities while there.

The second major argument for an Ephesian imprisonment runs basically as follows. The letters written to the Philippians and Philemon do not make sense if Paul is writing them from such a great distance from Asia as Rome was. They make far better sense, when Paul says things like "prepare a guest room for me" (Philem. 22), if he was much closer to Philippi and to the Lycus Valley than he would have been during house arrest in Rome. It is also asked whether it is plausible that Onesimus the slave would have fled all the way from Colossae to Rome and found Paul there. Ephesus is thought to be a much more likely destination.

Against this reasoning stand the following considerations: First, Paul's description of his condition in Philippians and also in Philemon suggests that although he is in chains, he has direct access to many friends and co-workers. In other words he has considerable freedom. These descriptions comport better with a condition of house arrest than with a condition of imprisonment. The only two occasions we know of when Paul was under house arrest were in Caesarea Maritima and in Rome.[9] Second, the letter to Philippi reflects that considerable time has elapsed since Paul has been there, enough time for the congregation to grow and develop leadership, for them to have sent Paul aid on various occasions, and for Paul to have seen his life work as extensive and possibly not far from drawing to a close. Likewise with the letter to Philemon: this letter apparently is carried to the Lycus Valley from Paul by one of the original founders of the congregation who since has left the area and is now returning, and time must have elapsed for Onesimus to have fled, been converted by Paul, worked with Paul, and now be sent back to his owner. Third, Paul was an inveterate traveler, indeed a professional one. There is plenty of evidence for the high degree of mobility of some persons between Rome and Asia, and Paul certainly was capable of being one such person. We must remember that when Paul says, "Prepare a guest room for me," he is not communicating by telephone or e-mail, but by a letter that was hand carried to his audience. This letter would not travel much faster than he himself would, and clearly, he

9. This is why some have even conjectured that Philippians was written from Caesarea. On the unlikelihood of that, see B. Witherington III, *Friendship and Finances in Philippi: The Letter of Paul to the Philippians* (Valley Forge, Pa.: Trinity, 1994), 25–29.

anticipates being free and following shortly after the letter to the same destination. Fourth, Rome was the slave capital of the empire. Estimates propose that as much as 50 percent of the populace of that city in Paul's day were slaves. If a slave like Onesimus really wanted to escape and get lost in a crowd of other such persons, Rome, not nearby Ephesus (close to the Lycus Valley), was the place to go. Fifth, remarks made in Philippians indicate Paul's contact not only with Caesar's household (4:22), but also with the praetorian guard or palace staff (1:13). These remarks are far more likely to point to Paul being in Rome than in Ephesus. On the whole, then, the theory of an Ephesian imprisonment, while not totally impossible, is without a firm foundation in any of the evidence we have at hand.

In Ephesus, as so often elsewhere, opposition developed in the synagogue to Paul's preaching (Acts 19:8). This in turn caused him to look for another venue to carry on proclaiming his message. On this occasion, Paul left the synagogue, taking some converts with him, and proceeded to set up shop in the hall of Tyrannus. Because of the large Jewish population in Ephesus, Paul was as likely to meet Jews outside as inside the synagogue, and furthermore, the Jews in this place were to one degree or another Hellenized Jews who would be interacting with Gentiles daily. The syncretism of cultures, as well as the syncretism of religion, is a major factor to consider in evaluating Paul's mission in Ephesus.

In antiquity an orator, to get not just a hearing but a following, needed an appropriate venue for proclaiming a message, whether in the home of a patron or in a public lecture hall. But when would a Jew like Paul be able to get access to such a public auditorium? Probably during the hours between 11 A.M. (the time when public affairs such as schooling or judicial activities came to a halt in a Greco-Roman city) and 4 P.M. This was the time of day when the building was least likely to be in use, the time for lunch and then naps rather than for speeches. Furthermore, most of Paul's clientele would have been those unable to come before the afternoon anyway since they would be working all morning. We must keep in mind that only a few high-status persons were likely to be Pauline converts in any given city. Yet Paul must have had a few patrons in Ephesus, for renting such a hall daily for two years (see 19:9–10) would have been an expensive proposition. Perhaps, Paul got a discount because he was prepared to use the hall when no one else wanted it. The venue of these meetings, coupled with their nature, would have suggested to a Greco-Roman audi-

An Ancient Letter

Most of the epistolary evidence that has survived to the present comes from Egypt, as does the document below from the first or second century A.D. This letter from a client to a patron contains the sort of deferential remarks that were customary for the client to remain in the good graces of the patron. In a world without a free-market economy, survival often depended on having and maintaining a good relationship with a patron.

Herm . . . [to Sarapion] . . . greetings, and that you may always remain in good health in your whole person for long years to come, since your good genius allowed us to greet you with respect and salute you. For as you also make mention of us on each occasion by letter, so I here make an act of worship for you in the presence of the lords Dioskouroi and in the presence of the lord Sarapis, and I pray for your safe-keeping during your entire life and for health of your children and of all your household. Farewell in everything, I beg my patron and fosterer. Greet all your folk, men and women. All the gods here, male and female, greet you. Farewell. Thoth 16th. (On the reverse side— To Sarapion, the lord). (*NewDocs* 1:57)

As G. Horsley notes, this letter seems to lack substantive content altogether. It appears to be mere flattery and obsequious remarks. The document is written in Greek, and notice that Sarapion is identified clearly near the end of the document as the author's patron. This in itself reveals the true function of this document. Here is a client who does not want his patron to forget him, as he needs his patron's benefactions. He does not ask for anything in this letter, but he wants to make sure that the flow of benefits does not stop. We gather from this letter that the relationship between author and addressee is not between near equals, who normally would call each other friends in such letters, but between a superior and a social inferior, perhaps a freedman who formerly had been Sarapion's

ence that Paul was some sort of philosopher or philosophical rhetorician, for there were no priests, temples, or sacrifices involved, which was the very definition of religion to the ancients, both Greco-Roman and Jewish.

Acts 20:31 shows that Paul spent some three years in Ephesus, and most of the proclamation time was spent in this lecture hall venue. Luke, using rhetorical hyperbole, says that all of Asia heard the Word during this period of time. This means that word got out into the surrounding region, including into the Lycus Valley, where churches were slave and had been manumitted. This would also explain the language of worship, which is not uncommon language in antiquity between slave and master. The reference to the Greek gods the Dioskouri, as well as to Sarapis, points to an author of Hellenistic background living in Egypt.

The reference to Sarapion's "genius" needs a bit of explanation. The Greek term refers to the spirit of one's ancestor, which was believed to act as a sort of guide, guardian angel, and inspirer throughout one's life—a meaning that carries over into one definition of the modern English word "genius." Thus, we must remember that in antiquity, great thoughts, ideas, decisions, and actions were believed to come by someone else's aid, not just from one's native brilliance. In this case, the genius, or spirit of the ancestor, has preserved Sarapion in good health and thus allowed the client to continue to address and benefit from his patron.

Finally, the reference to prayer reminds us that the ancients were more often than not very religious people who firmly believed that they depended on supernatural beings for life and health. The word "farewell" here is more than a goodbye; it means "I hope you fare well"— the original sense of the English as well. We should not assume that this letter is merely empty praise and flattery. Probably, the author truly is grateful for the benefits he has received and truly needs such benefits to continue if he is to survive and prosper in a world of patrons and clients.

founded by Pauline co-workers such as Tychicus, Epaphras, and others (see Col. 1:7; 2:1; 4:16; Revelation 2–3).

Letters to Corinth

Paul had plenty of time while in Ephesus to write letters to the Corinthians. In fact, he seems to have penned at least four, if not more, such letters. We know, for example, of a letter, probably now lost, referred to in 1 Cor. 5:9–10. This may be called Corinthians A. This in turn was apparently followed by a visit from certain Corinthian Christians—Chloe's people and Stephanas—which in turn prompted the writing of 1 Corinthians (which for clarity's sake can be called Corinthians B). The sad truth was, however, that 1 Corinthians did not by any means resolve all the issues it was intended to resolve, for it had to be followed by a short, painful visit to Corinth, then by a sharp letter of anguish (see 2 Cor. 2:3–9),[10] which finally was followed by 2 Corin-

10. Some have identified 2 Corinthians 10–13 as part of this sharp letter, and this is possible, but the reference to a past visit by Titus to Corinth in 12:18 counts against this, as does the lack in 2 Corinthians 10–13 of any reference to the man who accosted Paul during his short visit or the man's discipline.

thians (Corinthians D), or at least a part of it.[11] The sobering conclusion that we must draw after considering all the evidence is that even apostolic letters often did not suffice to change congregations, and that Paul's relationship with the Corinthian Christians was stormy at various points, though by the time he wrote Romans from Corinth, reconciliation seems to have taken place.

The contents of these Corinthian letters brim with life and circumstance. They are problem-solving letters, and Paul believes that the Corinthians have many theological ("there is no resurrection"), ethical (sexual and social immorality), and personal (their relationship with Paul, and the relationship between the weak and the strong, between high status and low status) issues to address. Knowledge and wisdom were assets that they prized highly and felt they had a great deal of. Among the varied converts in Corinth were libertines ("everything is permitted") and ascetics ("it is good for a man not to touch a woman"). It seems quite clear that the majority of converts there were Gentiles, and many of them had not adequately come to grips with leaving their pagan past behind.

In some ways, these letters give us the clearest glimpse into the life of the early Pauline churches. They reveal a highly gifted but highly factious group of Christians who are only partly socialized into the faith, and do not want to give up certain kinds of sexual relationships, visits to pagan temples, the right to litigate even against fellow Christians, the right to evaluate and critique their leaders on the basis of their rhetorical skills, and so on. These letters also reveal that Paul's commitment to using rhetoric was a significant missionary strategy, for it meant that he would seek to persuade, whenever he could, rather than command. He would treat his converts not only as responsible adults, but also as his partners and brothers and sisters in ministry. Cooperation rather than coercion was his desire in dealing with his converts. When all is said and done, these letters show an apostle who loves his converts but has been deeply wounded by some of them. These letters reveal the pathos of the apostle to the Gentiles, his pastoral heart, and also his profound struggles with his converts, even well after they have been converted.

Struggles in Ephesus

In the midst of wrestling through letters with the Corinthians, Paul also had to come to grips with difficulties in Ephesus, where he was liv-

---

11. Many scholars see pieces of several letters by Paul in 2 Corinthians. I have argued for its unity in *Conflict and Community*, 328–33, and in that commentary in general. Note that there is no textual evidence to support any partitioning of this letter into pieces.

ing. Ephesus was the magic capital of Asia, and Paul, if he performed miracles, faced the prospect of being seen as a magician or sorcerer. Paul and Luke both made the attempt to portray the Christian faith as the powerful alternative to the popular religion of magic and of consultation and control of spirits, as well as an alternative to astrology and fatalism. In other words, faith in Jesus was being portrayed as the real source of human and world transformation, which meant that these other means were impotent. It also meant that the emperor had no divine clothes. If Jesus was the savior of the world, others were not needed. In Luke's presentation of Paul and other early Christian wonder workers, miracles are not ends in themselves, but rather, serve conversionist aims. Miracles can and do change a person's belief system in regard to Jesus and his power.

Acts 19:11 serves as a heading for what follows, informing us that Paul was indeed a wonder worker (something Paul himself confirms in Rom. 15:19). The transfer of healing power from Paul to some items of clothing is mentioned in v. 12, such that various people were cured and some demons were exorcised. Success leads to imitation, and in v. 13 come Jewish exorcists in Ephesus attempting to use Jesus' name (and Paul's) to accomplish their exorcisms. These exorcists are said to be the sons of a chief priest named Sceva, and perhaps we are to think that since priests were the ones most likely to know the divine names and be able to pronounce them correctly, they would be the most likely persons to become exorcists.

Acts 19:15–16 appears as a sort of comic relief in an otherwise serious narrative. The demons do not recognize these amateur Jewish exorcists, and so they turn the tables by having the possessed man leap on them and exorcise them from the house naked and wounded. The upshot of this event was a much greater respect for the name of Jesus, and various Christians felt led to divulge their magical secrets, or turn in their magical charms. The power of magical charms, formulas, and spells lies precisely in their secret nature. Once the secret is divulged, the formula is rendered impotent. Here again, as in Corinth, we see partially socialized Christians having to come to grips with and renounce some of their past. Verse 19 relates how those who practiced magic went on to renounce the practice and even burned their books of secrets and of spells. Possibly, v. 18 refers to the actions of the lower-class Christians, and v. 19 to those of the upper-class ones, who could afford books—a very expensive proposition in antiquity. These actions can be seen as a further fulfillment of the apostolic decree, and also as clearing the way for the gospel. Verse 20 indicates that the purgation of magic allowed the Word of God to spread powerfully. This is, in a way, the climax of Paul's ministry as a free man. Hereafter it was to be troubles, travels, and trials.

Acts 19:21–22 recounts Paul's plans to go to Jerusalem, but by way of Macedonia and Achaia, and once having been to Jerusalem, to go on to Rome. We are told that Paul sent Timothy and Erastus to Macedonia, while he stayed a little longer in Ephesus. The riot is recounted in vv. 23–41, and shows Luke's flair for the dramatic. It is notable that the tale focuses on the economic impact of the gospel—less business for the silversmiths and less tourist trade in general if people believe the gospel. Gaius and Aristarchus, traveling companions of Paul from Macedonia, are said to bear the brunt of the verbal assault against the Christians, for the disciples would not let Paul appear. Once the uproar was over, Paul said his goodbyes to the Ephesian Christians briefly and then headed off to Macedonia (Acts 20:1). His hasty departure may explain why later he felt compelled to meet with the Ephesian elders in Miletus on his way to Jerusalem. He had some final instructions for them, since he would not likely be returning to Ephesus. Acts 20:2–5 recounts how Paul returned to Achaia for three months. In all likelihood, it was there and then that he wrote his famous letter to the Romans. We consider that letter briefly at this point.

A Letter of Introduction to the Roman Christians

Paul's letter to the Romans has been seen by many as the most crucial document that the apostle to the Gentiles ever wrote. Yet it would be a mistake to take it as a sort of summary of his gospel. It says nothing about his views on a host of important subjects, such as the Lord's Supper, and precious little about others, such as the resurrection. On the other hand, it does reflect his mature thinking about the status of Jews and Gentiles before God, both those outside and within the Christian fold. The letter is not written to a group of Paul's converts, and so it should not be seen as the same sort of ad hoc document as 1 Corinthians; nor can Paul without further ado simply assume the role of pastor or apostle to the Roman Christians, since he is not the one who led them to Christ. But on the other hand, this letter definitely is not a sort of generic document with no specific audience in mind (unlike, say, Ephesians). It serves as a kind of letter of introduction of Paul's thinking about the relationships of Jews and Gentiles both inside and outside the Christian community.

Paul wrote Romans sometime around A.D. 56 or early 57. Paul composed this letter fully aware of the situation that had transpired in A.D. 54 when the Jews were allowed to return to Rome after a four- to five-year absence. It seems likely that this included various Jewish Chris-

tians, who found them-
selves at a distinct disadvantage in terms of
numbers and leadership
positions. In addition, an
atmosphere of latent and
sometimes patent anti-
Semitism lingered in
Rome at the time. There
is a sense in which Ro-
mans can be seen as
Paul's apologia for the
Jewish Christians, and
also for the Jews, that
they should still be seen
as God's people, whom
God had not written off.
As Romans 1 says, the
gospel is indeed for the
Jew first, and also for the
Gentile; and as Romans
9–11 makes clear, God
still has a purpose for
Jews, even if temporarily
they have rejected the
gospel and been broken
off from the people of
God. Romans 11:13 is
unequivocal that Paul is

Illustration 11.5 Columns of a temple in the forum in Rome.

addressing Gentiles and wanting them not only to recognize the value
of their Jewish heritage but also to understand that God has not rejected the Jews in order to select a Gentile people of God. Rather, God
has arranged it so that in the end, both Jew and Gentile will stand equal
before him on the basis of his pure mercy, on the basis of grace and
faith (not the Mosaic law). Indeed, as Rom. 11:23–30 makes evident,
Paul believes that once the full number of Gentiles are saved, then, at
the return of Christ, a great many Jews will be saved by the same means
as the Gentiles.[12]

A careful read through Romans shows that Paul begins by dealing
with the status of Gentiles outside of Christ in Romans 1, then turns to

12. See the discussion of this in B. Witherington III, *Jesus, Paul, and the End of the
World: A Comparative Study of New Testament Eschatology* (Downers Grove, Ill.: Inter-
Varsity, 1992), 99–128.

the condition of Jews, and then gradually works his way to the condition of Christians, a discussion that climaxes in Romans 8. Romans 9–11 turns to the special issue of the status of non-Christian Jews. Of course, along the way Paul intersperses comments about Christians and Christian life, since that is his target audience, but clearly, he is proceeding somewhat systematically in dealing with the questions about the character and composition of the people of God. His comments in Romans 12–15 then address how all Christians should live, and learn to live together, whether they are Jews or Gentiles.

Romans 15 discloses that Paul is hoping to have the Roman Christians support him in his mission to Spain, which he hopes to undertake after taking the collection to Jerusalem. The collection is of paramount importance to him as he writes Romans, for 15:25–28 strongly suggests that he sees the collection as a way of cementing together the Jerusalem church and his largely Gentile congregations, and in a sense, as a way of reciprocating with the Gentiles providing material aid, since the Jews, and particularly the Jewish Christians, had provided a spiritual blessing to them. It may also be true that he sees the collection as a manifestation of the eschatological pilgrimage of Gentiles up to Jerusalem, joining forever with the Jews as God's people, which is what 2 Cor. 9:10–12 may suggest, as there Paul alludes to Isa. 55:10 and Hos. 10:12. But did the collection accomplish what Paul hoped? We now turn to that question.

The Collection

According to Acts 20:4, a group of Christians from Paul's Macedonian and Galatian and Asian churches accompanied Paul to Macedonia from Corinth and on to Troas. At Acts 20:5–6 the reappearance of the "we" indicates that Luke has joined Paul and the others on the journey from Philippi to Troas and beyond. Luke recounts in 20:7–12 the famous Eutychus episode in the church in Troas, and then Paul's farewell speech to the Ephesian elders in 20:13–37. He is preparing his readers for what will follow in Acts 21 when Paul reaches Jerusalem and is arrested.

The Miletus speech is the one closest in substance to Paul's own letters, not least because it is the only substantial speech of Paul in Acts that is addressed to Christians. The speech contains a sort of passing of the baton to the Ephesian elders as leaders of God's flock in western Asia, and ends with pathos as Paul makes clear that he does not expect to see them again. He also warns the leaders about coming persecutions and trials that they will face. The speech undoubtedly is a summary written up by Luke, and it makes evident that Luke does know about the heart of Paul's gospel of salvation by grace through faith in the Christ who died.

The collection for the saints in Jerusalem is a topic that becomes a rather frequent refrain in Paul's letters (Galatians 2; 1 Corinthians 16; 2 Corinthians 8–9; Romans 15). First Corinthians 16 makes evident that Paul did not turn this into a matter of taking up a collection in church on Sunday. Rather, on that day each Christian was to lay something aside for this collection. The famine relief was desperately needed in Jerusalem, and Paul had agreed, as Galatians 2 makes clear, that he would continue to remember the Jewish Christians in Jerusalem. Notice too how in 2 Corinthians 8–9 Paul leaves it up to the Corinthians to choose their own emissaries to accompany the collection to Jerusalem. Second Corinthians 9:2 shows that many in Achaia were prepared and eager to give. Apparently, Titus was sent to begin the collection before Paul returned to Corinth. Whether or not Paul's opponents interfered with this process is unclear. More clear is that Paul saw the acceptance of the collection as a validation of his ministry by the Jerusalem church. Paul sees the collection actually as a *leitourgia*, a public service but also as an act of worship of the Gentiles, offered up to the one true God. What is not certain is whether Paul actually received funds from the Corinthian church. It may be telling that Luke lists no Corinthian Christians in his roster of emissaries in Acts 20:4. But we must consider now what happened to the collection once Paul arrived in Jerusalem.

The journey to Jerusalem was uneventful, except that Christians at Tyre begged Paul not to go up to Jerusalem; and then at Caesarea, Paul, while visiting with Philip and his prophesying daughters, received another visitor, Agabus, who warned by prophetic gesture that Paul would be bound when he reached Jerusalem and handed over to the Gentiles (Acts 21:7–14).

What are we to make of Paul's reception recorded in Acts 21:17–26? Luke says that Paul was warmly received, but says absolutely nothing about the collection. Notable by way of silence is that the collection is nowhere mentioned in Paul's later Captivity Epistles either. Could the collection have been rejected? Here is what we know for sure. First, Luke sees the events recorded in Acts 21:17–23:35 as crucially important. In some of his most expansive treatment of anything, these chapters cover less than twelve days, while, for example, Acts 24:1–26:32 (where Luke is also present) covers two years (see 24:27). Second, by comparison with Paul's emphasis on the matter, Luke downplays the collection; indeed, some would say that he does not even mention it (but see Acts 11:27–30). Luke, of course, is writing well after the fact and knows how things turned out. As a companion of Paul on his last trip to Jerusalem, could he really not have known what happened to the collection? Then there is the volatile situation in Jerusalem by the time Paul and Luke arrived. J. P. Polhill puts matters this way:

> Josephus describes the period of the mid–50s as a time of intense Jewish nationalism and political unrest. One insurrection after another rose to challenge the Roman overlords, and Felix brutally suppressed them all. This only increased the Jewish hatred for Rome and inflamed anti-Gentile sentiments. It was a time when pro-Jewish sentiment was at its height, and friendliness with outsiders was viewed askance. Considering public relations, Paul's mission to the Gentiles would not have been well received. The Jerusalem elders were in somewhat of a bind. On the one hand, they had supported Paul's witness to the Gentiles at the Jerusalem Conference. Now they found Paul a *persona non grata*[13] and his mission discredited not only among the Jewish populace, which they were seeking to reach, but also among their more recent converts. They did not want to reject Paul. Indeed they praised God for his successes. Still they had their own mission to the Jews to consider, and for that Paul was a distinct liability.[14]

Marching into Jerusalem at this xenophobic moment with Gentiles from various parts of the empire would hardly have produced a positive response either from Jews in general or from Pharisaic Jewish Christians. Zechariah 8:20–23 would not be likely to be fulfilled on this occasion, nor would Jews be made jealous to follow Jesus. To the contrary, they would be angry, and be more prone to want to stamp out the fledgling Christian movement. Thus, coupling all this with Luke's and Paul's silence on the matter after the fact, it is safe to say that the collection did not accomplish what Paul had hoped in uniting the church.

But was the collection rejected? The answer seems to be no. Acts 21:17 says that Paul was warmly welcomed by "the brothers," but these may refer to the Christians connected with Mnason. This may be unconnected with the meeting that followed on the next day between Paul and James and the Jerusalem authorities. But we must remember what sort of person James actually was. He was a mediating figure, not a hard-line Pharisaic Jewish Christian. For this reason, it seems quite unlikely that the collection was simply rejected, even if it was an awkward moment to be receiving money from Gentiles. The Judaizers were a real presence in the Jerusalem church, but not in charge. How could

13. Not only with Jerusalem Jews but also with Diaspora ones, as the story of what led to Paul's arrest makes clear.
14. J. P. Polhill, *Acts*, NAC 26 (Nashville: Broadman, 1992), 447.

James pacify them and still not shame Paul and his converts by rejecting the collection? Paul had been right to fear that the collection would not be totally acceptable to all in the Jerusalem church (Rom. 15:31), a justifiable fear not least because his former strong advocate, Peter, was no longer there, nor were the other apostles.

Acts 21:19–20 shows that Paul is the one who does the greeting, and he relates what God had done among the Gentiles through his *diakonia*. In light of Rom. 15:31, this could be a reference to the practical service of the collection, but in light of Acts 15:12, it seems more likely to be a broader, generic description of what was accomplished among the Gentiles. The response of the Jerusalem church was to praise God, but then comes a recounting of the great things God had done in converting "thousands" of Jews in Jerusalem, something that made the Gentile mission more difficult to deal with, not less. This makes it possible that the church was worried about the impact of Paul's coming and of the collection on these new Jewish Christians, who were Torah-observant. The concern was that Paul might be teaching Jews in the Diaspora not to be observant. The rumors were: (1) Paul had taught all Jews who lived among Gentiles to forsake Moses; (2) he had taught them not to circumcise their children; and (3) he had taught them not to observe the customs. These complaints are understandable in light of texts like Gal. 4:9–11; 5:6, and Rom. 2:25–30. There is, however, no evidence that Paul went around trying to persuade Jews to be nonobservant, although certainly he was not insisting on observance either.

Acts 21:23–24 should be seen as a solution to the dilemma. Paul would undertake an action in Jerusalem that would demonstrate his support for Torah-observant Jewish Christians right at the heart of Jewish life, in the temple. This was thought to be a way to squelch the rumors about Paul. It is likely that the vow of the four men in question, since it involved shaving their heads, was a Nazaritic vow (see Num. 6:2–21). Paul is to join with these men in some fashion, go through a ritual of purification (from the uncleanness in Gentile lands perhaps? cf. *m. 'Ohal.* 2:3; 17:5; 18:6), and pay for the fulfillment of these men's Nazaritic vows, which involved costly sacrifices. Paying for others' vows was seen as an especially pious act (see what Agrippa I did, according to *Ant.* 19.294). Perhaps a good deal of the collection money actually was used to pay for these four men's vows and the sacrifices involved.

Some readers perceive a sinister side to this request, that it would put Paul at risk by placing him in the midst of hostile Jews. In fact, it would give them time to plan their attack on Paul, because Paul first had to appear in the temple and state in advance the day when he

would fulfill his vow (see Rom. 15:31). The problem with this suggestion is that James would never have consented to it. Nearer the mark is
the suggestion that if Paul performed this act, then perhaps the Jerusalem church could accept the collection in good faith. Verse 24b indicates that the desired outcome was that all would know the rumors
about Paul to be untrue. Verse 25 then has a restatement and commitment by the Jerusalem church not to go back on its agreement about
what was expected of Gentile converts, even though more was now
being required of Paul in a Jewish direction. Before turning in the next
chapter to what happened to Paul in the temple, here is the place to
consider the two documents in the canon that seem to have come from
James and Jude, for they reveal more of early Jewish Christianity in a
non-Pauline vein.

Ethics and Eschatology from the Jerusalem Leaders

Considerable debate continues about the authorship and provenance of the book we call James. Nevertheless, a good case has been
made that the letter was a real encyclical written by James the Just to
Diaspora Jewish Christians.[15] The character of the book points to an
author heavily indebted to the wisdom material found in Proverbs and
Ben Sira, and also in the Jesus tradition, in particular in the Sermon on
the Mount, alluded to over twenty times in James. The author appears
to be a somewhat Hellenized Jewish Christian, but one committed to a
Jewish wisdom agenda.

I submit that the function of this document is to reinforce the socializing process of new Jewish Christians, who due to pressure or persecution are now wavering in their faith. In addition, the author is concerned to help these converts reject a corrupted version of the Pauline
message, as James 2:14–26 shows. This last passage strongly suggests
a date in the middle to late 50s, after the first couple of missionary journeys of Paul had had their due effect. Nothing in the letter of James indicates that the author was a hard-line Pharisaic Jewish Christian. Indeed, the author seems to studiously avoid the topic of the relationship
of Jewish and Gentile Christians, concentrating instead on the gospel
for Jewish Christians—but then, this was the original agreement mentioned by Paul in Galatians 2. Peter and the other pillars would focus
on the gospel for Jewish Christians. In other words, the material in this

---

15. See, e.g., R. Bauckham, *James: Wisdom of James, Disciple of Jesus the Sage* (London: Routledge, 1999); B. Witherington III, *Jesus the Sage: The Pilgrimage of Wisdom*
(Minneapolis: Fortress, 1994), 236–47.

document comports well with the portrait of James derived from Acts and the Pauline letters, but also fills that portrait out more.

For one thing, in light of the focus of James and the focus of the decree in Acts 15, clearly, James's concern was with orthodoxy, in terms of honoring the one true God, and also with orthopraxy, with perhaps a stronger emphasis on the latter. Basically, the letter of James is about how Jewish Christians must live; very little is said about what they must believe. For another thing, the letter gives a strong sense of the practical nature of James's teaching. Like most early Jews, James was wrapped up in the matter of how to honor God in day-to-day living. Persevering in the faith and patience in suffering, being a good listener, bridling the tongue, avoiding favoritism, demanding responsibility of those who have more resources, praying for and laying hands on the sick—these are the staples of James's discourse. The concern for the poor and for orphans mentioned in James 1–2 also comports nicely with material in Acts 6 and elsewhere in regard to the concerns of the Jerusalem church. Notice that by and large, James stands in the wisdom tradition rather than focusing on the exposition and application of Mosaic law. What James seems most skilled at is practical advice, both to Jewish Christians, as in his encyclical letter, and to Gentiles in the decree.

Of a very different ilk is the little letter of Jude, one of the most neglected of the New Testament documents. Recent scholarship has shown that a very good case can be made for this document actually being from Jude the brother of James the Just and of Jesus. It is unlikely that a later Christian writer would have adopted the name of so obscure a figure for the sake of lending authority to his pronouncements.

We know little about Jude. He was one of four brothers of Jesus (Matt. 13:55; Mark 6:3) and was not a follower of Jesus during his earthly ministry. Rather, he became a believer through the Easter events (Acts 1:14). As for his vocation, it appears likely that Jude, unlike James, who stayed in Jerusalem, was a missionary, and Paul had heard about his travels (1 Cor. 9:5). His audience was Jews, probably in Palestine, but perhaps in the Diaspora as well. Obviously, the author of Jude knows Greek, but also it appears clear from his use of the Hebrew Scriptures that he knew the ancestral language, including probably Aramaic, to judge from his citation of *1 Enoch*.

The letter itself is very different from the letter of James, being an example not of sapiential material but of early Jewish Christian eschatological and apocalyptic thinking. Probably, he is writing to predominantly Jewish Christian churches, which favors the notion that he is addressing churches in the Holy Land and perhaps nearby regions such as Syria or Egypt, though the problem with antinomianism may suggest a Diaspora setting in a largely Gentile context. In light of possible Pauline echoes or phrases in Jude, some have thought that he was addressing churches in Asia Minor. Since he recalls the audience to the teaching they received from apostles other than himself, he apparently is not writing to churches that he himself founded.[16] Thus, he is writing at a time after various churches had been founded for some time outside Jerusalem, long enough to develop problems such as the interference of false teachers, but surely before the Jewish war and its disastrous climax. No date so well fits these requirements as the 50s, perhaps the late 50s.

Jude issues a strong warning about judgment on the immoral, including an example about judgment on immoral angels (referencing Gen. 6:1–4), which had long been a stock example of moral degradation in early Judaism (cf. *1 Enoch* 6–19; 86–88; *Jub.* 4:15, 22; CD 2:17–19). In fact, the author is mainly dependent on the *Enoch* material for his rendering of the story here. In addition, he draws on the *Testament of Moses* in v. 9 to speak about the devil wrestling with Michael the archangel over Moses' body.

In vv. 10–16, Jude excoriates the false teachers and reminds his audience that the Lord will return for judgment with a myriad of holy ones (which could refer either to angels or to the saints in heaven, likely the former; cf. Zech. 14:5; *1 En.* 1:9). Verse 18 indicates that Jude believes his audience is living in the end times, which would be characterized by false teachers running amok. Clearly, Jude sees his audience in danger from within due to false teachers, and in danger from without due to persecution. His basic message is one of persevering in the faith once given them, and he encourages them with the assurance that God is able to keep them from falling and apostasy (v. 24). It is entirely possible that Jude sees the scenario described in Jesus' apocalyptic discourse (Mark 13) being played out in his own days. In any event, his source material and the way he uses it in midrashic fashion suggest an author and audience familiar with the stream of Jewish apocalyptic tradition that produced a great corpus of literature in the intertestamental and New Testament eras. In the next chapter we will see what persecution looked like up close, as we consider the trials and tribulations of Paul and others during the period A.D. 58–62.

16. In all this, I am following the magisterial study by R. Bauckham, *Jude, 2 Peter*, WBC 50 (Waco, Tex.: Word, 1983), 14–17.

Chapter 12

Trials and Executions: Signs upon the Earth

A.D. 58–62

The Changing of the Guard

About Felix's rule as procurator in Judea, even the Roman historian Tacitus once remarked, "Felix practiced every kind of cruelty and lust, wielding the power of a king with all the instincts of a slave" (*History* 5.9; *Annals* 12.54). Tacitus perhaps is rather biased against anyone connected with the Julio-Claudian emperors and against freedmen as well, but in light of what Josephus also says about the man, we may take it that Tacitus is not too far off the mark. Acts 23 says that Paul was arrested during Felix's reign, which means before A.D. 59. But can we be more precise? The issue of Paul's native region comes up in the trial before Felix, and Paul says that he is from Tarsus in Cilicia. Until about A.D. 58, this region was still part of the combined province of Syria-

Cilicia. Felix does not transfer Paul's case to another official. He could have sent Paul to the legate in Syria, but that legate was also in charge of Judea and would have been none too pleased to receive a minor case like Paul's when Felix was perfectly capable of deciding it (he had full imperium in such matters). Had Felix sent Paul to the legate, he would have been creating more problems for himself, and so he agrees to hear the matter. All of this suggests that Paul was arrested sometime in A.D. 57 or a little after—before the provincial situation changed in Paul's home region. Felix procrastinated for two years on the matter of how to deal with Paul, and so he languished under house arrest in Caesarea until about A.D. 60, when Porcius Festus arrived as Felix's replacement.

Festus was greeted by a difficult situation on the verge of becoming pure chaos. He arrived in Judea in the tenth year of Agrippa II, A.D. 60. Bandit and zealot gangs plagued the land, a controversial preacher greatly hated by some of his fellow Jews but also holding Roman citizenship was under house arrest, and bad blood flowed between Agrippa II and the temple hierarchy in Jerusalem (see *Ant.* 20.182–196). Festus was a capable man, and he took matters into hand immediately when he arrived in dealing with the gangs (*J.W.* 2.271).[1] Paul was more likely to get a fair hearing from Festus than from Felix, although even Festus was not immune to the pressures of a volatile region and Jewish factions at odds with one another.

Ishmael ben Phiabi was appointed high priest by Agrippa II near the very end of Felix's reign (*Ant.* 20.179), but soon he was at odds with Agrippa over the building of a tower that would allow Agrippa to see into the temple courts, including seeing the sacrifices while reclining on his couch and dining. Acting in tandem with former high priests who were still influential, such as Ananias, Ishmael built a high wall to block Herod's view. But this wall also obstructed the view of the Roman soldiers who guarded the area, and Festus ordered it razed. The matter was appealed to Rome, with twelve Jewish leaders going to appeal to Nero. Nero, by this time married to Poppaea and influenced by her (who, if not a Jew, was at least a Jewish sympathizer), ruled in favor of the Jewish temple representatives. But there was a cost. The Jewish high priest Ishmael and Helcias the temple treasurer, who had taken a risk in standing up against Festus and Agrippa, paid the price. They were retained in Rome as hostages, and so Ishmael had to surrender his office (*Ant.* 20.189–196).

Clearly, a power struggle existed between some of the Herodian clan and some of the temple hierarchy and other Sadducees. Festus could

---

1. It was most unfortunate that he was to die prematurely while still in office in Caesarea, probably late in A.D. 61 or early in 62.

Illustration 12.1 The so-called widow's mite or lepta thrown by a widow into the temple treasury.

not have known this in advance. Indeed, he could not have realized that while it was natural in a provincial situation for the Romans to use the social elite as means of keeping things in line, this same elite was not united, and in fact was widely despised by many ordinary Jews, if not totally rejected, as in the case of the Qumranites. Thus, when Festus went up to Jerusalem to meet with the Jewish officials (see Acts 25:1–5), he was unaware that he was facing a house very divided. He did not know that the elite did not necessarily speak for the majority of Jews.

There was another problem that Festus would have to deal with. During his rule, Nero handed down a verdict exonerating Felix of any wrongdoing. Festus would have to manage the fallout from this decision. In addition, Nero authorized a reneging of the grant of equal civil rights to Jews, something that Claudius had made a formal right early in his reign (*Ant.* 20.183). It was by no means clear exactly what the cash value of this decision was. Did it mean that all Jews had no such rights, or only the Jews in certain cities who originally had been given such rights by Claudius (e.g., in Alexandria)? Whatever the decision meant, it made the situation in the Holy Land for Festus even more unstable. In this atmosphere of suspicion and danger at every turn, Paul came to trial. It is no wonder that in the end, he appealed to Caesar.

The Trials of Paul

In Acts 21, Paul is rescued from the irate Jewish crowd by the Romans, in particular by a tribune, who, initially mistaking Paul for a messianic figure, the Egyptian, is surprised when Paul speaks Greek to him (Acts 21:31–39). The reference to the Egyptian is interesting, as his activities may be dated to about A.D. 54 (cf. *J.W.* 2.261–263; *Ant.* 20.169–172).[2] This, of course, provides evidence that the events leading to Paul's arrest transpired considerably later.

Paul responds to the unfortunate suggestions that he is a false prophet or a revolutionary by trotting out his honor rating. He is a Jew, not an Egyptian, from Tarsus. To a large extent, people in antiquity were judged on the basis of their geographical and ancestral origins. Since Tarsus had a high honor rating, this reflected well on Paul. His family had citizenship not only in Tarsus, but also held Roman citizenship.[3] Perhaps, they had provided a necessary service to the Roman army, making tents for them, in recognition for which Paul's family was granted Roman citizenship. Paul, then, was a Roman citizen from birth. We need to consider this matter in more detail.

A Closer Look: *Paul the Roman Citizen (Part 2)*

In only two places does Paul's Roman citizenship become a significant issue: Acts 16 and 22. In both cases Paul mentions this only to Roman officials, and in both cases he does so to influence the conduct of fellow Roman citizens, to dissuade them from treating him improperly. When Paul in Acts is speaking to Jews, or Gentile pagans, or a Christian audience in a nonlegal setting, he never mentions the matter.

For obvious reasons, Paul does not mention his Roman citizenship within earshot of a volatile Jewish crowd. This would just be adding fuel to an already fast-burning fire. We also must remember that for Paul, his Roman citizenship was at least third in the list of important identity markers, if not lower down the list.[4] He had no need to mention it in his letters, since, apparently, his converts never challenged him about the matter, nor does he speak to Roman charges against him directly in the letters. But Paul's present situation demanded that he mention his Roman citizenship. The major benefits of Roman law went to those with the most honor from a Roman point of view, and this meant Roman citizens, especially the patricians among them.

2. It is worth pondering whether the Egyptian was trying to take advantage of the new situation brought about by the demise of Claudius in 54 and the rise of Nero.

3. This was perfectly possible. See B. Witherington III, *Acts of the Apostles: A Socio-rhetorical Commentary* (Grand Rapids: Eerdmans, 1998), 663, 682.

4. On Paul's identity, see B. Witherington III, *The Paul Quest: The Renewed Search for the Jew of Tarsus* (Downers Grove, Ill.: InterVarsity, 1998), 52–88.

Thus, the tribune Lysias had to ask a few questions before he proceeded to torture Paul to get the truth out of him. Lysias does not want to take an action that he later will regret, which would happen if it turned out that he was torturing not merely a Roman citizen, but his social superior. Since Paul was a citizen from birth, he had a higher status than Lysias, who had purchased Roman citizenship (Acts 22:28). Augustus had decreed that Roman citizens were exempt from torture as a means of judicial disclosure.

Paul, an inveterate traveler, quite possibly carried with him a certificate of citizenship, or at least a *libellus*, which vouched for citizenship and stated that the original was on file in a municipal register in one's hometown. The penalties for falsely claiming citizenship were so severe that Lysias could not afford to ignore such a claim. Paul's claim of Roman citizenship in a sense dictates how the rest of his story will play out in Acts, including whether he would be turned over to the Jews or would go on to Rome.

A few telltale signs from Paul's letters do reflect that he was a Roman citizen. First, he has a Roman name. The name Paulus is rare in the east, and may suggest high birth. Also, Paul's strategy of evangelizing Roman colony cities is best explained by some kind of natural connection he has with such cities. This may also explain Paul's desire to go to Spain, which was a major center of Romanization. Furthermore, Paul claims to be a Gentile to the Gentiles, but what would be his natural connection with them if he was not a Roman citizen? Finally, Paul's letters are peppered with Roman names. All other things being equal, this favors the case for his Roman citizenship, for it suggests that he related well to such people.

No formal trial scenes occur before Acts 24, but several pretrial hearings do take place. Since Paul is in Roman custody, Roman, not Jewish, proceedings are the order of the day. Thus, the scene before the Sanhedrin in Acts 23 must be construed as part of the discovery phase of the larger process. The tribune wants to discover the facts of the case so that he can determine whether Paul is guilty of some crime under Roman law. The important point about the hearing before the Sanhedrin is that Paul quite adroitly sets the terms of discussion for all that follows. He is the one who defines what the main bone of contention is. And of course, his real audience, whom he must make his point with, is Lysias the tribune, not the Sanhedrin. Lysias's subsequent letter to the procurator evidences that Paul had successfully achieved his aim. Thus, it is not just a matter of Paul seeking to extricate himself from a situation where he would be judged by the Sanhedrin; rather, he actually wants to be judged by the Romans instead of the Jews, and his words and actions support that aim.

One of the notable features about this and the subsequent hearings and trials is that Paul is presented as wishing to make the gospel the real issue, not himself. Thus here he says that he is on trial for the eschatological hope he believes in, including the resurrection. We must keep in mind that this tribune is the procurator's main representative in Jerusalem. From a historical point of view, there is no reason to doubt that he could require the Sanhedrin to come together and meet. It was within his power to act in a judicial manner *until* he discovered what the real issues, complaints, problems, and charges were, and then he would turn the matter over to the procurator. Thus, the tribune is present at, though not as a part of, the hearing before the Sanhedrin, and he intervenes only when order needs to be restored—once the row breaks out over what Paul said about the resurrection, a row that divided the house. As we have seen, the Sadducees did not believe in the resurrection but the Pharisees did, hence the division.

Acts 23:2 notes that Ananias is the high priest at this time. He had been appointed by Herod Agrippa I (a.k.a. Herod of Chacis) in A.D. 47 and remained in power until A.D. 58 or 59 (*Ant.* 20.103). Ananias was known for his pro-Roman sentiments, and thus it is quite believable that he would cooperate with Lysias in holding a hearing. This man was far from priestly in character: he allowed his own servants to steal the tithes reserved for the priests (*Ant.* 20.205–206), and he had supported violence against the Samaritans, which got him summoned to Rome (*Ant.* 20.131). However, Ananias's pro-Roman views are what did him in during the Jewish war, sometime in A.D. 66, when a follower of the Zealot leader Menahem executed him. Note that Paul makes his rhetorical move of mentioning the resurrection only after he realizes what kind of high priest he is dealing with. He knew that he would not get justice from this high priest. Notice also that some Pharisees stand up and declare at the hearing, "We find nothing wrong with this man," a theme that would be repeated at various points during this entire judicial process. But many disagreed, and Lysias's soldiers had to intervene to prevent Paul's being pulled to pieces.

Acts 23:12–35 shows that the inability of the Sanhedrin to agree on what to say or do about Paul led to less legal means of trying to eliminate Paul. A group of about forty plotters swore an oath not to eat or drink until they had killed Paul. Moreover, they sought to involve Ananias in the plot by asking him to summon Paul from the fortress to the Sanhedrin for a fuller examination. Along the way, the plotters planned to ambush Paul. Paul was alerted to this scheme by his sister's son, and then he was sent on to the Roman commander to alert him to the plot. This in turn led to Lysias writing a letter to Felix explaining the circumstances and stating that he found no charge against Paul worthy of imprisonment or death, and so would be sending him to Caesarea under guard to be dealt with by the procurator (23:25–30). Lysias presents the matter in a way that makes him appear to be above reproach, because, of course, he had not really rescued Paul from the mob in the temple, but rather, had "examined" him by flogging. The process of sending Paul to the provincial capital in turn meant that Paul's accusers would have to come to Caesarea and submit to the Roman way of handling matters. Paul was to be kept under guard in Herod's palace in the meantime.

Illustration 12.2 Roman male offering a sacrifice (note headcovering).

The trial before Felix is recorded in Acts 24:1–27, and is presented as a rhetorical duel between Paul and a hired gun named Tertullus. Verses 1–9 sum up the prosecution, vv. 10–22 the defense, and vv. 22–27 the fallout. It appears that the *extra ordinem* procedure was being used in this case. This looser process allowed the plaintiff to simply allege "facts" against the accused without necessarily producing any hard evidence or eyewitnesses, and then ask the procurator to deal with the matter. In such a case, the governor could render justice directly without a cumbersome legal process. Thus, the accusatorial, not the inquisitional, form of trial procedure is in play in Acts 24. The burden of proof rested with the accuser in such a case. The judge had great flexibility in deciding what the crime was, what the punishment should be, and whether action should be taken immediately or some time later—and later could mean much later. The famous historian Polybius was under house arrest for an amazing fifteen years, under suspicion without resolution of his case or a trial.

That the Jewish plaintiffs brought a professional rhetor with them showed how badly they wanted to get rid of Paul, as does the fact that the high priest and his entourage came in person to the trial. First, a pretrial hearing allowed the accusers to make their charge before Felix. Then, at the trial, Tertullus charged Paul with being seditious and with profaning the temple, while Felix, on the other hand, is praised for establishing the Pax Romana and good reforms in the land for a long time.[5] Paul is made out to be the same sort of fellow as the Egyptian, a major troublemaker and a plague in the land, and the implied hope is that Felix will deal with him as he would the Egyptian. These charges indeed were the sort that would grab the attention of a Roman ruler, as opposed to some sort of allegation about Jewish theology or eschatology. The end of Tertullus's speech urged Felix to examine Paul to see if these things were true, but Felix declines.

Paul, in his response to these charges, very appropriately limits his remarks to what he had been doing in the last twelve days in Jerusalem, for if the high priest had been able to produce, say, one of the Ephesian Jews who had raised the alarm when Paul was in the temple, and he testified that Paul caused an uproar in Diaspora synagogues, then the charge of sacrilege might be made to stick as well as the charge of sedition. Paul very effectively says that far from trying to pollute the temple, he was trying to purify himself there! It is interesting that the charge against Paul included the remark that it was the temple police who had seized him, when in fact it had been the crowd. This was a lie, perhaps meant to establish jurisdictional claim over Paul's case. But we must remember that Felix already had read his right-hand man's report to the contrary about the facts of the matter.

Paul's speech is in excellent rhetorical form, and includes a *narratio*, because the facts of the case are in dispute, as well as the interpretation of events. Paul establishes that he had not been disputing in the synagogues or in the temple; he had been purifying himself (Acts 24:12–18).

5. Which shows that this trial transpired late in Felix's time as procurator.

A Letter about Corruption

An interesting private letter from Egypt in the time of Augustus deals with an everyday problem of graft and corruption. It reads as follows:

> Syneros to his friend Chios, very many greetings. If you are well, fine. Theon brought along to me Ohapim, the public banker of Oxyrhynchos, who indeed spoke to me about the dishonesty of Epaphras. Therefore I say nothing more than 'Do not allow your own ruin because of those fellows.' Believe me, too much kindness brings calamity of the greatest kind upon men. Afterwards he himself will show you the significance of the matter, when you call him to you. But persevere. He who makes so large a profit from such a petty amount is willing to kill his master. Then I ought to shout out, if I read the situation aright 'gods and men'! It will fall to you to take revenge lest someone else may like to do it. (Reverse side—To Chios [slave] of Caesar). (*NewDocs* 1:53)

Chios is a public servant working as part of the household of Caesar, in this case abroad rather than in Rome. Epaphras has been engaging in some sort of dishonest monetary dealings and has made a good profit. Epaphras, then, would be a slave of Chios who has been taking advantage of the liberty Chios had given him to make investments and transact business on his behalf. This was not an unusual practice in this era. In fact, there were very wealthy slaves who had added to the net worth of their masters but also had lined their own pockets. Syneros thinks it not only an immoral situation but also a dangerous one, for the slave would no longer be dependent on his master financially, and indeed would have a motive now for eliminating his master and so becoming free of his control. Syneros is also fearful for Chios's reputation. Chios had better deal with the matter before it becomes too widely known and he finds his honor rating drop, not only with the banker in question but also with others. Here is a portrait of the dilemmas of everyday life and of the problems inherent to a system of slavery. It reminds us as well that first-century slavery was in many respects of a very different ilk than agricultural slavery in the antebellum South in the nineteenth century.

Paul then stresses that he admits to being a follower of "the Way," which still entailed worshiping the God of his ancestors, but in a particular manner. Once again, Paul focuses on the gospel and makes it the real issue under debate. At 24:17 he responds to the charge of sedition. He says that he had returned to Jerusalem to bring alms to his nation (probably an allusion to the collection) and to make sacrifice. The reference to money here may explain why Luke says that Felix delayed judgment on Paul, hoping he would offer him a bribe (24:26).

Perhaps in a moment of inspiration, Paul refers to some Diaspora Jews who stirred up the temple crowd against him, but who are not present to charge Paul with anything. Roman law took very seriously the failure of an accuser to be present at a trial to pursue the charges that had been leveled against the accused elsewhere. In fact, by A.D. 61, legislation was passed in Rome that prevented this from happening. There would be no trial if the accuser could not manage to be present. Felix adjourns the trial without rendering a judgment. We can only speculate that while he did not want to totally alienate a pro-Roman Jewish high priest, neither did he see any real case against a man who was a Roman citizen. Acts 24:23 suggests that Felix did not consider Paul a threat, as he relaxed the conditions of his confinement. He is placed in military custody with a centurion, but kept in the governor's palace, and allowed visits from friends.

We may be wondering where Luke is during the two years that Paul spends in custody. I suggest that he probably was with Paul a good deal, bringing him sustenance and necessities, but also using the time to gather a great deal of data from James and the Jerusalem church, and from Philip and his family in Caesarea, about the earliest period of Christian history. The years A.D. 58–59 may have been crucial for him as a historian gathering sources about the period A.D. 30–57.

Acts 24:24–25 recounts how Felix visited with Paul on various occasions, including at least once with his Jewish consort, and on that occasion Paul had spoken pointedly to him about future judgment for sin, about self-control, and about justice, three matters he definitely needed to hear about. Yet Felix was to leave office without doing justice to Paul, leaving him for Festus to deal with.

Acts 25:25–26 tells of the trial before Festus. Festus turned to Herod Agrippa for help in Paul's case, perhaps because Agrippa was a Jew but was not among the plaintiffs or defendants, but also probably because he had close ties with Rome. This part of the drama begins with the report that the Jewish priests lobbied Festus to transfer Paul to Jerusalem to resolve his case. Festus, however, asserts his own authority, and in essence starts the judicial process all over again by asking the accusers to come with him back to Caesarea, where he would examine Paul's case. Acts 25:8 shows that all the requisite parties were finally assembled in Caesarea, and Paul took the straightforward approach by saying that he had not offended against either the Jewish or the Roman law. In v. 9 Festus proposes a change of venue to placate the Jewish authorities, but Paul would still be judged by Festus.

Paul will have none of this, as 25:10–11 makes quite apparent. He is already standing before the judgment seat of Caesar, where he must be judged. Verse 11 shows Paul's good character. He is perfectly willing to be judged by Roman law and to die if he has committed some crime worthy of death under that law. He insists that if there is nothing to the Jewish charges, then no one can give him over to the Jewish authorities as a mere favor to them. Paul finally plays his trump card by stating plainly, "I appeal to Caesar." Only under great pressure does he exercise this right, when he feels that there is grave danger of not getting justice in the present situation. It needs to be stressed that Paul is not appealing a verdict already rendered, for none had yet been given.

When Augustus had set up the empire, he actually encouraged the appeal of cases from the provinces to Caesar, if they touched the *dignitas* of the emperor. This was a way of centralizing power even further.[6] The *Lex Julia* was clear that if a provincial procurator interfered with this process undertaken by a Roman citizen, the penalty was death (Ulpian, *Digest* 48.6–7). This right of appeal protected the citizen from coercion by the procurator. Of course, for Paul, there was another upside to the appeal: it gave him an occasion to testify for his faith before the emperor. Also, in A.D. 59, after five years of reasonably good rule by Nero, Paul had no reason to fear him more than Festus, or to doubt that he had a better chance at justice in Rome than in the volatile province of Judea.

Festus, however, was now in an awkward spot. If the charges against Paul were frivolous or untrue, how could he explain to Nero why he had taken up his time and the empire's money by sending Paul to Rome? If a Roman citizen had appealed to the emperor, what had been so grave about the situation that he felt compelled to do so? How would Festus explain this without looking incompetent or not in control of the Judean situation?

But as fortune would have it, and as Luke reports in Acts 25:13–27, Festus was about to get some help from an unexpected source. Herod Agrippa II and his consort, Bernice, arrived in Caesarea to officially welcome Festus to the region. Remember that this is the Agrippa raised in Rome, and who renamed his capital city, Caesarea Philippi, Neronias in honor of the current emperor. It would be natural for Agrippa to be seen by Festus as a Jewish authority superior to the high priest, since Agrippa was the one who appointed the priest and had control of the sacred vestments, and was curator of the temple treasury. It would be invaluable for Festus to be able to report to Nero that Agrippa had concurred with his judgment to send Paul along to Rome.

6. See the detailed discussion in Witherington, *Acts of the Apostles*, 724–26.

Bernice was a thoroughly remarkable woman. She was considered a woman of great beauty and intelligence. She was Agrippa's sister, and there were rumors of an incestuous relationship with Agrippa, on the Eastern pattern of consort/sister/wife (see *Ant.* 20.145–147). At the end of the Jewish war, she became the mistress of the conquering general, Titus, and she returned to Rome to live with him. Titus wanted to marry her, but since he was in line to be emperor, and Roman anti-Semitism being what it was, it was too much of a scandal to do so (see Tacitus, *History* 2.81; Suetonius, *Titus* 7). Titus, in the end, because of his political ambitions, dismissed Bernice and went on to become emperor in A.D. 79.

Festus's portrayal of himself in this passage is highly self-serving. In the end, he places the blame for his dilemma on Paul himself, due to his appeal, which Festus depicts as senseless because there were no substantive charges against Paul. But notice that neither Felix nor Festus was prepared to totally offend the Jewish authorities by dismissing the charges and freeing Paul. Festus is puzzled about what to tell Nero, and Agrippa says that he would like to hear the man for himself, and this leads to Acts 26, the climactic speech of Paul before a king in royal regalia. This fulfilled the promise of Jesus (see Acts 9:15).

Bear in mind as we evaluate Acts 26 that Paul is not on trial when this speech is delivered; rather, he is involved in a judicial hearing meant to help the procurator decide what to write the emperor about Paul. Also bear in mind that the primary audience of this speech is Agrippa, as is shown by Acts 26:1, where it is Agrippa who gives Paul permission to speak. Agrippa would understand much of Paul's rhetoric about his Jewish life and work. This, then, is an *apologia* for Paul's life, a testimony or witness delivered to Agrippa. Paul in this speech plays the role of a witness in his own defense, instead of rebutting charges and attacking his accusers. Rather, Paul makes an appeal to remain as he is, minus the chains. Much of the speech is taken up with a simple narration of events in Paul's life, leading up the point when he becomes a captive (v. 21). It does not relate the trial before Felix or what happened during house arrest. The main thrust of the account is to make manifest that Paul has lived the life of a pious Jew.

What, then, does Paul say about himself? To begin with, he spent his youth among his own people, and more particularly, in Jerusalem, which confirms, as already suggested in Acts 22:3, that Paul grew up a Jew in Jerusalem not in Tarsus (although, Jerusalem Judaism was also a Hellenized entity). Paul says further that he was a part of the strictest sect of Judaism, the Pharisees. At v. 6 he stresses that the reason he was being persecuted and pursued by his fellow Jews since becoming a follower of Jesus is precisely "on account of my hope in the promise made by God to our ancestors"—an apparent reference to resurrection and the eschatological state of affairs. In vv. 9–11 Paul recounts his actions against Christians, performed under the authorization of the high priest. Keep in mind that the family of Annas and Caiphas had held the high priesthood off and on throughout the Christian life of Paul. It is hardly surprising that latter-day members of this family would want to do in the man who had betrayed the cause that their relatives had commissioned him to fight for in the 30s.

Acts 26:10 hints that Paul as Saul was a member of the Sanhedrin, which is not impossible, but probably he was too young to qualify in the 30s. Whatever his status was, his vote was for doing away with Christians by execution. This raises the interesting possibility that Paul is trying to incriminate the Sanhedrin at this juncture, because they did not at that time have the power of capital punishment. In any event, vv. 9–11 paint a clear picture of Paul as a zealous persecutor, just as vv. 12–18 rehearse the by now familiar (to Theophilus) story of Paul's conversion. In v. 20 we learn something new: Paul proclaimed his new faith not only in Damascus and Jerusalem but also throughout the Judean region; or possibly, it simply means that he proclaimed the message "in every country, to Jews and to Gentiles." In any case, it will be seen by the end of the speech that in fact Paul has managed to make clear that the real bone of contention between him and the Jewish authorities is religious not political, in the narrower sense of the latter. Verse 20 makes evident that Paul is casting himself in the line of prophetic figures like John the Baptist, as he has called his own people and others to repentance and deeds worthy of repentance. Yet he would also make clear that the prophets had foretold that the Messiah would come, and must suffer and be raised from the dead, which is the gist of his message.

The mention of Jesus' resurrection in Acts 26:23 prompts an outburst by Festus that Paul is out of his mind, not unlike what the Areopagites were thinking when the same topic came up in Acts 17. What Festus actually seems to mean is that Paul's great learning has caused him to leave common sense behind—dead persons do not rise to life again. At this juncture, in a masterful rhetorical move, Paul brings Agrippa into the discussion by a direct question: "Do you believe in the prophets?" And then before Herod can answer, Paul answers for him that he knows that he does. Had Herod said no, it would have marked him as a bad Jew; had he said yes, Paul might have asked why he did not believe what the prophets said about the Messiah. It is hard to know whether Herod's words "In so short a time do you think to make me a Christian?" are said in jest, in sarcasm, in incredulity at the boldness of Paul, or in partial conviction. Whichever is the case, it is now Herod who has been put on the defensive. The meeting concludes without a conversion of Herod, but with a brief confabulation between Festus and his consultants in which the procurator states that Paul could have been set free if he had not appealed to the emperor. Hereafter, Paul would once more become a traveling man, now with the accompaniment of a Roman escort. He would finally reach the destination he had written about to the Romans some four to five years earlier—the Eternal City. But in order to get Paul out of town quickly, they had to set sail out of due season.

The Rough Ride to Rome

Adding up all miles of the nine or ten sea journeys Paul is said to undertake in Acts (beginning with 9:30), we find that he covered some three thousand miles by sea during his three decades of ministry. Second Corinthians 11:25 says that on three occasions during his ministry prior to the trip chronicled in Acts 27–28, he was shipwrecked. By the time of the journey to Rome, Paul was already a veteran traveler of the sea as well as the land. Here is the place to take a closer look at Paul the traveler throughout the empire.

A Closer Look: *Paul the Traveling Man*

Though without doubt Paul's catalog of traveling woes in 2 Cor. 11:25–27 reveals some of the perils Paul faced, it would be a mistake to assume that travel was more difficult and dangerous in Paul's day than in previous eras. In fact, a strong case can be made that the first century A.D. was a time when travel was the safest it had ever been in the Mediterranean world. Consider the words of L. Casson:

The first two centuries of the Christian Era were halcyon days for a traveler. He could make his ways from the shores of the Euphrates to the border between England and Scotland without crossing a foreign border, always within the bounds of one government's jurisdiction. A purse full of Roman coins was the only kind of cash he had to carry; they were accepted or could be changed everywhere. He could sail through any waters without fear of pirates, thanks to the Emperor's patrol squadrons. A planned network of good roads gave him access to all major centers, and the through routes were policed well enough for him to ride with relatively little fear of bandits. He needed only two languages: Greek would take him from Mesopotamia to Yugoslavia, Latin from Yugoslavia to Britain. Wherever he went, he was under the

> protective umbrella of a well-organized efficient legal system. If he was a Roman citizen and he got into trouble, he could, as St. Paul did, insist upon trial in Rome.[7]

This is certainly too optimistic a reading of the situation, but perhaps not by much. If the point of comparison is with the preempire situation, Casson is certainly right. Travel was easier and safer during the empire than in previous eras, not least because there were no major wars between regions or countries during that time.

In some respects, Paul can be compared to a traveling salesman hawking his wares. For example, he can be compared to the merchant Flavius Zeuxis from Hierapolis in Asia, who brags on his tombstone that he had rounded the cape at the southern tip of Greece some seventy-two times on sea voyages to Rome (about two to three trips per summer). Paul had a trade he could practice in various places, but what was its precise nature? It is not likely that he was a weaver of goathair cloth and linen, the sort of material often used by tentmakers, since the tools and equipment required by weavers would not go on the road, being too large and unwieldy. More likely, Paul repaired tents and made other leather products, carrying a bag of cutting tools, an awl, and a sharpening stone.[8] Paul may have been more of a risk taker than most salesmen and craftsmen, as he even traveled out of due season, as the references to rivers and shipwrecks in 2 Corinthians 11:25–26 show.

Many of the good Roman roads that Paul traveled had been in place for a long time. For example, the Via Egnatia through Macedonia was finished in 148 B.C., and by the time of Augustus, good roads ran through Asia and Syria and all the way down to Alexandria in Egypt. The major concern of Rome during the late republic and early empire was to build straight, all-weather roads suitable for armies to travel under any conditions, though of course, they also provided all-weather means of travel for merchants, sophists, and rhetoricians. It is ironic that the gospel of peace spread rapidly on means of travel that were intended for quite the opposite purpose. Latin mile markers dotted the major Roman roads. These Roman roads were not equaled or surpassed before the nineteenth century of our era.

7. L. Casson, *Travel in the Ancient World* (London: Allen and Unwin, 1974), 122.
8. See B. Rapske, "Acts, Travel, and Shipwreck," in *The Book of Acts in Its Graeco-Roman Setting*, ed. D. Gill and C. Gempf (Grand Rapids: Eerdmans, 1994), 7.

In addition, there were government-maintained hostels and inns throughout the empire, and even the ancient equivalent of AAA Trip-Tiks, telling the exact distances between hostels, and their locations and facilities. Of course, these facilities were mainly for the use of government couriers, but it is highly probable that a Roman citizen like Paul used them as well, and perhaps also Paul's own couriers of his letters. A letter carried by one of Paul's co-workers could take considerable time to get to its destination if it had to go over water to reach the destination, such as from Corinth to Rome or Rome to Philippi, or if it was sent in the bad season for travel.

In some parts of the empire, travel by land was possible almost year round, but travel by sea was more limited to the sailing season. Prime sea travel time was from May 27 to September 14. The Mediterranean was volatile from March 10 to May 26 and from September 14 to November 11, but still sailable. The winter storms made the seas treacherous after November 11 and until March 10, but still, some daring merchants in search of extra profits from products such as the grain from winter wheat would not infrequently take the risk.

There were no genuine passenger ships of any size in antiquity. One had to book passage on a merchant ship. The smaller ones would hug the coastline and go slowly from port to port, while the larger ones would occasionally venture out into the Mediterranean. On a big vessel and in good weather, travel from Rome to Corinth took five days, and Rome to Alexandria ten days. The latter was the usual route of the big grain freighters. Most travelers on these large ships booked passage as deck passengers, sleeping in the open or under a small covering or tent. They would have to bring their own cooking materials and clothes, and sometimes bedding as well.

Since the ships in question were sailing ships, they hardly ever left port on a regular schedule. Rather, they waited for the winds to be right. Thus, travelers needed to be constantly ready and near the port to sail on such a ship. Then, too, sailors were a superstitious lot, unwilling to travel on certain "accursed" days on the calendar (August 24, October 5, November 8, religious holidays). A sacrifice would usually be made by the captain before sailing, and if the reading of the entrails was not propitious and the omens were not good, the trip would be put off. These factors explain in part why Paul had time in Tyre and Caesarea to visit with fellow Christians on his way to Rome.

Obviously, the bigger the boat the safer the travel, and the biggest were the grain ships. The largest we know of was the *Isis*, which held a thousand tons of grain and could carry a thousand passengers as well. Paul's ride was provided by a medium-sized boat, much inferior in size and capacity to the *Isis*, as it would carry only three hundred passengers (see Acts 27:37). In addition, the boat Paul was on in Acts 27 was traveling out of due season. The outcome of the trip is hardly surprising, and it provides another example of how God's providence worked all things together for good in the life of Paul.

Acts 27–28 includes one of the most vivid narratives in all of Acts, an apparent eyewitness account by Luke of the adventures and misadventures of Paul on the way to Rome. The reason Luke includes this vivid and detailed account is in essence because he, as a Greek historian, must demonstrate that he was an eyewitness of some of the events he chronicled. In other words, though he summarizes other important stories of which he was not a part, this one he can tell in full because he was there. It is a matter of the amount of source material he had at hand. Here too, Luke reveals himself to be a Greek, a lover of sea tales (e.g., the *Odyssey*). But this story of the journey to Rome is no entertaining diversion. It is integral to the whole narrative that has been moving since Acts 1 from Jerusalem to Rome, from the Jewish capital to the Gentile capital, from a more Jewish church to a more Gentile one, with Paul being the bridge figure between the two.

Acts 27:1 says that when it was decided to send Paul to Rome, he was placed in the custody of a centurion named Julius from the Sebastiani cohort of the army of Syria and Judea (attested in *ILS* 2683 = *CIL* 3.6687). Since Claudius had prohibited the use of the name of his most illustrious ancestor, Julius Caesar, if one was not a Roman citizen, it is probable that this soldier was, like Paul, a citizen of Rome. This may in part explain why Julius treats Paul in such a kind fashion. But also, Paul was not a condemned man, so the centurion could hardly treat him as a criminal, especially in view of Paul's citizenship status.

Accompanying Paul on this trip is not only Luke (note the reappearance of the "we" at this juncture in the narrative, which continues right through 28:16), but also Aristarchus from Thessalonike, who, according to Acts 20:4, had accompanied Paul to Jerusalem with the collection and now was going to Rome with him. Notice that in Philem. 24 he is called Paul's fellow worker and in Col. 4:10 he is called Paul's fellow prisoner, another small indicator that we are on the right track in thinking that the Captivity Epistles originated in Rome.

Initially, Paul was definitely on the slow boat to Rome, riding a small ship that hugged the coast going north and put into port just north of Tyre. Paul was treated in a humane fashion, and he was allowed to go ashore and visit the Christians in Sidon, not least so he could be fed and cared for by someone other than the centurion. Paul visited with friends briefly, and then Acts 27:4 says that they put out from Sidon and were forced to sail under the lee of Cyprus due to contrary winds. Already they were sailing during the time of changeable weather and waters, and already there was danger. At this time of year, winds from the west and northwest prevailed, pushing a boat south and making it difficult to sail westward, as Paul's boat had to do to reach Rome. The boat managed to reach Myra in Lycia, a normal stopping point for grain freighters. It is thus no surprise when v. 6 tells of such a ship from Alexandria bound for Italy being in port there. It would be the centurion's job to secure passage on it for himself and his charges.

Even this larger grain boat had great difficulty sailing west and was fortunate to reach Fair Havens, on the south side of Crete, intact. Luke says explicitly that they were sailing after the Fast, which is to say, after the fall Day of Atonement. In A.D. 59, when this adventure transpired, that day fell on October 5. This was well within the parameters of the dangerous season for sailing, which was September 14 through November 11. Paul advised that the ship put into port for the winter at Fair Havens; otherwise, he believed, life and cargo would be in great danger. This should be seen as commonsense advice from a veteran traveler, not prophecy, for although the boat sails into a gale resulting in loss of cargo, only later does Paul announce the divinely inspired vision that the voyage would see no loss of life (Acts 27:22–26).

Under the rule of both Claudius and Nero, incentives were given to ship owners to sail during the dangerous season, and the emperor promised to recompense losses as well as pay a bonus if they would attempt it, so greatly was the grain needed in Rome during the off-season (see Suetonius, *Claudius* 18.2). It is thus not surprising that the owner of Paul's vessel, who was on board, decided to sail on. The emperors took such initiatives because grain shortages often caused major social unrest in Rome and its environs, and Tacitus (*Annals* 12.43) speaks of an insurrection during the reign of Claudius caused by such a grain shortage. It must be remembered that part of the largesse of living in Rome was a free dole of grain for many of the residents.

The attempt was made to sail past the point of Crete and around to the larger bay where the port of Phoenix was. They had not counted on the typhoon that hit them, a powerful northeaster. Cargo began to be jettisoned. Despair sets in, and Paul makes a speech to encourage everyone that they would survive, though the ship and cargo would be lost (27:21–26).

Paul proved to be right about this matter. A Gentile likely would read this story to suggest that Paul was innocent of any crimes, as otherwise, the miraculous rescue of Paul and all passengers (276 of them) would never have happened.[9] The boat drifted with the winds some 475 miles before running aground off of Malta.

Malta is a small island, only eighteen miles long and eight miles wide, located some sixty miles south of Sicily and 180 miles north of Africa. It was a major stopping point for grain freighters, which explains the presence of the ship *Dioskouroi* in port there (Acts 28:11). The culture of the island had been, and still was to a large extent in Paul's day, Phoenician. This was due to the influence of the Phoenician settlement in northern Africa at and around Carthage. Greek and Latin were spoken on Malta, but the native vernacular was Punic.

A reciprocal relationship is set up between the "chief man" of Malta and the Maltese people on the one hand and Paul on the other. The Maltese provide hospitality and aid, Paul provides healing, and then in turn the Maltese provide provisions when Paul leaves. The initial act of kindness involved the Maltese building a bonfire on the beach for those who had been rescued from the sea. From out of the brush that Paul had picked up came a snake, apparently a viper or a constrictor of some kind, which fastened itself on Paul's hand. The Maltese took this event as a sign that Paul was a criminal, until Paul survived the snake bite, at which point they saw him as a god.[10]

The father of Publius, the chief of Malta, was sick with a fever, and according to 28:8, Paul comes, prays, lays on hands, and the man is cured. This in turn led to the sick of the island coming to Paul and being cured. In gratitude, the residents gave Paul and his companions provisions and traveling funds to get them to Italy. After some three months or so on Malta, Paul and those with him, either in February or March of A.D. 60, sailed on to Italy.

At Last in Rome

The remainder of Luke's second volume, Acts 28:12–31, is devoted to Paul's reaching, and his time in, Rome. After they had made a brief stop at Sicily, a strong wind propelled Paul and his companions to Puteoli,

9. See G. B. Miles and G. Trompf, "Luke and Antiphon: The Theology of Acts 27–28 in the Light of Pagan Beliefs about Divine Retribution, Pollution, Shipwreck," *Harvard Theological Review* 69 (1976): 259–67.

10. If the snake that bit Paul was nonvenomous, then no miracle was involved, despite the ascription of divinity to Paul by the Maltese.

Rome

Rome began as a small agricultural settlement on the Tiber River around 753 B.C., according to first-century A.D. reckoning. It was thus an ancient city by the time of the New Testament era, and clearly the most important city of that age, for obvious reasons. The transformation of the settlement or village into an actual city seems to have been accomplished by the Etruscans somewhere around 600 B.C. This required the draining of marshy land, the building of a city wall, the paving of various areas, and the construction of public buildings. The Etruscans also developed this city into the leading metropolis in central Italy, including setting the pattern for Rome's legal and religious systems.

Though it was not called such, by the second century B.C. Rome possessed an empire in the western Mediterranean that included Spain, northwest Africa (spoil of the Punic Wars with Carthage), and southern Gaul. Already in this period, for administrative purposes, these territories were organized into provinces governed by senatorial proconsuls. This was to serve as the blueprint for the expansion in the east, which began even before the Julio-Claudian era.

The impact of the continuing expansion of the empire is that money and other resources, including human resources (slaves), flowed with great regularity into Rome, and the city gained considerable wealth and came to rival even Alexandria as a center of commerce and prosperity. Empire building proved to be profitable, especially for the upper echelon of Roman society, and the results could be seen in the city itself as massive building campaigns were undertaken by Augustus and other wealthy Romans. Augustus bragged that the city he took over made of brick, he left behind made of marble (Suetonius, *Augustus* 28.3).

The Mediterranean came to be seen as (and even called) a giant Roman lake, and the territories around it as sources of materials, people, and revenue to support and help build a greater Rome. Once Rome became a prosperous city, many throughout Italy and elsewhere in the empire sold farms and property to move to the capital and make a better living. But unfortunately, these now landless people often did not find sufficient work to allow them to live the good life, necessitating already in the second century B.C. the creation of a public welfare system. Rome became a city like many modern cities, with the same disparities between rich and poor, between well-built and poorly built areas, and with the same social problems—poverty, hunger, homelessness, and the like. The setting up of the dole of grain in 22 B.C. by Augustus was necessary to prevent social unrest in the city.

The city of Rome had certain natural advantages. There was the Tiber, of course, but also the indispensable resources of silex, with which Rome could be paved. Silex was provided by the lava flow from the Alban volcano, which came within a few miles of the city and provided the raw material for street construction. The city, having been built on seven hills, was quite difficult to take in battle. It was once called a "suspended city," meaning a city hung from several hills. In such a situation, dwellings had to be vertical in character, hence the *insulae*, or what we would call high-rise apartment structures. This mode of building, using mostly timbers, made Rome in the dry season a natural fire hazard as well. The technology of kiln-fired bricks fully developed only by the time of Nero, and reconstruction of Rome after the fire of A.D. 64 was on the more solid and sound basis of brick rather than timber for the most part, augmented by wider streets to help keep fires from spreading.

The means by which such massive construction projects could be undertaken was largely slave labor. Though Corinth had major slave markets, without a doubt Rome had the largest slave population in the empire. Slaves in Rome were not simply domestic servants; they were artisans, businesspeople, tutors, civil servants, and a number of other things. Of the fourteen major districts of Rome, none could have been run without slave labor, and all had a slave population. While certain ethnic groups, like Jews, lived in particular parts of the city, slaves were everywhere. A conservative estimate would suggest that at least a third, if not a half, of the population of Rome was slaves, meaning perhaps more than one hundred thousand slaves. The economy depended quite literally on slave labor, and nowhere was that more evident than in the Eternal City itself.

Needless to say, to deal with the big-city problems, Rome had an adequate police force, and a military presence was necessary. Ulpian states that the job of the city prefect was "to maintain soldiers on guard-duty to preserve quiet among the *populares* and to keep him informed about what is happening where" (Ulpian, *Digest* 1.12.1–12). Augustus for the first time made available more military manpower for the local magistrates to use. In fact, the city prefect had three urban cohorts, or fifteen hundred men, at his disposal. Also, in 22 B.C. Augustus set up the city watch, composed of six hundred slaves, a force that grew to almost four thousand by A.D. 55. Their principal task was to be city firefighters.

Rome was the most cosmopolitan of all cities in the empire; indeed, it was the empire in microcosm with representatives of every race, ethnic group, religious persuasion, and social status to be found in the empire. Under such circumstances, it is surprising that there was not more unrest in the Eternal City.

the major port for those traveling to Rome. According to vv. 14–15 Paul, Luke, and the others found Christians almost immediately in Puteoli. Clearly, Luke has no wish to portray Paul as the founder of Roman Christianity, though something may be said for the view that he was a pioneer of the gospel of universal salvation for Jews and Gentiles while he was in Rome. Perhaps, the form of gospel they had known heretofore was more like that offered by the Jerusalem Jewish Christians, though Paul's letter to the Romans suggests that there was a problem with supersessionism on the part of the largely Gentile Christian congregations in Rome.

Acts 28:14–15 relates that after Paul and his companions visited for a few days with Christians in Puteoli, Christians from Rome came some forty miles out of the city down the Via Appia to the Appian forum to meet him. Paul is depicted as some sort of dignitary, with a welcoming committee meeting him outside the city. This show of respect and affection reassured Paul that he had friends in Rome, even though he had to face the Roman judicial process when he got there. Verse 16 concludes the "we" section and the travelogue.

Note that Paul is portrayed in this passage as being under the most lenient form of military custody, having only a soldier guarding him and being allowed to choose his own lodgings. He is not in a prison or in a military camp. Furthermore, the soldier in question is not even a centurion, but simply an ordinary soldier. And notice that there is only one such soldier, where normally there would be two if the case was serious at all (see Acts 12:6). It appears that the duty rotated among Caesar's elite guard, and could have involved many different soldiers from the nine or so cohorts in this guard. Josephus says that the guard was rotated every four hours (*Ant*. 18.179–181), and we can well imagine Paul using these occasions as an opportunity to witness. In fact, I would argue that this is what Paul is likely referring to in Phil. 1:13. The situation described in Philippians, in which Paul is in chains but has ongoing dealings with his co-workers (2:19–20) and various Roman Christians (4:21), not to mention lesser members of Caesar's household, presumably slaves (4:22), corresponds well with the description in Acts 28. Since Paul's social standing cannot entirely explain the liberty he has while in Rome, it is necessary to conclude that the Roman officials deemed the case against him a very weak one. After all, the procurator of Judea had said that Paul could have been released had he not appealed to Caesar, for he had concluded that Paul was not guilty of any significant crime. We may also note Acts 28:19, where Paul brings Jews together to reassure them that he will not be engaging in a countersuit. There may well have been some fear of such action now that Paul the Roman citizen was in Rome and Jews were in a tenuous position there, having been expelled from the city within recent memory (A.D. 49) during the reign of Claudius. Notice that the Jewish leaders there freely admit that they had received no letters about Paul from Judea (Acts 28:21).

Furthermore, Acts 28:30 says that Paul lived in his rented dwelling for two years unscathed. That Luke mentions a specific period means that he knows that something happened after that—the custody did not continue indefinitely. The evidence as Luke presents it in Acts 21–28, evidence that shows Roman officials concluding at every turn that Paul was not guilty of any significant crime, and that he could have been released had he not appealed to the emperor, suggests that Luke knew of a favorable outcome after the house arrest. What else could Theophilus conclude? The alternative is to conclude that Luke and his audience knew that Paul met an untimely demise in A.D. 62—in spite of all the hints along the way that show no basis for this—and yet Luke did not feel compelled to explain this travesty of justice at the end of his account. This is very hard to believe in view of how hard Luke has worked to lay the foundation for the reader to think of Paul as acquittable and in good shape with Roman authorities. It is also hard to believe since Luke is arguing for the legitimization of the early Christian movement, and along the way defending Paul against any later suspicions about him. We also must remember how adamant the Romans were about accusers appearing at a trial to make their case. If Sanhedrin representatives did not follow Paul to Rome, then the case surely would have had to have been concluded with acquittal or dismissal (see Ulpian, *Digest* 38.14.8).

What we know of Nero at this time also supports the likelihood of the dismissal of Paul's case. First, Nero during his early years closely followed the advice of Seneca, who taught him that clemency was a great virtue, and of Afranius Burrus, the head of his praetorian guard, who was in charge of all provincial prisoners brought to Rome on appeal to the emperor for justice. It is quite possible that the centurion Julius had handed Paul's case over to Burrus personally; but even if not, he surely would have known the case well, since his soldiers would have been guarding Paul for two years.

Second, we know that Nero despised signing warrants of execution (Suetonius, *Nero* 16.2–17). It went against his training from Seneca. Nor did he show any real interest in dealing with the backlog of cases in the courts. Until the dark days later in A.D. 62 when he lost both Burrus and Seneca, Nero was not one to personally spend time on trials and appeals. All of this also suggests that Paul was released in A.D. 62 for lack of evidence or any real case against him.

This is in fact what Clement of Rome says was the case, and he was in a perfect position to know (*1 Clem.* 5:5–7). Paul, he says, did reach the furthermost parts of the West (i.e., Spain). Indeed, Paul may have been exiled there. Paul, of course, had expressed his intention to go to

Illustration 12.3 The Emperor Nero's image on a silver denarius.

Spain (Rom. 15:24). Finally, Eusebius tells us directly, based on ancient testimony, that Paul was martyred in Rome on his second visit to the city, having been released the first time. He says specifically, "Paul's martyrdom was not accomplished during the sojourn in Rome which Luke describes" (*Hist. eccl.* 2.22.1–7). If we take all this together, it seems much more probable than not that Paul did not die in Rome in A.D. 62, but rather, after the fire and after Nero gave up the virtue of clemency.

The book of Acts ends on a familiar note, with Paul meeting with Jews and others and trying to convince them about Christ (28:17–31). It is rather surprising that nothing is said about Paul's relating to or spending time with Gentile Christians in Rome, but much about his trying to reach Jews there. Could this have been an attempt to redress the imbalance in the Roman Christian community by injecting new Jewish converts? We know that there was a substantial Jewish community in Rome,[11] and that they had a powerful sympathizer in the person of Nero's wife, Poppaea Sabina. Nero was under her influence until at least A.D. 64–65, when he killed her by kicking her when she was pregnant. Yet on the whole, the inscriptional evidence suggests that Roman Jews were not a wealthy group of people, and for them to take on Paul would have meant the hiring of an expensive advocate skilled in rhetoric. Considering their marginalized position and general social and economic status, it seems unlikely that the Roman Jewish community would have taken on Paul in court without support and aid from Jerusalem, which Acts does not show was ever forthcoming. Everyone knew that the Roman justice system was heavily weighted in favor of Roman citizens.

Paul tells the Jews of Rome that he has done nothing against his own people or their ancestral customs; rather, he is on trial because of the resurrection, the hope of Israel. It is interesting that Acts 28:21–22 says that

11. The inscriptional evidence reveals at least four or five synagogues in Rome by A.D. 60. Philo speaks of a great Jewish sector of Rome beyond the Tiber (*Embassy* 155–157), though he is describing what was the case in the 30s. The estimates are of fifty thousand Jews in Rome in the early first century, but only twenty thousand during Nero's reign, presumably because of the expulsions in the late 40s.

Illustration 12.4 The interior of the Roman Colosseum today (built *after* the time of Nero).

The exterior of the Roman Colosseum today.

although the Jewish leaders in Rome had received no bad reports about Paul, they had heard nothing good about the sect of the Nazarenes, and so they consulted with Paul about the latter. As had been the pattern before, some Jews were convinced by Paul's arguments and became believers, but most were not, and his arguments set off a debate among the Jews he was evangelizing. The picture that Luke wishes to leave us with is of the unstoppable Word of God being shared freely and unhindered even in the capital of the pagan empire. He knows that the story continues, and since he is not writing a biography of Paul, he feels no compulsion to end this volume with a narration of Paul's death.

How may we evaluate Luke's historical purposes and the way he presents the Christian mission? Acts is an apologetic work, but not written for outsiders. Rather, it is intended to legitimate the faith of insiders and give them a strong sense of who they are and what God was doing in their midst. Luke, to be sure, respects Roman law and citizenship and customs, but he knows very well that Christianity is in various respects subversive. He knows that there is truth to the claim that Christians seek to turn the world upside down (17:6). It was the intent of Christianity to convert the world to the belief in the one true God, which meant revising or rejecting previous religious commitments, including those to the emperor. Luke does not try to hide this fact, because he is writing to insiders (even if they are neophytes in the faith) rather than outsiders. He cannot chronicle the triumph of the Word without chronicling the tragedy of its rejection by various Jews and Gentiles, that is, the tragedy of their failure to give up previous religious commitments. As a historian, he is more concerned with the success of movements than of individuals, in particular the Christian movement, and he believes that the Holy Spirit, not even Peter or Paul, deserves the lion's share of credit for that success. His is a chronicling of a God-directed movement. As such, it is a very different sort of history writing than modern historiography. It is more like Herodotus than like Churchill. We can learn a bit more about Paul and Christianity in Rome by considering the letters he likely wrote from there, to which we now turn.

The Captivity Epistles

Though the letters to Philippi, Ephesus, Colossae, and to Philemon have often been called "prison epistles," this likely is a misnomer. These epistles certainly do refer to Paul being in chains (cf. Eph. 6:20; Phil. 1:7, 14; Col. 4:18), and Philemon does speak of Paul being a prisoner of some sort, indeed, a prisoner of Christ (Philem. 1, 10, 13, 23), but none of this requires the conclusion that Paul was in a jail or a prison. To the contrary, reference to all the people Paul is in contact with and to the ready coming and going of his co-workers, not to mention the ongoing progress of his ministry, favors a situation where Paul is under house arrest. In other words, these letters could have been written either in the period A.D. 58–60, while under house arrest in Caesarea, or in the period A.D. 60–62. In my view, the latter is more probable, not least because of the atmosphere of danger conveyed by these letters: had Paul written them from Caesarea, he knew he could always appeal to the emperor, but in Rome he knew that the outcome of the judicial process would be final. We should note as well that at several points in these letters Paul suggests that he expects to be released (cf. Phil. 1:19, 25; Philem. 22).

Also, of course, debate continues about the authenticity of two of these letters, Colossians and Ephesians. Probably still a majority of scholars think that Colossians is by Paul, but Ephesians is more often than not attributed to a later Paulinist. This latter conclusion may be correct, but several things suggest otherwise: First, the style of Ephe-

sians has often been used as a strong argument for non-Pauline authorship, but in fact the Asiatic Greek of this letter reflects adaptation to the
audience, and more particularly, an adaptation of style to suit an epideictic form of rhetoric, a style Paul seldom uses (but see 1 Corinthians
13). Second, this letter is likely a homily with an epistolary framework,
and is a document meant to circulate through various churches, probably including Ephesus and the churches in the Lycus Valley. It is not
an ad hoc document like Paul's other genuine letters. These factors
must be taken into consideration. Third, the generic character of this
document extends even to the degree of direct copying from Colossians
almost verbatim toward the end (cf. Col. 4:7–9; Eph. 6:21–22), which
supports the notion that these two documents were produced together,
or at least that Ephesians was produced on the basis of Colossians, perhaps turning a homily into a letter by this addition. Fourth, even most
of the scholars who think that Ephesians is by a Paulinist rather than
by Paul do not think that the letter is un-Pauline (i.e., expressing ideas
antithetical to Paul's own thought). But if there is nothing un-Pauline
about the document, and if we take into account the reasons for the generic character and difference in style, then there is no good reason
why the letter could not be from Paul himself. I thus conclude that
these documents were dictated by Paul, and in the following order: Colossians was written first, perhaps in A.D. 61, and was sent out with
Philemon, and perhaps also with Ephesians, which may well have been
the Laodicean document referred to in Col. 4:16. The reference "in
Ephesus" at Eph. 1:1 is textually suspect, as the phrase is omitted in
some important early manuscripts. Whether one agrees with my ordering of those three letters or not, it seems clear that Philippians was the
last of the four to be written, for it conveys the strong sense that the
outcome of the long judicial process is not far off, and that Paul has
been under house arrest for such a period of time that he has converted
some of his guards! We may place its composition in A.D. 62.

Colossians and Ephesians share in common a household code (cf.
Col. 3:18–4:1; Eph. 5:21–6:9), though the Ephesians version of the code
proves to be much expanded and more Christianized. In both codes,
however, Paul is indeed humanizing the usual household rules as they
applied to Christians. We need to consider not merely what Paul says
in these codes, but their trajectory. By this I mean that these codes are
moving against the flow of the dominant patriarchal culture in their attempt to require as much of the father/husband/master as of the subordinate members of the household in terms of love and care. Paul is not
simply baptizing existing patriarchal values and calling them good;
rather, he is revising them within the context of the Christian commu-

nity. This becomes especially clear in the Ephesians code, where not only is the husband required to love his wife as Christ loved the church (that is, in a self-sacrificial manner that negates any sort of authoritarian posturing), but the whole discussion falls under the heading of the mutual submission of all Christians, male and female, to one another.[12]

The discussion of slavery in Colossians and Ephesians needs to be compared to what Paul says in Philemon. In this latter letter, Paul argues that slaves who are Christians are in fact brothers and sisters in Christ and should be treated as such. They are no longer to be viewed or treated as living property. And Paul asks Philemon to manumit Onesimus and send him back to work with Paul. Once again, Paul is dealing with an existing cultural institution, in this case slavery, and is pushing for more humane treatment of those who are enslaved (Colossians and Ephesians), and, where opportunity arises, for manumission (Philemon). Paul's theology of all being one in Christ and of there being no slave or master in Christ was a revolutionary teaching, which, unfortunately, was never fully implemented either in the first century or for many centuries thereafter.

Colossians and Ephesians are letters meant to encourage the audience to focus on the christological core of their faith by means of drawing on both hymn and creedal fragments that may already have been familiar to the audience, and the same can be said of Philippians 2. It is also true that these three documents focus a good deal on the church as Christ's body and on the need to be joined to the head, as well as to be united with each other.

Colossians and Ephesians also share a focus on knowledge. In Ephesians this focus is not brought to bear on some particular problem, but rather, serves the larger design of making clear the nature and unity of the church and the basis of that unity. Colossians is something of a problem-solving letter, but Philippians is more of a progress-oriented letter. There is the difficulty of the two women leaders needing to be reconciled, and a potential danger referred to as "the dogs," but on the whole, the tone of Philippians indicates a church functioning well, bringing Paul great joy.

Perhaps only the church in Philippi among the churches addressed in these letters is one founded by Paul. It seems that the churches in the Lycus Valley in Asia were founded by Pauline co-workers (e.g., perhaps Epaphras [Col. 4:12–13]), which may explain something of why Colos-

12. So much is this the case that the verb "submit" in Eph. 5:21 must be carried over into v. 22, which is elliptical. Whatever submit means in the inclusive statement in v. 21 is also what it means in v. 22. Indeed, the husband's loving his wife in a self-sacrificial manner is said to be his manner of submitting to his wife.

sians sounds rather different than 1 Corinthians. But none of these letters was written to churches in areas that neither Paul nor his co-workers had been. Thus, these must be seen as pastoral letters, and so in some measure different than the letter to the Romans. Also, not surprisingly, more of the shadow of death hovers over some of these letters, particularly Philippians. Notice, too, that there is absolutely no mention of the collection in these letters—something Paul was so obsessed with in the earlier letters.[13] Paul seems to be focusing on other things, and no doubt one of them was the church of Jews and Gentiles in Rome.

The Character of the Roman Church

In order to speak about the church in Rome in the early 60s, we must briefly back up and consider first what may have been the case with Christianity in Rome before Paul had anything to do with it, and then what Romans 16 may reveal to us in the middle to late 50s.[14]

P. Lampe in his landmark study makes a compelling case for the conclusion that Christianity in Rome began as an intra-Jewish phenomenon.[15] J. C. Walters sums up things well:

> It is most probable that Christianity made its way to Rome spontaneously as the personal baggage of Jews, proselytes, and sympathizers, who brought faith in Jesus as Messiah with them from the East [see Acts 2:10]. They came to Rome for commercial reasons, as immigrants, or against their will as slaves. It is not surprising therefore that early Christians were concentrated within the same regions as non-Christian Jews, both residing primarily in areas where foreign peoples were concentrated [e.g., in Trastevere and along the Appian way, but also in Marsfield and the Aventine.][16] Jews—and Gentile sympathizers and proselytes—who believed Jesus was Messiah not only shared a religious outlook with non-Christian Jews, but also a common socialization. They were part of the Jewish ethos and of the foreign population of ancient Rome. They assembled in synagogues with other Jews and may not have

13. There are other telltale signs of the lateness of these letters—for example, the household codes, and the reference to church officers such as bishops and deacons in Phil. 1:1. These are the kind of things or persons we would expect Paul to mention or discuss when he would no longer be personally present as the apostolic voice, when both moral structure and local leadership would have to be counted on instead of the apostolic presence and word. These letters push us in the direction of the Pastoral Epistles.

14. I am assuming with the majority of scholars that Romans 16 was in fact sent to Rome, and not elsewhere.

15. P. Lampe, *Die stadtrömischen Christen in den ersten beiden Jahrhunderten: Untersuchungen zur Sozialgeschichte*, WUNT 2.18, 2nd ed. (Tubingen: Mohr-Siebeck, 1989).

16. See ibid., 10–35.

gathered outside Jewish contexts in the earliest period. However, the dissonance created by the activities and/or words of Christians provoked tension, particularly over issues related to the observance of the Law and the inclusion of Gentiles. Eventually these tensions escalated into disturbances which gained the attention of the Romans, resulting in the Claudian edict of 49 C.E.[17]

We must assume that the edict of Claudius given in A.D. 49 had an impact on the Roman church, and perhaps particularly on its older Jewish leadership. In Rom. 16:3–5, Paul sends greetings to Priscilla and Aquila, who are back in Rome (cf. Acts 18) and have a church in their house. But notice that Paul then goes on to greet a number of people, and apparently a goodly number of house churches. This strongly suggests a lack of central leadership or a lack of a "great church" that all attended in addition to their household groups. This in turn may explain why Paul, even though he is not their pastor, must seek to reconcile the predominant Gentile Christians with the Jewish ones in texts like Romans 9–11 and Romans 14, where he speaks of strong and weak. The Jewish Christians are in the minority, and tension exists between them and the majority.[18] The summary by W. Lane is helpful: "Paul wrote to prepare his own visit to Rome, but also to seek reconciliation and unity in a fragmented church. The exegetical key to this approach is to be found in Romans 15:1–13: Roman Christians are to accept one another, just as they have been accepted by Christ. Paul addressed a troubled community struggling with an alienated constituency of Jews and Gentiles."[19]

Some of the preceding material helps us to understand Acts 28 a bit better. The interaction between Paul and the Jewish community is not a surprise if the Christian community had always shared the same social location as the Jews and in fact had been a part of the Jewish *politeuma* for many years. Bear in mind that the Jewish community in Rome saw itself in a tenuous position. The edict of Claudius might not be the last act of expulsion they would face. The evidence suggests that Jews worked hard not to adopt the values and habits of the larger culture, but this was not so much the case with the Christian community,

17. J. C. Walters, "Romans, Jews, and Christians: The Impact of the Romans on Jewish/Christian Relations in First-Century Rome," in *Judaism and Christianity in First-Century Rome*, ed. K. Donfried and P. Richardson (Grand Rapids: Eerdmans, 1998), 176–77.
18. Notice that in the list of the people Paul greets in Romans 16, Jewish names are in the minority.
19. W. Lane, "Social Perspectives on Roman Christianity during the Formative Years from Nero to Nerva: Romans, Hebrews, 1 Clement," in Donfried and Richardson, eds., *Judaism and Christianity*, 198.

Illustration 12.5 The Erastus inscription in Corinth saying that he paved the space before the theater to procure the office of aedile. He is the only Christian (Rom. 16:23) mentioned in this way in ancient inscriptions.

especially when it became a predominantly Gentile community.[20] Inculturation could threaten the very existence of the Jewish community, and if the Christian part of the community was moving in that direction, it could be dangerous, all the more so after A.D. 59, when Nero's "good" years were behind him.

At the close of this period, in A.D. 62, two disastrous events affected Christians. The first was a major earthquake in the vicinity of Colossae, which apparently leveled much of the city. The ancients saw such events as acts of God, and Jews and Christians often saw them as eschatological acts of God or the messianic woes. It is not certain whether the Christian communities in Colossae or Hierapolis or Laodicea were severely affected by the earthquake, but likely they were, for they met in houses, the structures most vulnerable to earthquakes.

The second event was in a sense even more earth-shattering as far as its effect on the leadership structure of the earliest church. Porcius Festus died in office, thus preventing a natural transition where one prefect comes before the previous one leaves, or at least only a short interval occurs in between prefects. Before Albinus arrived to replace Festus,

20. See G. F. Snyder, "Interaction of Jews with Non-Jews in Rome," in Donfried and Richardson, eds., *Judaism and Christianity*, 69–90.

the high priest Ananias, according to Josephus, "thought that he had a favorable opportunity because Festus was dead and Albinus was still on his way. And so he convened the judges of the Sanhedrin and brought before them a man named James, the brother of Jesus, who was called the Christ, and certain others. He accused them of having transgressed the law and delivered them up to be stoned" (*Ant.* 20.200). The stoning suggests that James was accused of blasphemy against the law. Such a charge is perhaps conceivable if James was as we have seen him to be—a mediating figure between Paul and the hard-line Pharisaic Jewish Christians. But on the other hand, James was known as "the Just" and as a Torah-true Jew, and even Josephus says that he was highly regarded in the city. So much was this the case that "those of the inhabitants of the city who were considered the most fair-minded and who were strict in their observance of the Law were offended at this" (*Ant.* 20.201). Thus, protest was made not only to Agrippa but also, when he arrived, to Albinus, with the result that Ananias was deposed, ostensibly for illegally convening the Sanhedrin.

Though James was replaced by another close relative of Jesus, a cousin named Symeon, it is fair to say that A.D. 62 marked the end of an era. The Jerusalem church would continue to live in an embattled atmosphere until something even worse happened—the breakout of the Jewish war in A.D. 66. It would no longer have a leader in close relationship with the other major leaders of the church elsewhere in the empire, including Paul. At about the same time that James was killed, it is probable that Paul was released from house arrest, as no substantive charges had ever been laid or proved against him. Yet, as we will see in the next chapter, this was only a slight reprieve, for in the next four to six years both Paul and Peter would lose their lives in Rome, before Nero took his own life in A.D. 68. To this darkest chapter in Christian history we now turn.

Chapter 13

Through the
Refiner's Fire

A.D. 63–68

The Decline and Fall of the Julio-Claudian Dynasty

For all the accomplishments of the Julio-Claudian dynasty during the first century A.D., the last five years of the final Julio-Claudian emperor were nothing to be proud of. Indeed, a strong case can be made that the real decline of Nero into viciousness and extreme vice began in A.D. 59, as the first five years were coming to a close. That was the year that Nero had his mother, Agrippina, killed, and Tacitus says that after this, Nero "plunged into all the excesses which a certain regard for his mother had had up to now retarded but not entirely controlled" (*Annals* 14.13). In fact, all three major Roman historians of this period, Dio Cassius, Suetonius, and Tacitus, held that Nero had always been inclined to vice, and it was a matter of his having been restrained by his counselors Burrus and Seneca, and by his mother. When they were re-moved from the scene, Nero indulged all his excesses and lost all sense of right and wrong (Dio Cassius, *Roman History* 61.4–5). Yet Tacitus stresses, I think rightly, that it was in A.D. 62 that the Nero whom Christians were later to see as a paradigm for the Antichrist really began his reign of terror. It was then that he began to break his earlier pledges and started to perpetrate his crimes outside his own immediate family. Certainly, behavior earlier in Nero's reign hinted that things could move in this direction, but it was not so blatant or persistent a form of behavior as it became in A.D. 62. The real Nero more clearly emerged in A.D. 62 when Burrus died and the evil Tigellinus, not a soldier or politician but a raiser of race horses, was appointed prefect of the praetorian guard. The alleged remark of the praetorian tribune Subrius Flavus to Nero in A.D. 65, when it was discovered that he had betrayed his oath of loyalty to the emperor, is brief but speaks volumes about Nero's latter years: "I began to hate you after you murdered your mother and your wife, and became a charioteer, and an actor and an arsonist" (Tacitus, *Annals* 15.67). Nero was not all that interested in politics unless it helped him to achieve his other aims. He fancied himself an artist and a musician and an actor, and he was willing to go to some lengths to promote his "artistic" agendas. For example, sometime in A.D. 61, Nero sent his freedman Acratus to plunder the great art treasures of Asia for Nero's first palace. The proconsul of Asia, Barea Soranus, objected, and conflict between the proconsul and the emperor ensued.

Nero fancied himself a philhellene, which is to say that he believed in the superiority of Greek culture. This is why he built and dedicated in A.D. 61 a Greek-style gymnasium in Rome with the purpose of establishing Greek athletics in Roman upper-class life. It also explains his going to the Isthmian games in Corinth to recite his poetry and sing. This "aesthetic" agenda of Nero, along with his professed desire to rebuild Rome, or at least a large part of it, in a more artistically pleasing style, is what was to lead to the speculation that Nero had set fire to the city in A.D. 64.

The fire, of course, changed everything, including the toleration of Nero's excesses. Indeed, the fire was apparently the straw that broke the camel's back and led to the conspiracy against Nero in A.D. 65. We need to remember that after the fire, Nero himself was on the hot seat, and his blaming of Christians for the fire was not an example of politics as usual with Nero, but rather, his using politics when expedient and useful to deflect criticism against his reign onto others. Nero had no great love for holding trials or sitting in the senate unless it gave him something he wanted or needed.

Illustration 13.1   The center of Rome. Christians were executed by Nero in the Circus Maximus not the Colosseum.

With the demise of Burrus and Seneca, Nero apparently increasingly took advice from Poppaea, his wife of Semitic sympathies if not Semitic origins, and from Tigellinus. We can demonstrate that Poppaea was influential in the period after A.D. 63, because Josephus tells of his own mission in A.D. 63–64 to Nero to secure the release of the Jewish priests from custody in Rome, and to overturn a decision of the procurator of Judea in favor of Herod Agrippa II. Josephus says that he owed these concessions to the influence of Poppaea, and he says that she was *theosebēs*, which might mean that she was a God-fearer, but at least that she respected the Jewish religion (*Ant.* 20.195). Yet if a friend of the Jews, she did not always exercise good judgment on their behalf, because she is said to have secured the post of procurator of Judea for the husband of one of her friends, Gessius Florus, the man whose behavior turned Jewish unrest into revolt in A.D. 66.

It is important to realize that Nero, while certainly immoral, was not demented. Indeed, in many ways he was quite shrewd, and recognized which side his own bread was buttered on. Consider, for a moment, the very matter of bread. Augustus, late in his reign, took on the responsibility for the organization of the corn/grain supply for Rome. During the empire, this became a major responsibility for the emperor. Naturally, the actual day-to-day details were delegated to another, in this case, the equestrian prefect. Nero knew that keeping the natives from getting restless in the capital was crucial to a long, stable reign, and so when in A.D. 62 a storm had destroyed two hundred corn ships in the harbor in Ostia, and a fire had destroyed another hundred vessels bringing corn up the Tiber, Nero cleverly avoided a general panic by having the spoiled corn dumped in the Tiber as a signal that more could be obtained. He appears also to have managed to keep the price of grain down by giving subsidies to corn dealers from his own funds. In the year of the great fire, with the city in chaos, Nero had grain supplies brought in from Ostia and elsewhere and he lowered the price of corn. Also remember that during the empire, a free distribution of grain was made every month to nearly 200,000 male citizens. Interestingly, Paul would have been eligible for his share once he took up residence in Rome.

Another sign of the shrewdness of Nero is that he supplied not only public assistance, but also public diversions in the form of entertainment. Miriam Griffin in fact calls Nero the greatest showman of them all.[1] He set up gladiatorial games, chariot races, elaborately staged plays, and the *Ludi Maximi* (which included tossing tokens to the crowd redeemable for jewels, slaves, houses, horses, and other things), and conducted special games called the Juvenalia and the Neronia. Nero no doubt would have fancied himself the P. T. Barnum of his day, the world's greatest showman. For example, at the coronation of Tiridates as king of Armenia, the king-to-be, after bowing down before Nero, was escorted into Pompey's theater, especially gilded for the occasion, where Nero gave a public performance on the lyre, after which he donned full charioteer regalia and drove a chariot around the arena while the crowds watched (Suetonius, *Nero* 13).

Nero spared no expense on spectacle. For one of his gladiatorial games, Nero sent a Roman knight to the Baltic Sea to bring back amber, which then was used to trim the weapons, the nets, and even the coffins (Pliny, *Natural History* 37.45). These spectacles served at least two purposes. First, they distracted the people from whatever difficulties were extant at the time. Second, the games allowed "the populace at large to see their Emperor and to make their feelings known to him, for they had few other opportunities for contact with their sovereign."[2]

Nero could appear magnanimous at such occasions, not only sparing the lives of losing gladiators who were popular, but also responding to a spontaneous outcry of some sort. For example, he instituted re-

---

1. M. Griffin, *Nero: The End of a Dynasty* (New Haven: Yale University Press, 1985), 109.
    2. Ibid., 110.

Illustration 13.2 A bust of Nero.

forms in response to an outcry at the games protesting the greedy, self-serving practices of tax collectors (Tacitus, *History* 1.72–73). Nero loved applause and the admiration of the crowds. But Nero also loved anonymity, sometimes visiting the theater in disguise, or wandering around the streets, taverns, and brothels incognito, indulging in fights and thievery. This is important for our purposes because after the fire in A.D. 64, Nero's behavior was virtually unrestrained, and even his earlier public displays of clemency were abandoned when it came to Christians.

Nero had always been involved in extravagant building and engineering projects (including trying to finish the canal through the Isthmus at Corinth), and without a doubt, the great fire of A.D. 64 presented Nero with new chances to pursue his passion in these matters. Rome was always prone to fire because the *insulae* normally were made almost entirely of timber and because fire-fighting equipment was scant, but the fire that began on July 19, A.D. 64, was no ordinary blaze. This conflagration lasted for six days, and then, after a brief hiatus, for another three days, leveling three of the fourteen regions of Rome, and leaving only four completely untouched (see Tacitus, *Annals* 15.38–39). The fire began near the Circus Maximus and spread north along the Palatine through the Colosseum Valley, destroying shops, homes, and temples in the very heart of the city.

The main locale of the fire appeared suspicious to many, since this was precisely the area Nero would want to reconstruct. While Nero perhaps could have ignored most criticism about the reconstruction, when he took the opportunity to build himself a new palace in the heart of town, the criticism became severe and unyielding. In fact, both Tacitus and Suetonius report Nero's desire to have the glory of founding a new city to be named after himself—Neropolis (Tacitus, *Annals* 15.40–42; Suetonius, *Nero* 55). Nero also had erected an enormous bronze statue of himself, 120 feet in height, which was to be placed on the Sacra Via in front of the Golden House, where all could see it.

The criticisms of Nero's megalomania could not be deflected by some of the wisdom he exhibited in the rebuilding. For example, Nero insisted on new building codes to prevent such fires in the future. The scale of the rebuilding was mammoth and was not completed by the time of Nero's death in A.D. 68. Imperial arson became a pervading and persistent suspicion, not least because the second fire began on Tigellinus's own estates. Both Suetonius and Dio Cassius later would conclude that the fire was an act of wanton destruction by Nero.

The unrelenting criticism and suspicion drove Nero to find a scapegoat—Christians. In fact Christians were accused en masse for the fire, and in order for their punishment to fit their crime, Nero used them as living torches to light his nighttime circus games (Tacitus, *Annals* 15.44–45). We must be clear, however, that Hollywood spectacles that show Christians being killed in the Colosseum are guilty of retrojecting a building into Rome that did not exist in Nero's time. It was in the Circus Maximus that they lost their lives. It is important to note that these acts by Nero show that Christianity could be and was distinguished from Judaism in A.D. 64–65. It has been suggested that Poppaea was responsible for helping to make this distinction from Judaism known, thereby keeping the blame from being fastened on those with whom she sympathized—non-Christian Jews.[3]

It can hardly be estimated how devastating these acts of Nero were on the Christian community of Rome, not least because it appears that both Paul and Peter were swept away in the wake of Nero's decision to blame Christians for the fire. Clement says of these two apostles that "the greatest and most righteous pillars of the church were persecuted and contended unto death" (*1 Clem.* 5.2). Although we have no evidence that Peter and Paul were both in Rome at the same time, it appears that they both died there somewhere between A.D. 65 and 68. I will say more about this later in the chapter.

3. See ibid., 133.

The spring of A.D. 65 had seen a nasty conspiracy against Nero by members of the upper class, which left Nero in no doubt that he had serious opposition in his own city and within his own patrician fold. Nero was publicly decried for serious crimes, including the murders of his mother and his wife, the burning of Rome, and perhaps most humiliating to Nero himself, the "crime" of his acting and chariot racing. We need to understand that this conspiracy was no small-scale operation, for it included senators, praetorian tribunes, centurions, and even a prefect.

Nero began to look elsewhere for adulation. The summer of A.D. 65 brought with it the second Neronia festival, which included Nero's first public stage performance in Rome. "The senate tried to avert the disgrace of Nero's participation by offering him the crowns of singing and oratory, but Nero was determined to win a real contest. First he recited part of his epic on the Trojan War and then, as he left the theatre, he was recalled by his public who urged him to display his other talents as well. . . . One of the presiding consulars, the future Emperor Vitellius, urged Nero to return to the theatre and perform on the lyre."[4] Yet the praise was hardly genuine, much less effusive. Perhaps this is why Nero decided to take his show on the road.

In A.D. 66, Nero went to Greece and participated in both the Olympic and Isthmian games, and of course, he always won. While there, he inaugurated the cutting of the Corinthian canal himself. He returned to Rome not as a conquering hero, but dressed as and acting like a triumphant artist. Griffin is surely right to see the trip to Greece as part and parcel of Nero's withdrawal from political life and descent into a fantasy world of the arts.[5]

Needless to say, all the lavish spending on rebuilding Rome, the emperor's many games and theater productions, and his travels abroad put a severe strain on the Roman budget. Perhaps this is why late in 65 and on into 66 Nero brought charges of treason against the conspirators, and also extorted money from their families in exchange for their estates not being confiscated and other family members not being dealt with harshly. In fact, Nero was in a very litigious mood from late in 65 through 66 and beyond, purging the city of his enemies, and probably this is also when Paul was beheaded (remember that unlike Peter, Paul had a previous record of being in custody in Rome). Nero's fears were not relieved by such actions, however, since more conspiracies followed, including a plan to kill Nero as he was on his way to Greece in A.D. 66.

4. Ibid., 162.
5. Ibid., 164.

The second plot against Nero sparked paranoia, with Nero regarding the whole of the senatorial order as his enemy. Nevertheless, Nero was determined to continue his artistic tours, and his closest friends at this point were his own freedmen, not senators or politicians. They flattered him and supported his plans to travel to Greece. Yet much was brewing elsewhere in the empire while Nero was neglecting his duties.

Nero was caught by surprise at the defeat of his governor of Syria by Jewish forces on November 8, A.D. 66. There were also rumblings of major revolt in Gaul, a revolt that in fact came to pass in March of 68. But Nero stayed away from Rome from mid-66 until early 68 A.D. Both within Rome and in the provinces, things were beginning to go drastically wrong for Nero. The events of A.D. 68, when Galba, Otho, and others decided to lead legions against Nero, with Galba declaring himself the legate of the senate and the Roman people in April of 68, were really just the climax of a process that had been fermenting for some time. As Galba's star and support continued to rise, Nero saw his armies defecting. The senate even plucked up its courage and declared Nero a public enemy, which made him a marked man. Nero considered fleeing to Alexandria, but in the end he simply hid in a villa outside Rome with a few of his freedmen. On June 9, A.D. 68, with soldiers coming for him, Nero managed to commit suicide with the help of his freedman. In ignominious fashion thus ended the Julio-Claudian dynasty that had begun and built the Roman Empire. We consider now the events of the 60s that led to the Jewish revolt.

Unholy Actions in the Holy Land

Josephus is unequivocal that under Albinus things went from bad to worse in Judea, but his account of that reign in *Jewish Antiquities* suggests a bit more balanced assessment than he gives in the earlier *Jewish War* account (cf. *J.W.* 2.271–276; *Ant.* 20.204). In the credit column, Josephus lists a few things. First, the work on the temple was finally completed during Albinus's reign. Unfortunately this meant that eighteen thousand workers now faced unemployment (*Ant.* 20.219–222), but a foundational wall collapsed, and so more work on the temple was required. Second, Albinus exterminated most of the *sicarii* (20.204). In part, this was an act of desperation, for the *sicarii* were getting bolder and bolder. They took to kidnapping prominent persons (e.g., Eleazar, son of Ananias and governor of the temple) and holding them until prisoners whom they wanted were released. Third, at the end of Albinus's reign, when he knew he would be replaced, he sought to clear up pending cases (unlike Felix), executing those deserving death and releasing those with trivial charges leveled against them (*Ant.* 20.215).

But in fact this amounted to releasing some thugs, just as Albinus earlier had released some of the *sicarii* supporters, which did not improve the general social climate in Judea.

In addition, Albinus had to deal with other sorts of violent gangs. Two of Herod Agrippa's relatives (Saul and Costabar) organized their own groups who, being a pro-Roman faction, plundered ordinary Jews (*Ant.* 20.214). There was chaos in various parts of the land, including in Jerusalem. Supporters of former priests and supporters of the existing priest feuded and engaged in rock throwing contests in the Holy City (*Ant.* 20.213). The rule of law and order was rapidly breaking down, which explains some of Albinus's desperate measures.

In the debit column, Josephus tells us that Albinus took bribes from the former high priest Ananias, who paid for such bribes by extorting money from the local populace. In addition, he increased the tax burden of the people. All said, Albinus inherited a situation already out of control, and as poor as his judgments were, they were better than his successor, to whom we now turn.

Josephus blames Gessius Florus, who ruled from A.D. 64 to 66, for being the final cause that set off the Jewish war (*Ant.* 20.257). Tacitus the Roman historian also recognized that the Jews' patience with bad procurators ran out when it came to Florus (*History* 5.10.1). It appears that Florus allowed open season for the bandits throughout the land, so long as he got his share of the plunder (*J.W.* 2.278). Indeed, Josephus even goes so far as to suggest that Florus deliberately incited the Jewish war to cover up his own misdeeds (*J.W.* 2.282–283).

In A.D. 66, Florus, with the legate for Syria, Cestius, visited Jerusalem during the Passover season. Numerous angry pilgrims surrounded these officials, demanding relief from the oppression of the bandits and indeed of Florus himself. Florus scorned them, and Cestius did not take any direct action, but simply promised that Florus would moderate his behavior in the future (*J.W.* 2.280–281).

The war broke out in various places, and surprisingly, one of the first of those was in the provincial capital of Caesarea. Recall that this city had significant Jewish and Gentile populations, not only because the city had been built by Herod as a Hellenistic city, but also because it was a seaport and the place where Rome's troops and administration were housed. On a Sabbath in A.D. 66, as the Jews were assembling for worship at their synagogue, a Caesarean Gentile simulated the sacrifice of a bird on a pot right in front of the synagogue. This action implied that the Jews were lepers (see Lev. 14:1–5), which apparently was a common calumny used by Gentiles against the Jews (see *Ag. Ap.* 1.304–313). Not surprisingly, a fight between the Jews and Gentiles in the city erupted. The synagogue leaders, fearing the worst for their synagogue, left the city carrying their Torah scroll and went immediately to Sebaste, where Florus was at the time. But Florus arrested them, ostensibly for carrying off the temple scroll from its proper location (in other words, for stealing a sacred object) (*J.W.* 2.289–292). Needless to say, this pleased none of the Jews in Caesarea, and things got so heated that Florus did not dare go back there.

For a long time the tribute to Caesar had not been paid by the Judean province (*J.W.* 2.403–404). To remedy this problem, Florus took the liberty of taking seventeen talents from the temple treasury. This resulted in another confrontation. Florus called a tribunal but at the same turned his soldiers loose on the city, and they plundered the Jerusalem market. They also took captive various persons and scourged and even crucified some (*J.W.* 2.305–308).

Agrippa's sister Bernice (in the stead of Agrippa, who was in Egypt at the time) appealed to the Romans to stop their violence (*J.W.* 2.309–314), while the aristocracy and chief priests appealed to the Jewish people to cease and desist from violence. Two cohorts of soldiers were brought in from Caesarea, but to prevent them from getting to the Antonia fortress, various porticoes of the temple that connected it to the fortress were destroyed. Florus decided to back out of the city and left word with the Jewish leaders that they were now responsible for law and order there, leaving them a cohort to reinforce that order (*J.W.* 2.330–332). Florus, the Jerusalem leaders, and Bernice all filed reports with Cestius about this matter. Cestius decided not to take military action, but instead sent an official to meet Agrippa and allow him to mediate the situation. Agrippa pleaded with the Jews to rebuild the porticoes and be prepared to pay the tribute in view of the great and irresistible might of Rome (*J.W.* 2.345–401). For a time, the people acquiesced, but they soon realized that Florus was not being removed as he should have been. This led not merely to more revolts, but even for a call for the banishment of Herod from Jerusalem.

Sometime, apparently in the early summer of A.D. 66, the *sicarii* managed to capture Masada, and the small detachment of Roman soldiers there was simply massacred. This strategic site also was the location of an armory, so now the "dagger men" had supplies to continue to carry on their guerrilla warfare. The chief of this band was Menahem, who happens to have been the grandson of Judas the Galilean (*J.W.* 2.433). This first locale captured by the revolutionary Jews was also to be the last holdout against the Roman forces in A.D. 72. In other words, Masada was the bastion of the revolt throughout the next six years. But other nearby fortresses were also taken over, including

Cypros, which guarded Jericho, and Machaerus, where John the Baptist had once been housed (*J.W.* 2.484–486).

Though what I have recounted so far could be regarded as preliminary skirmishes, it could be said that the first real declaration of war transpired when Eleazar, son of Ananias and governor of the temple, brought the traditional sacrifices on behalf of the emperor to a halt, sacrifices that had been offered since the time of Augustus (*J.W.* 2.197). Josephus calls this act "the foundation of the war with the Romans" (*J.W.* 2.409–410). Yet only a part of the temple hierarchy supported this move. Generally speaking, the older priests opposed the move, as did various Pharisees, but the younger priests and the temple police supported it. The dissenting group refused to reinstitute the sacrifices and strengthened their control over not only the temple precincts but also the lower city. The appeasers sent embassies to both Florus and Agrippa for help. Florus did nothing, but Agrippa sent three thousand troops to Jerusalem (*J.W.* 2.418–421).

Agrippa's forces fought for a week but could not prevail. Aided by the *sicarii*, the belligerents took the upper city and burned a series of major buildings—the palaces of Agrippa and Bernice, the house of Ananias, and, most importantly, the public archives building where the tax and debt records were. The Antonia fortress was then captured and burned, the troops there were executed, and Herod's palace was besieged (*J.W.* 2.425–432). Suddenly, Menahem, who must have been informed of these developments early on, appeared in Jerusalem from Masada with his entourage. He acted like a king and took over the lead in the besieging of the palace. Part of the palace was destroyed and Agrippa's troops and other Jews asked to leave, and were allowed to do so. The Roman troops hid in the northwest corner of the city in three Herodian towers. With the Romans cornered, Menahem went after opposing Jews and caught and killed both Ananias and his brother Hezekiah, who happened to be the father of the young priest who started this development, Eleazar. Seeking revenge, Eleazar caught and killed Menahem, but some of his followers escaped to Masada, including Eleazar son of Jair (*J.W.* 2.433–448). The Roman troops pled for terms, which were granted, but when they laid down their arms, the entire unit was executed except the Roman commander, who escaped death by agreeing to be circumcised and become a Jew (*J.W.* 2.449–456).

When word of the complete breakdown of Roman control in Jerusalem reached the countryside, pitched battles were fought in most of the major cities pitting Jews versus Gentiles. In cities like Caesarea or Ptolemais, where there was a majority of Gentiles, the Jews felt the brunt of the brutality, but in other cities the Jews prevailed. The in-

ternecine warfare even spread into nearby Egypt in Alexandria, but the
resident legions were able to quell the fighting in that locale (*J.W.*
2.487–498).

By September 66, Cestius Gallus knew that he had to take action. He
had four legions at his command but chose to go into action with one
legion and two thousand troops drawn from the other three legions.
With additional cohorts and cavalry that he brought along, he had
about two legions. Furthermore, various kings who were allies, including Agrippa II, supplied an additional fifteen thousand troops. As he
headed south, Agrippa accompanied him (*J.W.* 2.499–502). Moving
down the coastal road, this force burned some cities and captured others (e.g., Joppa). A portion of the force was sent east into Galilee, but
found very little resistance. Indeed, they were welcomed into Sepphoris (*J.W.* 2.510–511). The two portions of the army rendezvoused in
Caesarea in mid-October and marched on Jerusalem. This was the time
of the Feast of Tabernacles, which meant that many pilgrims were in
and around Jerusalem. On the way down to Jerusalem, both Antipatris
and Lydda were taken and burned. Clearly, the Romans were waging
war. They set up camp a few miles north of Jerusalem in Gibeon (*J.W.*
2.513–516).

To the Romans' great surprise, Jews came forth from the city, their
ranks swelled by pilgrims, and went on the offensive. They were aided
by an attack from the north by Simon ben Gioras and his forces. They
cut the Romans' supply train and made off with a myriad of the Roman
baggage mules. The Jewish forces for a time had the Romans pinned
down, since they were on the heights above them. Agrippa sent two
Jews to negotiate a peaceful settlement, but the rebels were having
none of it. They murdered one emissary and wounded the other (*J.W.*
2.517–526). Cestius chose to move closer to Jerusalem, and after a few
days assaulted the most vulnerable spot around the city, the north wall
of the temple. He had just about undermined the temple wall and broken down a gate, when the opposition suddenly got much stiffer, and
Cestius ordered his troops to retreat from the city. This act must have
suggested to the rebels that the Roman commander was weak or pan-
icking. After the Roman forces spent a night on Mt. Scopus, they retreated, and the rebels came after them. The retreat was halted at
Gibeon for two days, but began again, and the pursuers came after
them with full force, leading to disorderly, even frenzied, flight. As they
moved on to Beth-Horon, the Jewish rebels attacked with full force,
and when night fell, Cestius fled to Antipatris with only the remnants
of his forces with him. Eventually, over five thousand of Cestius's re-
treating troops were killed by the pursuing Jewish forces. The Jews rel-

ished their first great victory over the Romans, plundering the corpses and collecting the booty (*J.W.* 2.527–555). When word got out that the Jewish forces had won, the pro-Roman forces abandoned Jerusalem and fled. This included various Herodians, among them Agrippa's relatives Saul and Costabar, whom Cestius sent to Nero to report on the grave state of affairs in Judea, making Florus the scapegoat for what happened (*J.W.* 2.556–558).

The Jewish rebels knew that the Romans would be back. They also knew that the Romans were smart enough not to resume the fighting out of the normal season for warfare, which is to say, not before spring of A.D. 67 (cf. 1 Chron. 20:1). This gave them time to shore up the defenses of Jerusalem and prepare for a proper war. It also gave them time to set up a provisional government, and notice that the government they set up involved commanders in Judea and Galilee but not in Samaria. Interestingly, Samaria was not envisioned as part of the new Holy Land. As a clear sign of their independence, the Jewish authorities already began to mint coins in the spring of 67, including silver coins. "The use of silver coinage in addition to bronze was significant. Roman provinces were not allowed to mint in silver; by using this metal, the Jewish state was giving embodiment to a claim of independence."[6]

The formerly moderate and pro-Roman groups had to cast their lot with the rebels, and it is interesting that the rebels were not in fact chosen as the new leaders in Jerusalem or as generals of the new districts in Israel. Zealots such as Simon ben Gioras operated outside of these arrangements and plundered cities in northeastern Judea. This bears witness to a very important point: the Jews were not united in their opposition to Rome, and in fact were jockeying for position amongst themselves. There was "no national unity . . . and . . . interfactional conflict and personal ambitions were more the rule than the exception, a situation that would continue throughout the war."[7] Ultimately, this was perhaps the main factor that led to the failure of the Jewish war effort.

Note that Ananias, the son of Ananias the high priest, and Joseph ben Gorion were chosen to control Jerusalem, not Eliezar the Zealot leader. The radical leaders were marginalized not only in this selection process but also in the selection of the commanders of the districts, which were made by the leading men in Jerusalem (*Life* 28–29). The one commander whose name is of importance to us is Josephus himself, who later was the historian of these events. He was sent to main-

6. J. Hays and S. Mandell, *The Jewish People in Classical Antiquity: From Alexander to Bar Kochba* (Louisville: Westminster John Knox, 1998), 190.
7. Ibid.

tain order and prepare for battle in Galilee, apparently lower Galilee and Gamala in the Transjordan (*J.W.* 2.566–568). But the Galilee that Josephus had to deal with was far from united in regard to the war. After vacillation, Sepphoris opposed the insurrection. Tiberias belonged to Agrippa and was divided on the matter. Basically, upper-class persons and members of the governing class were opposed to the war. Then, too, Josephus had to deal with John of Gischala, a man who had been radicalized when his own town was burned by forces from other cities. He raised a group of men and retook his city, and thereafter he commanded a band of about four hundred extremists (*Life* 43–45). John opposed Josephus's leadership in Galilee. Although the two managed a brief period of cooperation, they soon fell out again and became such vicious enemies that John tried to have Josephus killed. He also circulated rumors that Josephus was in league with the Romans and would deliver Galilee to them. John even managed to have Josephus investigated by a delegation from Jerusalem (cf. *J.W.* 2.614–631; *Life* 122–125).

Once word got to Nero of Cestius's defeat, he determined to relieve him of his post. Nero chose Vespasian, a career military man with a proven war record (Tacitus, *History* 5.10). Vespasian immediately dispatched his eldest son Titus to Alexandria to bring the legion there up to Judea (*J.W.* 3.1–8). Vespasian was in Antioch by the spring of 67, and Agrippa met him there. Vespasian had at his disposal two full legions ready to do battle, in addition to which he got the same auxiliary support that Cestius had had, and also forces donated by Malchus II, the Nabatean king (from about A.D. 40 to 70). Josephus says that all in all, Vespasian had about sixty thousand soldiers at his disposal (*J.W.* 3.64–69).

Both sides made a few initial failed attempts to take cities. Josephus failed to take Sepphoris, and the Romans failed on the first attempt to take Jotapata (*J.W.* 3.110–114). Basically, Vespasian was biding his time until Titus and his legion arrived, which happened sometime in late May or early June 67. At this juncture Vespasian invaded Galilee with a purpose, and many of the Jews fled in advance of his coming. Josephus took refuge in Tiberias, and then moved on to Jotapata. The Romans surrounded the town, and the siege lasted several weeks. When it finally fell, the Romans executed the men in the city, but Josephus escaped and hid in a cave (having reneged on a pact to commit suicide if the Romans took the town). Vespasian's forces found him, and the general was going to send him to Nero for trial. But at this point Josephus, playing the role of a Jewish prophet, predicted that not only Vespasian, but also his son, would become emperor. As a result,

Illustration 13.3 Copper coin with Vespasian's image.

Josephus was retained as an aide-de-camp with Vespasian's forces. This is Josephus's version of what happened (*J.W.* 3.392–408), but apparently, it was believable to Roman historians as well, who repeat the tale in much the same form (cf. Suetonius, *Vespasian* 5–6; Dio Cassius *Roman History* 66.1.1).

Once Jotapata fell, Vespasian set up operations on both sides of Galilee, making Scythopolis in the east and Caesarea in the west his military bases, a wise choice, since they were mostly non-Jewish cities anyway (*J.W.* 1.409–413). Vespasian then set out to recapture Tiberias and Taricheae, cities belonging to Agrippa II. Part of this job proved to be easy, for Tiberias immediately surrendered when Vespasian arrived with his army. Taricheae, however, was another story altogether, for it had become a city of refuge for rebels fleeing as Vespasian's forces advanced. The city held out against the Romans, but Titus was able to breach the city's defenses from the side that had no wall. Many of the rebels attempted to flee across the sea of Galilee, but most were captured. Vespasian sent six thousand of the captives as slaves to Corinth to work on Nero's canal (*J.W.* 3.462–542).

After Taricheae, most cities in Galilee had no fight left in them, but the city of Gamala resisted. A month-long siege of the elevated city was required. Heavy fighting was involved even after the city wall was breached (*J.W.* 4.20–83). The only other significant struggle in Galilee took place at Gischala, which eventually surrendered, with John of Gischala fleeing by night to join the resistance in Jerusalem (*J.W.* 4.84–111). Galilee now had been "pacified" by November and winter was coming on, so Vespasian set up winter camp in Caesarea. The winter, however, did not mean inactivity, for several Galilean towns were garrisoned and some were rebuilt.

The winter season was indeed a winter of discontent for the Jewish forces, who spent their time wrangling with one another and even killing each other off. John of Gischala's arrival with an army in Jerusalem had strengthened the Zealot forces, and the more moderate forces found themselves at a disadvantage. There was a spate of killings eliminating moderates, including some of Agrippa II's own relatives (J.W. 4.138–150). John pitted himself against the leader of the moderate forces, Ananias the high priest, and John managed to convince the Zealots to call in the Idumeans to further strengthen their control of things (J.W. 4.208–232). This led to the decimating of the temple police forces and the murder of Ananias, along with various aristocratic families. The Idumeans finally got disgusted with all this internecine bloodletting and left. John, by default, became the real ruler of Jerusalem.

Though Vespasian could have taken advantage of the Jewish divisions, he chose to wait until the spring of A.D. 68 to resume the war effort. In late March, he took Gadara in Perea, and indeed, all Perea readily submitted to his control, except for the fortress at Machaerus (J.W. 4.410–439). Vespasian's strategy was to eliminate resistance all around Judea and then "pacify" the heart of Judea and Jerusalem last, the center of the resistance. Thus, Vespasian took various Idumean towns and western Judean towns, and he arrived in Jericho in June. Vespasian had Jerusalem surrounded, and he set up a ring of camps at fifteen to twenty miles outside the Holy City in all directions, including in Jericho, Emmaus, and Adida. The rebel strength was now confined to Jerusalem and the fortresses in the east—Machaerus, Masada, and the Herodium (J.W. 4.486–490, 550–555).

An interlude in the war occurred when Vespasian waited to see what would happen in Rome. He learned of Nero's demise on June 9, A.D. 68, when he was in Caesarea finalizing his plans to take Jerusalem (J.W. 4.491–496). The siege of Jerusalem was put on hold because Titus and Agrippa had been sent to Rome to salute the new emperor, Galba. But before these emissaries could reach Rome, Galba was assassinated in January of 69. Titus returned to Caesarea, but Agrippa went on to Rome to figure out what was happening and what the next move should be (J.W. 4.497–502). All of this plus the onset of winter put the siege of Jerusalem on a lengthy hold, which allowed rebel bands to regroup and pillage various areas. We must reserve the discussion of the climax of the Jewish war for the next chapter.

Peter, Paul, and Their Co-Workers

Here, we must consider the fate of Peter. Peter was not a Roman citizen, but simply a Galilean fisherman. As such, he would have not had the social status and advantages of Paul if on trial before a Roman tribunal. John 21:18–19 reflects a knowledge of Peter meeting an end, not of his own choosing, that involved a stretching out of his hands, likely a reference to crucifixion. More specific information comes in *1 Clem.* 5:4. Clement was in a position to know what happened to the church leaders in Rome, since he was a part of that church. When we couple the information of Clement with the later data in *Acts of Peter* 37; Tertullian, *Scorpiace* 15:3; and Eusebius, *Hist. eccl.* 3.2.1, it seems probable that Peter also lost his life during the Neronian crackdown, which began late in A.D. 64 and carried on into 65–66. We should conclude that he was crucified during that period of time. What is intriguing about all this evidence when compared with the traditions about Paul and his demise is that nothing suggests that Peter and Paul were ever together in Rome. We can conceive of a scenario in which Paul left Rome in A.D. 62 and was returned there as a captive after the fire in the summer of 64. Peter may have arrived in Rome while Paul was gone, and indeed may even have been crucified before Paul came to trial there, perhaps in A.D. 65 or early 66. Can we learn anything about Peter from the Petrine correspondence?

The vast majority of scholars are convinced that 2 Peter was not written by Simon Peter, not least because of its heavy dependence on earlier documents like Jude and its reference to a collection of Paul's letters, which must surely indicate that the author lives at a time after Paul's death and after the time when Paul's letters had been collected and circulated as a collection (2 Pet. 3:15–16). Apart from the testimony material in 2 Pet. 1:12–18, which has the same style as the material in 1 Peter, the rest of this document is in a style very different from the first epistle attributed to Peter. I have concluded elsewhere that 2 Peter was attributed to Peter because it contained a genuine Petrine fragment, his testimony about the transfiguration, which is preceded by a reference to his imminent departure from this life (2 Pet. 1:14–15).[8] Second Peter likely was written in the latter portion of the first century A.D. and may indeed be one of the last documents in the canon to be written. The testimony portion reveals that Peter made every effort to leave his charges with written instructions. This comports with the theory that 1 Peter was written by Peter during the 60s, before Peter's execution but after the Christian community had already experi-

8. See B. Witherington III, "A Petrine Source in 2 Peter," in *JBL* (1985): 187–92.

enced suffering. First Peter 5:1 speaks of the author as an old man and as someone who witnessed the sufferings of Christ. This comports well with the theory that the author is indeed Peter himself, though Silas has in fact written the document for him.

First Peter likely was written in Rome, as the greetings from the sister church in Babylon suggests (1 Pet. 5:13; cf. Rev. 18:2–24). The letter was in fact inscribed by Silvanus (Silas) for the author, who has with him Mark (1 Pet. 5:12–13).[9] This letter is written to Jewish Christians in Pontus, Galatia, Cappadocia, Asia, and Bithynia (1:1). This address to Jewish Christians comports with the evidence of Gal. 2:7–8 that Peter had been preaching the gospel to Jews in various places. This meant that his mission *field* would overlap with Paul's even though his mission *focus* would be somewhat different. The emphasis in Peter's case would be on reaching his fellow Jews. If the list of churches in this address is genuine, it gives a clue as to where Peter disappeared to once he left Jerusalem. He did not go to Rome in the 50s, but rather to the area we now call Turkey, probably by way of Antioch, as Galatians 2 may suggest. Presumably, Peter would have known about the expulsions of Jews from Rome in 49 and would not have ventured there anyway while Claudius still ruled, which is to say, not before A.D. 54 at the earliest.

Peter writes at a time when his Jewish Christian audience is undergoing suffering and trials (1 Pet. 1:6–7; 4:12–16). The letter has much discussion of suffering, about Christ as the suffering servant, and sacrifice for sins (1:11, 19; 2:21–24; 3:18–19; 4:1). The exhortation about governing officials, including the plea to honor the emperor (2:13–17), perhaps was an exhortation in due season because the emperor was now engaging in the persecution of Christians, and this may have led some to reject such human institutions. This is all the more likely to be the case with Jewish Christians if they were in sympathy with the struggles that their fellow Jews were experiencing in the Holy Land at that very time. Doubtless, they will have heard reports of the violence by the authorities against Jews, even moderate and peace-loving Jews in Jerusalem and elsewhere. The audience is exhorted to live an exemplary family life, turn the other cheek, and be prepared to testify to their faith when challenged to do so (3:1–16).

To the leaders of these various churches Peter says that they must act like shepherds tending their flocks (1 Pet. 5:1–5). Notice that he refers to these leaders as "elders," and there is no evidence of terminology that became common after Peter's lifetime being applied to these lead-

9. We will have occasion in the next chapter to speak about Mark in Rome and his gospel, but here it must suffice to point to Col. 4:10, which locates Mark in Rome.

ers in this letter. In the end, Peter calls his charges to humble themselves and be patient witnesses under duress and suffering. There is nothing in this exhortation that Peter himself could not have been responsible for. It bespeaks of a time when Christianity in Rome and elsewhere was under fire, and the 60s A.D. was certainly such a time. Peter himself was to follow the paradigm of the Suffering Servant, in all likelihood not long after he wrote this document, perhaps in 64 or 65.

Now we turn to another document that likely was written to the Christian community in Rome during this same period. It comes probably not from Paul but surely from someone in the Pauline circle. This is the letter to the Hebrews.[10] The most natural way to read Heb. 13:24b is that the author is writing to Christians in Italy, and some of their fellow Italian Christians send greetings. As for the date of this letter, there are several clues. First is the reference in 13:13 to remembering those who are now in prison and are being tortured in the body. Second is the call in 13:7 to "remember" the leaders who spoke the word of God. This suggests past leaders, as does the second half of that verse: "consider the outcome of their way of life, and imitate their faith." This indeed could be a reference to Peter and other Roman church leaders. The sequence of 13:7–8 echoes the material found in 11:1–12:2, where the author has discussed the great martyrs of the faith, including, finally, Jesus. Third, the audience of this letter is Jewish Christians who seem to have been losing heart and are in danger of not persevering in the faith. This fits well the situation that likely obtained in Rome after the gradual return of Jewish Christians to the city from A.D. 54 onwards. Fourth, as I have shown elsewhere, the author of this document knows several of the earlier Pauline letters, particularly Galatians and 1 Corinthians. This places Hebrews after A.D. 54.[11] Fifth, the first known user of Hebrews is Clement of Rome, as *1 Clem.* 36:1–6 shows. Sixth, the calling of the leaders in this church *hēgoumenoi* (13:7, 17, 24) points to Rome, as this is the designation used for them in *1 Clem.* 1:3; 21:6; 37:2, and in Herm. *Vis.* 6:6; 17:7. Seventh, Hebrews 10:32–34 speaks of an earlier persecution of the audience that involved confiscation of property. This comports well with what happened in Rome at the time of the expulsion in A.D. 49. Eighth, the reference in 9:25 to the

10. In my view, the most likely candidate is Apollos not only because of the elegance of the letter's style and its obvious knowledge of the Hebrew Scriptures, but also because of the way the author has been influenced by Platonism, much like Philo. If Apollos is the author, then it is germane to point out that he, like Philo, came out of Alexandria, that is, out of a Jewish if not a Jewish Christian environment that was quite Hellenized.

11. See B. Witherington III, "The Influence of Galatians on Hebrews," *NTS* 37 (1991): 146–52.

temple being entered year after year by the high priest comports with a date prior to A.D. 70, when the temple was destroyed (cf. 9:7).

The author of Hebrews seems to know that the readers are facing persecution and even execution. They are dealing with fear of death (2:15) and are in danger of losing heart (12:3), though they have not yet contended to the point of bloodshed (12:4). This suggests a time in A.D. 64, before the beginning of the public reprisals in the Circus Maximus. The author tries to overcome the readers' alienation and vulnerability by connecting them to other Christians in Rome (13:24). They are not simply to go into hiding, but rather, they should attend the fellowship and worship meetings with others. This exhortation is in part needed because these Jewish Christians seem to have been meeting in their own house church and had forsaken meeting with other household congregations elsewhere in Rome (13:17; 10:24–25). "The fact that the writer feels obliged to call for obedience and submission to the current leaders suggests that local authority structures were relatively fluid at this time."[12] They must have been fluid at the time Paul arrived back in Rome as well, and in my view, the Pastoral Epistles are the last documents to come forth from a Christian in Rome prior to the writing of Mark's Gospel.

The authenticity of the Pastoral Epistles—1 and 2 Timothy and Titus—is doubted by probably the majority of New Testament scholars, though numerous critical scholars, ranging from Jeremias to Kelly and more recently to L. T. Johnson, accept that Paul is responsible for one or more of these letters. Perhaps the least problematic solution to the question is to suggest that they were composed very shortly after Paul's death by one of Paul's co-workers in their own style and hand, based on authentic Pauline notes and instructions.[13] Three considerations favor this conclusion. First, the letters do not manifest "early catholic" thinking; indeed, they manifest an ecclesiology that seems rather primitive and thus suited to the end of or just after the Pauline era. There are no hints of monarchial bishops of the sort we find in Ignatius at the beginning of the second century. Second, the letters manifest a uniform style, and a non-Pauline style, but the content comports with Pauline teaching. Third, if the material found in these letters emanated ultimately from Paul while he was in Mamertine prison shortly before his death, he would have needed help to get the letters composed and sent. Paul's situation in the Mamertine would have been drastically different from his house arrest in Rome in the early 60s.

12. W. Lane, "Social Perspectives on Roman Christianity during the Formative Years from Nero to Nerva: Romans, Hebrews, 1 Clement," in *Judaism and Christianity in First-Century Rome*, ed. K. Donfried and P. Richardson (Grand Rapids: Eerdmans, 1998), 222.

13. On all the various solutions, see I. H. Marshall, *A Critical and Exegetical Commentary on the Pastoral Epistles*, ICC (Edinburgh: Clark, 1999), 79–92.

Illustration 13.4 The Circus Maximus, where Christians lost their lives.

Oral instruction to a co-worker—someone like a Luke—shortly before the execution, is the most likely means to have conveyed some of this information. Perhaps the personal testimony in 2 Timothy was hastily written out by hand by Paul near the end, but if so, the composer of these three letters rewrote his source material in his own style, by and large.[14]

What can we say about the end of Paul's life with any confidence? Eusebius gives this summary: "After defending himself, the Apostle was again sent on the ministry of preaching, and coming a second time to the same city suffered martyrdom under Nero. During this imprisonment he wrote the second epistle to Timothy, indicating at the same time that his first defense had taken place and that his martyrdom was at hand" (*Hist. eccl.* 2.22). Eusebius is quite clear that Paul's martyrdom did not occur during the imprisonment recorded in Acts 28. We may also point to *1 Clement* 5 which, as noted earlier, refers to Paul's release from house arrest and his traveling west, a tradition that reoccurs in *Acts of Peter* 1 and also in the Muratorian Canon.

From the previous discussion of Nero's dealings in the early and mid-60s, three points certainly favor the notion that Paul met his end after

14. Johnson, however, is right that the more Pauline material, in terms of style, occurs in 2 Timothy. See L. T. Johnson, *Letters to Paul's Delegates: 1 Timothy, 2 Timothy, Titus* (Valley Forge, Pa.: Trinity, 1996).

rather than before the fire of Rome. First, there is no evidence of any substantial case against Paul in A.D. 60–62, and Paul was a Roman citizen. It is likely that he would have been given the benefit of the doubt. The form of custody he was under in Rome suggests that the Roman authorities did not see Paul as a notable criminal. Second, before the fire in Rome, Nero was not looking for scapegoats, nor was he given to spending time hearing legal cases. Third, by contrast, after the fire in A.D. 64 and the Pisonian conspiracy of 65, Nero was in a litigious mode and also was looking for patsies to bear the odium for the fire. In my view, no period was so likely to have been the time when Paul and other Christians were executed or used as human torches in the circus as late A.D. 64 to early 66, thus, after the fire and before Nero went off on his extended "concert tour" in 66.

What, then, do the Pastorals tell about Paul's last days? First, Paul was very concerned about the matter of his close co-workers Timothy and Titus being properly prepared to carry on his mission. Second, Paul desired that Timothy and Titus exercise the authority granted them to set up a leadership structure in various places east of Rome. Third, these letters do not mention a trip by Paul to the west, but they do indicate that he went back east for a while to deal with problems. This is plausible not only because Paul was a good pastor who would go and deal with problems when they arose, but also because Philem. 22 shows that he planned to go back east to Asia. These letters also reveal that there continued to be significant problems in the Pauline churches, and significant defections by some of Paul's Gentile converts. Basically, these letters are stores of practical advice on how to keep the churches on track and faithful to the gospel originally preached to them.

If 2 Timothy does preserve authentic Pauline memories—and I believe it does—then notice that in this letter, unlike Philippians, Paul believes that his hour for departing this life is at hand (2 Tim. 4:6). In this letter, Paul says that at his first defense, no one came to his support; rather, all deserted him (4:16). This comports well with the desperate and fearful situation in which Christians in Rome found themselves during the period of reprisals for the fire in A.D. 64 through early 66. Probably, this is a reference to the Roman legal process whereby a preliminary hearing (*primo actio*) preceded a decision as to whether the trial would go forward or not. Apparently, the lack of support for Paul allowed the trial to go forward.[15] The supreme penalty Paul could face was beheading, which is the likely outcome of the trial in A.D. 65 or

---

15. The reference to being rescued from the lion's mouth (2 Tim. 4:17) indeed can be taken literally in the time frame in which these events transpired. Paul, being a Roman citizen, was not dealt with as ordinary Roman Christians were. He was not set alight and he was not thrown to the wild beasts. Nonetheless, his trial went forward, ending in his execution.

thereabouts. Finally, notice the greetings from Pudens, Linus, and Claudia, all good Roman names (4:21). It is possible that this Linus is the one who after the deaths of Peter and Paul was to become the leader of the Roman church.

Without question, the period A.D. 63–68 was one of the most turbulent in early Christian history. Christianity endured the loss not only of two of its greatest missionaries and apostles, Peter and Paul, but also of many others tortured and killed in the Neronian crackdown. The Jewish war had begun, and already in 68 the outcome looked ominous for those who hoped for peace without reprisals in the Holy Land. As the war reached its climax, and with almost all of the major apostles martyred, the time had come for the writing down of the gospel, lest the eyewitness testimony be lost. Oddly enough, the first to feel the need and the inspiration to take up the task was the cousin of Barnabas, who, so far as we can tell, played only a minor role in early Christianity, and in some respects, not always the most honorable of roles. A companion of Paul and later of Peter in Rome, he found his crowning achievement in the writing of the first Gospel. To that we turn in the next chapter.

Chapter 14

The Dawn of the Age of Inspiration

A.D. 68–70

Musical Chairs in the Palace

The death of Nero left a void at the top of the Roman pyramid of leadership, and several candidates sought to fill it. The first to try to fill the void was Galba, who seems to have been reasonably well accepted by both the senate and the military. There were, however, grave crises to face. Fiscally, Rome was in terrible shape due to the extravagances of Nero, not least in his building programs. Galba, as soon as becoming emperor, attempted to address this problem by raising taxes—never a popular expedient. He also attempted to make some cutbacks in expenditures, but this seems not to have impressed anyone very much. Galba made other missteps as well.

There had been, in fact, various military candidates for the emperorship, and various factions of the Roman army expected their favorite leader either to be the emperor or to have a significant post. In January of A.D. 69, the armies of the Rhine refused to renew their oath of allegiance to Galba. They wanted to champion their own leader, Vitellius. In panic, Galba recognized he needed to pick an associate, or fellow consul, who would appease some sectors of the military that he himself had not led. Unfortunately, he made the mistake of not picking either Vitellius, or even Otho, who was a close friend of Nero and at the time the governor of Lusitania. Instead, he picked a young senator whom he saw as no threat to him. This left Otho and Vitellius furious.

Illustration 14.1 Shrine from a Roman villa where household gods were worshiped.

Otho successfully arranged to have the praetorian guard do away with Galba, and the guard declared him emperor in mid-January of A.D. 69. This did not satisfy the army of the lower Rhine in the least, and so they marched on Rome, determined to set up their own man, Vitellius, in power. In fact, they went ahead and declared Vitellius emperor. Otho tried to make a deal with Vitellius but failed. Vitellius's army made it safely over the Alps in the midst of winter, surprising the forces of Otho. A brief civil war ensued, which Otho lost, and he then committed suicide.

Vitellius may have thought that he had no rivals once he set himself up in power in Rome, but since it appeared to be open season for military leaders to be declared emperor by their troops, he should have anticipated another such declaration. In July of A.D. 69, the governor of Egypt (Tiberius Alexander) and the eastern legions in general declared for the popular general Vespasian. The legions on the Danube rapidly followed suit, and indeed, Antonius Primus, their commander, even marched on Rome, catching the forces of Vitellius off guard. Primus won two clear victories, and Vitellius agreed to abdicate. Before that could be arranged, however, the praetorian guard made plans to kill Vitellius and also attacked and killed Vespasian's brother, who was Vespasian's liaison in Rome. Clearly, they had their own designs and sought to be kingmaker. Civil war looked likely to break out, but Primus arrived in Rome, captured and killed Vitellius, wiped out the remaining Vitellian forces, and made Domitian, the younger son of Vespasian, who actually was in Rome, the vice-regent until his father arrived. Having gotten used to fighting and pillaging in Rome, the army from the Danube could well have just carried on and sacked the city. But they respected Vespasian, and when Vespasian's legate, Mucianus, hastily appeared on the scene, order was restored by sending these troops back to where they came from. It was not until a few months later that Vespasian was able to make it to Rome, in the summer of A.D. 70.

The so-called year of the three emperors was a grim year indeed for Rome, which became something of a war zone. For Jews and Christians in Rome, both trying to survive the turmoil in the city and holding their breath in regard to what was happening in the Holy Land, it was a very dangerous and dark time indeed. In the wake of the loss of Peter and Paul, and in the midst of the mayhem, John Mark wrote the very first Gospel to help his audience get through the horrible time of suffering and trial without losing all hope for the future or all sense and memory of their sacred history. It was an eschatological time, and with the destruction of Jerusalem looming on the horizon, Mark wrote in an apocalyptic and eschatological manner. I will say more about this remarkable document shortly.

Titus and the Temple of Doom

Vespasian could hardly have known that he was about to found a dynasty after the suicide of Nero. Vitellius was widely disliked, and neither Galba nor Otho had wide support. The legate in Syria, Licinius Mucianus, believed, as did Vespasian's troops, that Rome could do better, and it was both the legate and the troops who proclaimed Vespasian emperor. This in turn led Vespasian to make certain strategic moves to secure control of the empire (*J.W.* 4.585–604). For example, Egypt had always been the major source of grain for Rome, indeed, the breadbasket of the empire. With governor Tiberius Alexander's support, Vespasian quickly gained the loyalty of the two legions in Egypt (his son Titus had already had associations with the troops there and had commanded some of them). Mucianus then was sent to Rome with an army to pacify the situation there. On December 21, A.D. 69, Vitellius was killed, and Rome eagerly awaited Vespasian, coming from Alexandria (*J.W.* 4.645–657). Before he left for Rome, Vespasian dispatched Titus to Caesarea with orders to finish the war and crush the resistance, even if it meant destroying Jerusalem (*J.W.* 4.658–663).

By the time Titus arrived in Caesarea, much had transpired in Jerusalem. Three major factions in the holy city were vying for control. John of Gischala and his six thousand Zealots controlled part of the lower city and the temple outer court, but another group of Zealots under Eleazar ben Simon, who had twenty-four hundred troops, controlled the temple inner court. Simon ben Gioras, who had been let into the city with his army by moderates hoping to counter the Zealots, had fifteen thousand soldiers and controlled the whole upper city and some of the lower city. Tacitus sums up the situation nicely: "There were three generals, three armies: the outermost and largest circuit of the walls was held by Simon, the middle of the city by John, and the temple was guarded by Eleazar. John and Simon were strong in numbers and equipment, Eleazar had the advantage of position: between these three there was constant fighting, treachery, and arson, and a great store of grain was consumed" (*History* 5.12.3). This situation was a recipe for disaster, not least because October 68–69 was a sabbatical year for crops, meaning that much less grain was available. As Hays and Mandell remind us, "By the time of the April-May 70 C.E. harvest season, the city was under siege."[1]

Titus took no chances, marching on Jerusalem with four full legions, Tiberius Alexander in tow as an adjunct to help with the Egyptian troops, and various auxiliary forces as well (*J.W.* 5.39–46). It must have been sometime before this juncture that Christians fled the city, and according to tradition, went to Pella. Near disaster befell Titus when he came within range of the city. He took six hundred cavalry and went to survey the city defenses. Suddenly, Titus and some of his cavalry were cut off from the main force by some Jews who had come forth from the city. Titus barely escaped, unscathed. Titus should have learned a lesson from this episode: cornered Jewish Zealots were prepared to risk much to survive and continue to fight for the cause of independence.

Titus decided that he would attack from the north, as had always been the strategy against Jerusalem, with its vulnerable north side. The plan of Titus involved breaching the third wall, taking the Antonia fortress, and then moving into the temple area. He placed one legion on the Mount of Olives and three on Mount Scopus overlooking the city

---

1. J. Hayes and S. Mandell, *The Jewish People in Classical Antiquity: From Alexander to Bar Kochba* (Louisville: Westminster John Knox, 1998), 196.

Illustration 14.2 A Roman battering ram (partially restored).

from the north. The Jews once more surprised the Romans by coming forth from the city and attacking those who were setting up camp on the Mount of Olives, with not a little success (*J.W.* 5.71–97). Despite the clear evidence of imminent disaster, the three sets of Jewish forces within the walls continued to fight with one another right up to the point when the Roman battering rams started hitting the city's defenses (*J.W.* 5.248–257, 275–279). Josephus himself was sent to present the terms of surrender to those within the city, but his plea went unheeded (*J.W.* 5.114).

Using a battering ram named Victor, the Romans broke down the outer wall in fourteen days, and then took only five more days to breach the second wall. This left the northern wall of the inner city as the next objective. Of course, psychological warfare was being waged both within and outside the walls. Within the walls, atrocities were committed to prevent desertion; outside the walls, prisoners were crucified near the city walls. "The soldiers out of rage and hatred amused themselves by nailing their prisoners in different postures; and so great was their number, that space could not be found for the crosses nor crosses for the bodies" (*J.W.* 5.451).

The siege tightened the noose around the city, and starvation became a very real prospect for those trapped within. Building earthworks is a slow task, and it took some weeks to effectively seal off the city and make it ready for the final assault with battering rams. In July of A.D. 70, the inner-city wall was finally breached, but John of Gischala had managed to build another wall inside that one. Yet even John's wall was finally scaled and the Antonia fortress was captured. Extremely fierce hand-to-hand combat prevented the Romans from immediately gaining access to the temple courts themselves (*J.W.* 6.25–32, 54–92). Titus thus decided to demolish the Antonia fortress, in part to demoralize the opposition and give them time to surrender. Another plea was made by Josephus to spare the temple from destruction by surrender, but only a few aristocrats defected. The majority resolved to fight to the death (*J.W.* 6.93–130). The walls of the temple precincts proved impervious to the battering rams, and so the walls had to be scaled, or burned and then the rubble scaled. Both sides set fire to parts of the porticoes around the outer precincts, and when the outer court was penetrated, the defenders hid within the inner courts.

At this point Titus held a war council. Should the temple be destroyed or not? The argument apparently considered both sides of the coin. To destroy the temple would be seen as sacrilege and would ruin the reputation of the Romans for clemency or moderation. To not destroy the temple was to leave it as focal point for future potential insurrections. The latter consideration apparently weighed more heavily in the general's mind in view of the turbulent history of the Judean province. Titus wanted the war over in such a way that the flames would not be rekindled again.

In the final assault, the temple was set ablaze. There is a story, probably legendary but perhaps partially true, that when the temple was set ablaze, the gold and silver coins in the treasury melted, seeping through the cracks in the massive Herodian stones. This, it is said, led to the soldiers turning the stones over to recover the precious metals. Hence the temple was left with not one stone upon another (cf. Mark 13:1–2). Titus and his chief commanders managed to enter the burning sanctuary, including the Holy of Holies, before it collapsed, rescuing some of its contents (*J.W.* 6.260). Celebrating their victory, some Roman soldiers set up their standards across from the temple's eastern gate and offered sacrifices to their standards. Titus was acclaimed *imperator* (*J.W.* 6.316; Suetonius, *Titus* 5.2). Though the temple was taken in August of A.D. 70, the mop-up operation elsewhere in Jerusalem lasted another month. Titus ordered the razing of the walls of both the city and what remained of the temple enclosure, except for the western retaining wall (now called the Wailing Wall) and three towers of Herod (Phasael, Hippicus, Mariamne). Titus kept as prisoners both John of Gischala and Simon to take back as trophies, along with the great

Illustration 14.3 Scale model of first-century Rome (note the aqueducts).

booty from the temple, including the menorah, for his triumph in Rome in A.D. 71. Though the war was not entirely over, because several of Herod's outlying fortresses remained in the hands of the rebels, for all intents and purposes, Rome had the victory.

Since it was already October by the time the operation was finished in Jerusalem, which was too late to set sail for Rome, Titus took a winter holiday with Agrippa in Caesarea Philippi, at which time, apparently, Bernice became smitten with Titus, which in due course led to her being Titus's mistress in Rome (Tacitus, *History* 2.2.1; 2.81.2). Despite Josephus's attempts to paint Titus as a man of clemency, we know that Titus used some of his Jewish captives to put on grisly spectacles with animals as well as gladiatorial games in both Caesara Philippi and in Berytus (Beirut). Hayes and Mandell are right to conclude that from "a certain perspective, it was an incongruous, incredible time. A Jewish king was entertaining the conqueror of his fellow religionists while enjoying shows produced by the further decimation of Jewish flesh. While Jerusalem's ashes still smoldered, the passion of an uncircumcised future Roman emperor burned for one of the last of the Hasmonean beauties."[2] Titus did something of a victory tour through Syria and then Judea, stopping in Jerusalem in the spring of A.D. 71 before

2. Ibid., 203–4.

going on to Alexandria in order to sail back to Rome. He left the conquest of the remaining Herodian fortresses to lesser Roman commanders. I will continue the story of what happened when Titus reached Rome in the next chapter.

Making Its Mark—Ancient Biography as Gospel

Perhaps writing anywhere between a few months and a year or so before the fall of the temple in Jerusalem, Mark took it upon himself to compose a narrative focused on the ministry of Jesus. But what sort of narrative was Mark composing? We now consider the genre of the Gospel of Mark.

A Closer Look: *Mark's Biography of Jesus*

Mention the term "biography," and immediately certain expectations are set up for the modern reader. It is precisely some of these expectations that have prevented readers today from seeing Mark for what it is: a "life of Jesus" in ancient form, complying with ancient expectations as to what a biography should look like. But first, it will be useful to canvass some other suggestions about the genre of Mark.

From time to time it has been suggested that we should see Mark's Gospel as an example of Greek drama.[3] Some, in fact, have gone so far as to suggest that Mark attended the theater (Herod's theater in Jerusalem?).[4] This suggestion has certain plausibility. Mark's prologue has not infrequently been compared to the prologue of a Greek play.[5] But what sort of drama would Mark's Gospel be? It is certainly not a Greek comedy. Nor does it have the ending of a Greek tragedy. Jesus' death is transcended by the resurrection. Even if the Gospel is seen to end at Mark 16:8 (on which, see below), the empty tomb and the Easter proclamation remain. Nor do we find in Mark the chorus that we find in Greek drama. We do have an author who occasionally intrudes into the

---

3. The following material in this "Closer Look" section appears in a somewhat different form in B. Witherington III, *The Gospel of Mark: A Socio-rhetorical Commentary* (Grand Rapids: Eerdmans, 2001), 1–9.

4. See M. A. Beavis, *Mark's Audience: The Literary and Social Setting of Mark 4.11–12*, JSNTSup 33 (Sheffield: Sheffield Academic, 1989).

5. M. Hooker, *A Commentary on the Gospel according to St. Mark* (London: Black, 1991), 18–19, notes this, and hints at the possibility that Mark might be seen as a drama. But she also points out that other Gospels have prologues, and certainly it would be difficult to read Luke's Gospel as a drama.

narrative, but that is a literary, not a drama, technique. Thus, although Mark's is a dramatic Gospel, with an interesting plot and plenty of controversy and pathos leading to the death of the main character, it does not seem to be a Greek tragedy. To the contrary, it is a book of good news rather than tragedy.[6] There are, however, two other types of ancient literature that Mark might be said to be an example of: the historical monograph and the ancient biography.[7]

Recently, the suggestion has been made by A. Y. Collins that Mark's Gospel be seen as some sort of historical monograph.[8] This theory has a certain plausibility because of the overlap between the characterizing features of an ancient biography and an ancient historical monograph. But when we look for the more specific telltale signs of a historical monograph, they seem to be almost entirely lacking in Mark's Gospel. For example, Mark shows no real interest in synchronisms with the events of the larger Roman world, unlike what we find from time to time in Luke-Acts. Furthermore, Mark shows little interest in historical causality or explaining the links between the various events in his narrative, with the exception of some of the material in his passion narrative. Furthermore, unlike historical monographs, Mark focuses not on a series of events and those involved, but on a singular person. People are mentioned in Mark's narrative only for their connection or interaction with the central figure, Jesus.[9] This is true even of John the Baptist. Furthermore, in light of Mark's portrayal of the disciples and the crowds, it

6. But see G. G. Bilezikian, *The Liberated Gospel: A Comparison of the Gospel of Mark and Greek Tragedy* (Grand Rapids: Baker, 1977).

7. Mark should not be compared to modern biographies of the psychological sort, which analyze a historical figure in depth and in detail and chronicle a life "from womb to tomb." Clearly, this is not what any of the Gospel writers are doing. Their accounts are episodic and they show little or no interest in the character development of the central figure. Nor can Mark be classified as myth, for what ancient myth recounts the crucifixion and utter shaming of a god?

8. A. Y. Collins, *The Beginning of the Gospel: Probings of Mark in Context* (Minneapolis: Fortress, 1992), 1–38.

9. In his recent commentary, J. Marcus, *Mark 1–8*, AB 27 (New York: Doubleday, 1999), 65–66, suggests that Mark's Gospel might be more of a historical narrative because stylistically he occasionally imitates the Old Testament historical narratives with phrases like "and it came to pass in those days." But the overlap between some features of a historical biography and a monograph can explain this similarity. He then goes on to suggest that it is the biography of a movement, but this ignores both the heavy critique of the disciples in Mark and, on Marcus's showing, the ending (he thinks the book ends at 16:8), neither of which suggests that Mark is trying to highlight the Jesus movement. To the contrary, he is focusing on one central figure who is the paradigm for his audience—Jesus.

seems clear that he has the sort of paraenetic purposes that more nearly and more frequently characterize ancient biographies than historical monographs.

Having glanced at the various other possible genres, we turn now to the possibility that Mark might be seen as an example of an ancient *bios*, an ancient biography of Jesus. Once again we must remind ourselves that this possibility must be assessed on the basis not of modern biographical conventions but of ancient ones. Yet determining the genre of a work means assessing not merely its form but also its content, at least to some extent. The content of Mark's Gospel is Jewish through and through. In its extant form, Mark's Gospel is a document written in Greek and reflecting the Greek rhetorical and biographical conventions of the era in which Mark lived. Is this surprising combination of Jewish content and Greek form possible in an ancient biography?

Here, I direct the reader back to the prolegomenon, where I discussed at length the genre of the Gospels in comparison to that of ancient biography. I concluded there that Matthew, Mark, and John (Luke-Acts is a related but different case), when judged by ancient standards, look rather like ancient biographies of the more religious or philosophical sort. In discussing Mark here, some additional considerations are important.

Neither the superscript nor the first verse of Mark's Gospel tells us much about the genre of the document. Mark uses the term *euangelion* to refer to the content of God's saving work, just as Paul does (cf. Mark 1:1, 14; 8:35; 10:29; 13:10; 14:9 to Gal. 1:7–9; Rom. 2:16).[10] That Paul and Mark can use this same term, and always in the singular, in works of two very different literary genres shows that *euangelion* had not yet become a technical term for a certain kind of literature. This also in a small way favors the claim that Mark's Gospel is early. It is not until at least the writing of the *Didache* that the term *euangelion* is used for a certain kind of text or document. Notice that the term is used in the plural in several sources in the second century (*2 Clem.* 8:5; Justin Martyr, *1 Apol.* 66.3; *Dial.* 10.2; 100.1).

It is important here to ask, In what way can we use the term "apocalyptic" of Mark's narrative, especially since, as C. Myers says, "Mark chose realistic narrative over the more highly fabricated fictions of apocalyptic"? When we speak of Mark's apocalyptic rhetoric, we are refer-

---

10. See C. Bryan, *A Preface to Mark: Notes on the Gospel in Its Literary and Cultural Settings* (New York: Oxford University Press, 1993), 33.

ring to the fact that he operates with an apocalyptic worldview that affects the way he casts some of his narrative and the shape of some of his characterizations, including that of Jesus.[11]

H. C. Kee, after having pointed out how Mark seems to show more interest in Daniel than in any other Old Testament prophetic book (and in general favors excerpts from apocalyptic material found in Daniel; cf. Isaiah 24–27; 34–35; Ezekiel 38–39; Joel 3–4; Zechariah 9; 12–14; Malachi 3–4), and in fact quotes from every chapter in Daniel, argues that Mark adopts Daniel's narrative strategy of presenting miracle tales in the first half of his work followed by a second-half focus on suffering and martyrdom. He further finds a series of traits in Mark that often characterizes apocalyptic works: (1) dualism—the new order is opposed to the old; (2) use of the combat myth, in this case the contestants being Jesus and Satan; (3) the theme of lack of understanding unless there is revelation of the divine perspective; (4) the narrative is bounded spatially from above by the supernatural world, and temporally from beyond by the climactic eschatological events, including final judgment by the Son of Man.[12]

Something now needs to be said about the superscript that designates this document as *kata Markon*, added, when more than one Gospel was circulating, to distinguish this one from others. M. Hengel some time ago made a convincing case that early in the second century, Christians held a deep conviction that there was only *one* Gospel, presented according to several different Evangelists.[13] Especially striking is P[66] (ca. A.D. 200), which has the clear heading "Gospel according to John." Hengel argues that from early in the second century there was a collection of the fourfold Gospel, and that the "Gospel according to . . ." had become the regular title for any and all these Gospels in order to differentiate one of these works from the other three. Already, the *Didache* had references to a written document, not merely an oral tradition called *euangelion* (*Did.* 8:2; 11:3; 15:3–4).

It has been suggested that the rise of the fourfold Gospel circulating together (presumably beginning not long after the writing of the Fourth Gospel) precipitated the prevalent use of the codex in Christian circles,

11. See C. Myers, *Binding the Strong Man: A Political Reading of Mark's Story of Jesus*, (Maryknoll: Orbis, 1988), 104; Marcus, *Mark 1–8*, 71–73.

12. H. C. Kee, *Community of the New Age: Studies in Mark's Gospel* (Philadelphia: Westminster, 1977), 45–66. See Myers, *Binding the Strong Man*, 103.

13. M. Hengel, *Studies in the Gospel of Mark* (Philadelphia: Fortress, 1985), 64–84.

for no scroll could contain even two of these Gospels.[14] There is now some manuscript evidence for a fourfold Gospel collection in the second century.[15] The implications of the circulation of the fourfold Gospel seems to include the following: (1) the notion that one Gospel was sufficient was rejected; (2) the notion that a harmony of the four Gospels was sufficient was rejected; (3) the notion that other Gospels beyond these four were equally valid and valuable was at least implicitly rejected.[16] Irenaeus's defense of the idea of only one Gospel in only four presentations, mounted in the latter third of the second century (*Against Heresies* was written about A.D. 180—see 3.11.8), reflects the prior existence and growing normativity of that collection.

But this entire process raises a pressing question about the Gospel according to Mark: Why was a Gospel by a somewhat obscure, non-apostolic figure like Mark accepted into this collection, especially when Matthew already contains the vast majority of his work? Would such a title really have been dreamed up in the second century, when there was pressing concern to connect all foundational documents closely with apostles? I think not, and there is further reason for thinking that the earliest Gospel was from the beginning indeed connected with one Mark, an early Christian.

Mark's work is, and would have been seen as a biography, and ancient biographies almost invariably had *known* authors—we think of Plutarch's *Lives*, or Suetonius's narratives about the Caesars, or Tacitus's *Agricola*, or Josephus's autobiography. Though internally, Mark's Gospel does not reveal the name of the author, the predication *kata Markon* is very likely to have some foundation in fact.

Mark's Gospel was to set up a blueprint that was to be followed by more than one subsequent Gospel writer. Our concern here, however, must be with Mark and its function for its original Roman audience. I believe that we find a key clue to the provenance of this document in Mark 13:14. The author is warning his own readers that the end of the temple will be the end of an era and that that end is near at hand. This end was predicted by Jesus to transpire within a generation of his death, which is precisely the time when it did happen, forty years after Jesus' death, in A.D. 70. But this is news that Mark's audience can only

14. See the discussion by G. N. Stanton, "The Fourfold Gospel," *NTS* 43 (1997): 336–39.

15. T. C. Skeat, "The Oldest Manuscript of the Four Gospels?" *NTS* 43 (1997): 1–34.

16. See Stanton, "Fourfold Gospel," 342–44; Skeat, "Oldest Manuscript," 32–33.

read about, not see (notice that he does not say "let the *viewer* understand," but rather, "let the *reader* understand"). The sacrilege of Titus entering and pillaging the Holy of Holies was indeed "an abomination that makes desolate," but to his credit, Mark does not edit his source to conform it to the actual events in A.D. 70. Instead, the background in Daniel rather than the foreground in A.D. 70 is what accounts for the shape of Mark 13:14.

The structure of Mark's Gospel reveals a great deal about Mark's focus. Approximately the first half of the Gospel is devoted to raising and answering the who question—who really is Jesus? When this question is answered at the climactic episode in Mark 8 at Caesarea Philippi, it is then, and only then, that in three successive chapters Mark clearly states Jesus' mission: the Son of Man did not come to be served, but to serve, and to give his life as a ransom for many (10:45), or as he puts it in 8:31, 9:31, and 10:33–34, the Son of Man must suffer many things, be killed, and on the third day arise. Put simply, it is the mission of Jesus to suffer and die for his people. The last third of the Gospel (Mark 11–16) records how Jesus fulfilled this mission.

Mark's narrative is indeed a passion narrative with a long introduction. The dark shadow of suffering hovers not only over Jesus but also over his disciples, who are called on to be prepared to undergo the same baptism of death he undergoes, and are warned at length in Mark 13 about their coming trials and tribulations. In this environment of misunderstanding, persecution, and suffering, it is no surprise that Mark chooses to make clear that the truth about Jesus can be known only by means of receiving the revelation of God about him. Thus, the Gospel has certain key apocalyptic and revelatory moments—the baptism, Caesarea Philippi, the transfiguration, the trial, the crucifixion—that make clear that God must reveal the messianic secret to people or they will not grasp it. The apocalyptic rhetoric of Mark is much like that in the book of Revelation, and not surprisingly, both arise out of the same sort of social setting of persecution and suffering, though it is likely that Revelation is responding to the suffering that transpired later during Domitian's reign in the 90s.

Note that Mark's Olivet discourse (Mark 13) has an A-B-A´-B´ character to it in which Mark speaks confidently about the events that will transpire within a generation (vv. 5–23 and vv. 28–30, both discoursing about "these things"), and then speaks more briefly and generically about the more distant eschatological events (vv. 24–27 and vv. 32–37). He disavows knowing the timing of the latter events (see v. 32), but affirms confidently that the former ones will transpire within a generation (v. 30). The former are the messianic woes, or beginning of the birth pangs, that augur the end of a world—the world of Second Temple Judaism. The latter reveal the end of days. Undoubtedly, Mark believed that he and his audience lived in the age of the messianic woes, which is also to say, the age when prophecy was being fulfilled—including Jesus' prophecies—and he sees it as his job to alert his readers to this fact. In this way, the audience will realize that God's plan for them was being worked out, and thus their task is to keep awake and not lose heart. They must become exegetes of their own experiences and of those of God's people in Judea.

Where did Mark get this valuable information? It is plausible that a good deal of it he gained through his contact with Peter, as later Christian tradition suggested,[17] but surely, he also will have drawn on what he learned in Jerusalem while the early church met in his mother's house. He may also very briefly have been an eyewitness as a youth of one or two of the final events in Jesus' life, if Mark 14:51–52 is any clue. In any event, he has presented a stark portrait of Jesus and his earliest followers, meant to help his own Roman audience, and perhaps other Christians as well, get beyond the dark days at the end of Nero's reign and the year of the three emperors. Little did he know that the cycle of violence would repeat itself at the end of the Flavian dynasty, just as it had cropped up at the end of the Julio-Claudian dynasty. I will have more to say on this score in subsequent chapters. What is important to bear in mind here is that Mark's Gospel provided a wake-up call to early Christians, reminding them that with the dying off of the eyewitnesses, the time had come for recording their own sacred story before it was lost and witnesses could no longer be consulted. In the next chapter, we will consider how others took up the challenge.

17. See the discussion of this matter in the introduction in Witherington, *Gospel of Mark.*

Chapter 15

Beyond Jerusalem, Jamnia, and the Julio-Claudians

A.D. 70–81

Under Vespasian All Was Interesting

Almost exactly one hundred years had passed since Octavius had set up the principate, and the Roman Empire had been born. Though Vespasian's career had looked quite promising in the 40s and 50s (serving with distinction in the army in Germany and Britain, obtaining the consulship in A.D. 51 and the proconsulship thereafter), sometime in the 50s he went bankrupt and had to mortgage his estates to his brother. Even worse, on one occasion he fell asleep while Nero was playing one of his recitals and became persona non grata in the royal palace. It was, then, something of a surprise when Nero offered him command in A.D. 66 of the legions that were to put down the revolt in Judea.[1]

What qualifications did Vespasian have to be emperor? Perhaps the chief one, in the wake of the year of the three emperors, was that he had the respect of the armies and could handle them if need be. Furthermore, he knew the value of fiscal responsibility, having experienced poverty himself. He had a goodly measure of common sense as well. Then, too, he had heirs who could follow him, at least one of which, Titus, looked quite promising as a future leader. Lastly, he had a sense of humor and was not a megalomaniac.

Vespasian was not inventive, but he was indeed a good mechanic,

Illustration 15.1 Statue of the Flavian emperor.

able to repair and tune up an already existing engine of empire. When he became emperor, he was already sixty and came to his task with none of the immaturity of Nero, but rather, as a man of experience. He knew how to deal with the various revolts extant in the empire, but he knew also that even more crucial was to deal with the financial and morale problems at home as well as the perception of disarray elsewhere in the empire.

Vespasian also had good fortune on his side. Tacitus reports that even before the time of Vespasian, there were prophecies of a world ruler coming forth from Judea (*History* 4.81; 5.13). Then in early A.D.

1. For a full discussion of the matters briefly canvassed here, see S. A. Cook et al., eds., *The Cambridge Ancient History*, volume 11, rev. ed. (Cambridge: Cambridge University Press, 1954), 1–44.

70, while he was in Alexandria, Vespasian reputedly laid hands on a blind man and a maimed man, and both were cured. This, coupled with the victory in Judea, led to belief that Vespasian was the divinely anointed man who had been prophesied as coming out of Judea to rule the world. Not until the time of Constantine and later would it dawn on Roman citizens that perhaps the prophecies had after all been about someone else—say, a Jew from Nazareth.

Before ever he arrived in Rome, Vespasian made his presence felt through his son Domitian, who initiated various measures to restore normalcy in Rome including: (1) a restoration of full civic status to those convicted of treason during Nero's reign of terror or during the year of three emperors; (2) the restoration of the Capitoline temple, begun with the laying of the foundation stone on July 21, A.D. 70; (3) a quashing of the revolts in the east and the west under the best generals. These measures showed that Vespasian stood for law and order, or peace and stability. When Vespasian arrived in Rome, he immediately struck a chord with the common people by personally helping to cart away the rubble from the temple and assisting with the reconstruction. He also took action to reduce the praetorian guard from sixteen cohorts down to its original nine, a smart move that made internal sabotage of his reign less likely. By the end of the year, he was able to hold a ceremony closing the doors of the temple of Janus, indicating that Rome no longer was at war, because the Jewish revolt and several other smaller revolts had been put down.

Vespasian was intelligent enough to know that at sixty years of age, he would already be subject to questions about the succession, and so once Titus had had his triumph, returning from Judea, Titus was kept before the public eye by making him a fellow consul in A.D. 70, 72, 74, 75, 76, 77, and 79. Domitian held the consulship with his father only in 71, but he held the censorship with his father in 73–74. All of this made very clear that heirs were being properly trained for the succession. The goal was to make evident that no one else would in any way be nearly as well prepared to rule after Vespasian than his two sons. Titus had as one of his duties command of, and controlling, the praetorian guard. This was to make sure that they did not disrupt the Flavian success and succession at any point.

Vespasian was a far more patient man than Nero, and not nearly so vain, but even he had his limits as to how much verbal abuse he could take from his opponents. In A.D. 71 he finally was goaded into banishing some Cynics (including the famous Demetrius the Cynic) who preached anarchy and all astrologers and philosophers. Notice, however, that Vespasian did not have them executed, only banished, which was usually all he did to his other opponents as well, including radical back-to-the-Republic patricians like Helvidius Priscus. When the calumnies went on for years, however, Vespasian reached his limit, and some opponents were executed.

Vespasian had to deal with an ever shrinking patrician pool of talent, and so he made it his priority, especially during the years he was censor (73–74), to promote both provincials and Italians to the senate and to other important posts. Having finished restocking the senate, at the end of his censorship Vespasian was able to dedicate the temple of Peace, into which he placed the spoils of the Jewish campaign.

Vespasian also had to deal on an ongoing basis with financial crises. For one thing, when the wars were over, many soldiers died, and he had to find money for their pensions. Vespasian himself was a frugal man, and had simply cut out the extravagances of the Neronian era, but this in itself did not save enough to deal with expenditures. Thus, it became necessary to impose new taxes on the provinces, including the *fiscus Judaicus*. This last involved the redirecting of the money that had been paid into the Jewish temple as a temple tax into the Roman coffers, since that temple no longer existed. Jews had paid two drachmas to their temple each year, but now it was appropriated for a very different temple, the Capitoline. Since nearly five million Jews populated the empire, this brought in considerable revenues. Vespasian also was much in favor of granting Latin rights to various provincials, including especially in Spain, but also in parts of North Africa and Switzerland. This move likewise brought more stability to the empire and more coins into Roman coffers.

Only a few notable events from the years A.D. 75–79 stand out about Vespasian's reign during that time. Titus, as noted previously, had been smitten with Bernice, the sister of Herod Agrippa. In A.D. 75 Herod and Bernice came to Rome and were greeted with great respect and honor. Bernice, perhaps because she thought she would become Titus's wife, behaved imperiously, even holding her own court, before which the famous rhetorician Quintilian pleaded a case (*Inst.* 4.1.19). Unfortunately, the memory of Cleopatra still existed in Rome, and when various Cynics slipped back into Rome and others joined them in protesting the apparently inevitable marriage with Bernice, things became difficult. The atmosphere of xenophobia and anti-Semitism had been thickened, and the marriage became impossible, and so Titus had to let Bernice depart, for he wanted to rule more than he wanted her.

As is well known, the Romans, like most ancients, believed in omens, whether as read in the heavens or in the entrails of animals. In A.D. 79, a bad omen appeared for Vespasian. A plague hit Rome and claimed

Illustration 15.2 The arch of Titus, displaying the captured menorah on parade in Rome.

many victims. Indeed, Vespasian perhaps was one of them, for in the late spring of A.D. 79, Vespasian's health deteriorated. He struggled to carry on for a couple of months, but on June 24, he struggled to his feet and died—as the saying goes—with his boots on, as a soldier. In only a short time, he was made a god by a grateful Roman people.

Post-Temple Judaism Reorganizes

After traveling through Syria with his spoils of war and Jewish prisoners on display, and revisiting Jerusalem, Titus was prepared to return to Rome and have his triumph. A full triumphal procession, unlike any in recent memory, was arranged, complete with floats illustrating scenes from the Jewish war (*J.W.* 7.116–118, 123–147). Paraded before Roman eyes were some seven hundred prisoners, including Simon and John of Gischala. The former was executed after the procession reached the temple of Jupiter, the latter imprisoned for life. The citizens of Rome watched as a golden table, a golden lamp stand (menorah), and a copy of the Torah looted from the Jerusalem temple were displayed prominently in the parade (*J.W.* 7.148–154). For the Jews and Christians (especially Jewish Christians) who watched, this humiliation must have been excruciating. The memory of the humiliation was perpetuated by the minting of coins that depicted a Jewess under a palm tree with the words *Judea capta* inscribed, and by the building of

Illustration 15.3 The Herodium, Herod's favorite fortress.

the arch of Titus, which to this day depicts the triumphal procession of the booty from the Jewish war.

Two immediate changes came in the Judean province after the fall of Jerusalem. First, the province was upgraded to one of senatorial concern, placing it under an imperial senatorial legate of praetorian rank. There would be no more equestrian governors like Pilate or Festus or Florus. The new governors would bring with them a fuller and more competent staff. Then, too, Judea was made a province unto itself, and not merely connected with the Syrian province. This meant that the governor in Caesarea did not have to consult with the legate in Antioch. He could simply act. The other major change was that the troops in the region would no longer be auxiliaries raised from the region itself. Whereas before there had been a few auxiliary units, now there would be a full legion in Judea, and the bulk of the troops would be stationed in the hot spot, Jerusalem. Sextus Lucilius Bassus became the first governor under this new arrangement. To Bassus fell the unwelcome task of rousting rebels from the caves and fortresses where they hid, in the process of the mop-up operation.

Late in A.D. 71, the Herodium was taken from the rebels, apparently without a major fight (*J.W.* 7.163). The Machaerus did not fall so easily. In the summer of 72, Roman troops built a major rampart to reach and breach the fortress wall, and when it seemed likely that doom was inevitable, the rebels surrendered in exchange for safe passage out of the

Illustration 15.4 Roman siege camp below Masada.

fort. Near this locale was a forest called Jardes, where some three thousand rebels hid. They were surrounded and killed summarily (*J.W.* 7.210–215). This left only Masada as a locale of a major rebel force, and it, of course, would be the hardest to take.

Bassus died while in office and was replaced by Flavius Silva, either in late A.D. 72 or early 73. Masada was commanded by none other than the grandson of Judas the Galilean, Eleazar son of Jair (*J.W.* 2.447; 7.253). He and his Zealots were determined never to surrender to Rome. Silva built various siege camps around Masada to make certain that none could escape. He chose to build a gigantic siege ramp from the west, and he used Jewish workers to supply his troops with food and water, and also with protection because the defendants were not likely, it was thought, to kill their own people. Once the ramp had been completed, the battering ram was brought up and it breached the first wall, only to meet a pliable wooden and dirt wall within that could not be battered down. This wall was fired and the final assault was planned. But according to Josephus, Eleazar and his lieutenants made a suicide pact to deprive Rome of its victory and prevent the enslavement of their families. Ten men killed all, and then one of the ten killed the remaining ones and then himself. When the Romans attacked the next morning, they found the fortress filled with corpses and silence, except for a few women and children who had hidden in a water cistern and survived to tell the tale (*J.W.* 7.320–406). Thus was the last Jewish stronghold taken. It was perhaps during this expedition that Qumran also was taken by the Romans, or perhaps at an earlier date when Vespasian was campaigning in the area.

In order to ensure the "peace," Vespasian ordered a military colony to be established in Emmaus near Jerusalem, and eight hundred soldiers were settled there. Several cities were made autonomous (Jamnia and Azotus among them), and a new city was erected by Flavius Silva and named Flavia Neapolis (modern-day Nablus). Since it was at Caesarea Maritima that Vespasian was first proclaimed emperor, it too was made a colony city.

Needless to say, Jewish religious life changed considerably as a result of the outcome of the war and the destruction of the temple. J. Hayes and S. Mandell ably sum up the heart of the matter:

> With the destruction of the Temple, the animal sacrifice cult came to an end in Jerusalem. Along with the loss of the Temple, the priestly guilds lost occupational usefulness and prominence. Worship became concentrated in the services of the synagogue, devoid of sacrifice. Many ritual demands of the scriptures were spiritualized and sublimated so as to be obeyed without being observed. Ordinary life was reinterpreted to replicate aspects of the Temple service—charity and good deeds were understood as sacrifice and the table in the home replaced the altar. The teacher-rabbi replaced the priest as the religious authority and interpreter of the will and word of God.[2]

Perforce, such an approach seems likely to have been necessary, for Josephus makes clear that there was no hope of reestablishing the temple and its sacrifices in Jerusalem. The city became primarily a Roman camp for most of the Tenth Legion. Structurally, Jerusalem basically had been razed to the ground, so that "those who visited it could not believe it had ever been inhabited" (*J.W.* 7.3).

In Jamnia, the city that Vespasian had used as a settlement center for refugee Jews who voluntarily surrendered to the Romans (*J.W.* 4.444), a rabbinic school was established by Johanan ben Zacchai. Johanan actually had requested and received permission from the Romans to establish this school. It is said to have replaced the Sanhedrin as the highest Jewish authority in the land, other than Herod Agrippa. In other words, it replaced the Sadducees' major source of power. This Jamnian school assumed priestly functions, like setting the religious calendar. Naturally enough, since the Sadducean religion had focused

---

2. J. Hayes and S. Mandell, *The Jewish People in Classical Antiquity: From Alexander to Bar Kochba* (Louisville: Westminster John Knox, 1998), 210.

on the temple, their influence was bound to decline after A.D. 70. Priests and priestly lines continued to exist, but without their traditional functions. They still received some support from the people, and the laws about the priesthood and the temple continued to be learned, as the people hoped for a future restoration of their worship center. It is probable that works like 4 Ezra and Baruch show how fervently various Jews hoped for the restoration of their "old time religion."

The houses of Hillel and Shammai began to assert themselves, and Pharisaic Judaism became the standard by which other forms of Judaism were measured. In particular, there were even some theological tests, such as a belief in resurrection, for being a good Jew. A complete reexamination of all the laws in the Torah was undertaken. On the whole, it appears that legislative and legal decisions made at Jamnia were seen as binding.

This raises the question about the *Birkat ha-Minim*. The traditional reading of this matter involves the conclusion that a benediction was added to synagogue prayers that would be impossible for Jewish Christians to pronounce, one in essence anathematizing heretics such as the followers of Jesus. This was seen as one of the factors causing the great divide between Jews and Christians. This twelfth benediction read, "For apostates let there be no hope, and the kingdom of arrogance uproot. In a moment let the Nazarenes and the heretics be destroyed; let them be blotted from the Book of Life, and with the righteous not be inscribed. Blessed are you, O Lord, who loves judgment."

Of late, however, there has been considerable debate about the nature and substance as well as the date of this benediction. It now appears likely that such a benediction did exist in the 70s, but *without* the second sentence about the Nazarenes, which seems to have been added perhaps at the end of the first century or the beginning of the second. It is possible, but highly uncertain, that texts like John 9:22; 12:42, and 16:2 reflect this addition to the twelfth of the eighteen benedictions. Whatever its date, it probably reflects the fact that followers of Jesus were still coming to synagogues in the Holy Land even at the end of the first century A.D. On the whole, once the rebels were dealt with, things seem to have been relatively quiet in the Holy Land in the 70s.

From Q to Matthew

The letter *Q* is a cipher for the German word *Quelle*, which means "source." It is used in New Testament scholarship to refer to the material shared by Matthew and Luke but not found in Mark as an entity. Some scholars doubt the existence of Q, and have explained this "double tradition" found in Matthew and Luke by arguing either that Luke used Matthew or that Matthew used Luke. This is a minority opinion. Most scholars believe that there was a source, largely made up of Jesus' sayings, that circulated independently of the Gospels and was used by both the First and Third Evangelists. But when and where would this source have originated? This question is especially a pressing one in view of the fact that Mark does not appear to know or use Q (though a very few scholars think otherwise). The question becomes even more pressing if Mark was in Rome when he wrote his Gospel and if Luke was in Rome when he wrote his two-volume work, and Luke knew Q and Mark did not. This may suggest a significant time difference between the writing of Mark's Gospel and the writing of Luke-Acts.

A few words of caution are in order in discussing Q. First, we have no his-

Illustration 15.5 Mosaic from the floor of a house in Magdala showing a Galilean fishing boat of the first century A.D.

torical evidence of any kind suggesting that Q existed prior to the writing of any Gospels. It well may have, but that cannot simply be assumed to be the case. Second, we cannot conclude, even with a careful reconstruction of Q, that this material characterizes a particular community's way of thinking about Jesus *to the exclusion of their using other materials*, such as Gospels or passion narratives and the like. For instance, we have no reason to think that there were Galilean Christians whose faith was based solely on sayings material and who did not believe in the redemptive nature of Jesus' death and resurrection.[3]

3. On this point, see M. Hengel, *The Four Gospels and the One Gospel of Jesus Christ: An Investigation of the Collection and Origin of the Canonical Gospels* (London: SCM, 2000), 1–55.

Third, the *Gospel of Thomas*, which most scholars date to the late first or early second century, and which represents a gnosticizing of the Jesus tradition, cannot be seen as proof that very early collections of Jesus' sayings existed before Gospels were written, much less that such collections were seen as whole Gospels or full faith statements of particular communities.

It may well be that early collections of Jesus' sayings did exist, but it would seem that someone like Mark, who was connected to the Jerusalem and Roman churches, and who traveled with early Christians such as Paul and Barnabas and visited significant cities such as Antioch, would have known of such collections. If he did, his Gospel certainly does not show it; and more to the point, since his Gospel strives to portray Jesus as a great teacher, he would have been apt to use at least some Q material if he knew of it. Thus, I must conclude that probably, the Q material as we know it was collected and written down sometime between when Mark wrote his Gospel in A.D. 68–69 and when Matthew and Luke wrote theirs in the 70s or perhaps the early 80s. It may well be that the death of the pillar apostles, the destruction of the temple, and the demise of the Jerusalem mother church prompted the collection and inscription of this material. The eyewitnesses of Jesus' ministry were dying off and the sacred traditions needed to be preserved.

The Q material is interesting because it focuses by and large on teaching materials from Jesus' ministry. Since it is likely that the Jesus tradition went from a more Jewish form to one more accessible to Gentiles, Matthew's version of the Q material is probably closer to its original form than Luke's version, though this matter must be judged on a case by case basis. A comparison of Matthew to Mark shows a certain re-Judaizing of some material taken by Matthew from Mark, which warns us that the more Jewish form of a tradition may not always be closer to the original form.

The vast majority of scholars who have focused on the Q material have noted a dominant theme of eschatological warning throughout. Indeed, this material also has a polemical tone, urging repentance in the face of coming judgment. In other words, this material seems to reveal a significant overlap between the message of John the Baptist and the message of Jesus at various points. The other dominant theme besides eschatology is wisdom. In Q, Jesus appears as both an eschatological prophet and a sage brokering revealed wisdom, a sage who teaches in the form of parables and aphorisms.

What does this tell us about Christianity in the A.D. 70s? It reminds us that Christians, like Jews, were stunned by what happened in the

Jewish war, and they felt their sacred traditions threatened by the loss of the original religious center of their faith in Jerusalem and the loss of most of the original apostles and eyewitnesses. It also lets us know that Christians realized the need to write down their own sacred texts and not simply rely on the Hebrew Scriptures. In other words, they were developing their own sense of religious identity apart from Judaism. One major impetus in this direction may well have been that outsiders such as the Roman authorities were able to distinguish Jews from Christians and did so after the fire in Rome in A.D. 64. This distinction made it possible for Christians to be persecuted as part of a *superstitio* throughout the empire. This in turn made the Christian communities look inward and secure their religious heritage.

The preservation of Q material in both Matthew and Luke shows that this material was highly valued in several parts of the church, and also demonstrates that the church had not given up on the eschatological and sapiential teachings of Jesus. Eschatological hope was still alive in the last third of the first century A.D., as was the need for foundational teaching from Jesus on matters of practical living, and the fleshing out of the dominion of God on earth.

Later, perhaps some years later than the production of Q, came the production of the second Gospel, Matthew. We must take it seriously when Luke says that "many" had undertaken to write an account of the foundational events. This indicates multiple attempts, which in turn implies that Luke's Gospel was likely written after both Mark's and Matthew's, and perhaps after other, no longer extant attempts at Gospels as well. Also favoring this conclusion is that Matthew takes over the vast majority of his Markan source (well over 90 percent) as though he has no other precedent or template for a whole Gospel document, while Luke uses only about 50 percent of his Markan source.

If Matthew wrote after Mark, while having a copy of Mark before him, some time must be allowed for the circulation of Mark's Gospel to locales other than Rome.[4] In addition, it appears that he is writing in a locale that has both a significant quotient of Jewish Christians and a goodly number of Jews and synagogues in the vicinity. Furthermore, he is writing at a time when the foundational role of Peter in the church is being highlighted even more so than in Mark's day and community. Matthew softens the hard edges of the portrayal of the disciples in Mark; they are persons who exhibit faith, even if at times it is "little faith," whereas Mark stresses the complete failure of faith at various junctures. This suggests that Matthew was writing no earlier than the

---

4. Most scholars think that Matthew was produced in the East, perhaps in Syria or even in the Holy Land.

Illustration 15.6 A scroll case from Qumran.

mid-to-late 70s, when Christians needed to find positive role models to emulate as they went forward into the world without the somewhat protective umbrella of being part of a recognized world religion like Judaism. This church needed wisdom to know how to live, and it is not surprising that under these circumstances this Gospel not only provided the reader with five teaching discourses of Jesus (the one like the other great Jewish teacher, Moses) but also portrayed Jesus as a sage who offers revealed wisdom from God.[5]

But who is the author of this Gospel? First, it seems highly likely to have been written by a Jewish Christian concerned to show that Jesus fulfilled the law, and indeed affirmed that the law was not to pass away. Second, in view of his high degree of dependence on Mark, this evangelist was not likely an eyewitness of the ministry of Jesus. Why would an eyewitness, much less one of the Twelve, need to rely on a secondary source written by a non-eyewitness like Mark? It may well be that the most famous source of this Gospel writer's material was Matthew, but Matthew probably did not assemble this Gospel. Perhaps the special "M" material, such as Matthew 1–2, which is not found in any other Gospel, goes back to the tax collector who was one of the Twelve. The Gospel then would have been named after its most famous contributing source. Whatever the case, this

5. On this, see B. Witherington III, *Jesus the Sage: The Pilgrimage of Wisdom* (Minneapolis: Fortress, 1994), 335–68.

evangelist offers a much fuller and more didactic Gospel than does Mark, and presents a much fuller account of Jesus' life. Like Mark's Gospel, Matthew's Gospel takes the form of an ancient biography offering up highlights from the words and deeds of Jesus. The Jesus of this Gospel comes across as a master teacher, but also as a divine messianic figure, even the Wisdom of God come in the flesh. The Jesus of this Gospel is Immanuel, God with his people, who promises to be with them always.

Luke the Historian

Either in the later A.D. 70s or perhaps in the early 80s, Luke sat down to write not only the history of the Jesus movement but also the history of earliest Christianity. It may be that in his mind the really crucial events for Christianity lay behind him rather than in his own day. More to the point, he may have worried that Christians in the 70s, focusing singularly on their own difficulties, were in danger of forgetting their roots. Thus, he decided to undertake something that his forebears had not attempted, never mind accomplished: write as a Hellenistic historian, analyzing his Christian sources as a historian in the Greek tradition would do. He was concerned that all sorts of people, including some of the social elite like Theophilus, be able to embrace this new faith as one with a long and rich heritage, and as a religion that could exist peacefully within the Roman Empire. He wanted to make evident that faith in Jesus Christ was not just for the least, last, and the lost, but also for the most, first, and the found. He wanted to make clear that God's unstoppable Word and Spirit could and would cross any and all geographical, social, and ethnic boundaries to create a people of God who worshiped the one and only universal Savior. Here, we need more detail about the nature of Luke's historical project.

A Closer Look: *The Work of Luke the Historian*

There were, broadly speaking, two sorts of historical traditions that Luke could have followed in writing his monographs, the Roman and the Greek. The Roman tradition, as represented by writers like Livy or Tacitus, basically involved a retired person writing up memoirs, with some reference to documents available on site in Rome, and occasional reference to previous historical works in the same tradition. Furthermore, Roman historians tended to be historians of a city, Rome, rather than historians of a race, much less of a world. Of a very different sort was the Greek tradition, represented by figures like Thucydides, Polybius, and Ephorus. Doing actual research, traveling to sites, consulting eyewitnesses, and actually participating in some of the events in question was of the essence of this tradition. In Luke's case, it is quite clear from his prologue (Luke 1:1–4) what his intent is; and his occasional synchronisms with world history, along with the "we" passages in Acts, confirm that Luke is attempting to write in the Greek historigraphical tradition.

Luke's work stands out from the work of a writer like Livy or Josephus, who seek to do an "archaeology" of one particular group of people, whether it be Romans or Jews. Luke is chronicling a particular historical movement that is ethnically inclusive and religiously focused. This religious focus is why Luke spends more time than Thucydides would have done on prophecies, wonders, signs, miracles, and the like rather than on political and military history. But Luke is not writing about secret societies or a mystery cult. He is doing microhistory about an evangelistic religion that necessarily and intentionally has a public face. Its deeds are not "done in a corner" (see Acts 26:26), and its revelations are meant for public proclamation.

How can we know that Luke's Gospel is not like the other three Gospels, an ancient biography? Several key clues reveal that Luke wants even his first volume to be seen as an historical monograph. First, there is the prologue itself (Luke 1:1–4), which signals this intent quite clearly. Nothing like this appears at the beginning of the other three Gospels.[6] Second, there are Luke's various synchronisms with world history, such as we find in Luke 3 or Acts 18. This sort of approach to writing the narrative is absent from Matthew, Mark, and John. Third, notice how Luke does not mention Jesus at all at the beginning of his work, but rather, begins with the story of John the Baptist. Because of the nature of ancient documents, it was crucial for a work to signal its character up front. Ancient documents were written without separation of words or sentences, without divisions or chapter markers, and written on papyrus, which had to be gradually unrolled. In such circumstances, authors were wise to signal the nature of the document and its major focus or subject in the first sentence or two. What Luke says up front is that he is chronicling "the things that have happened among us." In other

6. The prologue in John 1 is a theological, not a historical, prologue that orients the reader to the nature of the main character of the biography, Jesus.

words, his focus will be on events, deeds, actions, and so on—historical activities—not on personalities or an individual's biography.

Jesus' life is seen as coming forth from the history of Israel and leading into the history of the church. Luke is indeed the narrator of salvation history, and so not surprisingly, even his Gospel begins and ends in the lives of people other than Jesus: John precedes Jesus, and the disciples wait for power from on high so that they can continue this great work of God in history. Fourth, the ending of Acts comports well with the nature of Luke's history writing. He wants to indicate that the story is open-ended and continuing even in his own day. The Gospel went from Galilee to Jerusalem, and Acts chronicles the progress of the Gospel from Jerusalem to the heart of the empire in Rome. But still, much work remains to be done. Ancient biographies try to bring a story to a close with the death of the major figure of the narrative, but Luke in his Gospel deliberately makes a segue to the next chapter of the story by recounting the ascension in both Luke 24 and Acts 1, which makes clear that matters have not come to a halt, but rather, have been left in the hands of the disciples. The historic events continue, with other names leading the movement. More could be said along these lines, but we must now consider the rhetorical factor in ancient history writing.

Rhetoric, the art of persuasion, was a discipline that had affected, some would say infected, all other forms of ancient discourse and writing, including the writing of history. Historians like Luke came to their task hoping to persuade people about their subject matter, in this case about the importance and viability of faith in Jesus as the means of world salvation. One of the clearest signs of Luke's rhetorical interests is the amount of space and care he devotes to speech material in both his volumes. These speeches are, perhaps with no exceptions, only summaries of speeches, and they have been shaped by Luke so as to conform to rhetorical conventions in various ways—for example, in the structure of the speeches and also in their orientation, whether judicial, deliberative, or epideictic. Luke's aim is to set the record straight for Theophilus about the truth about Jesus and the movement of his followers. Since the story takes many surprising twists and turns, this will require some persuasion, some rhetoric. Luke uses his speech material to bind the work as a whole together and to stress its major theological and ethical themes: personal salvation, repentance, amendment of life, religious community, and the like.

An ancient reader would pick up the rhetorical signals and would expect a serious historian writing on a serious subject to write in a responsible manner, but nonetheless to engage occasionally in rhetorical hyperbole for effect to make clear the great importance and wide impact of the matter in question (e.g., Luke's use of the word "all" from time to time—cf. Luke 2:1 to Acts 11:28, claims about "all the world"). A less serious historian who was concerned more with rhetorical effect than with historical substance—for instance, Livy—might well fabricate large quantities of speech material to make a dramatic story that would impress and appeal to and entertain the audience. Luke, however, is not in the entertainment business, and since his story has to do with very recent events of the first century, and since his religious claims about these events hinge on their having really transpired in various parts of the empire as attested by various eyewitnesses, he takes a much more circumspect approach in handling his material, not likely creating source material out of whole cloth just for rhetorical effect.

Thus, in Luke-Acts we have a two-volume historical monograph that grounds Luke's audience religiously and locates them socially as part of a crucial historical movement that was changing the world. Luke wishes to make clear that this movement is in continuity with the heritage of the Hebrew Scriptures, but as a movement has gone its own way and is no longer simply a sect of Judaism or a part of the synagogue. Its legitimacy rests in being a fulfillment of the ancient sacred prophecies and promises in the Hebrew Scriptures, and thus it deserves to be recognized as a legitimate religion in the empire and not miscast as a *superstitio*. Luke is an apologist writing to new converts who need reassuring about what they have committed themselves to, and in the end he has written an effective two-volume work that makes clear that Christianity was not, and was not meant to be, a mere philosophy, or merely like ancient religions that focused on temples, priests, and sacrifices; rather, Christianity was a historical religion that sought to ground itself in a particular story and desired to live as a community shaped by that story.[7]

In regard to the composition of Luke-Acts, I offer the following hypothesis. A careful study of the Greek text of this two-volume work reveals that Acts has a stylistic roughness missing from the Gospel of

7. For an in-depth discussion of these topics, see B. Witherington III, *Acts of the Apostles: A Socio-rhetorical Commentary* (Grand Rapids: Eerdmans, 1998), 1–102.

Luke. I submit that the Gospel was revised, while Acts remains in its original form, and perhaps, Luke lost his life before he was able to revise his second volume. Taking the prologue to the Gospel seriously, we see that Luke embarked on his writing project only after several others had written at least a Gospel. Since Luke uses Mark, he surely must have taken up his pen after A.D. 68–70, and since he knows of other such attempts at Gospels, his work must have occurred later than the early 70s as well. This makes it likely that he wrote at least in the late 70s or early 80s. If Luke was in his thirties when he joined Paul on his travels in the early or middle 50s, he would have been sixty or so in A.D. 80. Perhaps his own age is partly what prompted him to write when he did, and perhaps the fact that he was getting old and not able to travel and consult eyewitnesses further about the period of the mid-60s to late 70s explains why he stopped the narrative where he did. Whatever the case in these conjectures, there can be no disputing that we would be lost in any attempt to write a New Testament history without his two-volume work. There are no other comparable chronicles of the early Christian period written during the time that the events were transpiring. This very fact may explain why Luke felt it so important to take pen in hand. In the end, Luke had no peers and apparently few imitators before Eusebius wrote centuries later. It is Luke, rather than his descendant Eusebius, who should be called the father of early church history.

Imperator Interruptus—The Case of Titus

It is quite possible that Luke was writing his monographs while Titus was ruling in Rome from A.D. 79 to 81. Accordingly, here is a good place to speak about the period of that short reign before concluding this chapter. On June 24, A.D. 79, Titus succeeded his father on the throne, the first naturally born heir to do so since the beginning of the empire. He was only thirty-nine when he became emperor, but he had been groomed for the post for a long time. Quite naturally, apprehensions arose when Titus took power, but these were to be quickly dispelled. There were to be no treason trials and no executions; indeed, Titus even publicly flogged informers. Titus had much going for him. He was handsome, very bright, and a war hero. In addition, he was fluent in Greek as well as Latin. He had not, however, produced any male heir (having only one daughter, Julia), and he spoke openly about his younger brother Domitian succeeding him. Nevertheless, he did not put much trust in Domitian, who was ambitious and harbored some resentments about playing second fiddle to Titus when Vespasian bestowed advancements.

Titus had his work cut out for him when he assumed the throne, especially because of natural disasters that happened in the first year of his reign. First, a fire in Rome destroyed the recently renovated temple of Jupiter as well as Porticus Octaviae with its major libraries. This necessitated a major rebuilding program. Then, on August 24, A.D. 79, Vesuvius erupted, destroying Pompeii and Herculaneum. Titus had a personal interest in this disaster, for he lost his close friend, the naturalist Pliny the Elder, who went to watch the eruption out of natural curiosity and stayed to rescue frantic victims only to be overcome by the fumes, ash, and lapilli. Titus acted quickly, assigning senators by lot to administer the ruined cities, and he gave the property of those who died without a will to those who lived but had lost their property and livelihood in the disaster.

Titus was a builder, like his father, who not only undertook the reconstruction of the temple of Jupiter but also completed the project that his father had begun, the giant Colosseum. He gave lavish games lasting one hundred days at the opening of this magnificent facility—surprisingly so, since he, again like his father, was a frugal man. And indeed, thereafter Titus became known not for lavish spending on himself, but for his munificence towards others. Suetonius (*Titus* 8) has this to say about the princeps:

> Titus was naturally kind-hearted. . . . He also had a rule never to dismiss any petitioner without leaving him some hope that his request would be favorably considered. Even when warned by his staff how impossible it would be to make good such promises. Titus maintained that no one ought to go away disappointed from an audience with the emperor. One evening at dinner, realizing that he had done nobody any favor throughout the entire day, he spoke these memorable words: "My friends, I have wasted a day."

He was merciful even to those who plotted against him, forgiving them, even promoting some of them. Titus was also to be renowned for the baths he built in Rome that were to bear his name.

Titus died under somewhat suspicious circumstances. He had barely reached his forty-second year when he was stricken with a fever and died quite quickly. On September 21, A.D. 81, he breathed his last at his ancestral country home in Reate. Rumors, never proved, circulated that Domitian helped him out of this world. Not surprisingly, his untimely demise was celebrated by Jews in the empire; otherwise, his death produced great mourning. Rome had enjoyed just over a decade of very stable government. It remained to be seen what would happen when the more mercurial and ambitious Domitian took the throne.

In general, after the disasters of the period A.D. 64–70, Christians had a certain amount of breathing room to regroup during the stable reigns of Vespasian and Titus. There was time to shore up community life, and even to write several historical works chronicling the foundational story about Jesus and his followers. Things would become difficult once more after Domitian took his place on the throne.

Chapter 16

The Dominion of Domitian

A.D. 81–96

The last twenty years of the first century A.D. saw the dying off of the remaining eyewitnesses and apostles. It also saw the revival of attention of a negative sort being given to Christians by Roman officials. We must consider first the contours of the emperor Domitian's reign.

Domitian as *Dominus*

Domitian was proclaimed emperor by the praetorians on September 13, A.D. 81. Domitian was a man of a very different sort than his brother and his father. Unlike Titus, Domitian apparently had not received a good education, as is reflected in the fact that others drafted his speeches, letters, and official rulings. Also unlike Titus, Domitian was no war hero. Indeed, his father had refused to send him on military campaigns, even though he requested it many times. Having gained an early taste of power in A.D. 69–70, when he ruled in his father's stead until Vespasian returned to Rome, "what Domitian wanted most was glory in war and a controlling hand in administration."[1] He possessed the temperament of a tyrant, and he was not able to win the hearts of his people as Titus had, due in part to his heavy-handed manner. His study of astrology left him both legalistic and fatalistic. He had few social graces and treated with contempt even those he was close to and broke bread with. What "fills Tacitus and Pliny with horror is no occasional act of vengeance or outburst of passion, but the fact that Domitian's cruelty was calculated and deliberate, conceived and carried out in pursuit of a definite aim."[2]

Domitian was a ruler insecure enough to view any near equals or even any powerful persons as threats. Much of his reign was spent trying to make sure that the senate, the army, and even the people saw themselves as his servants ready to heed his every beck and call. Indeed, he alienated many by insisting that everyone, even patrician senators, address him as *dominus et deus*, "lord and god" (Suetonius, *Domitian* 13.2; Dio Cassius, *Roman History* 67.4.7). To maintain control, he held the consulship seventeen times during his reign, far more than any other emperor.

Domitian had the opportunity for military fame early in his reign when trouble arose in Germany. The difficulties were not major, but Domitian made much of his victories there. After operations were completed in late A.D. 83, Domitian issued coins proclaiming his great victory, and he wore the garb of a military hero, even when attending the senate. He also assumed the cognomen Germanicus. To make sure that he was properly appreciated, he also took on the role of censor, and thereby controlled the personnel in the senate. At one point he even renamed the months September and October after himself, calling them Germanicus and Domitianus, a practice that was, not surprisingly, dropped after Domitian's death.

Domitian showed signs of being quite like Nero as well, in that he affected being cultured and was a panhellene. He wrote poetry and instituted quadrennial games in Rome following the Greek model. This meant that Rome would have its own Olympic games complete with chariot racing, athletics, and literature contests. Domitian attended these games in Greek dress wearing a golden crown, and even more galling to traditional Romans, he had the judges wear crowns bearing

---

1. S. A. Cook et al., eds., *The Cambridge Ancient History*, vol. 11, rev. ed. (Cambridge: Cambridge University Press, 1954), 22.

2. Ibid., 23.

his image alongside those of other gods he favored, such as Minerva and Jupiter. For his contests in the Greek manner, Domitian built an odeum and a stadium in the Campus Martius. He also held mock naval battles and wild-beast hunts. Like Nero, he was an emperor who knew the importance of "bread and circuses" to the ordinary people.

Like Nero, Domitian had a great taste for building and refurbishing, and wanted a lavish palace for himself. He restored various buildings damaged in the fires of A.D. 64 and 80, including the Saepta, the Pantheon, the temples of Isis and Sarapis (placing imported Egyptian obelisks in front of them), the baths of Agrippa, and the Porticus Octaviae, which had important libraries. To replenish the libraries, he sent scribes to Alexandria to copy many books in its great library. No expense was spared in the restoration of the temple of Jupiter, which was given columns of Pentellic marble, and doors plated with gold and gilded tiles costing some twelve thousand talents. He also had architects spend eleven years refurbishing the royal palace. Further, in a temple in Ephesus dedicated to himself, he erected an enormous cult statue.

If there was discomfort at home with the tyrant Domitian and his enormous taste for self-glorification, there was also major unrest abroad. In A.D. 86, the Dacian kingdom, which had recently been amalgamated into one entity, inflicted a crushing defeat on a Roman army. Domitian, to his credit, was able to deal with this crisis, suppressing the revolt of King Decebalus, but his troubles were far from over. In 88, news reached Domitian that the legate of upper Germany, Antonius Saturninus, had been acclaimed imperator by his legions and was in open revolt. This treasonous act completely shocked Domitian, a shock that never entirely wore off, as he became even more suspicious and tyrannical during the remaining eight years of his reign. Saturninus had planned well and had summoned barbarian tribes to assist him, but the legate of lower Germany, Norbanus, knowing what was afoot, took matters into his own hands before the emperor could arrive with reinforcements. Saturninus's head was cut off, sent to Rome, and put on a pike for all to view the fate of those who tried to overthrow this emperor.

Domitian never was able to exorcise his demons of suspicion, and increasingly from A.D. 88 he listened to numerous informers, few of whom had any reliable information. The emperor took action against all sorts of people. In 89, he banished philosophers and astrologers from Rome. A provincial governor of Asia and the governor of Britain were executed for treasonous acts that appear really to have been trivial infractions. Not long thereafter, two rhetoricians were executed for reciting exercises against tyranny and for lampooning the emperor. Important for our purposes is the clear evidence that it was not just Romans who bore the brunt of Domitian's rage; it was also provincials. For example, the wealthy Athenian Hipparchus, grandfather of the famous rhetorician Herodes Atticus, was tried and executed, and his lands confiscated. After the death of the famous patrician Agricola in A.D. 93, Domitian felt free to take direct action against any remaining prorepublican patricians. Various Romans who had written plays or memoirs of famous earlier Romans were brought up on the flimsiest of charges and condemned, with their books being burned. For example, Helvidius Priscus the younger had written a play about Paris and Oenone, but the paranoid Domitian thought it was a veiled critique of his relationship with his own wife.

To pay for his many building campaigns, Domitian imposed crushing taxation in the provinces, including the poll tax on Jews, which was so rigorously enforced that many Jews were taken to court when they did not pay promptly (Dio Cassius, *Roman History* 67.4.6; Suetonius, *Domitian* 12.2). Domitian's severity continued to shock those who remembered the clemency of Vespasian and Titus. For example, when three vestal virgins were found guilty of having lovers, the lovers were exiled, but the women were given only a choice of modes of execution. Later, when the head vestal virgin also was found guilty of this same infidelity, she was buried alive and her lovers were beaten to death with rods. Some of Domitian's severity was applauded by traditional Romans—for example, his restrictions against prostitutes. They were not allowed to accept legacies or inheritances, and child prostitution was discouraged. But far too often, Domitian exercised severity in unjust ways.[3]

This background brings us to the case of Flavius Clemens, a cousin of Domitian married to the emperor's niece Domitilla. They had been so much in Domitian's favor that he proclaimed two of their children his heirs in A.D. 90 and appointed the great Quintilian to be their tutor. In 95, Clemens was *consul ordinarius*, but as soon as he stepped down from office, he was summoned to answer the charge of being *athe-*

---

3. The interesting story in Eusebius (*Hist eccl.* 3.19.1–3.20.7) about the grandsons of Jesus' brother Jude appearing before Domitian as descendants of the royal Davidic line is believable, considering how paranoid the Flavian clan was about prophecy in general, and in particular, prophecies about world rulers coming from the East, supposedly about Vespasian and his kin. Eusebius is quoting an earlier source, Hegesippus, who has to be read critically. It is far more likely that Domitian would have executed these relatives of Jesus than have called off the persecution of Christians because of their eloquent testimony. See the discussion in R. Bauckham, *Jude and the Relatives of Jesus in the Early Church* (Edinburgh: Clark, 1990), 94–106.

otēs—not atheism in the modern sense, but rather, a neglect of traditional Roman religion. There is reason, on the basis of evidence from the catacombs (the Coemiterium Domitillae), to think that Clemens and Domitilla were Christian sympathizers if not Christians. Domitilla was exiled, Clemens executed.

During the last three or four years of his reign, Domitian resorted to a litmus test of loyalty for those brought up on trial before him (see Dio Cassius, *Roman History* 67.14.1–2). This test involved offering a sacrifice before the image of the emperor. Anyone who refused could be formally charged with "atheism" and punished accordingly. This, apparently, is what happened to Clemens. What Dio Cassius in fact says in defining atheism is that it involves "those who had been carried away into Jewish customs" (*Roman History* 67.14.2). Now Judaism, a religion long familiar to and recognized by Roman authorities was not likely to be branded in this fashion, even by Domitian. The majority of Christians whom Domitian was likely to come across, however, were former pagans, and the Roman authorities recognized Christianity as a "Jewish superstition," that is, a nonrecognized (by either Jews or Romans) offshoot of Judaism. This was a religion inappropriate for Romans to practice, not least because it meant not only abandoning the worship of the traditional gods, but also abandoning the worship of the emperor, and could in fact lead to polemics against such forms of worship. Under these circumstances, it is quite believable that Christians, like Clemens, underwent persecution and in some cases even execution at the hands of the ever paranoid Domitian, especially during the last three or four years of his reign. Christians certainly would not be hailing him as "lord and my god" (cf. John 20:28).

But there is even more to this story. It turned out to be a freedman named Stephanus, who had been procurator of Domitilla, who attacked and killed Domitian on September 16, A.D. 96, while ostensibly trying to hand him a document. In this environment, replete with knowledge of Domitian's persecutions, one of the last documents in the New Testament was written—the Revelation of John. And it is likely no accident that Thomas's climactic confession of faith in Jesus in the Gospel of John, "my Lord and my God," is a direct echo of what Domitian demanded of others. Indeed, the Johannine corpus in general was written under the cloud of tyranny that hovered over the empire during the reign of Domitian.

The End of the Herodian Line

We have very little information of any sort about what happened in Judea and Galilee in the A.D. 80s and 90s. Surely, early Judaism was regrouping, with Pharisees leading the way. But there can only have been strong resentment for what had happened to the tribute money, now diverted to the temple of Jupiter in Rome; and adding insult to injury, the tribute was now being exacted of all Jews, even Diaspora Jews, and indeed exacted with great stringency.

The remnants of the Herodian line finally died out when Herod Agrippa died sometime in A.D. 92 or 93. After the Jewish war, he had been rewarded with the district of Acra in Lebanon, and he had regained control of his four districts in Judea. With the demise of Agrippa II, these four districts reverted to being a part of the Judean province under the control of the procurator.

The Peter Principle

The reference to a widespread knowledge of Paul's letters (2 Pet. 3:15–16), among other features, make it likely that 2 Peter was composed well after the demise of Paul, and of Peter as well. The author has relied on earlier traditions from the letter of Jude and from a testimony of Peter to address his own audience. He asserts clearly from the outset that Christ is "our God and Savior" (1:1) and also "our Lord and Savior" (1:11; 2:20), claims that stand in contradiction to the claims of Domitian.

Especially notable is the eschatological material in 2 Pet. 3:3–13, where the author tries to revive a flagging hope that the Lord will return during the audience's lifetime. He lives in an age not only of stress and persecution, but also of ridicule for the eschatological hope: "Where is the promise of his coming?" (3:4). The author is writing to a church that had received correspondence from Paul, perhaps the church in Corinth or Philippi, or one in Asia or Galatia (3:15). But Paul's writing is well in the past, and various Christians, including the author of this document, are struggling to understand his words. The bulk of 2 Peter 2 is devoted to a diatribe against false prophets and teachers, adapted and adopted from Jude. The author refers to "your apostles," who spoke in the past to the audience (3:2). But the warning about the presence of false teachers and prophets and the reference to apostles having spoken in the past show that the audience no longer has apostles to consult. They must rely on traditions from earlier authorities like Jude and Peter and Paul for their guidance.

Second Peter is a document that reflects the condition of the church in the 80s and 90s, looking to earlier sources, especially apostolic sources, for inspiration, guidance, and exhortation. This document may well be the last document written within the New Testament era. It speaks of the absolute destruction of the world, and notice that there is no exhortation to obey and honor the governing authorities (cf. 1 Pet. 2:13–14; Rom. 13:1). In spirit, 2 Peter is closer to Revelation than to 1 Peter.

The Johannine Community and Its Documents

There is broad consensus among New Testament scholars that some relationship exists among the documents known as the Johannine corpus, which includes John's Gospel, Revelation, and the three Johannine epistles. There is also broad consensus that this literature was produced in the last decade or so of the first century A.D. Thus, this literature in part reflects and responds to situations that existed during the reign of Domitian. We must bear in mind that John's Gospel is not a transcript of what was happening in the time when the documents were penned; sometimes, Johannine scholars have been guilty of too much reading between the lines of the Fourth Gospel. Nevertheless, there are some clues in the Fourth Gospel and in the Johannine literature in general that help us to get our bearings, but each of these documents must be taken on its own merits.

We are fortunate that Revelation identifies its audience. John of Patmos is writing to a group of churches in Asia that are all on the same road and are mentioned in the order that one would reach them traveling on this road—beginning with the church in Ephesus, then Smyrna, Pergamum, Thyatira, Sardis, Philadelphia, and ending in Laodicea. The locales of the first and last of these churches also are places where there were Pauline churches; but perhaps some thirty years after Paul's death, these churches should no longer be called Pauline churches. This, of course, is based on the majority scholarly conclusion that Revelation was written in the A.D. 90s, not 60s. This conclusion needs some further explanation here.

The following seven features of Revelation favor the conclusion that this document was written in the 90s. First, the twelve apostles are mentioned as an integral part of the foundations of the new Jerusalem (21:14), and nothing in the initial letters to the churches suggests that any of these apostles are still alive when Revelation is written. In other words, the apostolic presence is in the past and in the future but not in the author's present. The author does not call himself an apostle; rather, he is a prophet or a seer (1:1–3). Second, the church in Ephesus has lost its first love, and the church in Laodicea has existed long enough to become lukewarm in its devotion. This likely reflects a time later than the Pauline era, for Paul complains about no such thing when he addresses churches in this region. In addition, Laodicea was one of the cities devastated by the earthquake in the Lycus Valley in

A.D. 62. The church there surely would have been affected by such an event. Had John been writing shortly after the earthquake, it seems unlikely that spiritual lethargy would be the main problem to be addressed. Third, the overall impression of the vision recorded in Revelation 12 is that the church, depicted as a woman, has been under persecution from Satan for a considerable period of time and is going through a wilderness period that calls for hiding. This description could fit the Jerusalem church in the 60s quite well; but the end of the vision speaks of Satan going off and making war on the rest of that church's children who keep the commandments of God and hold to the testimony of Jesus, and this may suggest a later time. Notice, for example, that the church in Pergamum had a martyr named Antipas, and lives near the throne of Satan (2:13), likely a reference to the emperor cult. This description better suits a time in the 90s, after the emperor cult and persecution in Asia had been a reality for some time.

Fourth, Revelation 13 clearly seems to be a critique of an emperor, but which emperor? On the one hand, the mortally wounded beast of Rev. 13:3 might be an allusion to the Pisonian conspiracy against Nero in A.D. 65, but in fact, Nero received no wounds, mortal or otherwise, on that occasion. On the other hand, there was indeed a rumor following Nero's suicide in A.D. 68 that he would come back from the dead, perhaps leading the Parthian hordes, and devastate Rome. The worship of the beast clearly seems to refer to the emperor cult, and the crucial verse on this is Rev. 13:15, where those who refuse to worship the image of the beast are to be killed. We saw previously that Domitian was in various ways like Nero, and in this context, the fear that Domitian might be Nero come back from the dead makes sense. We also saw that it was Domitian who used worship of the image of the emperor as a litmus test of loyalty. The descriptions in Revelation 13 better suit the time of the reign of Domitian—he was, after all, the one who insisted on the moniker "lord and god." Fifth, there is wide scholarly agreement that some kind of relationship exists between the ideas in Revelation and those in the Fourth Gospel. The focus on the Logos and the Lamb in both works, for instance, is hardly a coincidence. It appears that John of Patmos had absorbed some of the teaching in the Fourth Gospel, affecting the way he articulated his visions. In the Fourth Gospel, the climactic confession of Jesus comes in John 20:28 when Thomas worships Jesus, calling him "my Lord and my God." This acclamation and its placement in this Gospel seem to be a challenge to the claims of Domitian for the right to such titles. If, as many scholars believe, the Fourth Gospel was assembled during the reign of Domitian, then it is likely that Revelation was as well. Sixth, the Johannine epistles, particularly 2 John, speak of a time when many deceivers and antichrists are loose in the world, misleading the Christians. This is a time of internal divisions over the christological confession, and when some Christians are denying "Christ come in the flesh"; in other words, they are either denying the incarnation or taking a docetic or gnostic approach to the humanity of Jesus. We know that in the second century, such christological issues indeed arose in the Asian church, and it is more likely than not that these letters were written sufficiently close to that time to be dealing with the initial stages of this problem. Seventh, John 21, the epilogue to the Fourth Gospel, alludes to Peter's death and to the fact that the Beloved Disciple has died (at a time later than Peter), and the Evangelist clearly states that Jesus had not promised that the Beloved Disciple definitely would live until the second coming. This makes best sense if the Beloved Disciple had long outlived Peter, but finally had died and Jesus had still not returned.

In light of these seven factors, the following reconstruction seems to fit the evidence best.

The communities addressed in all the Johannine documents are in Asia, in and near Ephesus. The Beloved Disciple was a, or the, founding pastor of these congregations. He is "the old man" who addresses some of the outlying congregations in 1–3 John, probably writing from Ephesus. These letters may have been written as early as the late 80s, but clearly at a time well after these congregations have been well established and have had time to develop difficulties, fight false teachers, suffer schisms, and the like. Sometime in the early 90s, the Beloved Disciple (whose name may have been John, though the text of the Fourth Gospel does not say so) died.[4] In my view, this disciple was not one of the Twelve, but rather, a Judean disciple with close connections to the high priest who lived in Jerusalem and hosted Jesus and the others during Jesus' final Passover. In other words, he was an eyewitness of the Judean parts of Jesus' ministry but not one of the Galilean disciples.[5] After the death of the Beloved Disciple, someone in the Johannine community assembled and edited the memoirs he had written down (see John 21:24; cf. 19:35), probably in the early 90s. At some point in the early to mid-90s there was a crackdown in Asia on those either who were disparaging the emperor cult or preaching Jesus pub-

4. Several interesting conjectures are afloat as to who the Beloved Disciple was. For the argument that he was Lazarus, see F. Baltz, *Lazarus and the Fourth Gospel Community* (Lewiston, N.Y.: Mellen, 1996). For the argument that he was Thomas, see J. H. Charlesworth, *The Beloved Disciple: Whose Witness Validates the Gospel of John?* (Valley Forge, Pa.: Trinity, 1995).

5. See B. Witherington III, *John's Wisdom: A Commentary on the Fourth Gospel* (Louisville: Westminster John Knox, 1995), 1–46.

licly and causing the neglect of that cult. John the prophet was taken prisoner, tried, and exiled to the penal colony on Patmos. There he had various visions, which he wrote down, put into an epistolary framework, and sent off to the Johannine churches in Asia. This document likely went out before the end of the reign of Domitian, probably no later than about A.D. 95–96. Having looked at the social location of these documents, we now need to consider briefly their content, beginning with the epistles that seem to be the earliest of the documents.

The letters of John are in fact not all letters. First John is better seen as a homily of some sort, while 2 and 3 John are indeed brief letters. Second John is a letter written to a church, while 3 John is written to an individual church leader. We will examine these letters in reverse numerical order.

Some church members visited with Gaius in an outlying area. They have come back to the "old man" and made clear that Gaius is faithful to the truth of the gospel as the Beloved Disciple had preached it. Third John appears to be a letter of reference for the missionaries who have come from the Beloved Disciple's church and are now with Gaius. Verses 6–8 amount to a request for hospitality and then traveling funds for these missionaries to get them to their next destination. The church situation where Gaius is appears to be difficult. Apparently, the leader of the church in question, Diotrephes, has rejected the authority of the Beloved Disciple and has turned away his emissaries. Thus, the Beloved Disciple must appeal to another member of the church, Gaius, to host and help these missionaries. Things have gotten so bad that Diotrephes has spread false charges about the Beloved Disciple, and he refuses to welcome the missionaries, and even expels from the church those who do so (v. 10). Another Christian, Demetrius, is vouched for by the Beloved Disciple, perhaps because he is the bearer of this letter. The Beloved Disciple plans to come personally to deal with Diotrephes and the church crisis. In the meantime, Gaius will do well to host and help the missionaries sent from the Beloved Disciple's church.[6]

Second John is a word of encouragement to urge the congregation in question to continue to walk in the truth, particularly the christological truth. Notice that the Beloved Disciple rejoices that *some* of those he is writing to have been faithful (v. 4). This must be contrasted with

6. Third John 12 is interesting in view of its similarity to John 21:24, which suggests that this phrase about true testimony was used regularly by the Beloved Disciple to vouch for his own authority and veracity. This may well have been necessary, as he was not an apostle or one of the Twelve. Indeed, it may be that he referred to himself simply as one of the Ephesian elders, perhaps one of the original and church-planting ones (on which see Acts 20:17).

v. 7, which states that *many* deceivers have gone forth from the community into the world who do not confess the incarnation of Jesus, or the true humanity of Jesus, or both. The Beloved Disciple labels such deceivers as antichrists. Verse 10 gives explicit orders to bar from the house church those who do not teach the orthodox teaching about Christ. It has been conjectured, and is certainly possible, that this very letter was being used by Diotrephes as justification to keep out the missionaries referred to in 3 John. The Beloved Disciple, who does not call himself that, but rather, refers to himself as the elder or "the old man," says that he hopes to visit the congregation soon. It may be that 2 and 3 John were sent simultaneously by means of Demetrius, but we cannot be sure. What can be said is that the Beloved Disciple is dealing with a church in severe trouble. It has endured a church split, with many leaving and only some remaining faithful and staying. The language of orthodoxy and the polemics against betrayers and opponents reflects the seriousness of the situation the author is addressing.

First John appears to be a homily, perhaps preached after the crisis referred to in 2 John, for the antichrists again are mentioned in 1 John 2:18–25, and as in 2 John, they are said to have gone out from among the congregation. This, then, may be the sermon that the Beloved Disciple preached when he visited the congregation he had written to in 2 John. The sermon is characterized by stark contrasts between sinning and not sinning, between orthodoxy and heterodoxy, and between loving and hating the brothers and sisters. The Beloved Disciple believes that his spiritual children are in the middle of a spiritual warfare zone, and have a choice of believing and acting like children of God or believing and acting like children of the devil. The strong exhortations to love and unitive behavior reflect a community that has been fractured by tensions and divisions.

The two major exhortations of the sermon are the exhortation to faithfulness to the confession that Jesus has come in the flesh, and the exhortation to love one another and love God. Lack of such faithfulness and love is likely the schismatics' chief violation. Strong emphasis on Jesus having come by means of his incarnation and death and by the Spirit is made in 1 John 5:6–8. The author understands that to deny the incarnation or true humanity of Jesus is to deny his atoning death (see 3:16).[7] Finally, the author stresses that the key to having eternal life is faithfulness to the creed about Christ and to the command to love God and one another.

7. On the much controverted 1 John 5:6–8 and its correlation with John 3:5–6, see B. Witherington III, "The Waters of Birth: John 3:5 and 1 John 5:6–8," *NTS* 35 (1989): 155–60.

The Gospel of John is one of the great first-century documents, biblical or otherwise. This book is said to be shallow enough for a child to wade in and deep enough for an elephant to drown in. It, like Matthew and Mark, takes the form of an ancient biography meant to provide resources to help Christian teachers convince people that Jesus is the Christ and the Son of God (John 20:31). In other words, this Gospel is intended as a teaching tool for evangelism, particularly with Gentiles. Note that all the names mentioned in 3 John are Gentile names, and 3 John 7 refers to accepting no support from Gentiles. When we couple this with the references in John to going to the Greeks, and the hostile discussions with Jews and references to being cast out of synagogues, we may be reasonably sure that the main audience for this material is not a Jewish one. Indeed, it appears likely that this Gospel was put together after the parting of the ways between Jews and the followers of Jesus in this region. Perhaps a further confirmation of this parting between Jews and the Johannnine community is Rev. 2:9, which speaks of a "synagogue of Satan" in Smyrna.

The Fourth Gospel focuses intensely on Jesus. The author tries to establish clearly both the divinity and the humanity of Jesus. The prologue is the key to understanding Jesus, but of course, the characters in the narrative have not read that paragraph. They do not know that Jesus is the Word come down from heaven, nor do they know where he is going. The origins and destiny of Jesus reveal his identity, but the Fourth Evangelist believes that Jesus' words and deeds do so as well, and the latter is what takes up the bulk of the Gospel material. Basically, this Gospel has four parts: (1) a prologue and (2) an epilogue, in between which is (3) a series of seven sign narratives coupled with seven "I am" sayings and discourses, and then (4) a lengthy farewell discourse linked to a passion narrative. It is clear that the author is not following the Markan outline, not only from this general description of contents, but also from individual factors, such as the temple cleansing occuring at the beginning in the Fourth Gospel (John 2; cf. Mark 11), and John recording only one Galilean miracle also found in Mark, the feeding of the five thousand. Instead, this Gospel has the singular reporting of things like the healing of a man born blind (John 9) and the raising of Lazarus (John 11). In other words, it offers a reporting of Judean miracles instead of Galilean ones, which supports well the theory that the Beloved Disciple was a Judean disciple.[8]

---

8. Probably one of the telltale signs that the Fourth Evangelist is not the Beloved Disciple is that in the Epistles of John, the author calls himself the elder, or the old man. It is unlikely that a disciple would bill himself as the disciple whom Jesus loved, but it is understandable how his disciples, who revered him, would call him this.

The Fourth Evangelist, as a biographer of Jesus, understands that it is crucial to explain why Jesus died the way he did, since it was widely believed in antiquity that how a person died revealed his or her true character. Thus in John, from the very first chapter, Jesus is the Lamb of God who takes away the sins of the world. From the outset, he is destined to die in a salvific way, and to be the Savior of the world. And so a virtual parade of different sorts of people comes to meet with and hear Jesus—the Baptist, Nicodemus, the Samaritan woman, the Greeks, and so on. In this Gospel, Jesus does not call disciples; they are attracted to him by spiritual gravity. Also noteworthy is that John omits all stories of Jesus as an exorcist and concentrates instead on healings and nature miracles (including the unique story of the Cana miracle). Jesus appears as a sage whom the world should embrace, a healer whom the world can approach, a savior whom both Jews and Gentiles can relate to. The battle with Satan is further in the background, unlike in Mark. And there is no veiled messianic character here, again unlike in Mark. Rather, here Jesus speaks as the great I AM and offers lengthy discourses that Gentiles can ponder rather than enigmatic parables. Jesus presents himself as Wisdom come in the flesh, the veritable Logos, and his discourses are like those of the Jewish sapiential tradition (e.g., Wisdom of Solomon). Our author is a Jew, but is writing largely for Gentiles. Here is presented a Jesus who is user-friendly for all first-century audiences.

The Fourth Evangelist is a masterful storyteller, as tales like the healing of the blind man or the raising of Lazarus show. He also has a flair for the dramatic, creating both a crescendo of miracles (climaxing with the healing of the man born blind and the raising of Lazarus, which foreshadows Jesus' own resurrection) and a crescendo of confessions that become increasingly adequate until finally the confession of Thomas in John 20 matches the implications of the prologue and in fact counters the similar claims of a certain emperor.

Much more could be said along these lines, but here it is important to notice that this Gospel probably represents a very long period of reflection and meditation on the significance of the Christ event. The Beloved Disciple is an eyewitness, but he has ruminated long on the meaning of what he long ago heard and saw and touched (see 1 John 1), and has reflected deeply on how best to present this Jewish story to the Greco-Roman world. The Spirit indeed had gradually given him more and more insight into the story, and inspiration for how to tell the tale for a new day and audience. Thus, salvation is described as eternal life, and revelation as heavenly light. Notable by its absence is any significant emphasis on future eschatology. Rather, the focus is on receiving eternal life here and now. In short, the emphasis and the way that the message is presented are very different from what we find in Revelation, to which we now turn.

The Book of Revelation is an example of apocalyptic literature, and here we must look more closely at this genre of writing.

A **Closer** Look: *Apocalyptic Literature*

It is appropriate that this last excursus deals with literature that focuses on the last things. An apocalypse is, as the SBL Seminar on this subject has noted, "a genre of revelatory literature with a narrative framework, in which a revelation is mediated by an otherworldly being to a human recipient, disclosing a transcendent reality which is both temporal, insofar as it envisages eschatological salvation, and spatial, insofar as it involves another supernatural world."[9]

This literature attempts to give perspective to present mundane reality by setting it in the framework of both the supernatural world and the future.[10] In Revelation, for example, the author begins with the situation of the churches in John's own day, and tries to help them understand and endure their own experiences, which involve marginalization, persecution, suffering, even martyrdom, by giving them the divine perspective on their situation. This literature quite clearly is minority literature, and in particular, for those experiencing significant injustices in life. In fact, apocalyptic literature is literature that could have originated only once there was a viable belief in an afterlife or a final day of reckoning, where wrongs that go unaddressed in this life will be righted.

It is a mistake to assume that apocalyptic literature is simply about matters eschatological, for on the one hand, the focus can be on what happens up there in heaven rather than out there in the future (see e.g., the Similitudes of *1 Enoch*), and on the other hand, much eschatology, both Jewish and Christian, does not take an apocalyptic form. Apocalyptic is primarily a matter of the use of a distinctive form (visions with bizarre and hyperbolic metaphors and images). At the heart of apocalyptic is the revealing of secrets and truths about God's perspective on

9. J. Collins, ed., *Apocalypse: The Morphology of a Genre*, SemeiaSt 14 (Missoula, Mont.: Scholars, 1979), 9.

10. This material can be found in a fuller and different form in B. Witherington III, *Jesus the Seer: The Progress of Prophecy* (Peabody, Mass.: Hendrickson, 1999), 218–19.

a variety of matters, particularly issues of theodicy and justice, and its force lies in the belief that one lives in the age when the secrets are unveiled and the prophecies are beginning to come true. The images used in apocalyptic are plastic, malleable. Thus, the same images are used differently in Revelation than in Daniel. The Ancient of Days with the venerable white hair in Daniel 7 is applied to Jesus in Rev. 1:14. The image of the wounded beast that is antichrist could be applied to Nero or Domitian. The images are, in short, multivalent, and can be applied to a variety of persons. Also, they are aspective rather than descriptive. The dragon in Revelation represents Satan, but it is not a visual description of him; rather, it makes clear something about his character. These things need to be kept in mind when evaluating the Revelation of John.

John's revelations come in the form of visions, as Revelation 1 makes abundantly clear. He has written down their content and then placed them in an order within an epistolary framework. This last feature makes clear that the material is intended for a specific audience, and unlike many apocalyptic documents, Revelation is not pseudonymous. We know the name of the actual author, and accordingly, this book has no *ex eventu* prophecy—history written up as prophecy and then retrojected into the mouth of an ancient luminary. Apparently, early Christians had a problem with such pseudonymity and the attempted deception involved in such literature.

The Book of Revelation shows that future eschatology is still very much alive at the end of the first century A.D. We could have gathered this also from a noncanonical Christian document like the *Epistle of Barnabas*, which may well have been written just before or right after the end of the first century A.D. Like Revelation, *Barnabas* urges readiness in the face of impending judgment. Like Revelation, *Barnabas* links the epistolary form with eschatology and some apocalyptic images. The struggle between good and evil is highlighted in both works, including supernatural good and evil (see *Barn.* 2:1; 4:1–9), and the present evil age is expected to close with the arrival of the age to come and its final judgment. But John's Revelation does not simply include apocalyptic images; it is a full-blown apocalypse.

One of the most notable features of John's Revelation is the hundreds of allusions to Old Testament texts, which nonetheless are almost never quoted. These ideas and images are put into the mental blender of this prophet and are used in creative new ways to make clear that his audience lives in the eschatological age when prophecies come true. In his view, the death and vindication of Jesus have changed world history and set in motion the last things. In a threefold repetition of seven judgments, the author reveals the character of the messianic woes that God's people must endure and be protected from on earth. These judgments upon the earth lead up to the return of Christ, the rule of Christ with his saints upon the earth, the final judgment, and at last, the new heaven and new earth. The author wants his disciples in Asia not to be surprised at their suffering and difficulties. He wants to make clear that God will finally vindicate them and all of God's people. Neither beastly empires nor emperors will finally prevail, for God's yes will be louder than their no in questions of justice and redemption. Not surprisingly, God's sovereignty is a major theme in Revelation, as in all such apocalyptic literature.

The very existence of Revelation indicates that not only the author but also the audience has been marginalized or persecuted by various powers in the world. By the time this document was written, Christians were a known entity, long distinguishable from Jews, and indeed not infrequently in an antagonistic relationship with the synagogue. They had neither the blessing of Jews nor the endorsement of the Roman emperor and his minions. They were caught betwixt and between. Yet the Johannine community had their precious sacred texts—letters, a Gospel, and an apocalypse—to give them guidance even after they lost key leaders. They were, as John 1 all along suggested, people of the Word, not unlike their contemporaries in the synagogue who were focusing with new energy exclusively on the Torah, having lost the temple and the territory.

In this situation it is understandable how a document like the *Gospel of Thomas* could arise, perhaps early in the second century. The minority community of persecuted people of the Word could focus almost exclusively on the words of Jesus and turn their backs on the world, indeed, turn their backs on the goodness of physical reality. As the Johannine Gospel and epistles make clear, this was a deviation from the way the apostles and their co-workers interpreted the Christ and the Christ event that needed to be refuted and rejected, which is what happened in the second-century gnostic controversies.[11]

---

11. It is possible to see the *Didache* as a reaction to the sort of prophetic movement that a *Gospel of Thomas* may have come out of. The warnings in the *Didache* about itinerant prophets are noteworthy. I agree with the assessment that this work comes from a time when the church was becoming more of a localized phenomenon and less of a prophetic movement. The number of true prophets is dwindling and all of them are to be carefully scrutinized. Though the work clearly incorporates earlier material—for instance, about the Lord's Supper—it probably was put in its present form at the end of the first century or the beginning of the second. See Witherington, *Jesus the Seer*, 343–48.

Illustration 16.1 The Appian Way.

All Roads Lead to . . .

This study of New Testament history concludes with an examination of some material from the end of the first century A.D. that comes from the Roman Christian community. I am referring to the writings of Clement of Rome. I will then conclude this study by considering another work originating from Rome that is not unlike Revelation, the *Shepherd of Hermas*.

There can be little doubt that Clement of Rome was a key leader of the Roman church in the 90s. The *Pseudo-Clementines*, a later Christian romance, describes Clement as a Roman citizen with some connection to the Flavian family who was baptized and discipled by Peter, but most scholars would see this as entirely legendary. It is possible that he was a cousin of Titus Flavius Clemens, whom we have already had occasion to speak of in this chapter. And Irenaeus may well be correct in saying that Clement was the third bishop after Peter in Rome (*Haer* 3.3.3).[12] It seems likely that Clement of Rome is the Clement referred to in Hermas *Vis* 8:3, in which case he was one of the church's main correspondents with other churches. This comports well with what we find in *1 Clement*. I have chronicled somewhat the reign of terror that was the last few years of Domitian's reign. *1 Clement* 1:1 seems to allude to this situation by speaking of "the sudden and successive misfortunes and accidents that have befallen us." The author has lived through the deaths of Paul and Peter and others in "our own times," and sees them as outstanding examples for himself and his own audi-

12. Linus being the second.

ence (5:1–6:1). He has also witnessed the death of some of the elders whom the apostles had appointed in Rome (44:1–5). By the time *1 Clement* is written, the church in Corinth can be called ancient.

Clement is writing in response to a letter or report from the Corinthian church (*1 Clem.* 47:6), which seems to be struggling with the same divisive and factious tendencies that Paul had to deal with in the 50s. The Corinthian church turns to the Roman church for some wise counsel. It must be remembered that leaders of the Roman church, Aquila and Priscilla, also became leaders in Corinth, setting up a social network between the two groups of Christians (cf. Rom. 16:3; Acts 18:2).[13]

The problem Clement is dealing with is not unlike the one mentioned in 2 John. *First Clement* 44:6 and 47:6 deal with the fact that some persons had taken it upon themselves to remove "some from the ministry which they had fulfilled blamelessly." They were arrogating power to themselves. It may be, as Lane has conjectured, that house church owners were asserting authority over some of the elders in the church, perhaps as part of house church rivalries and honor challenges.[14] Clement must seek to vindicate existing authority structures that the majority of Christians in Corinth seem to support.[15] "Clement's role as a mediator engaged in conflict resolution was to conserve what Paul and the apostles had initiated by showing how the existing structures were expressions of the church's beliefs and that the values shared by Christians implied a commitment to a church order rooted in apostolic practice and grounded ultimately in the will of God."[16]

Like 1 Corinthians, which serves as a source for *1 Clement*,[17] this letter of Clement takes the form of deliberative rhetoric, trying to heal the divisions in the church and to work for concord and harmony (see 63:1–4). Clement appeals to examples, warns about bad behavior, extols the benefits of working for concord, and in general urges the same sort of beneficial behavior that Paul argued for in 1 Corinthians. Clement cites as proof that his advice is right from the Old Testament (e.g., 42:5, citing Isa. 60:17

---

13. See W. Lane, "Social Perspectives on Roman Christianity during the Formative Years from Nero to Nerva: Romans, Hebrews, 1 Clement," in *Judaism and Christianity in First-Century Rome*, ed. K. Donfried and P. Richardson (Grand Rapids: Eerdmans, 1998), 227–28.

14. Ibid., 229–30.

15. This latter conclusion is supported by Dionysius of Corinth's letter to Rome, written about A.D. 170, which shows that *1 Clement* was still read in that church in his day (Eusebius, *Hist eccl.* 4.23.11). If it was still a source of help, then it must have been received and preserved by the majority of Corinthian Christians.

16. Lane, "Roman Christianity" 240.

17. Which in turn tells us that Paul's letters were circulating to churches beyond the ones they were originally written to. See 2 Pet. 3:15–16.

LXX), the teaching of Jesus (e.g., 13:2; 46:7–8), and, of course, Paul (e.g., 47:1–4). He also knows another document that was sent to Rome, Hebrews. Yet Clement also has been influenced by and is happy to draw on his Greco-Roman heritage, referring to the legend of the phoenix (25:1–5), the Stoic portrait of cosmic harmony (20:1–12), and even to the Roman army as a model for proper Christian behavior (37:1–4)!

A leadership gap at the top opened after the apostles and their coworkers died. Apparently, we see the effects of this problem in *1 Clement*, and the same can be said about the next document to be considered, the *Shepherd of Hermas*, in which are reflected serious divisions between and within house churches. We need to consider that document as this chapter draws to a close.

Hermas, like Revelation, is not a pseudonymous document and therefore does not have *ex eventu* prophecy. Also like Revelation, *Hermas* has no significant recollection of past events, whether salvation-historical or primordial. But there are also differences between *Hermas* and Revelation. The former has no reference to resurrection or to cosmic transformation. The general ethos of *Hermas* is that eschatological fervor is waning but the apocalyptic form is still in use.

The author of *Hermas*, like the author of Revelation, is suffering from some sort of social deprivation and has little sympathy with the rich and complacent. He appears to have been a freedman of the lady Rhoda (*Vis.* 1:1). Clearly, he had family problems, but the transgressions of his wife and children are linked to his own (*Vis.* 7:1). The author is a contemporary of Clement (*Vis.* 8:3), but of a lower social station. One of the real significances of his work is that it offers views of a Christian who perhaps was more like the majority of Christians, someone not from among the social elite or even what we would consider middle class. He lives at a time when Christians are being persecuted. *Vision* 10:1 says that they had endured "whips, prisons, great persecutions, crosses, wild beasts, for the sake of the name." This cannot all refer to problems in the 60s, for *Sim.* 98.3 speaks of Christians in his day committing apostasy and idolatry (worshiping idols) in order to avoid persecution. This sounds very much like a reaction to the litmus test that Domitian was imposing on those he suspected of "atheism." Instead of being loyal, the double-minded decide to submit to emperor worship to save their skin. We may compare this to evidence elsewhere of persecution by Domitian (cf. *1 Clement* 5; Dio Cassius, *Roman History* 67.14; Eusebius, *Hist. eccl.* 3.17). The author of *Hermas*, then, is writing for the pressured and persecuted, and provides prima facie evidence that such persecution was by no means limited to Flavius Clemens's family.

Like other apocalypses, *Hermas* has the following features: (1) the author gets his knowledge through mediators who convey divine wisdom to him through visions and words (e.g., *Vision* 5; *Similitude* 111–114); (2) he has visions of a book, a tower, and a beast (*Vision* 2–4); (3) he requires an angelic interpreter, much like Zechariah in Zechariah 1–8, to understand his visions; (4) he feels compelled to write his visions down so that copies may be sent to churches (*Vis.* 8:2–3; *Sim.* 111.2).

Vision 4 presents the author's vision of the beast, which, as in Revelation, represents the empire. Here, unlike in Revelation, *Hermas* suggests that with sufficient faith and prayer, one can face down the beast and not have to suffer (22:8–9). Another interesting difference from Revelation is that this author holds out an image of the church as a tower or an eternally youthful bride (*Vision* 4), rather than setting before his audience the new heaven and new earth. The author of *Hermas* is concerned more with postbaptismal sin than with the second coming, more with purity of heart than with the pure and perfect realm of the new Jerusalem. The form may suggest apocalypse, but the focus lies more along the lines of what we find in *Barnabas* or the *Didache* in terms of the moralizing nature of the document. In *Hermas*, as in the *Didache*, prophets are problematic, and therefore criteria to judge the true from the false prophet are needed. We must bear in mind also the largely non-eschatological nature of the vision of *Hermas*.

What we learn about the church in Rome from both *Hermas* and *1 Clement* is that it is settling down in this city and preparing for a possibly lengthy life. Problems of authority exist, and with the power vacuum have come divisions and a lack of adequate church order. At the same time, as the prophetic movement of early Christianity becomes an institutional church, prophecy in various ways is being marginalized or domesticated, and the future eschatological bite is being taken out of the visions. The author of *Hermas* is no John of Patmos, but the contrast between the two reminds us that in the 90s, even under persecution, not all were looking for eschatological solutions to their problems.

Christianity had shown remarkable growth and resiliency in the first century. Partly, this was due to much sacrifice on the part of the missionaries, to Christianity's remarkable social networks, and to lack of competition other than the ever growing emperor cult. And as Christianity became more and more distinguished from Judaism, perhaps this also helped the faith to thrive, especially after the Jewish war had placed a strong stigma on Judaism in the minds of most Romans, including especially the Flavian emperors.

Scripture Index

Ancient Writings Index

Subject Index